FIFTY-THREE DAYS ON
STARVATION ISLAND

Also by John R. Bruning

Race of Aces: WWII's Elite Airmen and the Epic Battle to Become the Master of the Sky

Indestructible: One Man's Rescue Mission That Changed the Course of WWII

FIFTY-THREE DAYS ON
STARVATION ISLAND

The World War II Battle
That Saved Marine Corps Aviation

BY JOHN R. BRUNING

hachette
BOOKS

New York

Hachette Books
Hachette Book Group
1290 Avenue of the Americas
New York, NY 10104
HachetteBooks.com
Twitter.com/HachetteBooks
Instagram.com/HachetteBooks

First Edition: May 2024

Published by Hachette Books, an imprint of Hachette Book Group, Inc. The Hachette Books name and logo is a trademark of the Hachette Book Group.

The Hachette Speakers Bureau provides a wide range of authors for speaking events. To find out more, go to hachettespeakersbureau.com or email HachetteSpeakers@hbgusa.com.

Books by Hachette Books may be purchased in bulk for business, educational, or promotional use. For information, please contact your local bookseller or Hachette Book Group Special Markets Department at: special.markets@hbgusa.com.

The publisher is not responsible for websites (or their content) that are not owned by the publisher.

Print book interior design by Amy Quinn.

Library of Congress Cataloging-in-Publication Data

Names: Bruning, John R., author.
Title: Fifty-three days on Starvation Island: the World War II battle that saved Marine Corps aviation / by John R. Bruning.
Other titles: 53 days on Starvation Island
Description: First edition. | New York, NY: Hachette Books, 2024. | Includes bibliographical references and index.
Identifiers: LCCN 2023044665 | ISBN 9780316508650 (hardcover) | ISBN 9780316508681 (ebook)
Subjects: LCSH: Guadalcanal, Battle of, Solomon Islands, 1942–1943. | United States. Marine Fighting Squadron 223. | Carl, Marion E., 1915–1998. | Smith, John L. (John Lucian), 1914–1972, | World War, 1939–1945—Naval operations, American. | World War, 1939–1945—Aerial operations, American. | World War, 1939–1945—Campaigns—Solomon Islands. | United States. Marine Fighting Squadron 221. | Fighter pilots—United States—Biography.
Classification: LCC D767.98 .B78 2024 | DDC 940.54/265933—dc23/eng/20231109
LC record available at https://lccn.loc.gov/2023044665

ISBNs: 978-0-316-50865-0 (hardcover), 978-0-316-50868-1 (ebook)

Printed in the United States of America

LSC-C

Printing 1, 2024

To the following remarkable people:
For my father, mother, and Uncle Dean Cavanaugh, who showed me the
history that led to the life I live and love

For Jack Cook, my brother from another mother, who has always had my back

For Jeff and Annelizabeth Pullman, dear friends who have given me the space
to write and build the best memories of my life

And especially for Gus, the best plumber in New Jersey, whose
love of country and sense of loyalty has no peer. Yours is the
purest American heart I've ever met. They say history cannot be
changed by a single human being. If they only knew. . . .

FIFTY-THREE DAYS ON
STARVATION ISLAND

PROLOGUE

Midway Island
June 4, 1942

T HE SQUADRON'S DESTRUCTION WAS SWIFT AND BRUTAL. TWENTY-five fighters rose to Midway's defense. They faced 108 Japanese aircraft, which were crewed by some of the most experienced and best-trained aviators in the world.

The Marines piloted inferior fighters—a mix of Brewster F2A Buffalos and an early-production version of the F4F Wildcat, a variant that carried only four guns. These young Americans, most of them fresh from stateside training units, had exactly one experience with aerial combat. A few months before this historic day, a lumbering, obsolete Japanese flying boat had blundered into fighter range off Midway. Four pilots from the squadron intercepted and shot it down.

In six months of duty on the most remote American outpost remaining in the Central Pacific, the incident was the sum total of combat that the men of VMF-221 had seen.* Now, they faced the might of the Japanese Kidō Butai—the aircraft-carrier force that had devastated Pearl Harbor and had run rampant across the Pacific and Indian Oceans ever since.

The Americans received advance notice of the incoming Japanese raid, thanks to the radar system recently installed on Midway. The squadron

---

* In US Navy parlance, VMF stood for Heavier than Air Marine Fighter Squadron.

scrambled, using converging runways. In the mad dash to get aloft, the men nearly collided with one another at the point of convergence. It was every man for himself, and VMF-221 climbed furiously into the fresh morning and its clear skies.

If the Marines were straggled and spread out, the Japanese presented a disciplined, parade-like foe when the Americans spotted them two thousand feet below their stubby fighters. The bombers flew in tight vee formations, their Mitsubishi A6M2 "Zero" fighter escort herding them protectively along from above and behind.

The Marines dove in a gaggle to the attack. Their initial altitude advantage allowed a single pass at the bombers—but then the Zeroes set upon them. The Marines in their barrel-shaped Brewster Buffalos dodged and twisted and tried to dive away from the deadly attacks. The Zeroes easily stayed with the US fighters through every maneuver, their pilots snapping out short bursts with their cannon and machine guns.

The Brewsters exploded and fell into the ocean, trailing long streamers of flame. Here and there, a parachute blossomed, but most of the Marines rode their planes into the sea, wounded or dead at the controls.

Capt. Marion Carl, piloting one of the handful of F4F Wildcats the squadron possessed, made one diving pass through the bombers. The other two pilots in his division were set upon and crippled by Zeroes even as Marion opened fire on a Nakajima B5N "Kate" bomber.

Seeing the enemy fighters above and behind him, Marion maintained his steep dive, pulling away and out of the fight. He stayed low and fast until he was absolutely certain the fight was far above and behind him. Then he started a long climb up to twenty thousand feet. He was no coward, no shirker. Even alone, he knew his duty: defend Midway. But he wasn't going to be stupid about it either. Altitude, he knew, was king in air combat. He'd get above the enemy again and try to make a surprise attack.

Meanwhile, of the first twelve Marines who attacked the Japanese, only three survived their first moments of air combat. The squadron commander, Maj. Floyd Parks, was among those to die. A few minutes later, Capt. Kirk Armistead led the remainder of the squadron down into the fight. Five of the seven men with him died at the hands of the veteran

Zero pilots. The survivors limped home for Midway, their Buffalos shot full of holes, trailing smoke, and leaking oil or hydraulic fluid. Flying wrecks. If they could have landed anywhere else, they would have, but Midway offered the only friendly runway for thousands of miles.

By then, Carl returned to the battle area, still alone. Looking down on it, he could see that the fight had strung both sides out for miles. The stately bomber formations were nowhere in sight, but he could see a few straggling aircraft—Zeroes perhaps—below him. As he considered how to attack, a sudden rush of sound filled his ears: metallic thuds—like rocks thrown on an aluminum roof. It took a second for him to process the noise. *I'm under attack.*

A glance over his shoulder confirmed it. He'd failed to keep his head on a swivel and check his tail. Now a Zero sat tacked onto his tail, muzzle flashes flaring on its wings and upper cowling.

He broke hard into the tightest turn the Wildcat could perform. The Zero pilot, surprised by the maneuver, lost his chance, and what would have been a fatal burst of fire went wild.

The move saved Carl for only a moment. As he looked back, he saw the Zero easily turn inside him. The aircraft was stunningly maneuverable. He knew it would be only a matter of seconds before the Japanese pilot clawed back into firing position. The Marine played his final card: he rolled out of his turn and dove vertically away from his pursuer. As he did, he spotted a small cloud below him and raced for it. The Japanese pilot gave chase, hard on his heels and closing in for the killing shot.

Carl plunged into the cloud and pulled the Hollywood of Hollywood maneuvers. He cut his throttle and crossed his controls—stick full left, rudder full right. The Wildcat staggered and skidded. The Zero burst into the cloud and whipped past the F4F.

Now the hunter was in the crosshairs. Marion firewalled the throttle and gave chase. Both planes hurtled out of the bottom of the cloud, his Wildcat dead astern of the Zero. He triggered his four .50-caliber machine guns—and nothing happened. All four guns were jammed. His wild maneuvers had unseated his ammunition belts in their bays, and no amount of charging and recharging could get them functional.

The Zero escaped.

Marion kept working to clear his jammed guns, charging them in an attempt to pop the snagged rounds out of the chambers and get the weapons to feed properly again. Eventually, he got three working. He was back in the fight.

Nearly over Midway now, Carl could see smoke rising from multiple fires around the atoll. The Japanese bombers had done their work. The squadron had failed to protect their ground-bound brethren.

He sighted three Zeroes below him, all spread out and operating alone. He watched for a few minutes, calculating the odds. Then he picked out one and dropped down behind it.

The Japanese pilot made the same mistake Marion had earlier in the fight: he forgot to keep clearing his tail. He never saw Marion's Wildcat come swooping in behind him to nearly point-blank range. The American opened fire with his three guns. Their bullets converged on the Japanese fighter, shredding its aluminum skin. The Zero spun violently and rolled straight into the sea below.

Marion Carl returned to Midway with eight bullet holes in his F4F Wildcat. He found that only ten planes were left in VMF-221. More than half the squadron failed to return, but on closer inspection, it was actually worse than that. Besides Carl's F4F, there was only one other plane still operational. The others were shot to pieces.

They had gone out twenty-five strong. Fourteen pilots were missing. The squadron's leadership was largely dead or wounded.

All the Midway-based squadrons suffered catastrophic losses that day. The full scope of the disaster came into focus later in the morning, when the Marines' dive-bomber squadron returned from attacking the Japanese carriers. The counterpunch had been supported by a flight of Navy TBF Avenger torpedo bombers and four Army B-26 Marauders. One bullet-riddled Avenger—its pilot wounded in the neck, the radioman hit in the head, and the gunner dead in the rear turret—managed to crash-land back at Midway with sixty-nine cannon and machine gun holes in it. One other B-26, in similar condition, made it home. And the Marine dive-bombers? Their squadron lost ten of twenty-seven planes in that first attack, including their commanding officer, Lofton R. "Joe" Henderson. Two more missions cost the squadron successive new commanders and most of their remaining aircraft.

Midway was a shambles. It was the third time in six months that Marine Corps Aviation had faced the imperial Japanese, and each time, the units involved were almost totally destroyed.

Sumner Whitten, one of the Marine dive-bomber pilots lucky enough to get home that morning, was tasked with boxing up the personal effects of the men the squadron had lost. As he went about the grim work, he realized this episode was just the beginning of their war. Looking into the future, he could not even conceive how any of them would survive in the days and weeks ahead. The Japanese were simply that good.

At VMF-221's operations shack, the bewildered, broken survivors of the squadron congregated to figure out what had happened. Of the fourteen men missing, only one would show up alive after bailing out offshore and swimming back to the island. The rest died in that short and horrific inauguration into combat.

Captain Armistead was the senior surviving officer still on his feet. Eyes wide from shock and trauma, his closest friends dead, he knew the mantle of leadership fell to him. He was not up to the task. He turned command over to the squadron's senior sergeant, telling him he was in charge. Then he went into a bomb shelter and got drunk.

Marion Carl was disgusted by Armistead's behavior.

The war didn't stop for people's feelings. Half the squadron remained alive, and the men needed somebody to step up and take command in the crisis. He gave a thought to the great leaders he'd met in the three years since he joined the Corps. Robert "Bob" Galer, Joe Bauer—both great fighter pilots from whom he'd learned a great deal about the profession. They always led by example. But one man was sorely missed in the moment. Oklahoma-born Capt. John Lucian "John L." Smith had come to Midway with the squadron aboard the carrier *Saratoga* at the start of the war. He'd been with the VMF-221 until February, when the Corps ordered him back to Pearl Harbor to command a brand-new fighter squadron.

John L. was a man who led effortlessly. He could have picked up the men and gotten them mentally back in the fight. Smith led from the front and was almost unbeatable in the countless simulated dogfights he'd fought with other men in the squadron. Quick-tempered but quick with praise as well, he possessed that rare blend of charisma, skill, and fearlessness that other men naturally followed.

John L. Smith missed the fight and never returned to Midway after his February recall to Pearl Harbor. So on that terrible June day, there was nobody else who could step up and save 221 from its post-battle collapse in morale.

That evening near sunset, a scramble order reached the shattered survivors of 221. A second raid had been detected. Midway needed its aerial defenders.

The squadron now had only two planes that could still fight: Marion's Wildcat and the Brewster Buffalo whose pilot had returned unscathed.

Marion grabbed his parachute and ran to his waiting Wildcat, the fresh bullet holes in the fuselage unpatched. Capt. William C. "Bill" Humberd, who had joined the Corps about the same time Marion had in 1938, took the untouched F2A Buffalo. It would be the two junior captains against the Kidō Butai.

They strapped into their seats with their plane captain's help, flashed each other a thumbs-up, and then taxied for the runway. Marion gave no thought to the odds. No thoughts to survival. Only of duty. This was his job, and he would do it or die fighting.

PART ONE

THE FIRST HEROES HOME

ONE

JOHN LUCIAN

Washington, D.C.
November 9, 1942

LUNCHTIME IN WASHINGTON, D.C.: AN ELEGANT RESTAURANT filled with handcrafted wood features and murals that captured snapshots of American history. Thick, formal tablecloths. Heavy silverware so shiny it flared like muzzle flashes in the overhead lighting. Crystal glasses tinked as busboys refilled them with ice water. Dishes clattered. Tables were cleared. The restaurant hummed with impressive efficiency.

The place was packed with the upscale D.C. set. The women looked immaculate—tilt hats, pumps, batwing dresses, and nylon stockings. They sipped coffee and ordered $1.90 filet mignon.

Maj. John Lucian Smith stared at his menu. A month ago, he was starving on captured Japanese rice on a remote Pacific island nobody in the restaurant had ever heard of until August. The *National Geographic* map—all the aircrew had before landing on it—called it Guadalcanal. The Japanese came to call it "Starvation Island."

He glanced up and his hazel eyes wandered the room, missing nothing. He was a meticulous man with hyperaware senses that had kept him alive in the South Pacific. Now he couldn't shut them off.

Officers in freshly pressed uniforms chatted with their companions, eating artfully plated food without giving it a second thought. Those men had no concept of what they would face when they went overseas.

If they went overseas. One look was enough to convince John L. that some of these headquarters types would be content to the fight the war from the banks of the Potomac.

Starving in the jungle, racked by dysentery, malaria, and dengue fever. Men huddled in muddy foxholes, craving only a bit of normalcy. A cup of coffee. A bar of chocolate. Instead, dried fish and maggot-filled rice kept them alive. But being alive on that island wasn't really living. It was a test of survival instincts.

"I'll have the coq au vin Fontainebleau" came a man's voice from a nearby booth.

Yeah. These officers had no idea what they would face. The prewar military had been almost a sort of country club for the commissioned class. Polo matches, lunchtime cocktails, and colonial largess at postings in places like the Philippines. The Japanese demolished that mindset and killed anyone who clung to it in the first months of the Pacific War. John L. and the others had seen those types of officers fail in the clutch. More than one was shipped off the island, broken physically or psychologically, useless to their units. The others stood their ground, adapted, and rose to the challenge. War evolves men quickly to its realities.

But Washington was clearly beyond the war's reach.

John L. looked across his own table at the two men who had shared his summer ordeal. Marion Carl, a tall and lanky Oregon farm boy, sat beside Richard "Dick" Mangrum, whose red mustache was now tamed and trimmed. It had been a bushy caterpillar of a thing in the jungle, remarked on by all who wrote about him there. Dick sat rigidly, his spine straight, shoulders squared. Marion was, as usual, a bit more relaxed. Both were people watching from behind cups of coffee.

John L. hadn't seen either man since they arrived in San Francisco to flashing cameras and staccato questions from reporters. After that circus, Dick had gone home to his wife and kids in Seattle. Marion had stayed in California to visit family and old friends. He had also paid his respects to some of the families of the men they had lost. That took guts, and John L. appreciated it. Courage in combat was one thing; courage to meet the family of a man you watched die required something quite different. Long ago, John L. had learned that Marion Carl was *hard* and that he always did the right thing.

John L. had made some of those calls, too, since he had gotten home. For Marion, it was a personal obligation to lost friends and brother aviators. For John L., it was his duty as their skipper to give what closure he could to the loved ones of the men he had lost.

John L. spared the families the details of what happened to their fallen Marine. The country wasn't ready for the details. Their boy went quick. Didn't suffer. There was no talk of bombardment madness, no moments in muddy dugouts as broken men bled out while overworked surgeons struggled to save a lucky few.

He hadn't seen every family yet. His squadron, VMF-223, had lost almost two-thirds of its pilots in fifty-three days of combat. The ground echelon suffered terribly, too.

Yet 223 had it easy compared with Dick Mangrum's VMSB-232, a dive-bomber squadron known as the Red Devils. When he left Guadalcanal on October 12, Dick was the last Red Devil standing. The others were dead or missing or, like Henry Hise, in stateside hospitals. The last that Dick had seen of the young hard charger, Henry was partially paralyzed, his pelvis and back broken during a Japanese bombing raid.

Now the trio had been ordered to Washington, D.C., a universe away from the shrapnel-torn tents that had been their homes only a few weeks before. Here in this restaurant, surrounded by polite company in what could have passed as peacetime splendor . . . for the three survivors, it was disorienting to say the least.

Their new Marine Corps public relations handler, Capt. T. E. "Ed" Hicks arrived and sat down next to John L. Without preamble, Hicks began discussing the afternoon's itinerary. Meetings at the Navy Department a few blocks away on Constitution Avenue. A press conference afterward. In the morning, they would head over to Naval Air Station (NAS) Anacostia for a photo shoot. There would be a variety of photographers, including one from *Life* magazine, who would be angling for a cover shot of John L.

This was the first lap of the first Marine hero tour of World War II. John L., Dick, and Marion were the men who mastered air combat and came home without a scratch. The Navy wanted them on every front page, extolling the virtues of Marine Corps Aviation and the effort to hold the jungle hellhole they had defended. There would be speaking gigs at factories, war bond rallies, press conferences, and radio shows.

Later in the week, John L. was scheduled to be a guest on Kate Smith's eight p.m. prime-time show. Her rendition of "God Bless America" would become the beloved gold standard of the song for seventy years, until somebody dredged up the fact that she had cut two horribly racist tracks back in the 1930s. But in the moment, she was a beacon of patriotic sentiment that reflected the mood of the nation. John L. would be one of the first guests on the *Kate Smith Hour* with combat experience in the Pacific.

After Hicks finished outlining the itinerary, the men made small talk as they looked over the menus. Studious normality, but each felt untethered to the world they now found themselves in. Dick talked about his kids. Marion mainly listened. He was always the quiet one, but he could bust out a broad, white-toothed grin that could stop traffic. The papers called him the Zero Man—tall, dark, and handsome. A woman's dream in a Marine uniform.

John L., Marion, and Dick caught one another up on what they had been doing since they landed back at Hamilton Field, California, on October 22, nine days removed from a night of battleship shells raining down on their living area. They had been interviewed when they stopped over at Pearl Harbor en route to the States, but none of them had had any idea of what would be waiting for them in San Francisco. They were just Marines who had done their job and tried to survive while men they loved had died around them every day and every night.

After the press conference and photo blitz in Frisco, John L. went back to his hometown of Lexington, Oklahoma, wanting only to see his father and brother—and spend a quiet moment with his mom. When he arrived, he was greeted by a cheering crowd of at least sixteen hundred. Lexington had half that population, so folks from all over the county had flocked to see him, America's Ace of Aces, the Hero of Guadalcanal.

A hand-painted welcome banner stretched across a block in downtown. A family friend and neighbor had painted another sign that read "Birthplace of Maj. John L. Smith Marine Ace" and placed it in front of his father's house.

The hometown pride left John L. surprised and humbled, unsure of how to react. When he asked to be taken to the town's cemetery, a caravan with a state highway patrol escort drove him there from the train station. He stepped out onto the manicured lawn and walked among the headstones, holding a bouquet of flowers he'd purchased on his journey.

Halloween season, 1942. He'd come home to Oklahoma to lay similar flowers on his mother's grave.

He wanted to stay longer with her, but the townsfolk were restless. To greet him properly, school let out early that Friday and all the businesses closed. The festive atmosphere grew as the people gathered in the town square, where they waited for the caravan to deliver him to a freshly constructed wooden platform and a microphone with which his soft voice could carry across the crowd.

To his surprise, his eighth-grade teacher, Cora Burkett, was waiting for him on the platform. She took center stage and spoke of John L. with sincere fondness: "It was my privilege to have John as a pupil . . . and to know him even better as he and my own son chummed together through their high school days."

She spoke of how he'd always asked for more work after he finished his assignments early. He was not one to coast. He wanted to feed his active mind, so Mrs. Burkett would assign him projects and special errands to soak up some of his abundant energy.

"Today, those errands have grown into an immense job, and the successes he has achieved have not been just luck. Wise, constructive thinking coupled with pluck has brought him safely home."

John L. stood awkwardly and listened to the praise with an armored heart. He felt undeserving. When Mrs. Burkett finished, she ceremoniously gave John L. a gold watch. The city council had entrusted her with this job after the entire town chipped in to pay for this beautiful, heartfelt gift.

Then it was his turn at the microphone. He still had no idea what to say. He didn't want to be there, didn't want the acclaim. He just wanted peace and a decent night's sleep.

His smooth voice reached the eager crowd. He managed a thank-you for the gift; it had genuinely touched him. A stirring speech, if that was expected, was not to be that afternoon. John L. simply said, "What I did only parallels what twenty thousand others are doing out there, and what must be done by three million others before this thing is over."

The crowd cheered and applauded. John L. stepped away from the microphone. People lined up enthusiastically to shake his hand and share a moment with the hero of the hour.

"I'm tired," he said. His dad and brother met him at the platform stairs, saw the look on his gaunt face, and spirited him away.

The next day, the press fawned, extolling John L. Smith's soft-spoken, humble demeanor despite his being America's greatest fighter pilot—that is, except for one anonymous but astute reporter. In an uncredited *Norman (Oklahoma) Transcript* sidebar, the writer observed, "There is a look in Major Smith's eyes often seen in the eyes of men who came back from bitter fighting in the first World War. They fought heroic deeds, but said little upon their return. They have looked the nasty business of war full in the face at close range, and it is not a pleasant sight. That fact makes them even more determined to end the unpleasant business as soon as possible and get back to decent, ordinary ways of life. America owes a debt it can never fully pay to Major Smith."

IN THIS BEAUTIFUL AND ORNATE RESTAURANT IN THE HEART OF AMERIca's capital, the man whose country owed him that debt looked down at his cup of coffee. Like everything else in this place, the cup lent itself to the atmosphere. Fine china. Understated elegance. He brought the cup to his lips and savored the taste of the coffee, the beans hand ground for the nation's elite. In the jungle, on the rare days when they could get coffee, they had brewed it over an open fire and drunk it from tin mess cups. Bitter and harsh, but the buzz took the edge off the weariness.

A waitress hurried past their table.

"Pardon me," he said to her. She paused and looked irritated at the interruption.

John L. asked her for a bit more sugar.

Her eyes narrowed, irritation blooming to anger. She shook her head and harshly replied, "Sugar's rationed. Don't you know there's a war on?"

Marion and Dick exchanged glances. John L.'s face went red. The waitress stalked off, her duty to her country done. Perhaps it was the freshly polished shoes, new uniforms, and haircuts the three veterans had received that morning. It made them look like every other officer in the D.C. headquarters set—to a civilian, anyway. Anyone in the military would decipher the tossed salad of colorful ribbons on their left breasts and know these men had seen action. A lot of it.

"Hey, Skipper," Marion said, "you okay?"

Dick added, "John L., you look ready to explode."

John L. could be charismatic and magnetic, but he also had a temper. There were times Marion and Dick had seen him fly into a rage. They could see him now on the edge of losing control.

"Skipper?" Marion said again.

All at once, as if a switch had been thrown deep inside him, the tension drained out of the ace's face. His color returned. His self-control held. For a long moment, he stared at the ceiling, exhaling slowly, his eyes far away. He looked inexpressibly sad.

"Old men are we." He finally sighed.

Dick nodded. "Yeah. We're older." He was thirty-six, the eldest of the trio. Both Marion and John L. were twenty-seven. But nobody was talking birthdays.

TWO

LOST IN TRANSLATION

Navy Department, Washington, D.C.
November 9, 1942

IN A GENTLE WIND UNDER CLOUDY SKIES, ED HICKS LED HIS THREE Marine aviators across the National Mall to the Navy Department building on Constitution Avenue. The building had been thrown up by Franklin D. Roosevelt when he was the secretary of the Navy during WWI, ostensibly as a temporary wartime affair. He wanted it made of wood, but ultimately the need for fireproofing dictated its concrete construction. It was an ugly, spartan building built on the section of the Mall that became the site of the Vietnam Veterans Memorial a half century— and two more wars—later. Roosevelt came to hate the building so much that he once quipped, "When I first came down here in 1933, I said I didn't think I would ever be let into the Gates of Heaven, because I had been responsible for desecrating the parks of Washington . . . [with the building]."

The Navy Department of 1939 housed about three thousand officers and employees. In the fall of 1942, that number had grown to thirteen thousand. The place bustled with officers in their winter dark blue and gold braid uniforms filling the hallways along with hundreds of civilian employees flowing between departments.

Ed led the men through the Office of Public Relations, an unadorned bullpen filled with former reporters now in uniform; they were so new to Navy service that most were still getting used to calling their shift an "eight-hour watch." A short pause while the PR types gathered around to shake the hands of the three heroes. John L., Marion, and Dick suffered through the formalities with silent grace. Then Ed led them to a nondescript metal door, where he stood and offered them a few last words of advice.

A moment later, they stepped into the Navy Department's pressroom. Ed did not follow them initially, so the trio made their way awkwardly to a leather couch up front and sat down.

The room was filled with bored-looking civilian reporters and one lone Marine PR flack in the far back. In one corner, three pudgy military-age men played acey-deucey backgammon. In another, a gaggle of photographers, their cameras on nearby tables, smoked quietly as they played poker. A *New York Times* reporter sat at a desk with a big bag of roasted peanuts. Several other scribes stood huddled around the bag, cracking the shells and eating. A few others sat at desks with their own piles of peanuts. Skins and bits of shells lay scattered in halos around them on the floor. The place smelled of body odor.

One look at who would be asking them questions, and the three combat veterans retreated into themselves. They averted their eyes from the reporters and leaned into one another, talking in low voices as if the rest of the room weren't even there.

Their reticence was not mere nerves. It was a phenomenon the press has never understood. Combat separates the warrior from the civilian. Those who experience it and measure up know the true strength of their own souls. Like Dick and Marion and John L., they have been fire-tested. They've seen others break. They've seen fine young Americans die in a dozen horrific ways. In such moment, they know what it takes to measure up. You want their respect? Be fit. Be clean. Be professional. If you haven't been through the ordeal, at least respect those who have.

These reporters had yet to figure that out.

In the back of the room, one of the reporters stood up and walked over to a phone. He started to order a ham sandwich while the other reporters

gradually picked up notebooks and pencils while sizing up the three aviators. A few of the braver ones stopped eating, stood up, and moved closer
to the pilots on the couch.

John L. and Dick lit cigarettes. Marion wasn't a smoker. The Marines
ignored the oncoming reporters.

Ed Hicks came through the door. "Ladies and gentlemen," he began,
"I would like you to meet Lieutenant Colonel Richard Mangrum, Major
John L. Smith, and Captain Marion Carl. They left Guadalcanal in
mid-October and would be happy to answer any questions."

A woman from the International News Service (INS) demanded,
"Would you introduce them again? I believe I have them mixed up."

Marion and John L. exchanged glances. After all the combat they'd
seen together, they could read each other's minds with one look.

Let's. Get. The hell. Out of here.

Dick probably would have bolted with them if they had launched themselves from the couch. Instead, he took a long drag from his cigarette and
lawyered up. He was a University of Washington Husky before joining the
Corps. As an undergrad there in his hometown of Seattle and later in law
school, he had learned public speaking. The skill had served him well in his
military career. He could answer calmly even through grinding teeth.

Hicks didn't miss a beat and reintroduced the men. "Colonel Mangrum on the left. Major John L. Smith in the middle. Captain Carl on
the right."

The *Washington Evening Star* reporter scribbled, "Charles Mangrum.
John Smith. Marion Carl."

In her notebook, the INS reporter added what would become her lede:
"The Three Musketeers of the Air: a trio of handsome Marine flyers. . . . "

Silence followed. The other reporters gathered close around the couch
now, except for the one in back still trying to order his lunch.

A tall journalist with a bobbing Adam's apple broke the ice. "Colonel,"
he said, "how does it feel to be home?"

The question prompted Marion to bite his nails. John L. ducked his
head, crushed out his cigarette, and lit another, the ritual a defense
against having to answer.

That left Dick Mangrum. He thought the question over. *Where to even start?*

"We are glad to be back," he said in his lawyer's voice, "of course. But we are not unmindful that there is still plenty of fighting to be done back in the islands. What happens to our friends concerns us very much."

Unmindful. That word never would have occurred to either fighter ace on the couch. They stayed quiet and let Dick do the talking.

One of the overweight acey-deucey players raised his hand and followed up with "Do you expect and want to go back?"

Dick nodded. "Yes," he said. "We expect to go back soon."

"But do you want to?" the reporter pressed.

Marion heard the question. He'd go back if ordered, of course. During the Battle of Midway, his F4F Wildcat was one of two fighters still left operational after his squadron's first encounter with the enemy. The squadron was scrambled a second time. He and Bill Humberd climbed into their planes. He was ordered up a second time. Two men against the entire might of the same Japanese carrier force that had devastated Pearl Harbor. Earlier in the day, the odds had been 108 to 25 in Japan's favor. On that second mission, it was just him and his wingman. The scramble proved a false alarm, but it served to demonstrate the kind of man Marion Carl was. Fear would never trump duty in his heart.

He bit his thumbnail again. He'd go back because it was the right thing to do, even though there were days at Guadalcanal when life expectancy was measured in hours. He wasn't the praying type, but more than once he thought he'd sell his soul for a guaranteed week of life.

John L.'s eyes developed a distant look. He was a million miles away from that moment, thinking of the men he'd lost. Of the rain of naval gunfire that left him and his comrades cowering in mud-filled slit trenches. The sound of chattering machine guns and the sight of flaming aircraft and flailing men falling earthward—images scarred into his memory.

"There is fighting to be done. . . . It involves all of us," Dick answered simply.

The photographers started taking pictures, bulbs flashing. John L. and Marion looked nervous and miserable. Dick stayed calm.

Marion mumbled, "That's a relief. Flash without noise." The reporters didn't get the comment. John L. smiled bitterly, thinking of the artillery flashes that strobed the night sky on Starvation Island—and the crushing sound of thunder that always followed.

When the reporters didn't seem curious enough to pursue what he meant, the Oregonian rested his elbow on his leg and, chin in hand, went silent again.

Somebody asked Mangrum about attacking Japanese ships. He gave a vivid account of one dive-bombing mission he had led. The reporters were not impressed. They quickly switched to the topic that dominated all air war coverage: air-to-air combat.

They failed to grasp an axiom of Pacific War air combat: while the aces made the headlines, the bomber pilots made the history. After all, it wasn't Zeroes that destroyed the battle line on December 7. Nor was it the Wildcats that sank the Kidō Butai's four irreplaceable carriers at Midway.

"Colonel, what about these reports that the Japanese are now using a more heavily armored version of the Zero?"

Dick looked over at John L. *Coming your way, brother.* "My own activity was in connection with dive-bombing operations," Dick said. "Our job is to stay away from fighter planes. But Major Smith might know more about that."

All eyes went to John L. The room fell silent, save the reporter in back finishing his ham-on-rye order and the *New York Times* guy still cracking peanuts.

"What about it, Major?" the same reporter asked. "Are our planes more rugged than the Japanese?"

"I wouldn't know about that," John L. said slowly, "having never shot down any Americans—just Japs."

Then he added, "I've never seen a Zero except in the air."

The INS reporter seemed astonished by that. "Didn't you see some of the planes you knocked down?"

"No ma'am. I was too busy to go out into the bush looking for them."

John L. waited for another question. The reporters outwaited him. Finally he gave in and said, "It was quite difficult to tell where the Japanese ended and the jungle began."

"Dangerous things down there in the jungle?" somebody asked.

John L. shrugged. "No. Just a lot of flies and mosquitoes. And lizards. . . . They eat the flies and the mosquitoes."

He left out the snipers, the thousands of bayonet-wielding Japanese troops. The artillery fire, the banzai charges, and the constant bombings night and day from roaming Japanese planes.

"How's the nightlife on Guadalcanal?" The question came from one of the acey-deucey players.

The aviators studied their feet. Did they think there were swanky clubs and dance halls on Guadalcanal?

"Well, you went to sleep if the Japs left you alone," John L. answered.

Another silence. The ham and rye had at last been ordered. The reporter cradled the phone and drifted toward the couch.

"Are American flyers better than Jap flyers, Major Smith?"

Some of my pilots were commissioned in April. They were green as grass. Eager, but eagerness and inexperience get young men killed.

He knew he couldn't say what he was thinking, for domestic consumption. Ed Hicks looked intently at John L. This was the first substantive question of the session.

"If you shoot 'em down," John L. said, "you're better than they are. If they get you—well, that's all it amounts to."

Somebody mentioned that Captain Carl had been shot down behind Japanese lines. Marion didn't want to talk about it. "There's not much to tell."

The reporter for the *Washington Evening Star* jotted down, "Marion Carl—reticent to talk."

"Speak up, Captain," the reporter said. "You're among friends. Tell us about it."

Marion described the mission that nearly ended his life. How he escaped from his burning Grumman Wildcat fighter and spent the next five days in the jungle.

"What did you do during those five days?"

"Well, I just fooled around," the Oregonian deadpanned.

He was sharing a little of his ordeal when the INS reporter cut in and asked, "Why is it you boys aren't very tan?"

Colonel Mangrum looked away, letting the twenty-seven-year-old major field that one.

"Um," said Marion. "We've been gone almost a month, ma'am. Tropical sunburns don't last very long."

"Is it pretty hot in the Solomons?" she asked.

"Yes ma'am. It's pretty hot down there."

"Are any of you married?" another reporter asked.

Colonel Mangrum nodded. "I am. My wife's name is Virginia. I have two children, Harriet and Bryan."

John L., next in line, said, "Louise and I married in June of 1941. She lives in Norfolk. No kids."

Marion Carl's flat, quiet voice replied, "I'm a bachelor."

The press conference ended a short time later. The three Marines practically bolted for the door. Ed Hicks stayed around to answer any follow-ups.

There weren't any.

THREE

UP WITH THE WHITE AND GOLD

Grant Field, Georgia Tech, Atlanta
Saturday, November 14, 1942

A S THE HERO TOUR KICKED OFF, THE FIGHTING AT GUADALCANAL continued. John L., Marion, and Dick had lasted fifty-three days in the fight, at the end of which their exhausted squadrons were replaced by new ones cobbled together and thrown into the fray. Now, they found themselves in the unsettling position of being safe and comfortable stateside while so many of their friends continued to endure the hell of Starvation Island. Each day, they opened newspapers to see headlines about themselves on front pages crowded with news from Guadalcanal. They ignored the ink about themselves and eagerly read every scrap from their Pacific battlefield, hoping to learn more about what was happening to those who replaced them.

The outcome of the battle remained in doubt, with severe fighting on land, air, and sea. On the night of Friday the thirteenth, a wild melee between American and Japanese warships erupted in the waters off Guadalcanal. Among the ships destroyed was the cruiser USS *Atlanta*. With their cruiser ravaged by shell hits and torpedoes and about a third of the men killed or wounded, the surviving officers tried to tow the vessel to

Lunga Point, the center of the Marine beachhead on Guadalcanal. Ultimately the crew scuttled the cruiser three miles offshore.

Hours after the *Atlanta* went down, Dick Mangrum and John L.
Smith found themselves in the city of Atlanta, standing on the Georgia Tech sidelines, awaiting the start of the nation's Game of the Week:
the Georgia Tech Yellow Jackets versus University of Alabama's Crimson
Tide. All Atlanta was abuzz over the game, and the stands at Grant Field
were packed with thirty-four thousand fans of the white and gold that
autumn afternoon.

John L., Marion, and Dick had spent the week after the D.C. press
conference touring US Navy preflight training centers on college campuses throughout the Eastern Seaboard. At each stop, they gave
speeches to the next generation of aviators who would soon carry the
war forward against Japan. It was an exceptional experience. They had
joined Marine aviation at a time when there were fewer than three hundred pilots in the service. Now the wartime expansion program was just
starting to kick into high gear, and the Guadalcanal vets spoke to hundreds of would-be cadets on each campus. Ed Hicks told the three men
that there were scores of these preflight centers at colleges all over the
country weeding out the unfit and sending the rest on to basic flight
training. At this rate, thousands of new pilots would be hitting the fleet
every month in 1943. If only they had enjoyed those kinds of numbers
on Guadalcanal.

After the University of North Carolina at Chapel Hill, the aviators
took a day off in Atlanta before going on to Athens and the preflight
course at the University of Georgia. They needed a day away from the
unblinking eye of the national spotlight.

So when Georgia Tech's seventy-six-year-old president, Marion Brittain, invited them to Grant Field to watch Georgia Tech's "Team of Destiny," John L. and Dick readily accepted. Marion elected not to go.

John L. loved football. He'd played ironman ball back at Lexington
High School in Oklahoma. He went all out on every play, hammering
opponents and taking bruising hits in return. The Lexington Bulldogs

could never hope to match the other, larger high schools in their area, but they played their hearts out and went down hard in each defeat.

John L. honed his competitive fire by scrapping in neighborhood games as a kid. During one pickup game when he was five or six, he collided with a barbed-wire fence after a particularly rough play. The accident tore open his face from cheek to jaw and left him with a permanent crescent-moon scar.

It was a crisp autumn day, about sixty degrees but with a chill wind that forced the crowd to bundle up—topcoats for the men, fur wraps for a lot of the women. The Marines saw little distinction between the people in the stands now and the games they'd attended before Pearl Harbor. Overall, maybe the men trended a little older, with fewer military-age males in the seats. But the Marines noted there were still plenty of those too.

The country needed its rituals, and college football remained one of them, war or no war.

As the kickoff approached and both teams assembled on their sidelines, John L. and Dick grew increasingly sour. What the hell was the country doing? There were Marines still living off captured Japanese food on Guadalcanal. They were short of everything, from ships to airplanes, tanks, and rifles. Where the Army had the brand-new M1 Garand semiautomatic rifle, the Marines were fighting the Japanese in the jungle with forty-year-old Springfield bolt-actions. These people around them in the stands? They needed to be making the weapons, crewing the ships that took personnel out to the South Pacific. These college kids needed to be in the trenches with the mosquitoes and the countless tropical diseases that thinned the ranks of every Marine unit on the island. America needed its citizens to fight.

As the Tide kicked off to Georgia Tech, the game began with a swelling thunder of applause and cheers. John L. looked around again. All the energy. All the normalcy. It seemed divorced from the warrior's reality, his reality. The scene left him simmering mad at first. That gave way to profound despair. His eyes darkened with that deep, old man's sadness again as he turned his gaze away from the crowd.

America was fighting a war, but the people back home had no idea what that meant. Certainly, Pearl Harbor had touched everyone in the States. The sudden burst of patriotic fever, the long lines at the recruiting centers the day after. Within weeks, rationing became the order of the day, along with victory gardens, scrap drives, and calls for citizens to give their binoculars, telescopes, and German-made cameras to the military. America's industrial workers flocked to nascent defense factories. Women were welcomed into these workplaces—the legendary Rosies.

True, the edges of the country experienced moments of the war. The U-boat blitz along the East Coast the previous spring had left beaches littered with bodies and wreckage, all covered in oil. The coastal cities resisted the order to black out their lights so that Allied merchant ships were not silhouetted at night by them. The city leaders feared the blackouts would hurt the tourist trade. The bodies washing ashore every morning ended up taking care of that.

On the West Coast, there were constant fears of air raids. Los Angeles fought a battle against nonexistent Japanese planes for almost forty-five minutes in February. San Francisco went to full blackout a couple of times a month that spring. The fear was real, but the threat was not.

The edges felt the war, but the heartland remained free from those enemy phantoms. In the stadium that fall afternoon, it seemed to the Marines that their people were playing at war without any understanding of consequence.

Or sacrifice.

In its November 9 issue, *Time* magazine reported that the US Army had suffered 1,016 men killed in action during the first eleven months after Pearl Harbor. The government told *Time* that the Navy, the Marines, and the Coast Guard had lost an additional 4,453 killed in action—about half at Pearl Harbor.

This loss was a drop in the bucket compared with what was coming. The "We regret to inform you" telegrams trickled out of the War Department and destroyed individual families here and there with their grim news that their loved ones had been killed in service of the nation. The trickle would become a flood in the months to come, and in 1943, the tidal wave of casualties would reshape the social fabric of every town and city, from San Francisco to Portland, Maine. The country would grow hard, and the war would come home to every living room one way or another.

But this impending reality seemed a million miles away at Grant Field. To the Marines who had suffered and fought under circumstances no other Americans had ever faced, the festive atmosphere seemed at best indulgent, at worse clueless and callous.

AFTER TECH SCORED THE FIRST TOUCHDOWN, THE GAME DEVOLVED into a series of cheap shots and ultraviolent hits. Each play was a bloody battle on the line. Punches were thrown more than once. Young men staggered to the sidelines, bloodied by the violence. John L. and Dick's host, Brittain, grew concerned and said to his aviator guests, "The refs need to start calling penalties. They're losing control of the game."

Maybe a few months ago, they would have been thinking the same thing. Instead, John L. and Dick stared at the field and saw a gridiron dogfight. Americans against Americans expending energy that needed to be spent against the real enemies.

Before halftime, a dark-haired man in a trench coat approached them from farther down the sidelines. Long face, bushy eyebrows. He was carrying a notebook.

Lee Fuhrman recognized a target of opportunity when he saw one. A veteran reporter with the *Atlanta Journal-Constitution*, he'd been covering the city's culture and music scene for a couple of years now. Deep down, he was an investigative journalist with a streak of creativity that made his reporting a cut above. While at a Philadelphia paper a few years before, he'd covered the Lindbergh kidnapping trial. Over the years since, he showed his willingness to go to extraordinary lengths to get a story. Later in his career, he joined the Ringling Bros. and Barnum & Bailey Circus and became a clown for a week to gain insight on life under the big tent. He also possessed astute observation skills. While reporting on a car wreck, he spotted a single piece of rope in the vehicle—and connected dots that had eluded the police. He ended up proving the crash was a homicide and solved the case.

At first, Fuhrman tried to strike up a friendly conversation with Dick and John L., but they weren't having it. A staff photographer joined them and snapped a picture of the men flanking Brittain. Tight-lipped and sad-eyed, John L. kept his head down, arms rigid at his side. Dick stood ramrod straight, hands clasped at his waist, eyes fixed in the distance as if his ignoring the press would make them disappear.

But Fuhrman wasn't going anywhere. He came from gritty stock—his folks were Hungarian and Russian immigrants who reached America at the height of the East European famine at the end of the nineteenth century. He grew up hard and tough in a working-class New Jersey neighborhood, where his family spoke Russian at home. He knew how to draw people out.

Dick finally gave the reporter an in when he mentioned his family back in Seattle. Fuhrman pounced. He asked about his kids, and Dick's demeanor changed. He lit up as he spoke of them. "My boy, Bryan, is four and a half. We call him Zeke. My eldest is Harriet. She's seven and a half. We call her Trinket."

Fuhrman asked, "Why Trinket?"

"'Cause she's cute as a trinket," Dick said through a smile. "When I came home, Zeke asked, 'Daddy, is the war over?' I said no. Zeke said, 'Then what are you doing home?'"

The reporter laughed with Brittain. John L. said nothing. He'd heard the story several times already.

The ice broken, the bitterness the two aviators had been feeling poured forth. The game held no interest for them. They were appalled at the scene. The Sunday morning article Fuhrman penned from the encounter politely put it, "The football game was quite incidental to these two chaps, an interview brought out. For these men know what it is to get shot at. More than that, they know what it is to see their pals shot down, chaps they might have been 'horsing' with an hour before. That's why it was hard to get these men to talk of their own exploits, their feats which they shrug off with a casual phrase, 'It's a business, this war.'"

John L., roused from his silence by the bubbling mix of anger and disorientation, suddenly blurted out, "America needs to wake up."

Dick echoed the sentiment. "War is no picnic," he said. He glanced up and around at the cheering crowd, who made his point for him.

John L. drilled Fuhrman with his eyes. The reporter wrote the next day, "He looks at you with a cold eye. . . . He's a mighty tough cookie, this young Major Smith. That's the kind of impression he makes."

Eyes locked on Fuhrman's, John L. said, "This war . . . it means killing. It means men will not come home. It means the life of your own son, or your brother or your nephew. Or your neighbor's boy."

Fuhrman asked him about air combat.

John L. was blunt. "It is either kill or be killed. It's a job to do, and you try to do it."

He pressed for details, but John L. offered few. "It gets pretty damn businesslike. There's nothing personal in it. It's just your life or his. So you do your best to make it his life and not yours."

On the sidelines of Grant Field, Dick and John L. found a message they could get behind. They hated talking about themselves. They hated trying to explain combat to a civilian. But as they spoke to the journalist, they realized they could try to sound the alarm. America needed to get serious. Ball games and elegant silverware at lunch could wait. There would be time to play and live life again after America secured victory. The war's cost was about to strike the country full in the face as hard as those Alabama linemen could hit.

FOUR

THE BUCKS COUNTY PLAYHOUSE

Long Island City, New York
November 20, 1942

THE FOUR-STORY BRICK AND GLASS BUILDING TOOK UP AN ENTIRE block in the heart of Long Island City's industrial section. Sedans were parked bumper to bumper at the curb. The day shift had just arrived, and people lined up at the guarded entrance carrying lunch pails. Some workers were dressed in coveralls or chambray button-down work shirts. This was no prewar crew. Men in their sixties and seventies, some resting on canes, stood beside young women who looked to be still in their teens. Family groups lined up together. Brothers and sisters, a grandmother with her arm around her granddaughter. Scattered among the growing crowd were Black faces among the white. The company—the Brewster Aeronautical Corporation—was known for being progressive and hiring African Americans, though it had recently been caught asking prospective recruits about their religious affiliation, ostensibly to deny employment to Jews.

The line moved forward briskly, people chatting as they waited their turn to pull their time cards from a wall-mounted rack just inside the entrance. The sound of the time stamp kept a steady cadence.

John L. Smith looked on, standing beside Ed Hicks and Dick Mangrum, oblivious to this morning routine. As was so often the case since the tour began, his mind was back on Starvation Island. He'd lightened up a little bit in press conferences after the football game. The day before, he even playfully needled Marion Carl while meeting with reporters at the Biltmore Hotel. John L. teased him into revealing how Marion had been shot down. Still, he had more and more moments when he gazed off and was lost to the occasion, thinking about the squadron, his men. The shellings and the cries of the wounded.

Beside John L., Dick glanced over at his fellow Guadalcanal vet and saw dark circles again highlighting his gaunt face. John L.'s eyes radiated that familiar sadness. It was the look of a leader who had loved his men and now struggled with the grief of losing so many of them. He wore that weight like a lead shroud. Civilians didn't understand it, but other warriors knew the look, knew the heaviness of the burden, because they carried it as well.

"Get any sleep last night?" Dick whispered to his friend.

John L. shook his head. Mornings were the toughest for him. Being on all day and all night was simply too much to ask.

Dick nodded and looked back at the line of workers. He noticed that a select few in the line wore metallic wings pinned above their breast pockets. The wings flanked a small silver pentagon, within which was the Brewster logo, surrounded by the words "Since 1810"—the year the company had been founded. Above the logo were the words *Three Years' Service*. Those pins were few and far between. Three years ago, Brewster's entire workforce numbered 912 employees, and the company had broken $1 million in aircraft sales only the year before. On November 14, 1942, the Long Island City factory counted 8,874 men and women as employees. Altogether, the company now totaled 15,000 employees spread across factories in three states. Not a bad growth spurt for a business with $370 million worth of outstanding contracts to make aircraft.

The building here on Long Island could not have looked less like an aircraft factory. It looked like any other turn-of-the-century multistory industrial building in the area—brick, with wide factory windows designed to supply plenty of natural light to the production floors. There was no airfield in sight. When the Marines asked about that, Ed Hicks told them Brewster used to truck its finished aircraft in pieces over to Roosevelt Field for final assembly and test flights. Now it sent them to Bucks County, Pennsylvania.

That seemed a little inefficient.

Yet the Navy counted on places like Brewster. On their factory floors, the aircraft so desperately needed would be built. Victory in global war started at home, right here on the shoulders of these everyday Americans streaming into the building. The United States had failed in its first effort to mobilize for total war. In 1917, despite its many robust industries, not a single American-built aircraft fought in combat during the Great War. Production delays, rampant corruption, government ineptitude, inexperience, and poor designs all forced the nascent US air services to rely on French and British aircraft.

That could not happen again. The Marine Corps needed better aircraft than what it had at Midway and Guadalcanal. It needed lots of them—and fast. What the Marines were flying in the Pacific now was barely holding the line, and it is axiomatic that as your own technology evolves in response to combat experience, so evolves the enemy's. America was in a race to conceive, design, test, and deploy better aircraft than the Japanese at a time when the Imperial Navy had proven it was the technological leader in the Pacific.

Wrote one field-grade Marine officer in a report to his commanding general after Midway, "If we can't have adequate equipment, we should be relieved, because at present if a flat-top should visit us we might break up the bombers but no one would know how many we hit. At this time we are waiting for the news from Midway and I do not doubt it will be bad. Another glorious chapter in Marine Corps tradition, written in blood, incredible odds, etc. If the losses are what I expect, it would be better called murder without honor. We are next on the list. Do something constructive before it is too late."

The "something constructive" was being done in factories like this one all over the country. A new generation of fighters and bombers was just reaching full production. The prewar designs would have to soldier on in frontline service for a few more months, but a rising tide of new aircraft would soon replace them—and equip countless new squadrons that would be hurled against the Empire of Japan.

Ed Hicks led his Guadalcanal veterans through the visitor's entrance. A moment later, Dick and John L. were introduced to the company's senior management, which included the new president and CEO, C. A. Van Dusen. The Navy had selected him to run the Brewster Aeronautical Corporation after requisitioning it from the original founder in late April 1942.

Van Dusen gave the Marines a short introduction to the company. Notably in 1932, one of the company's designers purchased Brewster's struggling aviation subcontractor division for just over $29,000. The division subcontracted through the 1930s before building a dive-bomber called the SBA for the Navy and a fighter plane known as the Brewster F2A Buffalo.

John L. knew the Buffalo well. It was one of the prewar designs that equipped Marine fighter squadrons in 1941. In fact, the F2A was one of the first fighters he'd flown after joining VMF-221 at San Diego just before Pearl Harbor. He and Marion Carl had been together in that unit when it shipped out aboard the USS *Saratoga* a few days after the war began. By then, the F4F Wildcat had become the fleet's standard fighter aircraft. The Marines got the Navy's castoffs, and the Brewster planes formed the core of the Corps' fighter aviation units until after Midway.

Midway: in that one fight, most of Marion Carl's squadron had been destroyed in a matter of minutes. The F2A proved underpowered; it was also an unstable gunnery platform. It also lacked armor protection behind the pilot's head. In combat, the Brewster could not maneuver with, or escape from, the Japanese Zero. One of Marion's squadron mates actually wrote in his official after-action report that men sent aloft in the Brewster Buffalo should be considered lost the moment they left the ground.

In a bitterly scathing report that echoed this sentiment, a Marine fighter squadron commander wrote, "If the Army or Navy can't spare decent equipment, won't the Lend-Lease work both ways? We could use some Hurricanes."

John L. hoped that whatever Brewster was building now was better than the Buffalo.

After his introduction, Van Dusen gave the men a walking tour of the factory. The company's new state-of-the-art dive-bomber, the SB2A Buccaneer, was just now starting to reach service. Earlier in the month, the Navy accepted delivery of the first batch. These aircraft were intended to replace the aging Douglas SBD Dauntless that currently equipped all the US Marine Corps and US Navy dive-bomber squadrons.[1]

The Buccaneer, Van Dusen explained, would be the plane that Dick Mangrum and his men would fly when they returned to combat. Understandably, the Seattle native was anxious to get in the cockpit and test one out.

On alternating floors of the main building and in the nearby Ford Building, Brewster was making room to begin production of the F3A. This was the next-generation fighter, also destined for Marine Corps service. It was not an organic company design but rather a license-built Chance Vought F4U Corsair, the first Navy aircraft to surpass four hundred miles an hour in level flight. According to Van Dusen, the company's retooling effort for this new design was over 50 percent complete. It would be making the Corsair in a matter of months.

On the tool and die floor, the Marines met some of the oldest employees. Plenty of men here were in their sixties or early seventies. Peter Zimmerman, working at a half-century-old shaper machine, was eighty-six. A man who had been alive during the Civil War now helped build airplanes for America's defense.

Then it was time for the visitors to address the employees. The workers gathered on the main floor, sweat and grease stained, looking curious and a little dispirited. The company president introduced his guests to the rank and file, and one at a time, the two Marines stepped forward to speak a few words.

Dick went first. Always polished, always prepared, his speech struck just the right tone. Though he knew of the Buffalo's disastrous record at Midway, talking about that would not have boosted morale here. Instead, he spoke about the battles ahead and why America was turning the tide against the enemy in the Pacific. He emphasized one great strategic advantage: American engineering and technology crushed Japan's. To illustrate the point, he related a story of how Japanese trucks bogged down on Guadalcanal. "They were two-wheel-drive jobs that fizzled in the mud," he explained. American trucks kept going, no matter the conditions.

He added that whatever worked well for the Japanese came directly from American designs. It wasn't entirely true, but Mangrum was playing to his audience.

On Guadalcanal, the Marines used captured tools, vehicles, and even an ice machine without any problem because their assembly and instruction manuals were printed in English and Japanese.

The crowd roared and applauded. Dick finished on a high note. "We can't build the planes we fly. That's up to you fellows and women. The better you build them, the better we'll fly them. And the sooner you build them, the sooner we'll be home to park that Rising Sun on the White House mantelpiece."

The workers loved his words. Cheers echoed through the factory, and Dick offered a rare grin in return. "Build them right, and we'll all be flying home sooner than you expect."

After Dick stepped back from the microphone, John L. took his place. He spoke precisely, his voice deep and gravelly, touched with a bit of an Oklahoma drawl. He stressed teamwork and the accomplishments of his squadron and never shone the limelight on his own exploits. He finished quickly, so much so that another senior manager stepped to the microphone and asked John L. a few questions.

"Are the Japanese really fanatical in their disdain of death?"

John L. leaned to the mic. He paused, putting words together in his head. The crowd stared on expectantly. "Maybe so," he began, "maybe so, but I've seen many of them use their parachutes when the going got rough."

A ripple of laughter went through the crowd. John L. frowned, thinking of the men he loved, the ones his orders sent to their deaths, day in and day out. They climbed into the cockpit every morning without complaint. He would never get over that. They knew the odds. Knew the score. And yet, nobody shirked. They faced the Reaper every day, and more than half his squadron paid the price.

But they never once said they had had enough. Their strength kept John L. going. Little did he know that his own example held his men together at the same time.

"The Japanese are tough," he suddenly added. The laughter evaporated. "But our kids . . . " He hesitated. The English language comes up short in such moments. There are no words to describe what it took to keep fighting on Guadalcanal. So he kept it simple.

"Our kids, they're tougher."

Long Island City rocked with applause.

AFTER THE SPEECH, JOHN L. BID HIS HOSTS GOOD DAY AND DEPARTED the plant with Ed Hicks, bound for the nearby Grumman Aircraft Corporation's factory complex, where Marion Carl was test-flying its next-generation naval fighter, the F6F Hellcat.

Dick stayed behind, eager to test out Brewster's new dive-bomber. His hosts drove him to Roosevelt Field, where they boarded a company transport for a short flight to Bucks County, Pennsylvania, and the company's massive and brand-new factory-airfield complex northeast of Hatboro.

The VIP contingent disembarked to a waiting group of more suits. Dick shook hands all around, carefully taking note of everyone's name as they were introduced. They had time for a quick tour through one hangar where the SB2A Buccaneer was being assembled. As they walked among the workers assembling the dive-bombers, Van Dusen pointed out some of the plant's more famous employees. Cincinnati Reds pitcher Bucky Walters had just joined the assembly team, working as an aircraft inspector during the offseason. Jack Delaney, a professional boxer, also worked as an inspector. Ben Chin, an eighteen-year-old Chinese refugee who had recently made headlines in the local papers, stood beside an SB2A's fuselage with a rivet gun. He'd escaped to America while most of his family languished under Japanese occupation back in China. Building the SB2A was his way of fighting for their liberation.

Albert "Dolly" Stark, a former major league baseball umpire, ran the plant's recreational program. To attract workers to such a remote location, Brewster realized it had to create more than just an employment opportunity. It had to create a sense of community. Soon, well over a thousand Brewster workers played in baseball, softball, basketball, and badminton leagues or joined the fencing, boxing, or flying clubs. There was even a bowling alley and some shuffleboard courts to use after hours or on breaks.

The plant manager, P. M. Stephenson, pointed out the modern firefighting equipment the company had just installed in the hangars. "Just in case of an air raid," he said with complete sincerity.

The chance of an air raid in Pennsylvania was about as likely as a blizzard in Death Valley in August. It seemed absurd.

The truth was, Van Dusen and Stephenson had an ulterior motive in bringing the most famous Marine Corps dive-bomber pilot to Hatboro. For all the hosts' talk and showmanship, this plant was a chaotic disaster. Without the skilled workforce available in New York City, Brewster had to pull in whomever it could entice to come out to rural Pennsylvania for ten-hour shifts six days a week. Hiring and keeping employees turned into a major challenge, one that forced the company to raise its hourly wage to over a dollar an hour to lure people away from the aircraft companies in the Philadelphia area.

The extra pay made little difference to retention. Many conscientious workers—some with sons in the military—quit in disgust after only a few months when they saw the slipshod quality control, the disastrous labor relations, and the slacking off that was tolerated. The factory complex earned the nickname the Bucks County Playhouse. It did not take long for reports of malingering, work slowdowns, employee walkouts, and even workers' sexual liaisons in half-built SB2A fuselages to reach Congress.

The union took such an adversarial position against Brewster's management that walkouts over trivial things like a security guard chastising an employee for driving down a street clearly labeled off-limits to vehicular traffic became commonplace. When management found and fired six young women—all fresh hires—lingering inside fuselages on the production floor in what was probably part of a prostitution ring, the union retaliated by quitting work two hours early.

Hundreds of thousands of hours were lost to the union's walkouts and slowdowns. The head of the union had pledged not to strike during wartime; he found ways around that pledge with other tactics that undermined Brewster's ability to fulfill its contracts at every turn.

The Navy ordered the Buccaneer's prototype, known as the Model 340, in April 1939. It first flew two years later. A year after that, despite all the advance money, the new factory, and the full support of the federal government, Brewster had managed to deliver a grand total of twenty dive-bombers. Along the way, two of the company's senior executives were sent to federal prison for illegally selling arms to Bolivia. Despite being caught, the two raked in millions of dollars in commissions on the export version of the Buccaneer and Buffalo—while still behind bars. Yet, to face the Axis, the country needed every defense contractor it had, so the federal government continued to push money Brewster's way.

The situation at Bucks County grew so bad that the Navy seized control of the company in April 1942. It cleared out the old senior management and brought in C. A. Van Dusen to get Brewster productive. Six months later, hardly an aircraft had left the Bucks County Playhouse, and Van Dusen was getting increasingly desperate. The Navy was pushing him hard, and if he didn't get this ship turned around soon, he'd be sacked for sure.

Dick Mangrum was there to bring the war home to the workers at Hatboro, to show them that their daily jobs had real-world implications for the men at the tip of the spear. He was the wake-up call Brewster needed to get the union and management to settle their differences for the good of the country.

He addressed thousands of workers that afternoon in front of the hangar complex at Hatboro, giving a modified version of the speech from earlier in the day at Long Island City.

"The Japs have been very unhappy these past two weeks," he began as he sketched the victories the news had reported since he'd returned from

Guadalcanal. The crowd loved it, cheering and applauding. When the workers quieted down, Dick got serious and spoke of the hardships, the need for more aircraft, more men. He spared no feelings and pointedly told the crowd that the fighting so far was just the opening round. Much tough work—and many losses—remained ahead.

"We are ready now for the real tactical fight of this war," he said, but he stressed that the only way to win was on the shoulders of every man and woman in the crowd. Their dedication, their attention to detail and quality—those would give the Marines and the Navy the weapons they needed so desperately to drive the Japanese back across the Pacific. The victory would be won not just on the battlefield but also in the factories here at home.

Speech finished, Dick was escorted to a waiting SB2A Buccaneer out on the parking ramp of the company's airfield. It wasn't painted in the normal blue and gray Navy colors. Instead, it looked more like an Army paint job, a camouflaged mélange of greens, browns, and grays.

At first glance, it resembled an extended and more squat-legged version of the Buffalo, thanks to its outsized tail and barrel-shaped fuselage. Beneath the long greenhouse canopy on the underside of the fuselage Dick spotted a pair of bomb bay doors. Unlike the SBDs that he had flown at Guadalcanal and that carried their bombs out in the open, the Buccaneer carried its ordnance internally to minimize drag.

Dick climbed into the cockpit while a Brewster test pilot crouched beside him on the wing explaining the instrument layout. Every instrument and panel was labeled in a foreign language. What's more, the instruments were metric.

When Dick asked about that, the test pilot explained that this batch of 162 Buccaneers had originally been purchased by the Dutch air force for service in the East Indies. When the Japanese knocked the Dutch out of the Pacific War, the Navy took over the contract—but refused to pay the extra $12.10 per plane to change the cockpit plates to English and the instruments to US standard.

These SB2As were destined for two Marine Air wings, one at Cherry Point, North Carolina, and the other in Florida. They were the dive-bombers of the future, presumably after the Corps repainted them and fixed the mess in the cockpit.

The test pilot made sure Dick was familiar with the cockpit layout, then gave him a rundown on things to watch out for on his flight. The brakes were twitchy and would lock up if applied too liberally while taxiing. Make sure the tail wheel is centered before takeoff by lurching forward a few feet and then hitting the brakes again. That would get it in position and lock it in place.

Even with two and a half units of right rudder trim, the Buccaneer still pulled left on takeoff. The test pilot stressed not to correct that with the brakes. Use the rudder.

He finished up his lesson with a series of what-ifs. How to handle a stall, what to do if the aircraft suffered hydraulic failure (apparently fairly common). Don't roll it under 195 knots. Any slower, and the aileron controls were sluggish.

Dick was ready to go. He went through the engine start procedure and taxied out to the broad airstrip.

He centered and locked the tail wheel before easing off the brakes. As he began the takeoff roll, he realized that the test pilot wasn't kidding. The aircraft pulled hard left, thanks to the P-factor on the propeller blades and the torque of its 1,700-horsepower Wright Cyclone engine. He countered it with right rudder and felt the tail lift at just under sixty knots. A moment later, he was angling aloft.

The aircraft was a dud. Heavy on the controls, sluggish ailerons, underpowered. Dick saw perhaps a little potential in its top speed, which was about twenty miles an hour faster than the SBD Dauntless he'd flown from Guadalcanal. It could carry two 500-pound bombs, whereas the SBD could only carry one. That, he supposed, was another advantage.

Yet the plane was a wallowing slug, and its two advantages couldn't make up for its performance deficit in other areas. In combat, it would get its crews slaughtered by Zeroes as surely as the Brewster Buffalo had been earlier in the year.

All that effort he'd seen that day by thousands of Americans of all ages, genders, and races. All the money and strategic materials flowing from foundries and steel mills into these planes. All the nation's invest-ment in Brewster, including the factory outside Hatboro and the fronting of cash before a single plane had been delivered. And this was the final product: a mediocre aircraft that offered no significant upgrade from the aging SBD Dauntless.

Fifteen thousand people were laboring to make a plane that would do little more than trigger flurries of Western Union telegrams from the War Department to the families of the Buccaneer crews surely to die in battle.

No wonder the Navy was giving it to the Corps.

What was the poem one of John L.'s pilots penned on Guadalcanal?

> *The Army gets the medals*
> *And the Navy gets the queens*
> *But the guys who get a fucking*
> *Are the United States Marines.*

Dick returned to Hatboro and set the Buccaneer down on the beauti-ful new runway, knowing that for all its deficiencies, the SBD Dauntless would have to carry the load in combat for the foreseeable future. The Buccaneer was a dud.[2]

FIVE

THE GRUMMAN WAR PRODUCTION CORPS

Bethpage, New York
November 20, 1942

THE NOON WHISTLE BLEW, AND THE GRUMMANITES POURED OUT OF Plants One, Two, and Three. They were happy, chatting, excited. The news had just been announced over the factory complex's public address system: the Navy was going to award them their second "E" burgee in six months. It was the highest honor the service could bestow on a civilian corporation and its employees.

The flow of workers from each plant converged on the streets and alleys leading to the Plant Four parking apron, where a platform decorated with red, white, and blue bunting had been erected for the occasion. For the next thirty minutes, the Grummanites—as they proudly called themselves—would celebrate with the Navy their incredible feats of production.

The crowd gathered on the apron as a Paramount Pictures newsreel crew filmed the scene. Some of the workers took notice and began mugging for the camera, waving and catcalling to the crew. The cameraman panned across the scene as thousands more pressed onto the apron to share the moment. The men and women wore button-down spread-collar shirts and cotton jackets. Most took the opportunity to strike a match and light a cigarette. There was no smoking inside the factories, so the ceremony would be their only opportunity for a nicotine fix until their afternoon fifteen-minute break.

This was the Grumman War Production Corps, as the company called its employees. They were respected. They were well treated. The company ran with smooth efficiency and produced thousands of aircraft that the Navy and Marine Corps pilots came to love. The workers built their beloved aircraft without glitz or glamour, just rugged as hell—exactly like the people who filled the factory. Their planes defined American engineering at its finest. Grumman was everything Brewster aspired to be: successful, functional, a major part of the war effort.

Grumman's F4F Wildcat had been the one fighter capable of standing toe-to-toe with the Japanese Zero these past months. Where the Zero made short work of nearly every other Allied fighter plane, the stubby, underrated little Grumman put an end to Imperial Japan's string of victories.

Those who built these beloved fighters waited eagerly for the ceremony to begin. The atmosphere was electric. They had been through this once before, having no idea what a Navy "E" burgee, or pennant, was. It stood for excellence in production. It meant the Navy valued the company's contribution to the war effort above all others. Grumman would be the first aircraft company to receive two of them.

The Plant One band stepped onto the platform. Each factory in the Grumman complex had its own rec teams and clubs, including bands and orchestras. The musicians had put down their rivet guns and wrenches for a chance to do what they loved most: play some music for an appreciative audience.

When they burst out with a John Philip Sousa march, the crowd went nuts. The energy skyrocketed to the stratosphere. These men and women labored day in and day out, knowing that each plane they made could get one of their own community's sons or husbands home safe. That point was driven home after one of their own, Mildred Brittingham, received one of the dreaded War Department telegrams. Her husband, a Navy lieutenant, had been killed in action fighting a German U-boat in the North Atlantic. She worked through her grief on the factory floor, avenging the loss of the love of her life with every aircraft she helped build.

A door behind the grandstand opened, and the workers recognized the first two men through it. President of the corporation Leroy Grumman stepped to the platform first, followed by the company's general manager, Leon A. "Jake" Swirbul. Several more followed: Paul Gilbert, the company's beloved personnel director; a local judge; and a Navy lieutenant commander tasked with bestowing the honor on the company and crowd.

Then two other men in Marine Corps uniforms stepped through the door. The crowd, already cheering, went into a frenzy as they recognized Maj. John L. Smith and Capt. Marion Carl, Grumman's "two greatest customers."

John L., fresh from Long Island City and the tour at Brewster, unleashed a broad, boyish grin. Carl hadn't seen him smile like that since before Pearl Harbor. The sadness in his friend's eyes had vanished. Instead, they shone with genuine happiness. The skipper of 223 jauntily scrambled up the steps to the platform and waved at the crowd. A surge of voices met the greeting. Both Marines could sense it: this was a family moment, melding the men of war to the builders of their weapon of choice. This was what they needed to see: Americans at home totally devoted to the war effort.

Marion's cap was raked at an angle, making him look even more strapping and cool than usual. Women in the crowd pointed, and the company's newspaper later reported, "The girls murmured approvingly over Captain Carl's tall handsomeness."

The Oregonian, grinning as widely as his skipper, took station beside him and looked out over the crowd. He'd never seen so many cheering faces before. Not for him, anyway. He'd grown up on a muddy dairy farm in near-abject poverty outside Hubbard, Oregon. The entire population of his hometown was probably a third of the size of this crowd.

The scene was like a jolt of adrenaline to him. Carl had been coasting through the tour, totally uninterested in the press conferences and fluff that Ed Hicks had arranged. In fact, the day before, during another meet-the-press moment at the Biltmore, Marion had dozed off twice while Dick and John L. fielded questions.

This was different. Marion knew nobody in the crowd yet felt connected to them. The Wildcat wasn't the best fighter ever built, but it got him home countless times when others would have failed him. And when he was shot down, the armor in his cockpit almost surely saved his life. Somebody in this crowd had built that cockpit and installed that armor. Funny to think he owed his life to a stranger—man or woman—who could be present in this moment.

Even better, earlier that morning, he'd flown the planes destined to replace the F4F. He'd talked his way into an F4U Corsair, then climbed into Grumman's latest and greatest design: the F6F Hellcat. Square lines, rugged, blunt fuselage, the Hellcat looked like the bigger, badder brother of the Wildcat. It had power. It had maneuverability. It could climb like a hawk and dive like an anvil. One flight and Carl could tell this plane would be the weapon the Navy—and, hopefully, the Marine Corps— would hammer Imperial Japan with in the months ahead.

The ceremony began. The burgee—basically a pennant with an *E* on it—was hoisted aloft on a flagpole. The crowd celebrated as the burgee fluttered in the early afternoon breeze. Then Leroy Grumman asked the boys from Guadalcanal to say a few words.

To onlookers, they seemed almost abashed. Neither man had the speaking ability of Dick Mangrum. One reporter noted, "They were truly men of action, not words."

Still, John L. took center stage and knocked it out of the park with his first comment.

"There were times when the only planes over the Solomon Islands were TBFs and F4Fs."

At the mention of their fighter and torpedo bomber, the crowd's cheering rose to a new crescendo. John L. and Marion realized the extent of the ownership these men and women felt over the planes they produced. It was a beautiful thing to see.

"You can see who is doing the fighting down there!" John L.'s voice was strong and gravelly. It carried through the apron and echoed off the factory walls.

More cheers, and John L. waited. He could feel the electricity, the unseen connection between speaker and audience. The energy fired him up as nothing else had since Guadalcanal. And he brought the house down with his next line.

"Just ask the Japs what *they* think of the Grumman Wildcats!"

Marion had no idea how to follow that act. When his turn to speak came, he started a bit slow, thanking everyone for the tour of the factories earlier that morning. Marion was never one to get flowery or effusive. He was the steady-keeled hardscrabble dairyman's son who remained unmoved in every storm. He spoke with a directness that was often refreshing, sometimes astonishing. On this day, his straightforward ways sent the crowd in a fit of cheers yet again.

"I have flown Grumman planes at both Midway and Guadalcanal. I know the kind of planes you make from firsthand experience. From the records, both you and we know that your Grumman planes must be *plenty* good."

When the whistles and clapping ebbed, he added, "I hope to get back out there and have a chance to fly one of your new models. I know we'll try to do even better with them than we did in the past."

Marion thanked the Grummanites, then backed away from center stage. The ceremony concluded with Leroy Grumman presenting John L. with an American flag that had flown over the Grumman factory complex.

For a few minutes afterward, Marion and John L. stepped down onto the apron to meet and thank the workers face-to-face. The crowd surged around them. One man called out, "Hey, fellas, when you go out there again—get *me* one of those little yellow men. Send him back in an envelope!"

The Marines ignored the comment as they continued to shake hands. These pilots had seen the quality of the Japanese aircrew firsthand. They knew how formidable, courageous, and relentless they could be. There was no room in such a world for hurling a racial slur at these foes. The racism endemic on the home front had once informed the military's arrogant view of the Japanese. It led to a prewar sense of superiority that got thousands of Americans killed. The war made realists of the survivors. Skin color made no difference at twenty thousand feet—only skill behind the stick.

Marion and John L. were genuinely touched by the extent of the emotional outpouring for them as more workers rushed to say a few words of praise and thanks. One Rosie, eyes alive as if she were meeting a childhood hero for the first time, rushed to the front of the crowd and grasped Marion's hand. Surprised, he turned to her and was struck by her earnestness and beauty.

"Captain Carl," she said, "it was awfully good of you to visit us today."

Marion blushed. Actually blushed. The crowd saw it and started to laugh. The young woman released his hand and fell back into the crowd, her eyes and smile radiating adulation.

All too soon, the whistle wailed. The crowd reacted instantly. Time to get back to work winning the war. The throngs of employees flowed out of the apron and rushed back to their plants, taking a final drag on their cigarettes before flicking them to the asphalt. The two pilots watched them go as photographers prepared to take a few last photos of them with Grumman's senior managers.

Not long after, they repeated the ceremony at Plant Fifteen, which was several miles away from the main Grumman factory complex. Afterward, Leroy Grumman announced he would hold a cocktail party in their honor that evening at the Waldorf Astoria. The heroes of the hour would be treated to the best the Big Apple had to offer.

Marion was not a drinker, and he was exhausted after the outpouring, the speeches, the flying. He'd also been wrestling with bad news from home. His mother, still living on and working the dairy farm in Hubbard, woke up earlier in the week to find their main barn on fire. The entire herd of dairy cows had died in the blaze—almost two hundred head. His mother's ability to make a living had been lost in that fiery instant.

Worse, in the days that followed, rumors seeped back to Marion from friends in Oregon. All the front-page news may have generated a backlash. Many of his neighbors in that part of the Willamette Valley were first-generation German immigrants who came to Oregon after the Great War. There was considerable suspicion that the fire was sabotage inflicted by some who still held allegiance to Germany and was retaliation against anyone fighting against the Axis powers.

Despite all these reasons, he couldn't turn down this invitation. None of them could or probably really wanted to. A night in New York City, feted by one of the great industrialists of the era? That would be a night to remember, for sure.

Little did Marion Carl know, it was a night that would change his life forever and would ultimately define his death.

SIX

A LONG-STEMMED AMERICAN BEAUTY

Waldorf Astoria, New York City
November 20, 1942

DICK, JOHN L., AND MARION STOOD TOGETHER IN THE LOBBY OF the Waldorf Astoria. In a few minutes, they would head into the reception room where the cocktail party was being held in their honor. They were dressed in their best uniforms, hair combed, and freshly shaved. All had showered after their day at the aircraft factories.

Ed Hicks joined them a moment later. "Gentlemen, I have news," he said. Leroy Grumman had called over to the John Robert Powers Agency earlier in the day and asked if he could send four agency models to help entertain his Marine hero guests at the cocktail party. The Powers Agency contract included a clause that required each woman to be available for such events. The company promised to have four of its models at the Waldorf by five p.m. sharp.

The Marines regarded one another. Models. *New York models?* John Robert Powers had transformed the fashion industry and revolutionized the advertising business when he founded his company some twenty years before. The models his agency signed were legendary. They started with print work around New York but many found their way into theater and Hollywood. He was discerning about whom he signed. Refined, intelligent, charismatic, tall—and gorgeous—those were the features that defined a Powers model. So much so that his models were dubbed Long-Stemmed American Beauties.

Marion looked around his circle of friends. He pulled the bachelor card. "You guys are all married. I get first pick."

The other guys weren't thrilled by that, but with rings on their fingers, they couldn't argue the point. Besides, these women were anything but escorts—that was never the role of Powers models. Their role was to be hostesses and ambassadors for their city.

They headed to the reception room, where they found Grumman and the other senior managers waiting for them, cocktails in hand, wives on their arms. It was just a bit before five, and the models had yet to arrive. While Dick and John L. ordered drinks and made small talk with their hosts, Marion slipped away to post up beside the door. He wanted a good look at the models when they entered the party.

They did a few minutes later. None of them spotted Marion beside the door as they entered, dressed to the nines.

Marion never noticed the other three models, seeing only the one who didn't seem to fit the mold. She was shorter than the other three women and was not as opulently dressed as the others. She favored Italian shoes and had her dark hair pinned up. Victory red lipstick, crystal-blue eyes, and a warm smile revealing perfect teeth—her beauty transfixed him.

She had no idea the reaction she triggered in Marion. Instead, she walked straight up to Dick and introduced herself. The two began chatting amicably. Marion watched her from his corner across the room. There was something captivating about her. The way she carried herself. She moved with grace, seemed totally at ease in the middle of a room full of millionaires and national heroes. She had presence.

Marion couldn't take his eyes off her. She couldn't take her eyes off Dick. Tall and handsome in his own right, Dick had a smooth and engaging cocktail-hour persona. He would have fit in with the Grumman suits had he taken a different career path. He was also a gentleman, still in love with his wife, Virginia, as much as he'd been a decade and a half before, when they were wed. As they talked, he held his drink with his left hand, prominently displaying the wedding band on his ring finger.

Marion knew others considered him handsome, and people reacted to his boyish grin, but he was not a live wire at a cocktail party. He was an introvert, a man more dedicated than most to his craft of flying fighters. Long before the war broke out, his dream of becoming a pilot absorbed most of his time and energy. When he joined the Corps, the dream became the single focus of his life.

He'd dated over the years. Had girlfriends from time to time, but never anything serious. He was twenty-seven years old, was currently front-page news across the counter, and had nearly died a dozen times in distant, never-heard-of islands before Pearl Harbor. Yet, he had never been in love—and frankly knew little about it.

Staring across the room at the blue-eyed brunette, he felt a pull he'd never experienced before. He had been charmed before. Wowed by somebody's beauty. Those infatuations never endured. This felt different.

He took a step toward her. Then another. He had no plan, felt almost as if he were on autopilot. He found himself cutting in. Dick glanced at him, irritated at first. Then he remembered the deal and backed down.

"Marion Carl, meet Edna Kirvin," he said politely.

Edna held out her hand, which Marion shook gently. Her palm was soft and smooth; his was dry and calloused from hours behind the stick of a fighter. He felt an almost electric thrill at their touch. A look into her eyes, and he sensed she felt it too. She offered a vivacious smile that set Marion instantly at ease. As they chatted, he began to realize just how tightly wound he'd been for all these months. Listening to Edna, he felt the stress and tension drain away.

As they talked in the middle of the room, Dick totally forgotten beside them, Marion smelled her perfume. Bright, airy, liberating—a complex mosaic of scents that hinted of flowers, spring days, and oranges. It was soft and feminine, a bit mysterious with a texture and depth that utterly intoxicated him.

Marion Carl had just encountered Chanel No. 5 for the first time. Those half-ounce bottles of Chanel, resembling whiskey decanters, were hard to come by in 1942, seeing as the Germans occupied France. When they could be found, the price was far beyond something most women he knew back home in Oregon could afford: the 2024 equivalent of four hundred dollars an ounce.

The room vanished. For him, there was only Edna, maintaining eye contact as she laughed and smiled through the cocktail-hour inanities. Small talk. What was the point?

The point was not to let this woman get away. He found the words, kept the cadence. She responded and laughed. They sparked and kept sparking, Edna taken by the physique and handsome features of this tall and rugged Marine. He was a man far different from the others she'd met on this circuit, and she grew curious about him. She began to ask questions that drew him, inch by inch, out of his protective introvert's shell.

Cocktail hour ended all too soon. While others around the room chatted in happy clusters, Ed Hicks intruded on their couple's space to announce it was time to go do the *Fred Waring Show*, which was being broadcast from a ballroom elsewhere in the Waldorf.

Marion was scheduled to be interviewed on the program. He didn't want to say goodbye to Edna and cared not a whit about the radio show. His attitude intrigued Edna even more: a man who had absolutely no interest in fame. She was reluctant to say goodbye.

He asked her if she'd want to come see the show. She accepted on the provision that she call her mother and let her know where she was. Edna's answer impressed Marion; she was conscientious and from a caring family.

The *Fred Waring Show* started at six. Ed hustled Marion down to meet the legendary band leader backstage ahead of the broadcast. Waring's show had first hit the airwaves in 1933. Ever since, it had been a staple of American pop culture. His band, Fred Waring and His Pennsylvanians, dominated the airwaves every Friday evening on NBC. The show was sponsored by Chesterfield cigarettes, and Waring used the revenue to build his own dance hall and soundstage in Pennsylvania, where the show usually was performed. Over the years, he would often go on location to places like the Waldorf for special broadcasts.

Although it was ostensibly a musical variety show, Waring made a point of bringing veterans onto the program ever since the Pearl Harbor attack. As Edna sat in the audience that evening, the bandleader interviewed Marion Carl, and the nation heard his quiet, deep voice for the first time. Until that moment, Marion's fame had come entirely from newspaper interviews and radio news accounts of his exploits.

The voice that greeted America that night was genteel, even kindly. But a discerning listener could detect underneath it the solid steel of a man used to privation and hardship—someone who had persevered and thrived through every trial.

By the end of the show, Edna was completely smitten. He seemed a man without ego or pretense. He did have an ego, but it was totally invested in his flying, not in what he took as superficial aspects of life, like money and prestige and fame.

So when Marion asked Edna if she was hungry, she suggested dinner at the Twenty-One Club. They headed to West Fifty-Second Street to one of the most unusual clubs in the area. During Prohibition, the place had been known as Jack and Charlie's 21. It had been filled with secret passages and levers that would flip the counters and dump liquor down chutes into the city's sewer system in case of a police vice raid. Later in the 1930s, the place became renowned as the storage facility for wine collections of A-list celebrities like Frank Sinatra and Ernest Hemingway.

John L., Dick, and the Grumman managers may have accompanied Marion and Edna to the club, but the two were so fixated on each other, they never mentioned those companions later. They spent dinner in their own bubble of conversation.

From there, they moved on to the El Morocco, Leroy Grumman happily picking up the tab. The El Morocco, a staple of the New York café society set, was made famous by its blue zebra-striped decor that Jerome Zerbe made famous with his photographs of politicians, actors, mob bosses, and the local literati there.

Marion was a fish far out of water, but for Edna, this was her scene. She was comfortable anywhere, including sitting on the overstuffed seats of the El Morocco, rubbing elbows with the rich and famous. Marion assumed she was part of that crowd. She handled herself with such poise, nothing seemed to faze her or break her graciousness. For all her beauty, he couldn't detect a trace of arrogance. She was earthy, grounded. To his surprise, when he asked Edna her age, she said she was only nineteen.

The party shoved off from the El Morocco after a couple of rounds, Marion and Edna both barely drinking. The others were happy and lit, laughing and carrying on as they made their way from East Fifty-Fourth eight blocks to the Copacabana nightclub at 10 East Sixtieth, just in time for the next show.

They piled inside, Marion noting the over-the-top Brazilian-style decor. It was as opulent and overdone as the El Morocco, just focused on another continent. Opened in 1940 by mob boss Frank Costello and Monte Proser, the Copa featured some of the best café entertainment on the circuit. To compete with the Ziegfeld Follies, the club created its own chorus line revue, the Copacabana Girls.

This season, the Copa chorus line was the talk of the set. Nicknamed the Samba Sirens, the revue usually included six dancers. This season, it had a seventh, as the producer hired identical twins Lucille and Lois Barnes. Tall and slender at five feet seven and 114 pounds, the two dancers were frequently in the local news cycle.

All the dancers were. They performed three shows a night, seven days a week, for $280 a month. They worked on routines and knitted socks for soldiers overseas during the day, then performed between comedian Joe E. Lewis's sets until after midnight.

It was tiring, demanding work, but the opportunities open to Samba Sirens were not trivial. The act packed the Copa every night and made the owners millions. Eighteen of the original twenty-five dancers went on to Broadway careers or landed Hollywood contracts. This was ground zero for developing new talent, and the A-listers flocked to the club to get the first glimpses. The dancers' measurements were shared in the likes of *Life* magazine, their favorite perfumes discussed and emulated. The twins wore Surrender and Shocking, while most of the others preferred the dark and rebelliously sensual L'Heure Bleue, which came bottled in Baccarat crystal and cost far more than they could afford on their salaries.

The show began with the house band performing "You Just Can't Copa with a Copacabana Baby." The dancers emerged onstage dressed in glamorous costumes—slit skirts with risqué halter tops and outrageously large ruffled sleeves topped with ivory-colored ornate sombreros.

Marion and Edna watched, tucked tight together in a booth packed with the other members of the night's party. Drinks all around, but Marion had Coke. Edna nursed hers slowly. She was not about to get sloppy, though John L. and Dick had descended into happy inebriation. For that matter, so had the Grummanites.

After midnight, they moved on to the Stork Club, but not before Edna excused herself to find a pay phone and call her mother again.

When she returned to Marion's side, she smiled shyly and explained why she kept calling. "I told her before I went to the Waldorf that I was going to stay for only a half an hour, just like I promised Mr. Powers."

"What made you stay?"

"You."

The sparks ignited a full-on conflagration.

The Stork Club early Saturday morning was filled with pampered debs, stirring the bubbles out of their champagne with monogrammed solid-gold swizzle sticks. This was the haunt of the elite of the elite, the most prestigious club on the café society circuit. Marion was only dimly aware of the opulence and ostentatiousness. He fixated on Edna the entire time.

There in the Cub Room, something happened to both of them. They made an odd couple, the farm-boy warrior and the fashionista big-city model. But beneath those exteriors, they discovered kindred souls.

Tenacity defined Marion's soul. He'd entered the Corps at a time when it had fewer than fifty fighter pilots. Determined to become one of them, he battled fiercely for the only fighter pilot slot available when his class graduated from flight training. He'd learned that kind of never-quit attitude on the farm. You found a way to make it work, no excuses. Failure was unacceptable. That was just life in Hubbard during the Great Depression.

When Marion asked how Edna had become a Powers model, she told him that when she was sixteen and riding a city bus one day, she noticed an advertisement showing an attractive young model. She thought to her-self, "I'm as good-looking as she is. I bet I could do that."

When she went home and announced her intentions, her three broth-ers fell over laughing. They teased her mercilessly until, infuriated, she had a friend with a camera take some head shots. She sent the prints to the Powers Agency, and a few weeks later, the agency called and invited her in for an interview.

She showed up at the appointed hour, checked in with the reception-ist, and sat down in the lobby to await her turn. As she sat there, a man appeared in the lobby, came over, and started talking to her.

With three brothers, Edna never had any trouble talking to men. She chatted away happily until the gentleman excused himself and disap-peared into the building. A few moments later, the receptionist's phone rang.

"Miss Kirvin, Mr. Powers will see you now," she called.

Edna stood up, straightened her dress, and followed directions to John Robert Powers's office. When she stepped inside, she saw the man she'd just been talking to in the lobby.

"Congratulations, and welcome aboard," he said.

Either the conversation in the lobby was a happy accident, or the con-versation *had been* the interview. Either way, Edna scored the gig.

ANOTHER ROUND OF DRINKS HIT THEIR TABLE. NO ALCOHOL FOR EDNA or Marion, but the rest of the party had no restraint. They forgot the war for a night and the disconnect they had felt ever since coming home. The reprieve from that disorientation felt glorious and liberating.

It was a needed moment, a healing one. When Civil War veter-ans returned from Appomattox, they discovered that two wars had been fought: the one the civilians back home had learned about through the war correspondents like Ambrose Bierce and the war that they had actually experienced. These were competing visions, and the friction between them caused great turmoil and hardship for the soldiers. The war had been lost in translation by the journalists and the censors back home; they had created a sanitized version that was all heroics and dash. The realities the veterans knew were stored away in their hearts and memories, for every time they attempted to set the record straight, their people failed to understand. Ultimately, the home-front version of the war won out, and the memories of what it really had been like faded as that generation of warriors passed on.

John L., Dick, and Marion experienced the same thing. This night was the first step toward a long, slow surrender to the home front's version. For the moment, the disconnect was bridged.

Edna and Marion huddled close, legs and sides touching in the booth. It was intimate despite the public setting. They saw only each other, lost in the cadence of their communication as they moved well beyond the typical small talk.

Along the way, their conversation turned to their parents. To their surprise, they learned they had both lost their dads while growing up. For Marion, his father's death was not a traumatic event. He rarely spoke of him through his entire life. When he did, it was to mention his violent streak. But both knew what losing their family's breadwinner in the midst of the Depression meant. Marion's mother had stepped up to run the dairy and keep the family afloat. For Edna and her brothers, their father's death meant that their mother had to take over her husband's trucking business in Brooklyn, New York. Aside from maybe the front lines in the Pacific, there was no sphere in America more a man's world than the trucking industry and its Teamsters Union. It was a bare-knuckles, take-no-prisoners world that required ruthlessness and complete dedication. Her mother carved a place, earning the respect of her male counterparts and rivals in the business.

Two people from opposite coasts, one raised around more cows than people, the other never having even seen a cow except on a plate. When they dug below their differences, they found a vein of common ground that opened one to the other in a way they had never experienced.

Edna sensed that Marion was a man with many friends. None were confidants. They liked him but knew almost nothing about him. For his friends, he was an in-the-moment kind of person, his backstory unshared.

He never spoke of his feelings, of his emotional life. This part of him he kept tucked away under iron guard. Life on the farm had taught him this, and his time in the Corps reinforced it.

Back in Oregon, he'd also been raised in a culture where a man could only reveal his true self to one person: the love of his life. In Marion's world, that woman someday would be his only lifelong confidante, the person for whom he stripped his armored heart bare the moment he came through the door.

The group closed down the Stork Club at four a.m. One more call to Edna's anxious mother, who was waiting up for her in the family's living room, and they headed out the door. The party said farewell and split up in cabs, each going their own way home.

Marion climbed inside the cab with Edna, not wanting to miss a second of time with her before he had to say good night. As they rode along to the Kirvin house on the corner of Flatbush and Beverley Road in Brooklyn, another tumbler clicked into place between them. Alone now for the first time, a glass partition between them and the cabby studiously regarding the road, the couple snuggled in back together. Whatever had happened to them that night was still unclear. It was a jumble of emotions that pulled them together in such a way that both sensed everything had changed.

Edna ventured to a subject otherwise avoided: the war. So far, Marion had not volunteered anything. He was sick of reporters' questions and the vapidness of those press conferences. The articles produced from them bore no resemblance to what he'd experienced or seen.

In the safety of Edna's arms in the back of that cab, he took the first steps toward her in a meaningful way. He began to talk about the warrior's version of the war. Of Midway and Guadalcanal. Edna leaned against him, quietly listening as the story unfolded. He included the things the press missed, the censors removed. Before that taxi reached Brooklyn, Edna Kirvin became Marion Carl's one and only—his lifelong confidante.

PART TWO

SEVEN

THE SIXTY-MINUTE VETERANS

Oahu, Hawai'i
June 21, 1942

CAPT. MARION CARL STEPPED OUT OF THE PBY CATALINA FLYING
boat his friend Bill Hardaker had piloted out of Midway earlier in
the morning. The Navy ground crew descended on the big twin-engine
craft as soon as they taxied onto the concrete seaplane ramp at Ford
Island, Oahu, Hawai'i. He'd been out on Midway since Christmas Day,
1941. The last time he'd been here at Pearl Harbor, coils of smoke still
rose above the ruined vessels of battleship row. Glancing in that direction now, Marion saw no smoke over the wrecked superstructure of
the USS *Arizona*. Both the *Arizona* and the *Oklahoma* were still leaking oil, though, leaving a glistening slick visible from overhead as they
flew in.

As if what happened at Midway weren't enough of a message, seeing
the damage here at Pearl Harbor was another reminder that the enemy
Marion and his comrades faced was deadly effective at the art of war.

And what of him and his fellow Marines?

Fellow Marines. The handful that survived *one* mission against the
Japanese. Less than an hour of combat had destroyed VMF-221. Two
planes and a few pilots were all that the Marines had to work with at the

start of June 5, 1942. But the reality was even starker. Capt. Kirk Armistead's going off and getting drunk set the tone for what happened in the days that followed. The squadron's spirit had been broken, and none of the leaders stepped up to try to pull the men together. They sniped at one another. Groused. Drank to deaden the trauma. The collapse in morale was a complete disaster.

Marion was a captain in rank only. He'd started the war six months ago as a second lieutenant. At Midway, probably because he'd become a regular Marine officer instead of the reservist he'd originally been, the Corps promoted him to first lieutenant. Less than two months in grade, and he was promoted to captain. It happened so fast that he didn't even have time to order his first lieutenant's bars.

Yet Marion had survived his first contact with the Japanese, unlike the majority of his squadron. He now possessed something only about two dozen Marine aviators had on June 21, 1942: combat experience. He was a veteran now, thanks to those sixty minutes off Midway.

The aviator had faced the Japanese, escaped from near-certain death, and then dished a bit of payback at the end of the fight by flaming a Zero. Those encounters counted for something, with experience in such short supply. He'd fought smart, made the right decisions in the heat of the moment. As he thought through his experiences on Midway in the days after June 4, he took comfort in how he had responded. It gave him confidence—something that much of the rest of 221 had lost.

A few days after the battle, he confided in his diary that he was ready for another fight. In another man, those words may have been penned to give himself strength for the battles ahead—a man struggling with the grief and despair that most of the VMF-221 survivors were grappling with. That wasn't the case with Marion. Farm life in Depression-era Oregon tempered him to hardship. Death was not an exceptional event in that world—it was a part of life. Before he left the farm, the life had claimed a brother and his father.

He took the deaths around him on Midway the same way he handled death back then: he compartmentalized it. He focused on the immediate and threw himself into the tasks at hand.

Many of the remaining men of the squadron, without planes or a mission, sank into a torpor as a result of the idleness. They simply waited for relief and a ticket off the island and out of battle.

Marion felt lifelong contempt for what happened there on the atoll after the battle. As he caught a ride to the Royal Hawaiian, where he would stay during a short leave that first day of summer in 1942, he just wanted to forget Midway altogether. He knew that the battle was the first round in a long, long war. To survive it, he'd need a short memory. So he walled off the past and looked ahead, eyes locked on the future missions waiting somewhere over the Pacific's blue horizon.

THE ROYAL HAWAIIAN WAS A FAVORITE R&R LOCATION FOR BOTH AVIA-tors and submariners fresh back from grueling patrols. The most luxurious beachfront hotel on the island went from the play place of the rich and famous to party central for men fresh back from combat. The hard-core drinking and carousing that went on became the stuff of legends in later years as those who survived looked back fondly on the interludes beside the aquamarine tropical waters.

For Marion Carl, a man who drank little and didn't carouse, the time was spent waiting for his next assignment. He'd been so disgusted with what happened in his squadron that he had little desire to spend time with the majority of its survivors. Some of those men were whisked off the island and sent stateside after only a couple of days at the Royal Hawaiian, never to be seen again by Marion and most of the others. They ended up in training command. The others congregated in cliques as they waited for their next assignments. Some considered those little better than death sentences.

A FEW MILES AWAY AT MARINE CORPS AIR STATION EWA FIELD, CAPT. John L. Smith stared at a pile of paperwork sitting on his government-issue metal desk in his tiny office. Requests for spare parts. Requests for more aircraft. Requests for more personnel. He'd been wrestling with this stuff for almost sixty days since taking command of VMF-223 on May 1.

The Marine Corps' wartime expansion program had barely reached the freshly formed squadrons standing up at Ewa Field. Fighting 223 consisted of himself as its skipper, Capt. Rivers Morrell as his executive officer, one tech sergeant pilot, and ninety-two enlisted men. About thirty were regulars; the rest were basically civilians in Marine uniform celebrating their second summer since their high school graduations. They had gone to basic training like every other Marine and had done little else. Hastily trained, they embarked on troop trains and were sent west to San Diego. About half boarded the USS *Hilo*, and the rest filed aboard the escort carrier *Long Island*.

When they arrived at Ewa after their oceanic voyage, the air group staff lined them up in the barracks and had them count off, "223, 224, 231, 232. . . . " That's how they were selected and distributed to the four squadrons of Marine Aviation Group 23 (MAG-23). Skill sets had nothing to do with it, though MAG-23 had been horse-trading with VMF-224 and Dick Mangrum's dive-bomber squadron to get one guy who knew how to type to serve as John L.'s clerk.

Two officers, less than a hundred men, and nine overused Brewster F2A Buffalos that had been castoffs from the Navy's fleet carriers—that was John L.'s first command. He was a captain, and not a very senior one at that, so when he was pulled off Midway, he bounced between a couple of squadrons to swiftly learn some of the admin requirements of command. When he received orders taking command of 223, he was as surprised as some of the men senior to him. After all, he'd been in dive-bomber units most of his flying career with the Corps, but half a year of flying Buffalos made him qualified in these desperate times.

Along with his own fighter squadron, the Corps gave John L. a ring-knocker as his exec. Not just any ordinary ring-knocker though. He was a legend: Chattanooga, Tennessee, native Rivers "Bulldog" Morrell thrived at the US Naval Academy in Annapolis, Maryland. After his mother moved the family to Los Angeles, he made a name for himself as one of the best prep athletes in the county. A relentless work ethic earned him an appointment to Annapolis, where he joined the football squad. On the field as a brawling, fearless offensive guard for the Midshipmen, he showed natural leadership even as an underclassman. In 1936—his senior year season—he became the team's captain. In one memorable game, he recovered a critical fumble that helped secure a key victory that season. This tenacity on the gridiron belied a more gentle heritage—he was the great-grandnephew of one of Chattanooga's celebrated musicians and composers, Roy Lamont Smith.

Before the war, Naval Academy grads often stuck their noses up around "lesser" officers who went to other public universities and found other paths into the Corps. John L. was one of those men. After his years as a University of Oklahoma Sooner, he transferred from the Army to the Marine Corps, serving two years in artillery units before earning a coveted slot to flight school. He was devoid of pretention.

Fortunately, so was Rivers Morrell. Square-jawed, with a broad nose, dark hair, and dark eyes, he possessed rugged good looks that mirrored his personality. In the two months since he and John L. had started working together, they had formed an excellent, relaxed relationship. John L. could see that Rivers was a magnetic leader. Capable, devoted. He arrived early, left late. His ethic set the example. But with only three pilots in the unit, there was nobody to see his principled nature. That made it all the more impressive since it was genuine. That's how Rivers rolled.

For two months, they had stood alerts with their few working aircraft and pilots. Thirty minutes at sunrise, thirty minutes at sundown. Exactly what this routine was to accomplish is anyone's guess. In March, though, a couple of Japanese flying boats sneaked over Oahu to drop a few bombs one night. Other than that, the fight was far away, fortunately. Any actual interception would have revealed 223's feeble combat power.

In between alerts, the three pilots in the squadron—Tech Sgt. John Lindley, Rivers, and John L.—flew night intercept training missions with the Navy. Useful stuff, as learning to fly in the dark was not something the schools back in the States focused on. Still, a fighter squadron needed to be training for its mission: intercepting enemy aircraft, attacking ground targets, and escorting friendly bombers. Very little of that could be done with just a few planes and pilots.

On June 21, the two shattered Midway squadrons, VMF-221 and the dive-bomber crews of VMSB-241, began dribbling back to Oahu. Some men, like Marion, rode back on PBYs. Others were stuffed into the cramped fuselages of the Boeing B-17 Flying Fortress bombers that had been based at Midway for the duration of the battle. The men didn't return as integrated squadrons, and they left their few remaining aircraft back on Midway for whoever would take their place.

John L. was informed by Marine Aircraft Group 23 HQ that the surviving fighter pilots who did not get sent home would be spread among the units forming at Ewa to give them a kernel of combat-experienced veterans.

The Oklahoman couldn't wait to get them. Anyone, really. Yet, their arrival and distribution would have to wait at least a few days. For now, the Midway vets had earned some beach time in front of the Royal Hawaiian.

Little concrete information had filtered back from Midway to Ewa, other than the fact that many Marine pilots had died. The Corps presented seven men of VMF-221 to United Press reporter Frank Tremaine, who dutifully wrote a heroic account of the fight over Midway. The story stressed that the Marines had squared off against four-to-one odds—and still crushed the Japanese. The article ran under a headline proclaiming that 221 had shot down no fewer than forty-three aircraft.

Charlie Kunz, a second lieutenant whom John L. didn't know, was quoted in the article, which ran in the Honolulu papers on June 23. Kunz described how he had shot down two Japanese planes and how Zeroes had then chased him to the deck. Machine gun rounds inflicted two grazing wounds on the side of his head as he twisted and dodged the Japanese attacks. Once again, the lack of head armor in the F2A Buffalo showed incredible lack of forethought by the aircraft's designers.

Marion Carl was also interviewed. He spoke concisely of seeing his two flight mates, Clayton Canfield and Capt. John Carey, shooting down several Japanese planes before Zeroes deluged them. Carey was wounded. Canfield covered his flight leader all the way back to Midway, Zeroes nipping at their heels. After Carey crash-landed, Canfield pancaked on the runway, too, a Zero still on his tail.

The paper made it sound like an incredible Marine victory. There was no ink spilled on the squadron's losses, nor on its state after the battle.

John L. knew that the casualty figures said something else. The list of the dead and missing from VMF-221 was a long one and included several men he knew and had served with when he was in the squadron at the start of the war.

Capt. Herbert T. Merrill was one of those men. Herb had been a three-sport letterman at the University of New Hampshire—tough, aggressive to the point of recklessness. He would have been a great addition to VMF-223, but during the defense of Midway, his Buffalo was set afire by Zeroes. Badly burned, he bailed out at two thousand feet and ended up in the water about two miles from the reef surrounding the atoll. He was rescued three hours later. Now he was in the naval hospital at Pearl Harbor, recovering.[1]

On the Honolulu front page that day, next to the story of VMF-221, was an article detailing the experiences of two Korean Americans sent to Midway as civilian mechanics tasked with maintaining the B-17s temporarily deployed to the atoll. Both were born and raised in Hawai'i. During the Japanese raid, they helped pass ammunition to Marine anti-aircraft guns. Of the Marine pilots he saw take off that morning, Clarence Choi said, "Those pilots were mere kids. . . . Somehow I had the feeling they'd turned into men between the time the action started . . . to the time the smoke finally cleared."

Those "men" were to serve as the nucleus for the expanding Marine Air Corps, increasing it from around two hundred aviators before the war to already several thousand in the summer of 1942. The problem was the vast majority of these thousands had just graduated from flight school. They had virtually no time in combat aircraft, and there were almost no combat aircraft with which to train them. What the Corps had was already forward deployed—or destroyed at Wake and Midway.

How were they going to survive, let alone win the war, with the mess they were in right now?

EIGHT

SURVIVORS AND TRUMPET PLAYERS

Ewa Field, Oahu, Hawai'i
July 1, 1942

JOHN L. SMITH SAT AT HIS DESK AND STARED AT PAPERWORK THE squadron clerk delivered a few hours before. He shook his head, riffling through the pages.

Desperate. Desperate times.

His squadron had just received a small influx of pilots, with more promised to come in the next few days. Additional enlisted men flowed in as well. It looked like a good start on paper—until a closer look revealed whom he'd been given. A kernel of Midway survivors fleshed out with grass-green trainees whose wings had just been pinned on them at stateside bases. Traumatized survivors and raw newbies. It was not a good combination.

Second Lieutenant Eugene Trowbridge's experience in the Corps was typical of the new guys. He and several others had sailed to Oahu in May on the USS *J. Franklin Bell* before ending up in MAG-23, then ultimately with John L. in 223.

A little over a year earlier, Trowbridge had been a senior at MacPhail School of Music in Minneapolis, playing trumpet with the hottest swing bands in the local clubs. He'd served three years in a National Guard coast artillery unit as a way to help pay tuition. Then, after graduation in June 1941, he was accepted into the Naval Aviation Cadet (NAVCAD) program. Ten months of training and a commission in the Marine Corps later, he was deemed ready to defend his nation at the controls of the fastest fighter aircraft the Navy possessed. Never mind that he'd flown one of those types of planes only a couple of times at San Diego before shipping out. Never mind that he had only a few hundred hours of total flight time, having earned his wings on February 6, 1942. The Corps gave him his second lieutenant's bars a month later, on March 20.

Eugene was all of twenty-three, a young man with no ambitions beyond serving his country and playing music. Until he arrived with 223, his life's biggest achievement had been conducting the Barnum and Bailey Circus band whenever it came to Saint Paul.

This situation was dire, and men like Trowbridge were to be thrown into the cauldron of combat against Japanese pilots who had been flying in combat since before he'd even started college. The young men would be ground up. John L. knew that. He suspected that everyone else did as well.

With these three rookies came five veterans of the Battle of Midway, fresh from their leave at the Royal Hawaiian. Of those, Marion Carl was the biggest addition to the unit. John L. had known Marion for a long time, knew he was a clutch guy and a great aviator. Joe Bauer was generally considered the best pure fighter pilot in the prewar Marine Air Corps, and word got round that Carl had fought him to a draw in several mock dogfights. If he really did that, he wasn't just a solid officer; he was one of the Corps' top fighter pilots.

John L. knew that Marion was also a man who did not whitewash anything. Carl would give him the straight scoop on what had happened at Midway. Unvarnished, blunt assessments—Marion Carl excelled at those.

The other Midway vets included Roy Corry, 2nd Lt. Hyde Phillips, who had not flown on June 4, and 2nd Lts. Clayton Canfield and Bill Brooks. Brooks was still fighting malaria when he reported in for duty, eager to do whatever was asked of him but hamstrung by recurring fevers that left him shivering in his barracks bunk.

John L. rose from his desk and went to talk to Marion Carl. He wanted the straight scoop from a man he respected. What had happened at Midway? The two conferred behind closed doors, where Marion was in no mood to sugarcoat anything. After a week at the Royal Hawaiian, he had been on a road near Bellows Field, an Army Air Force post, and had watched a P-36 pilot miscalculate a low-altitude loop. As the pilot tried to pull out, Marion's stomach turned as he saw there was no way he was going to make it. Sure enough, the plane ran out of altitude and impacted at the end of the runway. The P-36 exploded, and the wreckage burned furiously as the crash crews raced to the scene.

The sight of such foolishness angered the normally even-keeled Oregonian. The incident stayed with him after he joined 223. These were times when every plane and pilot were needed for the fight. Losing new kids like that was senseless, a waste. If they were ever going to turn this mess around and really take it to the Japanese, such recklessness had to be stopped. As it was, a senseless aerobatics display resulted in one more victory for the enemy.

The accident was even worse than Marion had thought at the time. The pilot was a seasoned captain in temporary command of a fighter squadron. His was also one of six fatal crashes among the US Army Air Forces fighter squadrons on Oahu in the seven days since Carl had returned from Midway.

So when John L. asked him what had happened at Midway, Marion unleashed a firehose of blunt truth. The pilots were barely trained. Some of those he took up and practiced dogfighting with before the battle he considered hopeless—they never should have been assigned to fighters. Maybe they could have contributed as transport pilots or perhaps bombers—but the fighter game was not something they would ever master.

Errant leadership, poor training, poor pilot selection for a fighter unit—the list of organizational and personnel mistakes that cost 221 so many lives was a long one. Then the day of the interception came, and the scramble became nothing more than free-for-all chaos with little attempt to consolidate the squadron once it was aloft and deconflicted from the departing strike aircraft.

Marion spelled out all the mistakes until John L. brought up the survivors now with 223. How useful would they be?

Carl considered the question carefully. For most of them, "The shock was a little bit too much for them to handle."

It was hard to blame them for that. A few months before June 4, they were civilians living happy civilian lives, far from danger and death and high-speed combat. They knew nothing of violence and war beyond the imagery of the gallant knights of the air, as Hollywood portrayed air combat.

Morale and building a fighting spirit into VMF-223 was going to be a challenge.

The overarching lesson from Midway was this: one combat mission could not overcome the general lack of training and flight time the survivors possessed. So the experience the VMF-221 veterans brought into 223 was of limited value, even if it was the rarest thing in the Marine Corps at the moment.

Training was the only antidote for the weaknesses that destroyed 221. Relentless, focused training. That was going to be difficult with just nine worn-out Buffalos and an empty spare-parts storeroom.

The situation changed two days after the new pilots arrived. The squadron's Brewsters disappeared, replaced by eighteen F4F Wildcats. The new batch was a mix of fleet-abused, well-traveled F4F-3s fresh off the Navy's carriers, plus a couple of brand-new F4F-4 variants straight from the Grumman factory back on Long Island.

It was like Christmas in July. John L. would have the tools to train his new pilots after all. Yet, with all the shortages around the fleet, the appearance of so many Grummans raised some eyebrows. Why was 223 a priority for such things after two months of languishing with next to nothing?

John L. learned the answer on the morning of July 5 when he received an order to report to Col. Claude Larkin's office. Larkin, known as the Sheriff, had been a Marine longer than most of John L.'s second lieutenants had been alive. Though he missed combat in World War I, he had served in Cuba and throughout the Caribbean in the 1920s before going to flight school in 1930. During the Pearl Harbor attack, he'd been wounded repeatedly while directing the defense of Ewa Field. He ignored the wounds and received no treatment until long after the last Japanese bomber vanished on the horizon. His leadership that day earned him a Navy Cross.

That July, Larkin was the senior Marine aviator west of San Diego, with his headquarters there at Ewa. After Midway, he wasn't sure how long he'd remain in command. Once the battle revealed the many weaknesses John L. had just learned about, Larkin gambled his career to effect rapid change. He wrote a letter to President Franklin D. Roosevelt detailing the many shortcomings, from training to equipment and aircraft, and personally handed it to James Roosevelt, the president's son. After the fact, Larkin passed word of his deed to his superior, Lt. Gen. Ross Rowell, and asked him to go easy on him should he be court-martialed for circumventing the chain of command. The fact was everyone knew the situation had to change quickly, and if getting the president's attention is what it took, so be it. Lives were at stake, as well as the outcomes of future battles. At 0 to 3 against the Japanese, Marine aviation needed a win.

Waiting to report to Larkin that morning was Col. Richard Mangrum, skipper of VMSB-232—one of the two dive-bomber outfits in MAG-23. John L. sat down next to Dick and waited for Colonel Larkin to call them into his office.

The two Marines were soon ushered in. Larkin stood behind his desk, shook their hands, and dropped an anvil. "Your squadrons have been selected for a special assignment. This is top secret, and nobody—not even your executive officers—are to know where you are going. You have between four and six weeks tops to be ready for a special mission in combat in the South Pacific. In any case, be prepared to depart on August first." To do what wasn't yet clear.

Larkin went on to say that John L. and Dick's men must all be qualified to operate on carriers. John L. went through his squadron roster in his head. Aside from Marion, Rivers, and himself, none of his pilots had any experience flying from carriers.

John L. stole a glance at Dick. He was mentally going through the same process. A month to get carrier qualified and combat ready? How would they do this?[1]

This assignment wasn't optional. The special mission was happening. Either they would be ready for it, or they wouldn't.

After the meeting, John L. sat down with Rivers and Marion—whom he'd made the squadron's operations officer—to discuss what to do. They would have a small window to cycle the pilots through carrier qualifications. The USS *Hornet* had returned from Midway and would be operating out of Pearl Harbor for a short period. That would give them a flight deck. The pilots needed three landings and three launches to get qualified. If the leaders prepped them ahead of time, with all the planes the squadron now had, John L. figured they could get all ten of his guys qualified within a couple of days.

That would solve one problem. But what about the legion of others? The men had virtually no tactical instruction. They barely had any time in fighters, and few had fired live ammunition more than once or twice. John L. had never trained anyone, let alone set up a training program for a squadron. He was groping in the dark.

They all were.

Clearly, the timeline would not allow for proper training. They would have to focus on one or two key things and just make do.

What were those key things? A fighter pilot's job is to shoot down enemy planes. If he can't shoot straight, he can't complete the mission. John L. decided that marksmanship was the single most important aspect of their trade, and they would focus on it.

Tactically, they would change things up. First, John L. switched the basic formation they would fly. Before the war, they had flown in three-ship vees, two sections to a division, for a total of six planes. Now, they caught up to the US Navy and US Army Air Forces basic tactical formation—two-plane elements in four-plane divisions. This formation would be the basic building block of VMF-223 from here on out.

Beyond the formation change, John L. realized he didn't have the time to train the newcomers in all the complexities of air combat tactics. They had no time to develop tactics that could overcome the Zero's general superiority to the F4F. John L. simply ordered his men to avoid Zeroes and never dogfight them. The Americans' priority targets would be Japanese bombers in all missions except escorting their own aircraft to a target area.

They would use hit-and-run attack whenever possible. From altitude, they would push over into what the Navy manual called *overhead passes*— the steep dives down onto a target like what Marion Carl and the other VMF-221 pilots used at Midway. One pass, maybe two, then head for the deck at top speed—the Midway vets discovered that the Zeroes could not stay with that maneuver.

Nor could John L. wait until 223 was at full strength. With the clock ticking, every day—hell, every daylight hour—counted. They would get to work at once with whomever they had on hand. With five Midway vets, three greenhorns from the USS *J. Franklin Bell*'s contingent, Rivers, and himself, VMF-223 stood at half strength. But half strength was better than no strength. The men of 223 climbed into their Wildcats and got to work.

NINE
THE *HILO* MELTING POT

July 6, 1942

THE DAY AFTER THE MEETING WITH COLONEL LARKIN, ANOTHER wave of second lieutenants arrived for VMF-223. They were part of a group of ten fighter pilots and seventeen dive-bomber pilots sent from San Diego aboard the converted luxury yacht USS *Hilo*. Pressed into service as a fast transport, the *Hilo* was supposed to be a PT boat tender. The aviators spent the voyage crammed among drums of high-octane gasoline, doing their best to ignore the possibility of a submarine attack. One torpedo would have turned the yacht into an inferno.

When the *Hilo* arrived at Pearl Harbor, the twenty-seven Marine second lieutenants disembarked and reported in at Ewa for their assignments. Half the fighter pilots went to Bob Galer's VMF-224, and half reported to John L. Smith's 223. The dive-bomber pilots were split between Dick Mangrum's squadron, VMSB-232, and the other dive-bomber unit in the air group, VMSB-231.

The Oklahoman could tell from his first meeting with this bunch that they were different. Exuberant and spoiling for a fight, they had bonded on the nine-day voyage to Oahu. Now, they would get to fly together in their first fighter outfit. It was the adventure of their lives. They bragged about the "Japs" they were going to bag. The raw reality of combat had yet to temper them. They stood in stark contrast to the more sobered, and sometimes morose, Midway veterans.

To John L.'s surprise, the *Hilo* boys were even more unprepared for the crucible ahead than the other second lieutenants already in the squadron. Instead of sending better-trained and more-prepared pilots in this lot, the Fleet Marine Force had cut every possible corner to get these men to Hawai'i. Only a couple had gone through the Advanced Carrier Training Group program at San Diego. Those few weeks of fighter pilot finishing school at least gave the graduates a few hours in F2As or F4Fs. These men came virtually straight from the schoolhouses at Corpus Christi, Texas, and Pensacola, Florida, where the most advanced aircraft they had piloted was the North American Aviation SNJ trainer.

Their lack of experience complicated the situation the squadron faced. With only three or four weeks left to get ready for combat, these guys faced an extraordinarily steep learning curve. At the same time, the obviously tight-knit nature of their nascent friendships was something 223 needed. In the days since the men began flowing in, the Midway vets tended to keep to themselves. The *Hilo* second lieutenants had formed their own clique. These five could be the heart of something 223 really needed: connection. From that, a fighting spirit could be built.

It did not take John L. long to figure out there was something more between these guys than their trans-Pacific journey. Two of them, Elwood Bailey and Zenneth "Zen" Pond, had lived in the same part of rural Michigan. Pond had grown up in Jackson, Bailey on a farm outside the crossroads village of Parma, a few miles away. They met at Jackson Junior College when they took a civilian pilot training class together in 1940. Both had grown up enamored with the great Hollywood aviation epics like *Hell's Angels* and *Dawn Patrol*. They built balsa and tissue-paper model airplanes and trolled the local drugstores for the latest installment of WWI pulp fiction magazines like *G-8 and His Battle Aces*. That love of aviation defined their lives, and when they met, it was as if they'd each discovered a brother from another mother. In short order, they were the best of friends.

Along with a third pal, Bailey and Pond pooled every dime they possessed and bought a Piper J-2 Cub. When the weather was clear, they would devote their days to pushing that tiny plane around the skies over Jackson. Bailey was all of twenty years old, Pond only a bit older. It was an idyllic passage from adolescence to manhood.

It was Zen who joined up first. The three friends had talked it over on many occasions. They had even taken the Army Air Corps entrance exams to see if they could qualify. Zen passed easily. He was whip smart and a focused, determined young man. Instead of the Air Corps, he chose to go Navy. When asked why, he'd tell people he was the third-youngest of eight children in his family. His kid brother had gone into the Navy and was serving as a sailor aboard the battleship *New Mexico*. He'd laughingly tell anyone who would listen, "I'm going to be out there, protecting him from above."

In May 1941, Zen said goodbye to his brother aviators and headed off into the NAVCAD pipeline. The Navy had just relaxed its education standards and started taking aviation cadets with only two years of college. Usually, a four-year degree was required to even be considered for naval aviation. In this case, the global emergency worked in Zen's favor.

On his first stop in the pipeline, Pond shone. Prospective cadets had to go through E-base (elimination base) training, where they were introduced to the basics of military life and were exposed to a little bit of flying. Zen finished at the top of his class, earning the Knudson Trophy for "highest honors in flying ability, industry and officer aptitude."

A month later, Elwood Bailey joined the Navy as well and followed along behind his best friend in the pipeline. Elwood ended up training at NAS Jacksonville, Florida, while Zen went through the program at Corpus Christi.

They both performed so well, they were given the option to choose the Marine Corps. Only the top 10 percent of every flight school class earned that chance. Both took it, and they received their wings and commissions in March and April 1942.

The winds of war blew the two friends together again in San Diego at the end of May. They were delighted to run into each other. In the last couple of weeks before they shipped out aboard the *Hilo*, they were again thick as thieves.

As their departure date loomed, Elwood proposed to his high school sweetheart, Eunice Roberts. She came out from Parma by train and arrived in San Diego just days before the men left. Zen stood up for Elwood as his best man at the hastily arranged wedding. The newlyweds got exactly one day together. Then the *Hilo* sailed.

Eunice stood on the dock and waved goodbye to her husband, who, as always, was shoulder to shoulder with Zen. Both men waved back at her as the *Hilo* slipped into the harbor and headed west.

Aboard ship, Zen and Elwood soon made friends with another freshly minted husband, George McLennan, who went by his middle name, Noyes. Nobody in the Corps would ever call a fellow Marine Noyes—it was just too snooty sounding—so he quickly became "Scotty." The new nickname was an everyman name, a camouflage for a sharp social distinction that existed between him and the other pilots. In civilian life, his privileged upbringing would have separated him from the others, so he was fine with the new nickname. It made him part of his new tribe.

Scotty came from the elite Chicago suburb of Lakewood, where his dad was partner in the Jackson Street insurance firm, Marsh & McLennan. Whereas Zen grew up with seven siblings, Scotty grew up with seven servants, including two from Sweden and one from China. The silver-spoon life included summers on a Canadian lake, dressage lessons, and hockey come winter. To ensure an Ivy League pedigree, his folks packed him off to Hotchkiss, an elite prep school in Connecticut. He excelled at everything, including debate, basketball, and football. While at Hotchkiss, he filled out to six feet one, 150 pounds, and grew into leadership roles throughout the school. He captained his class baseball team, ran the 880 in track, and skated every winter for the hockey team. Summers were spent back home, laughing and playing with his hometown friends as he rolled through the streets in his dad's convertible.

He was accepted to Yale, where he played for the school's hockey team and displayed a ruggedness that made him a formidable presence on the ice. While there, he met and fell in love with a debutante named Margaretta "Peggy" Purves, the daughter of a New York City bond broker. The match was a perfect one. Both hailed from the same class, but Peggy's family was just a little bit beneath the station Scotty's had secured—they only had three servants.

With the European war situation worsening, Scotty elected to do his part for his country. Duty and honor mattered to him. Privileged as he was, devotion to country was a bedrock of his personality. He joined the NAVCAD in the summer of 1941, reporting into the E-base in Brooklyn, where he met Willis Lees, another fighter pilot who ended up on the *Hilo*.

On May 26, 1942, Scotty married his debutante in a well-attended ceremony on Long Island. He wore his Marine uniform and looked strappingly handsome, his lieutenant's bars only a few weeks old proudly on his shoulders.

Four weeks later, he found himself aboard the yacht turned PT boat tender, turned troop transport, surrounded by the sons of farmers and electricians he would have never consorted with as a civilian. Despite their socioeconomic differences, Scotty and the rest of the men bonded anyway. He was an easygoing, likable young man, and he had two things in common with his brother Marine aviators: their love of flight and women.

When Scotty reported aboard VMF-223, John L. detected no sign of the snobbery and sense of superiority so often encountered among the Ivy League class. Instead, he saw a young man, trim and fit, with earnest gray eyes and close-cropped, naturally curly brown hair. He was down-to-earth, eager, and committed to his new role as a Marine Corps fighter pilot. With time, John L. sensed, the new man would develop into a fine officer.

With time. He sincerely hoped the kid had that luxury.

Rounding out the quintet from the *Hilo*'s American melting pot were two men the polar opposite of Scotty. Ken Frazier was a New Jersey boy, the son of an electrician who worked for the local power company, and Kenneth Chambers was a black-haired, blue-eyed country boy from an unincorporated village in Miami-Dade County, Florida.

Southern farm boy and Yale hockey player. It was a hell of a way to wage a war.

After meeting the *Hilo* pilots, John L. realized he couldn't run the outfit as a traditional Marine unit. Before the war, rank distinctions were
strictly adhered to in the squadrons he joined. There was protocol and
military procedures that his old skippers followed, including the golden
rule for all officers of the era: never get too familiar or informal with your
men. The protocol and procedures established generations ago were in
place as a result of hard-won, painful lessons. Each generation added its
twist, but by and large, they had become the bedrock of the Corps—
of the Navy, really. Getting too friendly with junior officers and men
could compromise a skipper's ability to make critical decisions in combat.
Ordering men to do something that might very well get them killed was
tough enough. Doing so when the men being ordered into harm's way
were not just subordinates but close friends—that was something all too
many leaders in prior wars discovered they simply could not do without
destroying themselves emotionally.

John L. faced a significant challenge on this point with 223. This bunch
of second lieutenants the Corps had just given him were Marines in name
only. For God's sake, Ken Chambers had just received his wings in April
and his Marine commission on May 26, 1942. He hadn't even been an
officer for two months yet and had only been in the Navy's pipeline a year.

Talking with them, John L. sensed a civilian's resentment toward military authority. These men were individuals. E-base was not basic training, where the drill sergeants broke you down and destroyed that boy
you'd been before showing up at Parris Island. Any rebel in the barracks
would be swiftly turned into an example. By the time they graduated,
they were Marines to their marrow: riflemen first above anything else
they would later specialize in. The civilians they once were were long
gone, replaced by proud members of America's most elite branch of the
service. Sure, they would go on to raise hell in bars and brothels the world
over, but these men were trained to respect and exist within the rigid
order and stratified authority that made the Corps function.

His new second lieutenants would not respond well to the traditional
way of doing business. He could not tyrannize them into competence,
could not be a rules-obsessed martinet and expect them to gel as a

squadron in the brief time they had. By nature, he was quick-tempered. He'd have to keep his temper in check and only flash it to drive home a particularly vital lesson after one of his second lieutenants screwed up badly.

John L. was not one for long speeches; he was not a cheerleader either. He didn't micromanage. Instead, he gave orders and trusted they would be carried out, supporting his men every way he could to make sure they succeeded. He set the example with his work ethic and his dedication to the squadron. He led with a natural air of authority. Anyone who met him for the first time could sense the gravity of his character. Men *wanted* to follow him.

Perhaps in ordinary circumstances, he'd have run the squadron by the book. Salutes. Rigid respect for rank, keep the relationships with the pilots and his subordinates on a strictly professional level. Ride them from above as the Old Man whose word was god.

But in July 1942, with this group of young Americans and the task set before them? This was no ordinary circumstance. These kids needed a softer approach. John L. was the kind of man and leader who could adapt to the situation and modify his approach to be more effective. That's exactly what he did that summer. As the training schedule took shape, the squadron's internal culture began to develop as well, established by John L. with Rivers and Marion backing him up.

From the outset, John L. blurred the lines that normally divide officers by rank and squadron position. He told his men to call one another by their first names or nicknames. To the pilots—even Chambers, the most junior man in the unit—the skipper would forever be known as Smitty. Captain Carl? Everyone called him Marion. The familiarity bred a closeness John L. knew the squadron would need in the weeks ahead if they were to gel into a fighting organization.

In the days that followed, the skipper spent almost every waking minute with the squadron. When he wasn't flying with them, he was teaching them what he'd learned from his own mentors. Marion and Rivers did the same. When their workday ended, they gathered as a squadron to chew the fat and get to know one another. It was surprisingly egalitarian, though everyone always knew who was in charge and what was expected of them.

They stayed at Ewa. Leaves were rare that July, and the men lived together in the barracks. They ate, slept, and flew together six days a week. Being cloistered at Ewa helped the squadron bond. It also gave the core leadership—Rivers, Marion, and John L.—the chance to get to know their pilots in a way that in ordinary times might have taken months of service together.

These moments confirmed just how diverse their backgrounds were. Howard Marvin had been a prewar chicken farmer. He was a wheeler-dealer, constantly on the prowl to make a buck. Hyde Phillips, who had been with 221 at Midway but had not been assigned to fly on June 4, came from the New York literary scene. His father was a writer, and one of his brothers was the editor of *Elks* magazine. Elwood Bailey spoke of fishing with his sister at a remote lake on the Michigan Peninsula. Summer fish fries, a childhood spent outdoors exploring the Michigan countryside. Despite the Depression and the razor-thin margin his family subsisted on, his stories of home sounded idyllic.

Then there was the newest and greenest of them all: Ken Chambers. He'd turned twenty-three the day after the Marine Corps gave him his commission less than two months before. He was the squadron's underdog, the most junior officer in a unit filled with junior officers. He'd grown up in perhaps the most unusual township in Florida, a little place called Princeton, which had been founded by Gaston Drake, a graduate of the college by the same name. When the first buildings went up in the village's tiny downtown, he made sure they were painted Tiger black and orange. The town grew up around his sawmill, which supplied lumber throughout South Florida through the early 1920s.

Ken Chambers came from dirt-poor farm stock. His dad grew up around Madison, Florida, lost an eye working the fields, and was exempt from service in World War I as a result. He married and managed to buy a farm outside Princeton, where the family raised tomatoes and pole beans. The Depression wiped them out, and by the late 1930s, his family subsisted on two part-time incomes and less than six hundred dollars a year. His dad worked fields that others owned. His mom drove a bus for the local school district. The six hundred dollars they made, as minimal as it was, made them among the wealthiest in their neighborhood. Some of the people on Ken's block barely scraped together a few hundred dollars a year. His world was the poverty of Depression-era farm life. He dove into high school sports, was active in the Future Farmers of America, and found ingenious ways to make do on a shoestring budget that barely fed the five mouths in the family.

Flying seemed a great escape from the grind and the grim life on the ground. Ken Chambers and his cohorts around Princeton were first exposed to aviation in the 1920s by the crop dusters that blew into the area to spray the local crops before moving on to the next county. By their early teens, many of Ken's peers had already found ways into the cockpits of those crop dusters. The lure of flight drew them skyward, and once there among the clouds, they found the reality of it even better than the fantasy. When war came, many of Princeton's sons ended up flying in combat.

After he finished high school, Ken's folks somehow found a way to help him pay for college. He was a good and conscientious student, and he thrived at the University of Miami, in Coral Gables. An education was his ticket to prosperity, the gift and promise of the American dream.

Midway through school, with war appearing an increasing certainty, Ken registered for the draft, then volunteered for the NAVCAD program. The Navy accepted him, and he finished in the top tier of his cadet class. Having an officer in the Chambers family—a fighter pilot, no less—must have made his folks proud.

Even more so after Pearl Harbor, when news broke that two local boys had been killed aboard the battleship *Arizona*, Princeton's sons and daughters flocked to the uniform, vowing revenge. Chambers had been in the training pipeline for all of about five months, but his commitment was redoubled. His younger brother, Clyde, chose to follow in his footsteps and joined the NAVCAD program as well.

Ken Chambers was a hard guy not to like. Sincere, eager, and willing. His ability to hold his own between Scotty McLennan and Hyde Phillips underscored how much the Marine Corps made equals of men who were anything but in civilian society. In the process, the rich and poor alike discovered many commonalities in their lives, especially when it came to sports. Of course, the one unshakable connection between them would always be their passion for flight.

IN THE FIRST DAYS AFTER THE *HILO* BOYS JOINED THE SQUADRON, John L. focused on gunnery training. Ostensibly, every pilot arriving in Hawaiʻi was supposed to have gone through fifty-four hours of additional flight time at San Diego's Advanced Carrier Training Group program. There, they were supposed to get familiar with the F2A or F4F and practice gunnery, bombing, strafing, and basic air-combat maneuvering. Virtually none of the 223 pilots had finished the full ACTG syllabus. Essentially, John L. was starting from scratch.

The squadron expended thousands of rounds a day, either on targets on the ground or at towed sleeves in the air. Marion Carl, who was the best deflection shooter in the squadron, gave clinics on the basic gunnery passes they would use. He taught them how to calculate lead while piloting a fighter moving at 440 feet per second and trying to down a plane moving equally as fast.

The second lieutenants quickly discovered that aerial marksmanship was not just a science. It was an art form, a feeling you'd develop in your gut. Ken Frazier, who was captain of his high school rifle team back in Jersey, quickly showed a natural bent for this. Overhead passes, high sides, low sides. As he gained familiarity with his F4F, his gunnery shone. As a kid, to supplement his family's meals, he would often stalk small game like rabbits or birds in the woods around his family's home. Frazier had that gut sense before he ever sat in a fighter's cockpit.

Some of the other guys—especially those who had never fired a shotgun or rifle in their childhoods—struggled to get the hang of it. The math and physics behind hitting a plane moving in three dimensions with a firing platform doing the same thing was dizzyingly complex. When factoring in the muzzle velocity of their M2 .50-caliber machine guns and gravity's effect on their bullets (known as bullet drop), the science behind aerial marksmanship required a deep mastery of math. As if that were not enough, the Wildcat carried its guns in the wings, two .50s in each, paired together midway from the root and the tip. They were raked ever-so-slightly inward so that their bullets would ultimately converge at about three hundred yards. Shoot at a target beyond that three-hundred-yard mark, and the bullet streams would cross and potentially pass the aircraft on either side. Shoot under that, and the same thing could happen. The sweet spot would be about a hundred yards on either side of the convergence point—or point-blank range.

Between gunnery missions, the veteran pilots in the unit took the second lieutenants up individually to work them out, assess their flying ability, and teach them rudimentary air combat tactics. Marion Carl developed a standard speech he gave all the new guys. Prior to Midway, when he took Clayton Canfield up for his first lesson, Marion stared intently into the young second lieutenant's eyes and said, "I want you to lock in on my wing. Stay with me, and stay close."

Canfield dutifully obeyed. Once aloft, he stuck to Marion through every maneuver he performed. Then Marion took things up a notch to see how much more Canfield could give him. The senior man rolled into a turn so tight that Canfield struggled to remain on his wing. Canfield pulled tighter and tighter, working so furiously to stay with the Oregonian that at one point he failed to even notice they were inverted.

Staying with Marion Carl through maneuvers like that separated the men from the boys. It took confidence, skill, and experience to fly a fighter as Marion did. He didn't expect everyone to follow him, especially not on that first evaluation flight, but he did expect everyone to improve—and quickly.

After a Sunday off, the squadron assembled on the flight line at Ewa for another long day of training. That Monday morning, Marion selected Ken Chambers as his student for the next flight. He pulled the young man aside, gave him the same speech he'd given Canfield and the others. The kid met his gaze with solemn intensity. Marion couldn't help but like Ken. They both came from hardy stock and lived hard lives in their days before the Corps. In their childhoods, both had seen levels of adversity that the other men in the squadron had not. Farm boys in cockpits. Kindred spirits.

They took off from Ewa and headed to twelve thousand feet, Ken tucked on his wing. The kid was raw but trying.

Marion leveled off and headed out over the water. Once clear of shore, the Oregonian threw his F4F into a series of tight maneuvers, watching all the while as Ken tried to stay with him. Each maneuver became progressively more difficult. Ken was hanging in there.

After a few maneuvers, Marion switched to doing some mock dogfighting. They chased each other around the sky for a while, and then Marion twisted into a tight turn. On the edge of graying out, he looked back to see if Ken was on his tail.[1]

There he was, not far behind, struggling to get on his tail. An instant later, Ken fell out of his turn. His F4F's nose sagged toward the water and the plane went into a steep dive.

Marion called to him. No answer. He called again and again, but silence greeted every transmission. The Wildcat plummeted through five thousand feet, the nose of his fighter never wavering as the aircraft gained speed.

A few seconds later, the F4F made impact with the water just offshore.

It took a month for Ken's remains to make the long journey home. On August 27, his coffin lay at the Church of the Nazarene in Homestead, Florida, where friends and family gathered to hear a Navy chaplain from NAS Opa Locka deliver Ken's eulogy. Clyde Chambers, then in E-base training in Georgia, received emergency leave to fly into Homestead and say goodbye to his older brother. The funeral procession then drove to Palm Cemetery in nearby Naranja to lay him to rest.

Second Lieutenant Oliver Kenneth Chambers was the first Marine from Princeton, Florida, to die during World War II. He was also the first VMF-223 pilot to be lost. He would not be the last.

TEN

THE COLDEST EQUATIONS

Ewa Field, Oahu, Hawai'i
Mid-July 1942

CAPT. JOHN L. SMITH SAT IN HIS OFFICE AT EWA FIELD, A POOL OF
light under his desk lamp revealing a blank piece of paper. The rest
of the room was swathed in darkness. It was hours after the last flight of
the day, and the men had long since stowed their gear and gathered to
eat and shoot the breeze. He desperately wanted to be there with them,
laughing, drinking, and forgetting the war for a bit. He needed that connection; it was the best part of the prewar Corps.

They were good kids, these young guys fresh from the States, and he
was growing fond of them. In return, he could see them responding to his
leadership. The squadron was born from fragments, but these evenings
helped them all come together and learn about one another.

Thinking about them now made the task at hand even more difficult.

In the eight months since war had come to America, John L. had yet
to see combat. This did not mean he was immune to its effects. He'd
served with VMF-221 for many months, both stateside and at Midway. Those pilots were his brothers. So were the dive-bomber crews in
VMSB-241 who attacked the Kidō Butai. He'd known some of them
for years, having first been trained as such a pilot. In fact, 241's skipper,

Maj. Lofton "Joe" Henderson, had been a dear friend. Joe and his wife used to spend nights together with John L. and his new bride, Louise, when they were all together in San Diego in 1941. Joe was a great leader, and John L. modeled much of his approach with 223 on how his friend handled rank and leadership responsibilities.

On June 4, as Marion Carl and the rest of 221 fought for their lives over Midway, Joe Henderson led his squadron of obsolete dive-bombers straight into the Japanese carrier task force. Unescorted, without any support, they stood no chance.

No chance. So far this war was little more than a series of lost causes John L.'s friends were thrown into, always outnumbered, outgunned, and outmaneuvered.

Joe seemed to sense his fate long before he ended up on Midway. At times in San Diego, when it was just the two of them drinking together, Joe revealed a fatalistic streak he hid from everyone else. He was not optimistic about his future. On June 4, the Japanese fulfilled that dark prophesy. While he was flying at the spearpoint of his formation, Zeroes singled out Joe's SBD Dauntless. It burst into flames, rolled over, and went straight into the water. No survivors.

His death hit John L. hard when he heard the news a week or so after the battle. He drowned his grief with liquor and tried to write Joe's wife, Ade. The words wouldn't come. Instead, he wrote Louise and told her of their friends' death. "I don't have the heart to write Ade and tell her about it."

John L. was a man of great physical courage. He never showed any fear in the air, despite the years of flying in worn-out, poorly performing prewar aircraft the Marines received secondhand from the Navy. He'd seen too many accidents and engine failures to have any doubt of the hazards he risked when just getting aloft for a few hours.

Yet, under the Oklahoma-tough facade, John L. loved easily and hurt even easier. For a warrior to be so built, it was a weak spot, his Achilles' heel. Loss. Death. He tried to consign those things to a narrow corner of his heart as best he could, but they never stayed there. In moments of stillness, when the bottle sat before him, the people he'd lost paraded across his memory. And he ached.

Midway's casualty roster hammered him center mass. Joe Henderson was the top of the list, but John L. had also known many of the men killed with both 241 and 221. Some were brothers he'd served with for the majority of his time in the Corps. The war wasn't even a year old, and it had already torn apart his circle of friends. They were the men he had wanted to serve with in combat. Instead, they were thrown into different units, their time in the Corps seen as the bedrock for the frantic expansion the service was now undergoing. Each old hand was to be the cornerstone for these squadrons full of second lieutenants who knew nothing of service and sacrifice, or the risks that they faced.

Seems that no one is destined to serve with whom he would like these days.

Scattered to remote outposts, his friends began to die. With them, the old Corps started to die as well. Those unique bonds—the deployments to the Caribbean, breakfasts on verandas, fine tablecloths, and servants bringing heaping plates of food. The camaraderie he'd found in such moments surrounded him with like-minded young men who respected one another. And what greater gift can a man give another beyond respect?

This new reality was ugly, and tonight's duty was a reminder of that. John L. stared at the blank page and wondered what the hell to write. He'd known Ken Chambers for all of a week. There was no camaraderie to connect them. He'd not even had time to evaluate his flying ability. The prewar closeness that defined his life nested in Marine aviation simply wasn't there with Ken. You'd think it would be easy to write a letter home, given the distance and unfamiliarity he had with his lost second lieutenant, but that was not the case.

This was his pilot. Under his command. His responsibility. Ken's death was both a measure of the moment and an indictment of the system that produced him. Desperate hours, bodies needed in cockpits. The training command cut every corner possible to send these kids west to face the Japanese. By the book, Ken should have arrived at 223 with weeks' worth of flights in Buffalos or Wildcats back at San Diego. But there was no time for that. He and the men who arrived with him—they had families. Loved ones, girlfriends. Kid sisters and younger brothers who hero-worshipped their older aviator siblings. These young men mattered to their people. To the Corps, in the moment, they were filler. Cannon fodder to be thrown against the Japanese in hopes of stemming the imperial juggernaut that had flattened all who opposed it, from Burma to the Dutch East Indies, the Philippines, and New Guinea.

These new flyers were here to buy time for America. The bill for the prewar neglect of the military had come due, and men like Ken Chambers paid that debt with their lives. Good kids. Ernest young Americans, eager and willing to do anything for their country. The Corps needed to be the measure of these men, not the other way around. But in this moment, the darkest hours of Marine aviation, the trough between the swells rising around them was deep. And there was no other option. For the sake of the country, these half-trained men would go to war.

It was unconscionable.

The country, the Corps, owed men like Ken Chambers a better chance than he had received. On that last training flight, Marion had done nothing wrong, of course, though Ken's death had hit the captain hard. He'd simply been trying to show the Florida farm boy how to survive against Zeroes. Ken was so green that he'd never maneuvered as violently as Marion showed him. He'd never had the time to build the muscle mass for such flying. Fighter pilots needed core strength. They needed upper body strength. They needed to be exposed to high-g maneuvers so they could learn their body's tells as gravity drained the blood from their brains. Telescoping vision. Then the edges would go gray. A second or two later, the g-forces would cause a blackout and the pilot stood a good chance of losing control of the aircraft.

With time and experience, pilots learned where their own threshold was. They learned little tricks to stave off the effects of g-forces for just a second or two longer. That may not seem like long, but in combat, every second, every bit of the envelope you could push, might just give you the edge over your enemy. Those little things separated the good pilots from the great.

In a matter of weeks, Ken Chambers went from sedate cross-country flights in SNJs to trying to stay with one of the Corps' best fighter pilots in a mock dogfight. It was simply too much to ask of these kids.

Yet there was no other choice. Ken's death was a wake-up call for everyone in 223. The training schedule could not be modified to account for their inexperience. There was no time for that. The pilots would either measure up to it or die trying. Learning from Marion, John L., and Rivers was their only path to surviving the crucible ahead. It was a cold equation, the coldest John L. had ever seen. He detested it. But with their departure looming, there was no other way. Those who made it through the next month would be as combat ready as any other Marine aviator that summer. He would do everything in his power to see to that.

Those were things he could not write to Ken's family back home. There would be no explanation of why their son had had to die, just some futile words of solace about how much he'd been liked by everyone in the squadron. How he did his job to the best of his abilities. Left unsaid was the Corps' failure to impart the abilities needed for life.

Long into the night, John L.'s pen hovered above that blank piece of paper, the words lost in his grief.

ELEVEN

THE PALMYRA SIDESHOW

Ewa Field, Oahu, Hawai'i
Mid-July 1942

THE NEXT MORNING, JOHN L. WAS ALL BUSINESS. AFTER A SHORT meeting with Rivers Morrell and Marion Carl, he briefed his understrength squadron on the day's mission: carrier qualifications. Fortunately, Bob Galer, VMF-224's blunt and fiery skipper, had some landing signal officer (LSO) experience. He would be working with both squadrons on dry land at Ewa, teaching the rookies to follow his instructions as they practiced that day. The field included a section of runway designed to duplicate the dimensions of a typical US aircraft carrier. Both John L.'s 223 and Dick Mangrum's rookie second lieutenants of VMSB-232 set about practicing their carrier landings on that stretch of runway.

Of course, working to perfect carrier landings on Ewa's concrete runways was the best way to avoid an early grave and a damaged ship. Every naval aviator learned that getting aboard a flattop on the high seas was the single most stressful act of flying they would ever face. Not even attacking a Japanese fleet would generate the fear and heart rate of a night carrier landing in foul weather. Get aboard in those conditions, and you were the best of the best.

Baby steps first. John L., Marion, and Rivers worked with each division, coaching them on the intricacies of these dangerous approaches. One at a time, the men in training swung around the pattern, using the hand crank in the cockpit to lower their F4F's wheels into place. As they lined up on final approach, the squadron's experienced members would watch from above, letting Bob Galer do his job from the end of the runway. There he would stand, wearing a white helmet, yellow paddles in hand, arms outstretched. The paddles and Galer's arm position telegraphed to the pilot exactly what he needed to do to bring his plane aboard safely. If he got into the groove and had his speed right, his nose slightly high, and his wings level, Galer would give him the *cut* signal by raking one paddle across his throat. Once the greenhorn saw that, he was to pull the throttle back and drop onto the deck.

The squadrons worked throughout the day perfecting their landings and short takeoffs. Both 232 and 223 took turns taking their directions from Captain Galer. When everyone had several opportunities to practice and get it right, the old hands took their divisions out to sea, where they rendezvoused with USS *Hornet*.

The big fleet carrier, fresh back from the Battle of Midway and its first engagement with the enemy, was off Hawai'ian shores conducting mock air group raids, antiaircraft drills, and other maneuvers. In between these maneuvers, the ship took aboard John L.'s pilots, one at a time. To be carrier qualified in the eyes of the Navy, each man needed three successful landings and three launches.

A myriad of things could have gone wrong. A hard landing could cause an F4F to bounce over the arresting wires stretched across the deck. Each fighter carried a tailhook that, when lowered on landing, was supposed to catch one of those wires and bring the aircraft to a quick stop. Miss the wires, and the Wildcat could careen into aircraft spotted farther ahead on deck. Countless accidents had been caused that way, some with truly gruesome results. Deck crew members chopped to pieces by spinning propeller blades, pilots or gunners trapped in burning aircraft with flaming pools of avgas spilling around them and preventing hope of rescue. Those were the realities of naval aviation, and such accidents happened all too frequently.

On this day, John L.'s rookies impressed everyone. Though there were some shaky landings, there were no accidents. The boys got aboard without major incident. The launches were also accident-free. Flaps down, engines roaring, the F4Fs trundled down the flight deck on their spindly landing gear. At the moment the planes ran out of wood planking and careened into the air, some of them dipped below deck level, the pilots hand-cranking their wheels up to get the aircraft as aerodynamic as possible so they could pick up enough speed to start a slow, painful climb away from the whitecaps.

They all made it. To Marion and John L., it was a minor miracle.

Then it was VMSB-232's turn. Dick's squadron included thirteen pilots. Like 223, the majority were green second lieutenants; there were also a few prewar regular officers and a salting of Midway veterans. Although they had worked hard to prepare for this day, one pilot, Tom Moore, was declared not ready by Galer. Instead of landing his own aircraft, Lawrence "Larry" Baldinus, or "Baldy," one of the squadron's rock-solid prewar aviators, put Moore in the rear seat so the new man could see how an old hand brought his plane aboard.

Baldinus made a perfect landing, catching one of the first arresting wires. As he taxied forward, Moore turned around to watch the next pilot in line come in. This was young Arthur O'Keefe, son of a highly decorated WWI Army officer. Raised in San Diego, California, he was an inveterate shutterbug and developed into an accomplished photographer while still a teen. Using profits from a tropical fish business he had started, O'Keefe purchased a Leica 35 mm camera before joining the Navy. He graduated third in his flight class, accepted a commission in the Corps, then packed his photography gear and headed to San Diego. He'd been shipped out on the *Hilo* before he'd had any Advanced Carrier Training Group experience. The fastest plane he'd flown before that July was an SNJ trainer. His lack of experience cost him on this day as he attempted his first carrier landing.

He muffed his approach. Just as he cut his throttle, the LSO waved him off frantically. He shoved the throttles forward. The SBD's engine roared. The bird hit the deck tail high, its left wing catching on one of the arresting wires, tearing the tip off and causing the Dauntless to career across the flight deck. For an instant, it appeared to be heading straight for Tom Moore and Larry Baldinus. Moore saw the props looming large like "a spinning sword that could slash a man in half 3,200 times a minute."

O'Keefe's aircraft struck the catwalks on the edge of the flight deck, pitched over the side, and plunged into the ocean. The Hornet's claxon sang out, and men scrambled to the side to get any glimpse of the pilot.

The SBD flipped upside down as it struck the water, engulfing O'Keefe in the blackest water he'd ever seen. The Dauntless sank quickly, even as Art worked furiously to free himself from the cockpit. He finally escaped and swam to the surface. His years spent surfing in the San Diego area probably saved his life that day. Slightly injured and sheet-white with fear, he was scooped out of the water a few minutes later by an attending destroyer's crew.

Later, he was most upset about his errant approach. Losing a precious aircraft was a blow to the squadron, and he'd been doing everything he could not to let Dick Mangrum and his fellow pilots down while he learned on the job. The Navy then rubbed salt in the wound by refusing to compensate him for the Ray Bans he lost in the crash.

It was a near-run thing that could have turned truly disastrous. They lost a precious combat aircraft, but everyone survived to learn and grow from the mishap. Both O'Keefe and Moore went back and tried again. This time, both men trapped aboard ship without incident and qualified, along with the rest of the squadron. Fortunately, there were no other major incidents—another minor miracle to go along with VMF-223's good fortune.

To get so many second lieutenants ready for carrier ops in such a short time deserved a celebration. But there was no room in the schedule for that. The best the men could do was a night together on post.

In fact, most of the second lieutenants had yet to go into Honolulu. Beyond Ewa, their only experience of Hawai'i since their arrival that July was going a hundred yards off post to bring their laundry to a series of shacks inhabited by some of the island's Japanese Americans. The shacks were filled with American flags and cutout magazine photos of FDR, a touching sight to some of the Marines. The women there processed their laundry for them with meticulous care. That was it for local color and off-base adventures. As John L. later said, "We flew the pants off" the second lieutenants that month. There was no time for frivolity.

ON JULY 17, THE ESCORT CARRIER USS *LONG ISLAND* STEAMED INTO Pearl Harbor, its deck full of factory-fresh fighters and bombers. The carrier also brought a final contingent of pilots from the States. They were divided among the squadrons in MAG-23: Galer got about half of the men. John L. received four more grass-green second lieutenants. And Dick's unit picked up two more very poorly trained dive-bomber pilots. Later that day, two more pilot second lieutenants, Cloyd "Rex" Jeans and Charles "Red" Kendrick, joined VMF-223 after a couple of weeks' worth of training with another fighter unit at Ewa. The squadrons were now at as close to full strength as they would get.

A final, late addition to VMF-223 arrived fresh off the attack transport USS *Zeilin*. Tech Sgt. John D. Lindley reported aboard as the squadron's only pilot from the Naval Aviation Pilot (NAP) program. While most naval aviators received commissions before joining the fleet, a select few enlisted men were admitted to the cadet program every year. They were the best candidates, experienced men who had served for years as air or ground crew. John Lindley had done both. Universally, NAPs were among the most respected aviators in the fleet.

Marion and John L. liked Lindley right away. He cut a rugged figure, muscular and trim, with a slightly rounded jaw and worldly eyes. One good look at him, and anyone would recognize that this man had seen rough times that had hardened him. He was tough, not in the barroom-brawl sense of the word, but soul tough. A survivor where others would have broken.

His toughness was no surprise. Born in Maud, Oklahoma, to a desperately poor farm family, John lived a Steinbeckian existence with his mother, father, and brother between the wars. His dad, always seeking a better place to make a stake, moved the family to California's East Bay in the mid-1920s, settling around Berkeley amid the vast orchards that once defined the area. Apricots brought the family only the illusion of wealth, and by 1930, the Lindleys uprooted again, driving through the American Southwest to settle on another farm outside Clovis, New Mexico. It was a familiar scene for them: harsh weather, harsh life. Unpainted clapboard house in a part of the country where indoor plumbing had yet to become a thing. Sunrise each morning brought only rugged, soul-sucking work on the land that netted little compensation. The family scratched out a meager existence, but surviving was never really living. By the mid-1930s, as the dust bowl swept the Midwest and displaced millions of families just like the Lindleys when they had been driven from Oklahoma, every travail of their hardscrabble life was imprinted forever on John's parents' faces.

They joined the great migration west once again in 1938, trying their hand in Southern California this time. They settled in Camarillo, a farm community that also happened to have the state mental asylum within its small town city limits.

After a short time in San Diego as a twenty-three-year-old product of the Depression, John joined the Marine Corps in February 1939. Five months later, his father died. The older man passed on before he could see his youngest son marry another Oklahoma native, Adabar Marsh, who had been born about ninety minutes away from Maud five years after John. Her father, a glass cutter by trade, came west searching for a better life about the same time as the Lindleys. While John's family stayed rooted in agriculture, Adabar's dad found new work—building ships in the San Pedro yards in California.

John excelled in the Corps. His fitness reports were excellent. He went into aviation after basic and became a radioman in reconnaissance and utility squadrons. In 1941, after two years of service, he applied for one of the few coveted NAP program slots open to enlisted men. He thrived in flight training, even battling back from a spell in the base hospital at Pensacola in January 1942 to finish the program and earn his wings in April.

He arrived with 223 as probably the most rounded and best-trained pilot in the squadron, after its three senior officers. Older than the second lieutenants, he was more settled and mature. His family had grown, and before he left the States, he and Adabar had welcomed their first child, a baby girl, into the world.

Both John L. and Marion considered him an excellent and welcome addition to the outfit, especially after they learned he'd actually gone through the entire Advanced Carrier Training Group program in San Diego before shipping out to Hawai'i. This meant he'd flown fighters, received tactical instruction, and had qualified to fly carrier ops. A new pilot with those creds in the summer of 1942? They were worth their weight in gold.

This latest infusion of replacement pilots to VMF-223 would be the squadron's last. They would be of questionable use since none of the other new guys fresh from their *Long Island* voyage had any experience operating from carriers. The *Hornet* was no longer available, and it was not clear when these men might get a chance to qualify before they departed on their special mission. That reality made Lindley's arrival even more welcome.

This headache was suddenly compounded when, the day after their arrival, MAG-23 gave John L. a new assignment. He and Bob Galer were ordered to detach fifteen of their pilots for temporary duty at sea that would last about a week. Losing a week of training with their squadron's combat departure date looming was bad enough, but when John L. was briefed on what their mission would be, the loss had to be even harder to take.

Palmyra Atoll was a backwater outpost some eleven hundred miles south of Pearl Harbor. Since the fall of Wake Island in December 1941, the atoll had been defended by a reconstituted VMF-211. With more F4F Wildcats arriving in Hawai'i every week, getting the F2A Buffalo out of operational service was a top priority after Midway. Palmyra's defenders still flew the deathtrap, and it was well past time to get them Wildcats.

The plan called for fifteen Marine pilots to go aboard the *Long Island*, which would head south with a couple of destroyers as escort. Off the atoll, the pilots would be launched in F4F Wildcats. They would deliver those birds to Palmyra and fly back to the *Long Island* in 211's aged F2A Buffalos. The original plan probably called for the men to sail back to Pearl with the flattop. But to cut down their time away from their training at Ewa, the plan evolved to have the pilots return to Palmyra and fly to Oahu aboard a long-range transport aircraft.

It seemed like a pointless, busywork mission any other squadron could have handled at a time when John L. and Bob both needed every hour in the air to get their second lieutenants ready for combat. More important, an actual carrier operation aboard a baby flattop like the *Long Island* was probably asking too much of his freshly qualified second lieutenants, especially in the fussy, unstable Buffalo. The *Hornet*'s flight deck was about 800 feet long and 115 wide. The *Long Island*'s was about 450 fifty feet long and 69 wide. It took experienced, capable pilots to operate from such a postage-stamp-sized flight deck—and even then, accidents were not uncommon.

It was a mission for only the squadron's best pilots. Even with his best, John L. had to reach down deep into the ranks of the second lieutenants. In the end, he picked Rivers Morrell, Marion Carl, John Lindley, Roy Corry, Zen Pond, and Ken Frazier. Pond and Frazier were the weakest of this group because of their lack of training but were the best pilots among the squadron's second lieutenants. John L. expected that Rivers and Marion would see them through.

While they were detached on this ferry run, John L. intended to stay at Ewa with the rest of the men and train them every day. He would redouble their efforts to get them ready for combat. They were running out of time.

On the night of July 21, Rivers led the 223 pilots over to Pearl Harbor, where they boarded the *Long Island* and found bunks, along with Bob Galer's pilots. Exactly why the two squadrons were picked for this mission is lost to history. Nobody was happy about the diversion, and it split both outfits up at a time when they were still working hard to gel. Perhaps the high command felt a carrier operation like this one would give the pilots vital experience for their trials ahead. Or perhaps there were just no other Marine fighter pilots on Oahu who could carry out the mission. Either way, orders were orders.

The next morning, at 0735, the *Long Island* cast off from Pearl Harbor's Pier F-1 and steamed south. Destroyers *Mustin* and *Anderson* joined the flattop on the open sea. It took the little task force four days to reach Palmyra. On the morning of the twenty-fifth, the Marine pilots climbed into the Wildcats spotted on the *Long Island*'s deck and prepared to take off from the baby flattop's truncated deck.

The old hands had no issues. For 223, Rivers and Marion launched first, gained altitude, and settled down in an orbit over the carrier to watch the new guys get aloft. John Lindley, Pond, Frazier, and Midway vet Roy Corry all joined them in the pattern. The VMF-224 pilots had no problems either. Soon, the fifteen Wildcats turned for Palmyra in two loose formations about twenty minutes apart. On landing, one of the pilots—possibly Marion Carl—lost control and crashed. Though he walked away, the F4F would be out of operation for a while. That nobody was hurt getting down on that rough jungle strip was a blessing, but the most difficult part of this mission still lay ahead.

The defenders of Palmyra had their new planes. The old ones now needed to go aboard the *Long Island* for the journey back to Pearl Harbor. These, the last of the Navy's F2A Buffalos serving in line squadrons, would be relegated for use as trainers until enough Wildcats were available to take their place.

Heading out to the flight line, Marion found the Buffalos to be in mediocre condition. Palmyra lacked adequate maintenance facilities. As was the case everywhere else, spare parts were in short supply. Already castoffs from the Navy, these birds were worn-out. Several couldn't even be started, so their assigned pilots sat out the mission to await the transport flight back to Ewa later in the day.

Rivers led the 223 contingent into the air early that afternoon, the pilots tucked into formation and turned for the *Long Island* with 224 leading the way. About a half hour later, the carrier came into sight, and the Buffalos began a slow orbit around it. One by one, the pilots dropped into the pattern and prepared to land aboard the carrier's tiny deck.

One of the first to swing into the groove on final was a 224 second lieutenant named Howard Walter. Inexperience left him overcorrecting his approach as he tried to follow the LSO's guidance. He muffed it badly, his Buffalo heading for the deck in a port skid as the young pilot fed in too much rudder. The LSO didn't notice the skid, thought he was good to go, and gave him the cut signal. Walter chopped his throttle, and the Buffalo came down on the deck at an angle, snagging the third wire before trundling right off the deck into the portside catwalk. It hung there, precariously balanced half-on and half-off the deck, the Buffalo's tailhook still biting into the arresting wire. Walter frantically unstrapped himself and scrambled out of the cockpit, fearful that the aircraft would pitch overboard. But the wire and hook held.

It took twenty minutes to clear the aircraft from the catwalk and reset the deck for landing ops. All the while, the pilots above orbited, checking their fuel gauges every few minutes with low-grade concern. Most were closing in on half a tank. If another plane fouled the deck, they might have to return to Palmyra.

Landings resumed. Marion watched as a couple of 224's second lieutenants went in next. Unsteady and lacking confidence, their approaches would have been savaged by their skipper in the prewar Corps. But it was different times now, for sure. All that mattered was that they get down without killing themselves or others. That was the success threshold for the day.

They made it, like fledglings returning to the nest on youthful wings, more sense of adventure than sense. The deck crew got the aircraft forward, and 223's turn began.

Next up was Ken Frazier. Lean face, dark eyes, dark hair, Ken exuded confidence both in the air and on the ground. He'd held his own with Marion, Rivers, and John L. throughout their few weeks of training together, impressing the old hands with his aggression in the air. The squadron's three leaders were convinced that Ken would be a real fighter pilot—if he lived long enough.

He banked onto final approach, getting into the groove behind the *Long Island*. Beside the flight deck, he spotted the LSO, whose paddles and signals would guide him in. Ken followed the LSO's guidance exactly and made a near-flawless approach. It was an impressive feat for a new guy, and the old hands watching from overhead took note of it.

As he reached the carrier, the LSO gave him the cut signal. Ken pulled the throttle back. The Buffalo sank onto the deck and caught one of the arresting wires. A split second later, the starboard landing gear suddenly collapsed. The F2A skidded to a stop on one main wheel, its right wing grinding along the deck planks. The bird's three-bladed prop struck the deck, bending the blades like flower petals and damaging the engine with the sudden impact.

The weary old Buffalo slid to a stop. Ken, who was unhurt, released his straps as the deck crew swarmed toward him. A moment later, they helped him out of the cockpit, and he walked away from the badly damaged fighter on rubber legs, his face a mask of calm.

In carrier operations, you can sometimes do everything right and still court disaster. Nevertheless, any landing you walk away from is a good one.

It took almost another half hour to clear the flight deck and resume landing operations. This was the gut-check time. They'd either get down or have to return to Palmyra. And the window for that option was quickly closing as the Buffalos' thirsty Wright Cyclone engines drained their fuel tanks.

Zen Pond was the big question mark. He'd done just okay qualifying aboard the *Hornet*. Though earnest, eager to learn, and capable, he had a rawness that sometimes got him in trouble. For him, this would be an acid test. Rivers and Marion watched with great interest as Zen turned onto final and followed the *Long Island*'s wake to the deck. He trapped aboard without incident.

Everyone heaved a sigh of relief. The squadron's second lieutenants had managed not to kill themselves or anyone else. John Lindley, Marion, and Rivers made it aboard without any snags. The birds were pushed forward, one at a time, and later taken below.

Mission accomplished.

When 224's pilots finished getting aboard, the Marines said farewell to the *Long Island* and boarded a small boat that ran them over to the destroyer *Anderson*. The tin can raced to Palmyra to put them ashore before turning back to chase down the *Long Island*.

The next morning, the fifteen Marines flew the eleven hundred miles back to Oahu aboard a transport plane. The entire Palmyra diversion cost VMF-223 the use of two senior officers and four men for almost a week. Instead of flying together, learning one another's habits in the air, getting better acquainted with their aircraft, and honing their tactical skills, they spent most of the time at sea, bored out of their minds. Losing two mentors like Marion and Rivers, who could work with the new guys, also left John L. desperately short of experienced aerial teachers at a crucial time. With time to train so short, the Palmyra sideshow represented a big loss for 223.

The squadron reunited on the twenty-seventh at Ewa, where they furiously tried to make up for lost time. They flew every day, sometimes making several flights. John L. stayed focused on two things: gunnery and hit-and-run diving attacks. He kept it basic, using the time he had to ensure that at the very least, if given an opportunity, his newbies stood a better chance of hitting something when they entered combat than they did when they had arrived at Ewa.

One bit of bright news: while the Palmyra operation was underway, MAG-23 received new aircraft. On June 24, VMF-223 received a full complement of factory-fresh F4F-4 Wildcats. Before their arrival, the squadron had been training on a mix of older four-gunned F4F-3s and an odd F4F-4 when they were available. The F4F-4 model incorporated two more guns in the wings for a total of six, but the extra firepower came at a cost of an aircraft that was nearly five hundred pounds heavier than the earlier variant—with no extra horsepower. Like it or not, the new and more sluggish Wildcats were going with them.

Performance deficit aside, having newer aircraft was a relief. The F4F-3s they had been flying were weary, offered less protection, and required more maintenance than the fresh lot. To some, getting these birds was sort of like GIs getting a steak dinner aboard ship the night before they assaulted a beach. The new planes meant the task at hand was rushing toward them, and they were running out of time to prepare.

By Friday the thirty-first, VMF-223's young aviators ended the week totally exhausted from the training pace. They looked forward to a weekend when they might get a day off. But on Saturday morning, John L. received a sudden alert order from MAG-23 headquarters telling him to have his squadron ready to depart by August 4 aboard the *Long Island*. Their destination was still classified, but John L. was told they would be heading somewhere in the South Pacific.

They didn't even get a month—let alone six weeks—to train as a complete squadron. The men were not ready, John L. knew that. So did Marion and Rivers. Throwing them into battle against the sort of pilots the Marines faced at Midway would get half of them killed.

This likelihood didn't matter. There was literally nobody else to do the job. So, the orders were given. They would be heading into battle, new pilots with their new aircraft at the tip of the spear and, in the van, a leader they all had just started to trust.

That morning, Marion Carl, who also served as the squadron's engineering officer and had gotten to know each individual F4F Wildcat better than anyone else did, selected the one he liked the best for himself. He asked his ground crew to paint a black number thirteen on the fuselage. Marion got a kick out of that, as if he were flipping the bird to superstition.

Once the ground crew had finished, he climbed into the cockpit and, with the rest of the squadron, flew over to Ford Island and parked his new mount. From there, cranes hoisted 223's Wildcats onto the *Long Island*'s flight deck.

There were a million little details that needed to be done to get the squadron aboard ship by Tuesday, but John L. knew that whatever lay ahead would be the trial of their lives. His men needed a chance to say goodbyes and blow off some steam. So he gave them a last Saturday night out in Honolulu before they would leave the bars and women behind.

Virtually the entire squadron—pilots and enlisted men—raced off post that evening to cram every second of living into their short liberty. Meanwhile, John L. and a skeleton crew stayed back at Ewa and worked through the night to prepare for the movement.

John L. still faced a significant personnel problem. The last batch of pilots who had come into the squadron had no carrier training at all. They were desperately raw and only had about two weeks to train with him.

Looking for help, he went to see Bob Galer and asked if VMF-223 could swap out its least experienced pilots for some of Bob's men. Bob and his 224 would be following John L.'s unit soon enough, but they had not yet received their alert order. Nor had they had a chance to get carrier qualified, so they were probably going to remain at Ewa for another ten days to two weeks, minimum. That would give these raw new guys a chance to get a little more experience in the cockpit.

Bob agreed to the swap. John L. gave him the four pilots who had arrived with the *Long Island* on July 17, plus Bill Brooks, the Midway veteran. Bill had been plagued with recurring bouts of malaria through the month and was dog sick that weekend. Hopefully, a few extra weeks would give him the time he needed to recover.[1]

The next morning, Sunday, August 2, MAG-23 sent John L. and Dick Mangrum a nasty surprise. Instead of shipping out on Tuesday, the *Long Island* would sail later that day. Both officers were ordered to get to Pearl Harbor with all haste.

What followed was a mad scramble that would have been comical if not for the seriousness of the moment. Together with 2nd Lt. Clarence Moore, John L. flew over to Ford Island in an SNJ trainer, where MAG-23's senior leadership waited for him and Dick Mangrum. They were summarily informed they would be leaving for the South Pacific by 1700 hours. Instead of two more days to load and prepare, the pilots and the advanced echelon would get only a half day.

Less than half a day, really. The men were scattered all over Honolulu, hungover and sleeping off memorable nights. None of them had packed their personal gear for the movement, let alone completed all the packing of the squadron. They still needed to bring spare parts and vital equipment over from Ewa to load aboard ship. A quick discussion with Capt. James Duke Barner, the *Long Island*'s storied skipper and a legend in the golden age of aviation, revealed that the carrier had minimal available space for the two squadrons and their aviators, equipment, and ground echelons. The carrier was being pressed into service as a stopgap transport, and even while the officers talked, bombs, crates of small-arms ammunition, and other supplies destined for the South Pacific were being hoisted aboard. Every compartment, magazine, and spare deck space below would be used to stack as much gear as possible, leaving precious little storage for MAG-23's two units.

Bunk space would also be at a premium. Each unit would get about fifty mechanics and ordnancemen for their advanced party, which meant another hundred bodies aboard ship. The rest of the two squadrons' ground echelons would follow a few days behind them aboard the troop transport *William Ward Burrows*. Whatever was left off the *Long Island* could be stuffed aboard the troopship—hopefully.

There was one small saving grace that Sunday morning. Mangrum's VMSB-232 dive-bombers had just been loaded aboard the *Long Island*, joining John L.'s Wildcats on deck. The aircraft were the one indispensable part of this process. So as long as they could find their men in Honolulu, both squadrons had a fighting chance to get aboard and depart at the ordered hour.

Making all haste, John L. flew back to Ewa and sent the shore patrol and Army military police out after 223's partying men. The patrols fanned out in Honolulu in search of the Marines, rousting them out of beds or pulling them away from breakfast tables, churches, or brothels with barked orders to report immediately to their squadrons. Through the morning and early afternoon, word spread around the city that the Marine aviators had been recalled to base. The men dribbled back to Ewa, feeling dejected and anxious. Yet, when told they were shipping out that afternoon, they cleared the cobwebs and got to work, frantically loading trucks with everything they could for the drive over to Ford Island.

With the shore patrol still rounding up members of the squadron, the assembled men made their way to Ford Island, where they crammed gear into every nook and cranny they could find aboard the *Long Island*. Space was at such a premium that 223 even stashed things in the rear cockpits of Mangrum's SBD Dauntless dive-bombers.

It was a pell-mell, chaotic mess. As the *Long Island* prepared to depart, a few men from the squadron remained unaccounted for. One, Lt. Howard Marvin, finally showed up right at the last minute. Another enlisted man, named Engle, could not be found. He was hastily transferred to 224 and missed the departure.

At 1754 hours, the *Long Island* steamed out of Pearl Harbor. The Marines had had no time for proper goodbyes. They had dropped everything for one frantic push to get the squadrons onto the ship. Now, the pilots and men stood on the flight deck or on the catwalks as their little converted flattop passed the remains of the battleship *Arizona*, a sheen of oil from its ruptured tanks still glittering on the surface of the water. They didn't know where they were going. They didn't know what their mission would be. They just knew they were going to war, and for some of them, this would be their last sight of Oahu's friendly shores.

TWELVE

THE RED DEVILS

Aboard the USS Long Island
August 1942

MAJ. RICHARD C. MANGRUM SAT IN THE *LONG ISLAND*'S NARROW wardroom, drinking coffee and listening to the hum of the ship's engines. For the moment, he was alone. That was a rare thing in the cramped confines of this cargo ship turned baby flattop. Just after sunrise out here somewhere in the middle of the Pacific's seemingly endless expanse, the *Long Island*'s massive engines churned the Marines along at eight knots. Between endless speculative talks and the long hours of staring at bulkheads from their bunks, they spent their days at sea thoroughly bored. There would be no flying until the men of VMSB-232 reached their destination. The inactivity made these days even longer for the pilots.

Now, a few hours after breakfast, most of Dick's pilots lay in their racks, reading or chatting with their cabinmates. Others played Hearts, a card game that had become 232's unofficial favorite pastime of this voyage. Day or night, there always seemed to be a cluster of second lieutenants doing their best to screw one another over with the queen of spades. Hearts required concentration, which was a good way to keep the tension at bay.

Two of Dick's junior officers always stood watch on the ship's quirky bridge, which was *under* the forward edge of the flight deck. Two men, twenty-four seven, for four hours at a time. There was little they could do while on watch, but any chance to learn something about the Navy and Corps was a plus. Like John L.'s squadron, Dick's 232 was full of civilians turned Marines. There had been time enough to teach them how to fly— barely—but they knew little about being a Marine officer yet.

Meanwhile, on the flight deck that morning, the squadron's gunners busily honed their marksmanship. The *Long Island*'s deck crew had respotted one of the squadron's SBDs with the tail pointed seaward. The gunners took turns climbing into the rear cockpit, charging the twin Browning .30-caliber machine guns, then loosing off bursts at weather balloons the sailors would release for them. It wasn't exactly like shooting at a swiftly moving Zero, but it was the best training they could manage while at sea. The squadron's gunners were a mix of well-traveled old salts and civilians turned warriors who had joined the Corps in January or February 1942 and went through abbreviated training before ending up on Oahu assigned to their first squadron.

Dick took another sip of coffee and thought about the chaos of the past seven months. This departure for the South Seas ranked as the most tumultuous of his entire career. He'd joined the Corps in 1928 and served aboard carriers on land on the West Coast. He'd flown almost everything in the Corps' inventory, as both a reservist and an active-duty regular officer. He'd stood watch in fierce storms and flown through harrowing skies in the glorified box kites that passed as aircraft in the early 1930s. Yet nothing in those fourteen years of service came close to his experiences since Pearl Harbor. December 7, 1941, represented a pivot point in history, a moment that changed everything in his world, from top to bottom.

Dick had spent parts of his career in Washington State and California, but in 1941, he joined VMSB-232 at Ewa Field, Oahu, Hawai'i. Back then, he was the squadron's executive officer, performing so well that he knew the Corps would give him his own outfit someday soon.

For him, December 7 started normally enough. He'd been drinking coffee, just as he was now, going through his Sunday morning ritual. His wife, Virginia, was nearby in the kitchen, cooking breakfast while he read the paper at the table, savoring a bit of Sunday morning peace before the kids woke up and wrought chaos.

The sound of aircraft engines pulled his head out of the newsprint. Through a nearby window, he saw the first waves of planes race past, bound for Pearl Harbor. It took a moment for him to process what his eyes beheld. Tight formations of low-flying aircraft—he knew that this sort of precision demanded flawless flying. Just a glance would tell any professional aviator that this squadron was exceptionally trained and expertly piloted. Which outfit were they from? They were a hot bunch for sure.

Then he saw the Japanese Rising Sun on the fuselages.

He bolted from the house to his car and sped to Ewa, getting strafed along the way by a marauding Zero. He arrived just in time to see all but one of the fifty Marine planes parked at the base go up in flames as Zeroes raked the field with cannon and machine gun fire. In the middle of it all there was the Sheriff—Colonel Larkin—barking orders, totally exposed to the Japanese planes overhead, whose guns had already left him wounded and bleeding.

Dick would never forget that day. Corpsmen rushed dying men to waiting vehicles, using blankets for stretchers. The dead littered the area, and the field's ramp was smothered in thick clouds of smoke, fed by the fires of dozens of burning aircraft.

Dick hadn't seen combat since that day, but he saw enough of the Japanese to know that all the prewar chatter about them was nonsense. *They were buck-toothed. Night blind. Couldn't fly in daylight either. Their planes were all bad copies of European designs way past their expiration date. In a shooting war, Americans would make short work of them.*

Pearl Harbor disabused them all of that racist crap. What he witnessed of the Japanese attack was nothing short of the most professional and capable aviation force he'd ever seen. The day left him with lasting pain and a sense of humiliation at being caught by surprise. But beneath those emotions, the professional warrior in him felt admiration for what the Japanese had pulled off.

He and his skipper made plans to start training the hell out of their pilots. They had a good crew, lots of old hands with plenty of flying under their belts. These pilots eagerly wanted revenge just as much as Dick did. Given a chance, they might have done some damage to the Japanese. But it was not to be. Marine Scout Bombing Squadron 232 possessed not a single intact aircraft with which to train on or attack the enemy. Weeks passed without any replacement planes reaching their books. Worse, by the time a few worn-out SBDs returned from carrier service to be passed off to the Marines, the old prewar 232 no longer existed.

On January 7, 1942, MAG-23 HQ gave Dick command of the squadron. His former skipper, Maj. Ira Kimes, moved up to group headquarters. At last, Dick had his own combat command. He'd waited his entire military career for this opportunity. But in the months that followed, it seemed as if his only role was to peel his squadron apart bit by bit to feed his experienced men into the stubs of new squadrons being formed.

SOME REAL CHARACTERS ENDED UP BLOWING INTO THE SQUADRON during all the turmoil. Pvt. Jack Stanner embodied that dynamic when he appeared in front of Dick's desk one day in early 1942. Dick had just finished reading through Stanner's service record book (SRB)—which was inches thick—and couldn't possibly fathom why the private had been sent to 232.

Private Stanner, an eight-year veteran of the Corps, had served at Shanghai with the 4th Marines, a line regiment. Throughout his career, he avoided promotion as he bounced all over the Pacific from China to the Philippines and eventually, Hawai'i. His penchant for drunken brawls just might have been a factor in his lack of rank. A detective might call this penchant a clue.

For Dick, a straight arrow with no time for brawlers, Stanner's extraordinarily long disciplinary record caused alarm. Why had the Corps sent this malcontent to him? Even worse, Stanner possessed no obvious skills that could be an asset to a dive-bomber outfit. The man was a drummer.

A drummer.

During their first meeting, Dick eyed him coldly. Stanner stood at attention at the end of the major's desk. Average build and height. Dark eyes, dark hair, sharp nose on a long, narrow face that ended in an undersized chin. He looked like a soda jerk.

This man was a brawler?

"You have the worst disciplinary record I've ever seen," Dick began, lifting up the SRB. Stanner's eyes darted to the paperwork. Dick's eyes, meanwhile, focused for a moment on his new private's right arm. Beneath Stanner's uniform sleeve, Dick could make out a series of tattoos. One looked like a crude black-ink image of a sundial strapped around his right wrist. Or maybe it was a compass. Either way, it resembled a prison tat, probably done by one of his fellow enlistees during a previous cruise.

"The worst," Dick reiterated.

"Yes, sir," Stanner replied uncertainly.

"Private, you have no discernible skills either. I think you're in the wrong place."

Stanner replied, "Major, I requested this transfer. If you will take me, I will make you a good Marine."

Dick asked why he'd requested the transfer. Stanner told him he'd been the bugler at Ewa on December 7. He'd been blowing the Church Call when the Japanese attacked.

Enough said.

Still glaring at him, Dick said slowly, "All right, Private. You've now got your chance to be a good Marine. Dismissed."

Stanner turned into a squadron project. He was put in the ordnance department, where he learned to load bombs under the squadron's SBDs. Later in the spring, he worked his way into the rear cockpit as a backup radio-operator/gunner for the squadron. The extra flight pay meant the world to him. He'd joined the Corps in the depths of the Depression to escape poverty in his home state of Michigan. He was quickly promoted to corporal—after eight years in the Corps. At twenty-six, he was finally making headway in life.

A few weeks before the squadron sailed on the *Long Island*, Stanner came to Dick and asked him for a twenty-four-hour pass. The

Washingtonian decided his drummer turned bomb-loader had earned it and sent him away happy.

The next day, the shore patrol brought Stanner back to Ewa and deposited him in front of Dick's desk, along with a list of charges and witness statements.

As the musician stood at attention, face covered in purple-blue bruises, eyes blackened, hair askew, Dick carefully read the paperwork. The shore patrol report contained several familiar phrases in Stanner's SRB, including "drunk" and "fighting." When Dick finished, he looked up and asked, "Okay, Corporal. What's your side of this?"

"Major, I swear to God, I only had a couple of beers!" Stanner blurted through swollen lips. "I was on my way back to Ewa. At the bus station. Then a couple of soldiers approached me and started running down the Corps."

Remembering the insults changed Stanner's demeanor from pleading to renewed anger. In a postwar letter, Dick noted that Stanner lost track of where he was, swept up again by the "monstrousness of the occasion." The corporal's face turned bright red, highlighting his bruises as he practically yelled, "Major, no fuckin' Dogfaces can talk to me like that! So, I popped 'em."

"Yes," Dick said. "I see from this report that you did 'pop' them, Corporal." Outnumbered and intoxicated, his bad-boy drummer had beaten the crap out of the soldiers. It was hard not to be impressed.

"Confined to station for sixty days," Dick told him. "Dismissed." The major knew they would be leaving long before the punishment expired. Dick could have tossed him out of the squadron, but where they were going, he was going to need every brawling, fighting Marine he could lay his hands on. Where 232 went, their drummer would go with them.

Stanner looked relieved as he left. Major Mangrum tried not to smile as he watched him go.

Welcome to the Red Devils, where even the musicians will beat the hell out of you.

For all the trouble he caused, Stanner's loyalty to the Corps and devotion to his new trade at 232 became bright spots for Dick, especially since plenty of other places in the squadron caused him concern. His green second lieutenants topped the list. Aside from a few experienced pilots—himself; his executive officer, Maj. Fletcher "Brownie" Brown; Capts. Bruce Prosser and Danny Iverson; and Lawrence "Baldy" Baldinus—the squadron was full of pilots who barely knew how to fly and who had no idea how a squadron functioned in the field.

As Dick ran through these challenges in his head, Tom Moore, one of 232's Midway veterans, walked into the wardroom to get some coffee. He saw Dick sitting alone, his brow furrowed as he stared into his coffee lost in thought.

"Morning, Skipper."

Dick nodded a welcome in return but said nothing. Tom got his coffee as 2nd Lt. Oliver Mitchell entered the wardroom. Seeing Tom, Mitchell grinned broadly. The two men had developed an unusual rapport. They had crossed the divide between combat veteran and rookie in a way few others had done so far in the squadron. It was black humor that bonded them.

"This is what twenty-five feels like," Oliver called.

"I wonder what twenty-six would feel like," Tom answered immediately. It was their own personal call and response, and they never failed to laugh at it.

Oliver had joined 232 from the *Hilo*'s contingent. Dick was glad to have him. As dark as the greeting was between him and Tom, Oliver's constant humor kept everyone laughing. Dick had made him the officer in charge of the parachute department, but Oliver was really functioning as an unofficial morale officer. Since getting aboard ship almost a week ago, the squadron's pilots would gather around Oliver while he entertained them with bang-on imitations of Hollywood celebrities. He had a particular knack for nailing Bob Hope, and of course the rendition would not have been safe for radio—or the silver screen, for that matter. The guys howled at his filthy one-liners.

Dick concluded that Oliver's sense of humor made him a vital part of the squadron. The pilots were deeply divided between the Midway vets and the new guys; each group generally stayed away from the other. The new guys found the old hands depressing and bleak. The old hands found the new guys clueless and overeager. But with only a few weeks' time in the squadron, Oliver used his sense of humor to help bridge that gulf.

THE INEXPERIENCE OF THE NEW GUYS CONTRASTED WITH DICK MANgrum's combat veterans. The Midway clique included Bruce Prosser, Danny Iverson, and Tom Moore. Like John L. Smith, Dick had sat down and listened to their stories from the battle. He learned how his friend Maj. Lofton "Joe" Henderson had died on June 4. He'd been flying around his formation, checking on his boys as they approached the Japanese fleet. As they spotted the carriers and closed up to begin their attack on those vital flattops, he tucked in beside a young second lieutenant named Jesse D. "Doug" Rollow and flew with him almost to the push-over point for their attack.

Seconds before they rolled into their dives, a Zero targeted Henderson's SBD. Tracers laced the sky right over Rollow's head. They speared into Henderson's Dauntless, which burst into flames right beside Rollow. For a moment, the second lieutenant could see Joe Henderson trapped in the fire-wreathed cockpit, burning alive.

As Joe's plane spiraled into the sea, the Zeroes hacked the rest of the formation apart. Half the Dauntlesses followed Joe into the sea. Danny Iverson barely returned to Midway, his SBD riddled with over two hundred bullet holes. Tom Moore only just got back, his Dauntless so badly shot up it was good for nothing but scrap metal. Bruce Prosser returned in similar shape. All three assured Dick they had escaped death by pure luck.

"There is no way we will survive if we don't have fighter escort," Iverson told Dick over and over. In fact, he told anyone who would listen. Without Wildcats keeping the Zeroes at bay, the SBD didn't stand a chance. The bomber was too slow, too sluggish when burdened with a bomb, and while it could take tremendous damage, the Zeroes carried a deadly 20 mm cannon in each wing. A hit in the right place—the engine, a fuel tank—and it was all over for the two men in the SBD.

As they trained through July, Dick could see just how traumatized by Midway his veterans were. In three missions, they had lost almost all their men and aircraft. Their squadron did not collapse like 221 did, but the shaken veterans returned to Midway plagued with nightmares, their nerves on edge. Young Rollow, assigned to VMSB-231 after the battle, epitomized the fraught nerves. One night at the Ewa officer's club, another Marine disparaged Henderson. Rollow overheard the harsh words. He rose loyally to the defense of his beloved skipper. Words were exchanged, heated further by alcohol. When the other Marine refused to retract his statements, Rollow drew his Colt .45 pistol and opened fire, shooting between the other man's feet.

After that incident, Dick kept a close eye on his own Midway vets. They weren't on the hair trigger that Rollow was, but their trauma was expressed through their fatalism. Like VMF-223's veterans, they were convinced the second round with the Japanese would kill them. They saw the odds through the prism of Midway. Nobody survived long against the Japanese. Why would this be any different? Especially since the Red Devils were even less experienced than VMSB-241 when it had flown into the maelstrom of flak and tracers over the Kidō Butai.

Meanwhile, the new second lieutenants knew so little, they didn't know what they didn't know. They were eager, boastful, full of fight. They saw the Midway vets as men who'd had the fight knocked out of them. It made for squadron tension that Dick could simply not bridge on his own in the short time the men worked together. So, as they steamed that morning for the South Pacific, his squadron was a reflection of polarities: naive overeagerness on one end and a black cloud of fatalism on the other.

Fortunately, besides Oliver Mitchell's soothing humor, Dick had another ace in hand: 2nd Lt. Lawrence Baldinus. One glance at his rank, and most would dismiss "Baldy" as another rookie with two left feet on the rudders. But he was far from that. In fact, he was one of the old-timers, a Depression-era Marine who joined the Corps out of Chicago in 1931. Between his stint at basic training and his experience at Pearl Harbor, he'd pretty much done everything in aviation a Marine could do. Now, he was one of those lug-nut guys who kept the wheels from falling off.

Dick had worked feverishly since he took over 232 to ensure that Baldy stayed with him. Over and over, as the squadron was peeled and stripped, he cut deals to keep his old-timer. They had served together for almost two years by that July, and Dick knew Baldinus better than anyone else in the outfit. He was a Czech immigrant whose family fled first to Warsaw, then to the United States. Rumors about Baldy's past circulated throughout the squadron and suggested he'd been orphaned by WWI. His family's home had been destroyed in the fighting on the Eastern Front. His parents killed by artillery. In the chaos of war, he and his siblings were forced to subsist on rats while living on the streets.

One look at his hard, blue eyes and rugged features, and new guys believed the rumors. The fact is, he was a year old in 1913, when his parents reached America's shores and all the promise its freedoms offered. They initially settled in Michigan, then moved to Chicago by 1930. Baldy's father, Wencel, found work in a local steel mill. At eighteen, Lawrence got a job in a factory that made springs. It was a dirty, hard life for little pay at the bottom rung of the second industrial revolution. The Depression made the life even harder, and Lawrence fled the poverty of the civilian world for the Corps' three squares and a cot, joining up in 1931.

Initially, he served in Marine aviation as an aircraft mechanic. Later, he became a radio operator and communications specialist, earning a seat aboard Marine Corps reconnaissance aircraft. In that role, he flew with some of the legends of Marine aviation. While serving aboard the USS *Saratoga* and the Navy's first carrier, the *Langley*, Baldy flew with Joe Henderson. Their careers would crisscross in the years to come.

In 1937, as a corporal, Baldy earned a slot in the coveted NAP program and reported for flight school at Pensacola early that year. He learned to fly with the likes of Bob Galer and Floyd "Red" Parks, both future fighter pilots of the early Pacific War.

Baldy ended up in dive-bombers, serving in VMSB-232 for over two years. During that time, as an NAP sergeant, he flew with Rivers Morrell, Fletcher Brown (232's executive officer), and Dick Mangrum.

In the spring of 1942, Baldy received an "involuntary" commission to second lieutenant. He didn't want to be an officer, but Dick needed an experienced hand with bars on his shoulders. Overnight, Baldy went from one of the hardest-working and most respected noncommissioned officers (NCOs) in VMSB-232 to one of the lowest-ranking officers in the squadron. The switch resulted in a significant pay cut for him, but it set the stage for one of Dick's best decisions for his squadron.

As all the new second lieutenants joined the unit in July, Dick pulled Baldy aside. He told him to live with the new guys, show them the ropes. Teach them to be Marines and aviators. Dick ran 232 in a much more traditional fashion, unlike John L.'s easygoing, informal approach. The stratified rank system precluded Major Mangrum from mentoring the second lieutenants. The squadron only had two captains and one first lieutenant—and they would be so overworked that they wouldn't have time to mentor the new guys either.

Baldy was the perfect solution. That July, he moved into Ewa's Bachelor's Officers Quarters with the second lieutenants and quickly became like an older brother to them. He steered them away from trouble, answered their countless questions, and showed them the discipline and professionalism needed to do their jobs. On the more technical side, he taught them tactics, shared insight on the intricacies of the SBD, gave them tips to help their flying, and covered for them when they screwed up.[1] As the squadron's communications officer, Baldy also selected the gunners and assigned them to pilots.

Dick knew that, with more time, the men would be well served by Baldy's guidance. But the war could not wait. Baldy would soon guide his ducks through hostile skies.

Dick stole glances at Oliver Mitchell and Tom Moore, who sat across the wardroom, periodic bursts of laughter emerging from their otherwise quiet conversation. Oliver's humor seemed to be the first bridge between the new guys and the veterans. It gave Dick hope that the squadron might yet fully gel.

As the dynamic among the pilots took shape in Hawai'i, Dick worked his guys as hard as he could. Through July, they had gained about sixty hours of experience on their aircraft as he focused on teaching the boys how to drop bombs. Lots of other requirements—including getting carrier qualified—interrupted what he thought was the most important element of their mission. Still, he'd taught them how to roll into a dive from above ten thousand feet and arrow down on a ship at a near-vertical seventy-degree dive.

For all his experience and outstanding leadership, Joe Henderson hadn't had time to teach his VMSB-241 the more challenging tactic. Instead, at Midway, he led his squadron into a much shallower—but technically easier—glide-bombing attack. It was easier on his inexperienced pilots, but it made everyone more vulnerable. In the end, the tactic allowed the Zeroes to stay with them and chop them to pieces.

Dick resolved to avoid that mistake. He just wished they had more time to practice. As it was, Baldy proved to be one of the best bomb-slingers in the squadron. He consistently nailed the targets they attacked on these training missions. His ability to clobber those targets solidified him as a role model.

A few of the *Long Island*'s officers drifted into the wardroom now, chatting and laughing as they grabbed a mug and teed up at the coffee pot. Dick stood up, greeted them, and headed for the flight deck to watch his gunners practice. These young privates—Marines for only a few months—were eager beavers, absorbing everything Baldy had taught them. And they were getting better with those twin .30s mounted in the rear cockpit of their SBDs. Those light machines would mean the difference between life and death someday, and the men pulling their triggers would have their pilots' fate—and their own—on their shoulders.

That was a ton of responsibility to put on teenage boys turned Marine privates, some of whom hadn't even finished high school before joining the Corps. He wondered if they would be up to the task when they met the enemy.

He reached the flight deck and stood to one side, watching the gunners take turns in the SBD's cockpit. The swabbies released a balloon. The gunner waited until it gained some separation from the ship, and then he'd open fire with short, controlled bursts.

These kids had already lived through unbelievable trials during their childhoods. At eighteen, they were veterans of the dust bowl, the

Hoovervilles. They'd seen their share of soup lines; their fathers saw their share of unemployment lines. The young men had scrabbled to survive in a society with no social net beyond the charity the local churches provided. They were proud and hard. Tough as hell too. Like 232's bad-boy drummer, they weren't afraid to use their fists. Thanks to countless schoolyard scrums, they knew how to take a punch. They had been kicked and knocked down again and again by Depression-era life. Each time, they grabbed their bootstraps and got to their feet.

They were survivors. Just like his pilots. But he couldn't shake the feeling that the Corps was sending them into a fight that would be too much for them to handle. Would they measure up in the moment of battle? They were tough. He'd have loved to train them properly—they would have made a fearsome force with more time.

He just wanted to know what the Corps expected of him and his men. Would they be flying from carriers? It seemed likely, given the urgent push to get everyone carrier qualified. That meant they would probably backfill some US Navy carrier air group that had taken heavy losses. This wasn't the primary role of Marine aviation, but it certainly was one of the secondary ones. That would be rough duty. Pitching decks. Rain squalls. Navigating over water after a mission, searching for that sliver-sized deck through inclement weather, fuel tanks draining alarmingly fast—these aspects of naval aviation at sea had to be learned through experience. Even then, every landing was an event. Every takeoff was a gut check. They never got easier.

Flying into combat from a carrier? With this squadron? Dick would be hard-pressed to bring half of them home.

He didn't want to think about those odds. Instead, he focused on Dennis Byrd, his personal gunner, as the young man took his turn in the back seat of the SBD. Byrd was a hard charger, quietly eager, with an exceptional work ethic. Like so many others, Dick's gunner was a hardscrabble Depression kid. Six years after he was born in a log cabin on a Central Texas farm, his mom died of tuberculosis. His father was a stationary fireman for the local railroad. He worked seven days a week at the lathes that rebuilt the giant steam engines dominating the heartland in the 1920s and 1930s. Dennis's family eked out a living, bunking down in a two-room shack through the depths of the Depression.

Dick once asked Dennis why he'd joined the Corps. "Twenty-one dollars a month and three square meals, sir. Never had that before."

Mangrum liked the kid. He was hard and a good shot, but most of all, he was totally loyal. They made a good team.

On the deck now, the sailors released a balloon, which floated up beyond the stern. The wind caught it and whisked it quickly away. Dennis charged the twin .30s, swung them toward the balloon, and fired a short burst. He nailed the target. Fired again, stitched it again. Cheers rang up as it deflated and fell into the sea.

That was the kind of marksman you wanted guarding your back. Flying an SBD in combat was a team effort. Dennis would cover their tail while Dick attacked the enemy. When in a dive, Dennis would call off the altitude so that Dick could focus on the target, not having to worry about checking his altimeter. At a thousand feet, they would release the bomb and pull out, then Dennis would swing around and man his guns again while Dick concentrated on getting them home.

It took time to develop the fluid communication and synergy to make a good crew. The two men hadn't had that time, of course. Still, there was something special between Dick and this twenty-one-year-old Texan. They clicked from their first flight together. From what the pilots had told Dick, most had the makings of great chemistry with their gunners too. No issues there, thank God, as the squadron in flight would be one team made up of twelve two-man teams. One breakdown in that dozen, and somebody would die. One failure of situational awareness. One gunner distracted and not checking his bird's tail. That's all it took for a Zero to get among the squadron and start inflicting casualties. The margin for error was nil.

This thought brought Dick right back to the central question of this entire endeavor: In whatever lay ahead, was the Corps asking too much of his greenhorns?

He could feel his gut grinding at the answer.

THIRTEEN
WHAT DARK HOURS WOULD COME

Suva Bay, Viti Levu, Fiji Islands
August 13, 1942

L T. COL. CHARLES J. FIKE, CAPT. JOHN L. SMITH, AND MAJ. RICH-
ard Mangrum stood in the *Long Island*'s tiny ready room and stared
at the Navy officer sent from COMSOPAC (the South Pacific command)
headquarters at New Caledonia to brief them on their mission. He'd
landed in Suva Bay aboard a weathered PBY Catalina amphibious patrol
plane, then came aboard the *Long Island*, which was tied up alongside
Kings Wharf.

He looked tense, worn-out. Overworked. If he was trying to project
confidence and authority, he'd missed the mark. This was an officer with
the smell of defeat about him. It made John L. and Dick uncomfortable.

The officer reached into a messenger bag and produced a folded map.
Carefully, he opened it up and laid it onto a metal table. The map showed
a string of islands running southeast to northwest. An elusive name
that Dick had heard back at Pearl Harbor—Guadalcanal—marked a
lima-bean-shaped blob of land at the southeast side of the map.

The Navy officer pointed to Guadalcanal and began to talk. An Allied
amphibious task force had invaded the island on August 7, putting ashore
the bulk of the 1st Marine Division. The Japanese had been building an

airfield on Guadalcanal that, if completed, would allow them to base long-ranged Mitsubishi G4M "Betty" bombers on the island. Command determined that this advantage could not be allowed to happen, as it would imperil the sea lanes to Australia.

To counter the threat, America had sent in the Marines. An ad hoc, hastily assembled invasion force reached Guadalcanal and rushed ashore, encountering minimal resistance. The ground Marines pushed through the primordial jungle to seize the airfield from fleeing Japanese rear-echelon troops. Across Savo Sound, though, Marines taking the anchorage at Tulagi ran into a desperate Japanese special naval landing force unit whose men fought to the last breath and bullet. The enemy had to be cleared out of every cave, trench, and bunker with point-blank attacks by Marine Raiders and paratroops, who suffered heavy losses in the process.

The night after the invasion, the Japanese sent a surface task force into Savo Sound—the gap of water between Tulagi and Guadalcanal— to intercept and destroy the transports unloading off Guadalcanal. They surprised a screening force of Australian and American heavy cruisers with their attendant destroyers.

The battle was a one-sided massacre. Over a thousand Allied sailors died as four cruisers, *Quincy, Vincennes, Astoria,* and Australia's *Canberra* all went down. The crushing defeat prompted the Navy to pull out and steam south, taking most of the supplies and equipment for the 1st Marine Division with them on the transports, which hadn't had time to unload.

Adm. Frank Jack Fletcher's carriers departed the area as well. They were currently operating several hundred miles south of Guadalcanal, offering "distant support" while remaining out of range of Japanese land-based bombers stationed at Rabaul, New Britain.

The Navy's sudden departure left the Marines on Guadalcanal on their own with about three days' worth of ammunition, minimal food, and minimal vehicular support. The line units established a loose perimeter around the Japanese airfield, but it was thin and full of holes, and it wouldn't withstand a concentrated attack by a properly equipped Japanese force.

Fortunately, there didn't seem to be such a force on the island. As the Marines dug in, the Japanese bombed the island daily while their rear-echelon troops who had been building their airfield hunkered down in the jungle or in indigenous villages to await help.

The lack of a well-equipped Japanese force in the area gave the Marines a chance to finish the airfield that the Japanese had started. Using captured equipment, they worked furiously to complete it. The briefing officer explained that it would be finished in a few days.

Dick Mangrum took all this in with a solemn game face. He asked if their two squadrons would backfill the Navy's carrier air groups. The briefing officer shook his head and produced an aerial photograph from his messenger bag. He handed it over to Dick, who studied it intently. The photo showed a roughly flat airfield hacked out of jungle and coconut groves. No hangars. No dispersal area or revetments. No buildings of note at all.

Dick gave the photo to John L., who gave it a long look, his face hardening. This was going to be rugged.

Both squadrons would be launched from the *Long Island* by catapult. The Marines would fly to Guadalcanal to be the first squadrons to use the new airfield once it was completed.

The Navy officer told them the Japanese from Rabaul bombed Guadalcanal every day around noon. They would get off the ground sometime around sunrise, fly down the Solomon Islands, and pound the Americans. Aside from a few antiaircraft guns, the mud Marines could not defend themselves. That's what VMF-223 was for.

Dick asked what would be expected of his men. Close air support and stopping any Japanese reinforcements coming by sea was the answer. The Marines on the island expected those enemy reinforcements any day now. Intelligence and air reconnaissance showed the Japanese marshaling strength at Simpson Harbor, Rabaul, their main naval base in the region. A counterinvasion by this force would surely come before the end of the month. It would be up to VMF-223 and VMSB-232 to stop that effort.

Dick Mangrum had no idea how they were to carry out this assignment. His men had no experience with close air support. They had never even trained with a ground unit. As far as hitting a ship? They had spent July bombing stationary targets on a land range. Hitting a ship and hitting a bull's-eye painted on the ground were totally different. A moving ship, countering the dive-bomber's approach, required tactical creativity, a lot of practice, and serious skills.

This mission? It was beyond his men's capabilities.

The briefing went on. Bad news piled onto bad news. Malaria was endemic on Guadalcanal. There would be no major resupply, just what could be carried on old WWI-era destroyers converted to fast transports. Those little ships would dash into Guadalcanal, unload their gear as quickly as possible, and then make a break for it to the south. The Japanese already had proved adept at hitting Allied ships that stuck around too long.

Fuel was in short supply. The Navy was trying to deliver a stockpile, but so far, little had reached the perimeter. Spare parts? The units in the New Hebrides barely had any for the defense of those crucial islands to the south of Guadalcanal. There would be minimal spare parts. There were hardly any bombs on the island, so VMSB-232 would have to catapult off the *Long Island* with a 500-pounder slung under every Dauntless's centerline. This arrangement would create a whole host of challenges, given the *Long Island*'s catapult system and lack of speed.

For John L.'s men, there was an additional piece of ugly news. The Japanese liked to come over Guadalcanal above twenty thousand feet. To use the diving-attack tactics he had taught his pilots, they would need to be somewhere around twenty-two to twenty-four thousand feet. These altitudes required oxygen.

None of their F4F Wildcats were delivered with oxygen systems. Worse, the squadron had no oxygen tanks. Out in the middle of nowhere, these devices simply could not be conjured overnight. Such things had to come from stateside stocks.

How could they stop the Japanese when they couldn't even get to their altitude?

They asked questions. Reinforcements? Minimal. Command arrangements? In flux, but for the moment Colonel Fike would be the air component commander. Whom would they report to? Gen. Alexander A. Vandegrift, commander of the 1st Marine Division. Or maybe somebody on his staff. Was there an air liaison officer? Unknown.

The questions provoked more questions. Few had any answers, and when the Navy officer did have one, it was grim. He promised that more aircraft and squadrons would be sent into Guadalcanal as soon as possible, but they would be the vanguard and on their own for a while. How long? No answer.

By the time the Navy officer departed for his PBY and the long flight back to New Caledonia, the three Marines felt gut punched.

This was a crazy, ad hoc mess with chains of command that made no sense and had no integrated planning that included the Marine Air component.

Fike looked at his two squadron commanders and asked, "Well, what do you think of that?"

"We're an afterthought," Dick said bluntly.

John L. concurred. This entire operation had been planned months ago, and they weren't even plugged into it until after it looked like a lost cause. Fike agreed but stressed they would have to hold until help arrived. In the meantime, as MAG-23's executive officer, he'd be the overall Marine Air commander once they got on the ground.

Lieutenant Colonel Fike was one of those guys who had been around the interwar block. Appointed to Annapolis on graduation from high school in Elko, Nevada, in 1920, Fike spent the next decade in uniform doing a variety of duties, including legation guard duty in Nicaragua, flying combat there in the late 1920s, and duty with Fighting Squadron Six (VF-6) in Hsin-Ho, China. In the 1930s, he served aboard the carrier USS *Ranger*, spent time on the *Yorktown*, and then joined a dive-bomber squadron in 1940. He was briefly the executive officer in that outfit, which included perennial bad boy and future legend Gregory "Pappy" Boyington. By the fall of 1941, Fike had served all over the Pacific, the Caribbean, Central America, and both with the Atlantic and Pacific fleets. He'd even done a stint on a heavy cruiser as the officer in charge of the Marine detachment aboard the USS *Portland*.

In the months before Pearl Harbor, Fike took command of VMF-2, which was later redesignated VMF-211. Stationed at Ewa, his cadre of experienced pilots was a who's who of future Marine Air legends, including Medal of Honor recipient Henry Elrod, Maj. Paul Putnam, and the king of Marine fighter aviation, Harold "Joe" Bauer. At first glance, Fike was an officer with all the pedigree and seasoning a subordinate could want. Yet, he was not attentive to details. He loved to fly, but he was inconsistent, a character trait that dated back to his high school days, when his classmates dubbed his favorite hobby "sidestepping class reports."

To Dick and John L., Fike's seat-of-the-pants reputation contrasted with his clear courage under fire, as his Distinguished Flying Cross from Nicaragua attested. Both men knew that bravery did not always equate to good leadership. Fike's role on Guadalcanal would be a staff one. He'd plug in with the 1st Marine Division staff, plan how to use the squadrons, and provide the overall vision of how the Marine aviators could best join this fight. This was a job that required a detail-oriented mind, a knack for relationship building with ground pounders, and the ability to inspire the men under his command to stay solid in what surely would be a very tough fight ahead. John L. and Dick Mangrum were not sure Fike was up to the task.

While that uncertainty was concerning, both squadron commanders realized they had no control over who would lead the force, so they focused on issues they could control. Their first task: brief their men, after a short shore leave. For now, the two squadrons piled out onto Kings Wharf to see what trouble they might get into in town.

The big score came through Zen Pond, who "appropriated" a jeep. The men went careening into town, eager to play tourist. They quickly discovered that the local constabulary had the place locked down tight. Melanesian cops stood on little platforms in every intersection while others patrolled the streets in pairs. They were formidable—tall with bleached blond hair that added almost half a foot to their height. Clad in thigh-length blue jackets with high collars and long sleeves, they wore no shoes or pants. Instead, they wore a lighter blue skirt flanged with white.

Their bare feet showed all the leathery toughness of a life spent without even sandals. As they walked, they swung wicked-looking clubs. The young Marines gazed in awe and not a little fear and resolved to avoid them at all costs.

Still, there were bars in town with cheap liquor and lots of it. The pilots, gunners, and a few members of the ground crew with them began polishing off shots, but no fights broke out. Everyone behaved, keeping one eye on the roving patrols of gigantic cops.

Others, like Marion Carl and Eugene Trowbridge, ducked out of the bar scene and spent their four hours of freedom poking around the shops.

The next morning, August 15, 1942, the *Long Island* and the *Alwyn* steamed out of Suva and into the open sea, bound for Vila Harbor, Efate, New Hebrides, the last US base before Guadalcanal. As land vanished to their rear, John L. and Dick called their squadrons together. The men gathered in the ship's wardroom, tense and expectant.

Dick looked around at the young faces, seeing the stress in their eyes. The uncertainty, the unknown nature of their mission—it was taking a toll.

"Okay, gather round," Dick told the men as he pointed to the naval officer's map, now stretched across a wardroom table. The men gazed down at the paper, looking at unfamiliar names on a string of islands.

"Well, gentlemen," Dick said simply, "this is our destination." He pointed to the lima-bean-shaped island in the southeast corner of the map. The men squinted to read its name, but Dick said it for them. "It is the island of Guadalcanal. Since we've been on this ship, the First Marine Division landed there and captured an airfield. We're going to fly from the *Long Island* to that airfield."

John L. produced the aerial photograph of the jungle strip. He put it on the table, and the men regarded it. Though nowhere near as seasoned as either skipper, they knew enough to understand the primitive nature of where they would be going.

John L. spoke, "We're heading for the Solomon Islands. Our Marines have taken Guadalcanal at the bottom of the island chain. The Japs are plenty sore about this, and they are sending air raids over every day. This means we're going to see action, and plenty of it."

The men had questions, plenty of them, but the skippers had few answers. They stressed that that all of them would have to stay flexible.

Later that night, somebody retrieved an old copy of *National Geographic* in the ship's library of magazines. The issue included a story on the Solomon Islands. Fletcher Brown remembered reading it during the run to Suva Bay and told the others about it. The article made the rounds through both squadrons, the men trying to absorb every detail—including the fact that the indigenous tribes in the islands were known for cannibalism and head hunting.

Were they friendly? No way to tell from the article or the information the two skippers possessed. Best to not get shot down and end up in their hands.

Over the next twenty-four hours, as they steamed for Efate, the tenor changed in both squadrons. They grew serious. The tension ratcheted up. The new guys stopped jawing about how many Japanese planes they were sure to shoot down and instead began asking the Midway veterans more questions. They listened intently, and the answers they received left them shaken. The veterans were in no mood to be optimistic. Where earlier in the voyage they were morose and fatalistic, the closer they steamed to their destination, the less of a filter they had in public spaces.

Roy Corry, in particular, obsessed over his impending death. As the 223's gunnery officer, John L. put him charge of making sure all the F4F's .50-caliber machine guns functioned smoothly and were properly bore-sighted. Remembering the many feed jams the pilots had suffered at Midway, Corry spent hours with each fighter, getting the *Long Island's* deck crew to swing its nose out to sea so that he could test-fire each gun personally.

Marion was an outlier among the Midway vets, being one of the few who weren't depressed and tense. True, he liked to nap and developed a rep long ago for his remarkable ability to fall asleep anywhere, no matter what was going on around him or how loud it was. But being a natural introvert of few words and grabbing a few z's was far different from the conviction among some that they were dead men walking.

The squadron came to depend on Marion Carl's experience and John L. Smith's leadership, with Rivers Morrell backing up the skipper. Marion was a straight shooter. He assessed everyone in the squadron on their abilities on the ground and in the air, then kept those assessments to himself unless asked. If asked, he'd speak directly and hold nothing back, good or bad. He was a genuinely honest young man with a black-and-white sense of the world. During those tactical discussions, the men listened closely to John L., but they hung on Marion's words—few that there were.

Yet, for all their tactical knowledge and air time, the first innovation didn't come from either John L. or Marion. It came from the most unlikely of sources: one of 223's rich kids, Scotty McLennan.

Yale had been a natural place for Scotty in the orderly world back home in the States. His family had the means, and he had the prep school pedigree, the physical fitness, and the mental acuity to thrive in its Ivy League halls. His intelligence and eloquence were the first things the squadron's leadership noticed. He was quick to adapt, learned on the fly faster than most, and possessed a chessboard sort of mind where he intuitively saw three or four steps ahead of everyone else. That latter ability made him a fighter pilot of considerable potential. With experience, his flying would catch up with his mind and make for a deadly combination in the air.

One afternoon, during one of the wardroom tactics discussions, Scotty pitched a new idea, a twist to the Navy's standard overhead pass. The new tactic would allow the Marines to quickly reverse back on their target and hit it again. John L. had drilled into the men that they would make one pass and then get out of Dodge. That was the key Midway lesson that John L. took away from all the reports. When VMF-221 made its initial attacks on the Japanese bombers, it caught the escorting Zeroes out of position. The Buffalos and Wildcats screamed down in fast dives and hit the bombers, flaming several. But then the Marines pulled up and prepared to make a second overhead attack. That's when the Zeroes tore into them.

John L. spent July teaching his men to never give the Zeroes that opportunity. One pass, and hightail it out of there. Live to fight another day. Get a bomber in the process—that was the way an outnumbered, outgunned squadron flying inferior aircraft could survive in combat.

Scotty wanted to give them a reasonable chance to get a second shot at the bombers without making them vulnerable to the fighter escort. He walked through what he had in mind. John L. and Marion listened. When Scotty finished, the two old hands exchanged glances. They dissected it, looking at every angle and possible downside. Ultimately, John L. pronounced it a promising innovation, and they would try it at some point once they got to Guadalcanal.

On August 17, 1942, the *Long Island* dropped anchor at Efate. The men watched from the flight deck as the ship's crew unloaded the bombs and crates of ammunition stacked below and sent them ashore.

Blessedly, the Marines received one final shore pass. They piled into launches and headed for the little French town built around the harbor. As they motored across the harbor, Melanesian locals came out in wooden canoes to welcome them, holding up coconuts and bunches of bananas to sell.

For 232's Tom Moore, this last trip ashore before Guadalcanal turned into a quest for some sort of peace with his fears. Two years before, he'd been working in Hollywood in a major studio's animation department. The global war took his quiet life of making cartoons and bent it totally beyond recognition. Strange how events so far away could alter a young man's course in what had been peacetime America.

Tom was raised in Brooklyn, where his dad was a beat cop who barely made enough to keep the family afloat. After he finished high school, Tom played around with the idea of becoming a merchant seaman. He spent two years at the US Merchant Marine Academy in Kings Point, New York, graduated in 1936, and gained the captaincy of a sixty-five-foot charter fishing boat. During his second summer, all of twenty years old, Tom impressed Dave Fleischer, a charter client who happened to be a Florida-based producer of legendary Hollywood cartoons. He lured Tom away from the sea with the promise of a steady seventeen dollar a week paycheck colorizing, frame by frame, Popeye and Betty Boop shorts that were played before the main attraction at theaters around the country.

In Florida, where the studio was based, he fell in love twice: first with one of the company's artists, Janet, and then with aviation. He spent every spare nickel on both passions, flying and courting between his hours as an animator. Eventually, his passion for flight led him into the Marine Corps.

Older than most of the other men in VMSB-232, Tom possessed more self-awareness and emotional intelligence. Normally, he was not the type to dwell, but the experience at Midway left him with profound self-doubt. The fear he'd felt at Midway, the trauma of watching so many of his friends go down in flames, clung to him through the remaining days on the atoll. He didn't want to be governed by fear, yet after Dick's briefing, he felt captive to it again.

For the past two days, he'd fought a war within himself, struggling to find the virtues and strength he knew he needed for the ordeal ahead. "Confidence and valor—those were the qualities I wanted for my own," he wrote. "I needed them to light what dark hours would come."

Confidence and valor. They were words thrown around a lot by people who never embodied them. Tom wanted to believe they defined his own character. Then came Midway and June 4's pell-mell scramble to get airborne, followed by the attack on the Kidō Butai. Those virtues ran into a buzz saw of flak and fighters, where to Tom, they vanished like childhood fantasies. The cold reality of combat disabused him of his self-assessment. Fear dominated every moment, made simple tasks complex, and sent his sense of self plummeting in the wake of his near-miraculous survival.

Confidence and valor, he concluded, were illusions in his own soul.

He needed them to be a real part of his bedrock if he was to survive and get back to his artist wife. At night, in his bunk, the fear returned and smothered him over and over. He'd lain awake, shuddering at the memories of bullets ripping into his SBD, his wingman afire and falling into the sea.

In sheer desperate, psychological self-defense, he created a mantra and whispered it repeatedly to the darkness.

"I am not afraid. I'll come back. It's just not possible for me to die."

No matter how many times he said them, those soundless words felt empty. Hollow. The mantra would be split apart by the thought that he'd cheated death. His survival was a fluke; all it would have taken was a single piece of steel to strike him, and his dark-haired wife—his great love—would get that shattering yellow telegram from a stoic Western Union deliveryman.

By the time the *Long Island* reached Efate, Tom's nightmares had penetrated daylight. Asleep, he saw the fires that consumed his friends. Awake, he could not escape the fear of what that terror would do to him in combat again. Far worse than anything else he could imagine was not measuring up. Disgracing himself even as the battle consumed his life.

He didn't want to go out that way. And so, the war within his head raged so furiously that something snapped. He gave himself up like an offering to fate. No more clinging to the life he knew back home. No more thoughts of his dark-haired artist, her gentle caresses, and those long kisses they shared during their Florida courtship.

Those things he consigned to a box and stuffed away in his mental attic. Another life. Another time, another Tom.

He used the fear to strip away his identity, kill the hope that every man carries into combat. He became a fatalist. He would not survive, and that acceptance allowed him to make peace with fate. Death would come "according to expectation . . . and in the final moment there would be no place . . . for disappointment."

When the launch he'd boarded touched the dock at Efate, he gave no thought to hitting the bars. This journey had driven him to the brink of madness. He concealed his inner battle from his squadron mates, not wanting to lose their respect or erode morale, so he had no one to talk to, no way to offload this burden.

Surrendering hope was his way of saving his sanity. His life was an offering now, but before he reached that final moment, he needed one final act of living. He sought out a priest. He needed Confession and wanted the priest to grant him the sacrament of Communion.

While waiting for the liberty boat, he mentioned his plan to Charles McAllister, one of the other young pilots in 232. Charley asked if he could come along. Tom suspected he was battling similar internal demons. Charley been part of the *Hilo* batch of pilots who arrived in mid-July, half-trained and grass green. He was a New York kid, raised in the shadow of his small town's city hall, his house kitty-corner to the local Catholic church his Irish family attended. He'd married just before shipping out, like many of the other second lieutenants. The odds looked as long to Charley as they did to Tom, though for perhaps different reasons. Charley barely felt comfortable in an SBD. He loved to fly, but with only a few dozen hours in it, he didn't even know what he didn't know yet.

They went off in search of a church. The pair found a village at the bottom of a steep, jungle-covered hill. To Tom, it looked like a typical tiny burg he had run across along US Route 66, when he drove across the country to San Diego before shipping out. They located the general store and went inside to ask for directions. Piles of crates, random products, and heaps of empty burlap bags lay scattered and stacked everywhere. It was like a hoarder's cave. They wove their way to the counter, where the owner—a wizened, stooped old man—told them how to get to the church.

They climbed the hill, following the old man's words like breadcrumbs until they saw a cross glittering white against the cobalt sky and standing watch over a run-down collection of buildings made from every conceivable material. The church stood beside a fenced-off schoolhouse and yard, where dozens of kids played in the tropical sun. The two Marines watched them, innocents lost in their games of imagination. It made Tom feel weary. His imagination, no longer the joyous escape it had been in his own Brooklyn childhood, had long since become his worst enemy.

A nun kept watch over the children. She noticed the two Americans standing at the fence line, sweating through their khaki uniforms. Approaching them, she asked in French what she could do for them.

Tom used his high school French to convey they wanted to see a priest. The nun shook her head and said their parish priest was away and would not be back for several days. Then she thought it over and added that the bishop might be able to help them. He lived at the top of the hill. She pointed to a dilapidated structure farther up the road.

The two Americans made their way to the bishop's door. Sixty-something and bent over, the short French man of the cloth welcomed them into his modest home with a quiet "Good day. Enter, please," in broken English.

McAllister went first. The bishop led him into an adjoining study, leaving Tom alone. He stood in what must have passed for the bishop's living room. Sparse, worn, and aged furniture, cheap. Weary looking. The windows were frosted and dirt stained, letting little light in. The place seemed more gloomy than spartan, a reflection of the life the bishop had chosen here at the edge of the known world, bringing the word of God to the few inhabitants of this tiny island. To Tom, though he counted himself a Christian, it seemed an unfathomable way to spend a life.

McAllister returned with the bishop several minutes later. Second lieutenants without the time or opportunity to sin had little to confess. Tom, on the other hand, had much to get off his chest. He followed the bishop deeper into his house. Once seated, he began to talk, switching to English when his schoolhouse French failed him.

It took a long time to say what he'd come to say. The words, broken by two languages, revealed a good heart in this young American. He was earnest and wanted to be the measure of his responsibilities. Midway had robbed him of his confidence that he would rise to the moment. The bishop listened, offering words of comfort when appropriate. Maybe some of the holy man's thoughts were lost in translation. Or maybe the bishop just didn't have the right words. Either way, when they finished, Tom did not feel the peace he'd sought. At least he did have the comfort of knowing that when the moment came, his conscience would be clean.

Maybe that would be enough.

After the bishop gave them Communion at the church, Tom and Charley walked back to the little village to do some shopping before they returned to the ship. Tom wanted to send something home to his wife and to his folks back in Brooklyn.

While they shopped, Scotty McLennan slipped into the local post office, a letter in hand. Had anyone seen its envelope, they might have been surprised that it was not addressed to his newlywed wife, Peggy. Instead, it was addressed to his older brother, Bill.

John L.'s diamond in the rough had listened to the briefings. He sized up 223 and the mission laid out for it at Guadalcanal. He listened to the Midway vets and asked questions of them whenever he could. Their answers, combined with their general level of training and the situation they were going into, left Scotty with no illusions of what they faced. He knew his own limitations as well.

The odds were not good. Instead of seeking the peace of Confession, he sat down and wrote his brother a letter before heading ashore. Scotty had a way with words, but he kept this letter simple, blunt, and honest.

Bill had stood up for Scotty at his wedding, his brother and best man. As Scotty wrote this letter, he thought of that day, Peggy looking radiant in her starched chiffon dress, its train edged with four-inch pleats, her tulle veil held in place with a coronet of orange blossoms and orchids. They were a striking couple, with him in his Marine Corps uniform. Both people tall, fit, and lit up with that extra fire for life that being in love brings.

He needed Peggy to be okay. She wasn't strong enough to survive his death on her own. He knew this about her and had worried about it ever since it was clear he would be heading for combat.

In the letter, Scotty minced no words. He told his brother that the situation was grim. He was probably not going to survive. He needed his brother to be prepared for that and to help care for the family after his death. His final sentences enshrined his mortal wish. He wanted the comfort in knowing that Peggy would be okay after he died. More than anyone else, he trusted his brother to take care of her for him, and so the letter concluded with that last request.

The words written, he sealed them in the tomb of that envelope and sent it on its hazardous, 8,000-mile journey back to Illinois.

As he left the post office, the sad duty done, he felt sure Bill would honor his wishes. His brother always had his back. As kids, they were nearly inseparable. Bill and Scotty had been through scraps and school-yard dramas that tested their loyalty to each other. It never wavered.

His family would be okay at home without him. The dreaded yellow telegram would not blow up their world, destroy their lives, destroy Peggy. Bill would pull them through. Scotty counted on that, and it gave him the comfort he needed to face the will of fate.

He would face whatever the future held, heart and mind clear, and do everything he could to measure up to the moment and not let the squadron down. Valor. Confidence. They could not be illusions. They had to be his guiding forces to face the coming storm.

FOURTEEN
FAREWELL TO NORMALCY

Between the New Hebrides Islands and the Solomon Islands
August 19, 1942, 1400 hours

SECOND LIEUTENANT HENRY HISE, LATE OF THE UNIVERSITY OF
Texas, stood on the *Long Island*'s bridge with a pair of binoculars in
hand. Officially, he was the junior officer of the deck. What that meant,
the Texan did not really know—beyond observing how things were done
by the officers and men who actually knew their jobs. He mostly tried to
stay out of their way.

The previous summer, he'd been in Austin waiting to go to flight school
after finishing up another term at the university. He'd joined the Navy
after the Army Air Corps rejected him for being "too tense." He sailed
through cadet training, which earned him an offer to join Marine aviation. After all of three hours of flying with the Advanced Carrier Training
Group in San Diego, the Corps put him on the *Hilo*, bound for Ewa. He
arrived in early July with the first batch of pilots to join VMSB-232.

Two months removed from the States, he scanned the skies around
America's first escort carrier in the middle of the South Pacific while the
little task group churned along at twelve knots. It was a hazy day, which
limited visibility. To compensate, the officer of the deck had posted a couple of extra lookouts on the flight deck above the bridge.

The mood aboard ship had changed after the Marines left Vila Harbor the previous day. They sailed through contested waters now, facing an enemy that, aside from the Battle of Midway, knew only victory. Anything could happen, and that possibility made the crew jumpy.

For this run to Guadalcanal, the *Long Island* picked up the light cruiser *Helena* and another destroyer as escort. To Hise and the other second lieutenants, the *Helena* looked like a battleship: huge, sleek, and studded with big guns. They were disappointed to learn the truth: only the big flattops rated fast battleship escort.

Hise searched the horizon. A whole lot of nothing lay ahead, just gray waves and gray skies. Nearby, a sailor stood at the ship's wheel, holding steady on a northwesterly course. The ship would maintain this course until tomorrow afternoon, then pivot almost 180 degrees into the southeasterly trade winds to launch the two Marine squadrons.

Over the past twenty-four hours, the Marines had encountered several aircraft. After the stories of the air attacks around Guadalcanal had spread among the crew and aviators, the *Long Island* considered each plane hostile until otherwise proved friendly. The ship carried only a few air defense weapons, pathetic armament for 1942 after the loss of so many Allied ships to air attack. Although Hise thought the *Helena* and the two destroyers seemed to have a little more in the way of antiaircraft guns, the best defense against an air attack was interceptors. The *Long Island*'s crowded deck included John L.'s nineteen F4Fs, but they were largely positioned aft, with 232's Dauntlesses arrayed in front of them. There could be no quick squadron launch should Japanese aircraft appear. In a token effort, the *Long Island*'s deck crews pushed a single F4F forward and prepped it on the catapult, ready to be the small task force's lone aerial defender should the worst happen. Hise did not envy the fighter pilot who landed that duty.

In the middle of his watch that midafternoon, one of the flight deck lookouts reported two ships on the horizon, a battleship and a carrier. Friend or foe? The lookout wasn't sure. Hise and the officer of the deck peered hard through their binos at the horizon thirty degrees off the starboard bow. Two distant lumps gradually materialized in the haze.

Taking no chances, the officer of the deck ordered the *Long Island* to general quarters, an order that would send the crew to their battle stations. Since the ship lacked an automatic alarm, the watch on the bridge included a musician who sounded general quarters by playing a bugle through the public address system.

The bugler grabbed his instrument, stepped to the microphone, and tried to get the first note out. Nothing but slobber and a guttural honk came out of the instrument. Hise looked at the young musician, who was so shaken at the thought that they were about to be engaged by a Japanese task force, he couldn't get a note out of the bugle.

Nearby, the *Helena* spotted the ships too. The cruiser went to all ahead full, leaving a big wake as it trained its six-inch-gun turrets on the approaching ships. The destroyers did the same with their five-inch batteries. It seemed like paltry firepower against the devastation of a battleship's broadside.

The bugler tried again, summoning all his poise in the face of the fear the Marines felt on the bridge. Any second, a rain of fourteen-inch battleship salvos could fall on them, and the *Long Island*, built as it was atop a merchantman's hull, possessed no armor plating anywhere. The vessel was a glorified cargo ship with a flight deck. With fueled aircraft on deck, bombs and more aviation fuel in unarmored storage areas below, the ship was a tinder box no amount of survival gear and lifeboats could mitigate. It would be a slaughter.

The bugler managed to blow a rough and squawky version of general quarters that drove home the urgency of the moment. Men throughout the ship scrambled to their battle stations. VMF-223's alert pilot dashed across the flight deck to the F4F sitting on the catapult. As the pilot strapped himself into the cockpit, Captain Barner, the *Long Island*'s rugged skipper, reached the bridge and ordered the crew to prepare to launch their lone bird.

Down in the living spaces, Arthur O'Keefe, the 232 pilot who had crashed and nearly drowned during carrier qualifications on the *Hornet* the previous month, was running for his battle station in the squadron ready room when he slipped and fell, bruising his hip so severely that he couldn't walk. He was carried to sick bay while the rest of the men from both squadrons streamed into the ready room. Adrenaline and fear mingling, they asked one another anxiously if anyone knew what was going down. Nobody did. They were stuck belowdecks with no situational awareness. It was an eerie, claustrophobic way to go into battle, especially for aviators used to open skies around them. They settled down in the ready room seats, waiting for somebody to tell them what was happening.

Meanwhile, the lookouts on the flight deck watched the ships grow on the horizon as the distance between them narrowed. The crews on all four ships in the task force grew tense, expectant.

At eight miles, through the afternoon haze, the unknown ships flashed a series of recognition signals with their blinker lights. The lookouts studied the flashes. Morse code. The letters matched the recognition signals for the day. Friendlies, thank God. Another few minutes passed, and the lookouts detected the familiar shape of the oldest, and largest, carrier remaining in the US Navy: the USS *Saratoga*. With it was either a fast battleship or a heavy cruiser.

The lookouts breathed a sigh of relief and reported the *Saratoga*'s presence. The tension drained away and the crews secured from general quarters. The *Long Island*'s surface escorts trained their guns back in and cut their speed, maneuvering to form a screen around the baby flattop again.

The Navy had sent the fleet carriers *Sara*, the *Enterprise*, and the *Wasp* to cover the *Long Island*'s final run to the launch point. These three carriers represented 75 percent of the Navy's remaining flattops. Committing them to protect the *Long Island* underscored to the Marines the vital nature of their mission. To get them to Guadalcanal, Adm. Chester Nimitz was risking the most important ships left to the Pacific fleet.

O'Keefe was the lone casualty from the incident. He was so badly injured that Dick Mangrum pulled him from the flight roster. The young pilot would have to rejoin the squadron later, once it was on Guadalcanal. O'Keefe's injury was a bitter blow to the Red Devils, as it meant Dick could only take eleven SBDs to the new airstrip at a time when every bird was needed.

Dick broke this piece of bad news to Lt. Col. Charles Fike later that evening when Dick and John L. met with their air group executive officer to go over the final details for tomorrow afternoon's mission. Beyond O'Keefe's loss, there were no other surprise developments. The men were as ready as they would ever be, though all three officers knew the next day's operation would demand a lot out of their young pilots. The margin for error was slim. Despite their inexperience, both squadrons needed to be almost perfect to pull it off.

The three leaders went over the most concerning aspects of the launch, talking through the best ways to mitigate risk. The biggest unknown would be the weather and the wind. Once the launch began, the *Long Island* would be sailing away from Guadalcanal at maximum speed. If they had an accident or if the catapult went down with a mechanical issue, the delays would put the ship farther and farther away from their destination. In that scenario, fuel consumption for the planes already airborne would become a concern. The squadrons would have to go into Guadalcanal piecemeal if an accident or a mechanical failure disrupted the launch.

Beyond the disadvantage of the prevailing winds, two other factors would make the launch very tricky, even for experienced pilots like 232's Midway vet Bruce Prosser, who had about seven hundred hours of air time. The *Long Island*'s crew believed that if the wind didn't pick up, the Dauntlesses would never get airborne with the 500-pound bombs they had been ordered to carry to Guadalcanal. If they got a ten- to twelve-knot breeze over the deck, and if the *Long Island* could maintain at least fifteen knots, then mathematically, they could get the SBDs aloft. Fifteen knots under these conditions was a tall order for the *Long Island*'s mediocre engines. So far the Marines had encountered light breezes of less than six knots. They would need a miracle in the morning for the conditions to be just right.

Should the wind not pick up, they would have to either scrub the launch or take precious time pulling the bombs off the SBDs so that the aircraft could get airborne—time in enemy patrolled waters that increased their chances of discovery and attack.

While the SBD crews prayed for wind, John L.'s fighter pilots faced a

unique problem with their F4Fs. Their little Grummans lacked hydrauli-
cally operated landing gear. Instead, the pilots used a small hand crank in
the cockpit to manually pull the wheels up. It took almost thirty turns to
get the job done. This would mean that after being catapulted off the *Long
Island*, the pilots would have to frantically crank up the wheels, even as
their Wildcats lingered on the bare edge of a stall just above the waves. The
longer it took to trim the aircraft for flight, the greater the chance one of
the pilots would end up in the Pacific, especially if there was minimal wind.

On the plus side, John L. had effected a second trade and swapped out
his four remaining least experienced pilots for better-trained ones when
the *Long Island* stopped at Efate. He and Marion Carl had gone to see
Lt. Col. Harold "Indian Joe" Bauer, skipper of VMF-212. Bauer's squadron had been in the South Pacific for months now, defending the New
Hebrides and America's most forward bases in the region.

Over lunch, John L. had asked if Bauer would be willing to make a
trade so his guys could get more flight time before being thrown to the
combat wolves. Bauer immediately agreed, and one of his officers, Loren
"Doc" Everton, offered not only to go with 223 but to select the other
seven pilots as well. Bauer thought these suggestions were good ideas,
and the pilot swap was made, with Everton's oversight. Two of the 212
pilots would fly Wildcats off the *Long Island* with the rest of John L.'s
guys while the others would get to Guadalcanal with the ground crew
via fast destroyer-transport.[1]

Altogether, the Marines would go into Guadalcanal with eleven SBD
Dauntlesses and nineteen F4F Wildcats. They would be facing the pride
of the Imperial Japanese Navy and hundreds of aircraft based at Rabaul.
Until help arrived, they would be outnumbered and outgunned. But the
Marines already on Guadalcanal depended on the arrival of these reinforcements for their very survival. Dick, John L., Fike, and their men
would have to give this risky launch their best shot. The meeting ended,
and everyone headed to their bunks for a final night of fitful sleep aboard
the little carrier.

The next morning, Captain Barner ordered all aircrew to attend
a final briefing on the ship's catapult and how the operation would be

conducted. To the astonishment of both squadrons, Fike didn't bother to attend. Apparently, he decided the briefing wasn't worth his time, since he intended to take off last. With a clear deck, he wouldn't need to use the dangerous and tricky catapult.

Fike's attitude infuriated Captain Barner, an old-school aviator who took pride in the example he set as an officer and a leader of men. Fike may have been in overall command of the Marine aviators aboard ship, but Barner was the skipper of the deck they would be using for the launch. His word was law. Fike's refusal to take the same risks as his aviators prompted Barner to take immediate action. He summoned the lieutenant colonel and informed him that as the senior Marine officer, Fike would naturally be the first off the catapult. Fike was anything but pleased by this direct order.

Fike now found himself in a serious predicament. The briefing was over, and with the launch scheduled for early afternoon, there would be no time for him to get a play-by-play on how the *Long Island*'s cat operations worked. Though a longtime veteran with prewar deployments aboard fleet carriers under his belt, he'd crashed several times on landing.[2]

Fike probably had little to no experience with catapult launches—let alone ones made with a rail set forty-five degrees off the port bow. His carelessness made him singularly unprepared for the afternoon ahead.

Throughout the morning of August 20, the men of both squadrons made final preparations for the catapult launch. They packed up their gear and stuffed it into their aircraft. Every SBD was crammed with spare parts, food, and personal items, weighing it down even further. Bruce Prosser, 232's operations officer, looked over his SBD with alarm. There had to be a few hundred extra pounds among all the gear and parts crammed into the cockpit and tiny baggage compartment. In normal situations, the SBD could handle the weight without issue—the Douglas could carry a thousand-pound bomb under the fuselage. But these were not normal times. Every extra pound loaded aboard the SBDs diminished the odds that the planes would remain airborne after their wheels left the deck.

Later that morning, Arthur O'Keefe limped up to Dick Mangrum. Art remained in significant pain, and Dick could see that just standing was an effort for the young pilot. Yet, Art let loose with an impassioned plea not to be left behind. He swore to Dick he could still fly and get his bird off the deck. Dick was skeptical and didn't think Art could handle the rudder with his injured leg. The two men went up to the flight deck, where Art climbed into his SBD and, though wincing in pain, showed Dick that he could move the rudder bars. That convinced Dick, who cleared him to fly the mission. The determined young second lieutenant, relieved and happy, limped off to get his remaining gear.

As noon approached, Fike gathered with both squadrons belowdecks to give a final briefing and supposed pep talk to his aviators. Marion, Dick, and John L. stood near their air group executive officer as he painted the situation at Guadalcanal and the men's role in it. Instead of firing them up, he left them slack-jawed and stunned by his words, "Men, your job is to buy time with your lives until the Navy and Corps can get more planes and men to Guadalcanal."

Their own acting commanding officer had just told them they were cannon fodder.

A greater blow to morale could not have been delivered, and Fike seemed oblivious to the destruction his words wrought. Dick and John L. realized they would need to do damage control. Unfortunately, there was no time before the launch to do that. For now, they gritted their teeth and just listened as Fike took a wrecking ball to the spirit of both squadrons. By the time he finished up, practically everyone in the room despised him. He was no longer the enigma—the brave and decorated combat veteran who administratively ran things by the seat of his pants. Now he revealed himself to be a callous son of a bitch unwilling to share the same hardships as the men under his command. With that one speech, he lost all moral command authority. The men would salute him. They would acknowledge his rank. But they would never respect Lieutenant Colonel Fike again.

The pilots sat in stunned silence in their ready room chairs, mulling his words.

Marion Carl reflected the prevailing opinion formed that day on the *Long Island*. "Fike was a poor excuse for an aviator, or even maybe for a Marine," he recalled later. "There wasn't too much respect for Fike."

The wait for the order to begin the mission turned into an awkward, depressed mess while above them on the flight deck, the *Long Island*'s crew fueled and armed the F4Fs and SBDs. The ship's ordnance men carted the 500-pound bombs to the SBDs and hung them under their fuselages. When that was done, the mechanics fired up their engines to warm them in preparation for the launch. In the rows behind the SBDs, the F4Fs sputtered to life. Soon the entire flight deck hummed with the sound of thirty-one engines running smoothly.

While the crew attended those final details, Captain Barner left the bridge to say a few words to John L. and Dick. He had good news to deliver. The wind had picked up over the past hour, and if it held, they should be within the margin needed to get the SBDs aloft.

"We'll get your ground crews in by boat," Barner promised the Marines. Dick would go to Guadalcanal with one mechanic, instead of the usual gunner, in the back seat of one of the SBDs. John L. would have nobody to care for his F4Fs until the rest of 223 arrived by sea. The sooner they arrived, the better. The squadron would not remain operational for long without its wrench turners.

As he spoke, Barner surveyed the squadrons and saw the expressions on the men's faces. He later pulled Smith aside and said, "They need you right now, Captain. Good luck and good hunting."

John L. knew he was right, though he didn't tell Barner why his aviators looked so shell-shocked. Instead, the captain thanked him for all the support. They shook hands warmly, then Barner returned to the bridge to prepare for the launch.

Shortly after 1300, a voice blared over the ship's public address system, "Pilots, man your planes."

In the ready rooms, the young Americans scooped up their flight gear, slung their parachutes over one shoulder, and headed for the flight deck and their waiting aircraft. It was gut-check time, the first of many to come in the fifty-three days ahead.

FIFTEEN
THE REAL LEADERS EMERGE

Aboard the USS Long Island, *180 miles southeast of Guadalcanal*
August 20, 1942

C HURNING THROUGH THE CALM PACIFIC WATERS AT MAXIMUM
speed, the *Long Island* billowed thick black smoke from stacks
located just below the starboard side of the flight deck. The engines
strained mightily, making the ship shiver like an old minivan pushing a
hundred.

Dick Mangrum stood on the deck, nose into the wind. It was a good,
stiff breeze, a combination of the sixteen knots the *Long Island*'s engine
crew miraculously delivered combined with an unexpected uptick in the
trade winds. The breeze over the flight deck had to be close to thirty
knots total now. That gave them a narrow margin for success—as long as
the trade winds held.

He glanced over at his gunner, Dennis Byrd, already up in the rear
cockpit of their Dauntless, securing the small hoard of supplies around
his seat. The identification numbers MB-21 ran along the fuselage sides
beneath Byrd's station, flanking the Stars and Bars. Byrd smiled and gave
him a thumbs-up. He was a Texas boy, eager and loyal with a bit of an
edge beyond his years. Mangrum liked the kid a lot and saw how much of
an honor it was to Dennis to be chosen as the skipper's gunner.

Behind MB-21, Tom Moore climbed into his SBD's cockpit. Bruce Prosser was already strapped into his seat, canopy open with a deck crewman standing on the wing next to him. All along the rows of SBDs and F4Fs, the Marines prepped for their departure. The thunder of the engines made talking almost impossible, so the deck crew communicated with the flight crew members with hand signals.

It was time to go. Dick hiked up onto the wing of his SBD and eased into the front cockpit with the assistance of one of the *Long Island's* sailors. The swabbie helped him strap into the pilot's seat, gave him a thumbs-up, and slipped off the trailing edge of the wing. The SBD sounded flawless, its engine throaty and smooth. The *Long Island's* men had taken meticulous care of these aircraft, a fact that would serve both squadrons well in the days to come.

Dick Mangrum's entire career was built for this moment. He was a leader, articulate with enough dash, polish, and charisma to be sometimes characterized as a knight-errant. Yet for all his years in the Corps, this mission would be his first real test of combat leadership. Since Fike elected to take an F4F to Guadalcanal, Dick was behind 232's SBDs. As much as Captain Barner wanted Fike to lead the way, the executive officer would only lead off VMF-223. That meant Dick and Dennis would be the proof of concept today. If they ended up in the drink, the launch would probably be paused and the bombs pulled off the SBDs. The launch could be scrubbed altogether, especially if the wind died down.

In the rear seat, Dennis lowered his head and began to pray with his arms folded over his machine gun mounting ring. His forehead touched its cold metal as he whispered into engine cacophony, "Please Lord, give us a safe flight."

Dick went through the preflight checklist: *Master armaments switch: off. Master electrical: on. Generator charge rate: five amps and twelve volts. Fuel pressure: normal at 6½ pounds. Oil pressure: 65 pounds.*

All in the green. He opened the cowl flaps, put the prop pitch to full-forward high rpm, and made sure he was drawing fuel from the reserve tank. That was always the first one to drain on a loaded SBD.

Almost there. He fed in two degrees of right rudder trim to compensate for the gyroscopic effect of the prop's rotation. Next, he set the aileron trim a half degree right to compensate for the forty-five degree crosswind they would have to contend with after their wheels left the deck. Finally, he lowered the flaps to full down to maximize lift.

He was ready to go. He gave the signal to the deck crew, who cleared him to move. Dick released the brakes and eased toward the eighty-foot-long catapult track. He had to be precise and line the SBD up exactly with the track under the center of the fuselage, tail wheel, and main.

He inched forward, walking the brakes, guided by the deck crew, until they gave him the signal to halt. As Dick locked the brakes, more sailors ducked under the wing to rig the catapult bridle. While they worked, Dick went over his checklist a final time. In back, Dennis made sure his guns and radios were locked in tight. More problematic was all the miscellaneous gear stuffed around him; spare parts, extra food, boxes of Hershey bars the ship's crew had given him, personal items, tools. The rear cockpit included a control stick for emergencies if the pilot was somehow incapacitated. Should the catapult shot cause any of the gear to shift, something could potentially get jammed around that stick and cause a crash. Dennis did his best to make sure this wouldn't happen, but managing all the gear was real seat-of-the-pants stuff. The Dauntless was built to drop bombs, not transport its own supply of engine parts.

Dick called Dennis over their intercom and asked if he was set. Dennis took a deep breath and confirmed. Moments later, the Washingtonian looked down at the catapult officer standing off the SBD's starboard wing. The two men made eye contact. Dick nodded. In return, the catapult officer raised an arm and spun two fingers in the air—the signal to go to full throttle.

The Dauntless's 1,100-horsepower Wright Cyclone engine roared, shaking the bird as it strained against its brakes. One last test, and then they would be cleared to launch. Dick checked the magnetos, switching the left one off, then back on, then the right one. No drop in power. Everything remained in the green.

With the prop spinning at twenty-eight hundred rpm, Dick and Dennis braced themselves for the shot. Part of the crew brief that morning stressed the importance of the pilot locking his right arm in place against his stomach so the force of the launch didn't cause him to reflexively pull back on the controls, sending the aircraft into a steep climb with the almost-inevitable stall and crash into the ocean. Dick secured his left hand on the throttle controls with his thumb shoved under its mounting bracket to make sure the force of the launch didn't cause it to slide backward and cut power at the critical moment they got airborne.

It was now or never. Mangrum pushed his neck and head tight against the seat's headrest, gave a quick salute to the catapult officer, then tucked his right elbow into his stomach even harder while loosely gripping the control stick. The catapult officer fell to one knee, his right arm fully extended. A second later, he dropped it and pointed three fingers to the deck. That was the signal to launch.

The gunpowder catapult fired with a bang, sending the SBD careening along the track. The zero to seventy knots in one second flat pinned Dick against his seat. The edge of the deck rushed at them. It was exhilarating—and terrifying.

The catapult's cylinder reached the end of the track and slammed to a sudden stop, sounding like an artillery shell detonating. The entire ship shuddered violently as MB-21 shot off the end of the deck, the bridle falling over the lip of the flight deck.

The sudden switch from wheels on the deck to forward flight just above stall speed in three seconds flat caused the SBD to sag toward the water, losing altitude the bird didn't really have to lose. The rest of 232 saw their skipper's SBD vanish from view as it dropped below the flight deck.

Dick furiously worked in the cockpit, pulling up the landing gear and trimming the aircraft for flight, fighting the crosswind as he did so. The waves rippled below, getting closer and closer. With a clunk, the wheels tucked into their wells, reducing drag and giving the SBD a surge of extra speed. The Wright Cyclone labored hard as Dick slowly retracted the flaps. Painfully, the SBD leveled out. Dick kept the bird just above the water and in ground effect, waiting until the air speed indicator passed 150 knots, at which point he started a shallow climb away from the carrier.

Proof of concept accomplished, the rest of 232 took heart as they saw the SBD reappear in the distance, above the flight deck. The skipper had just delivered a flawless performance. Encouraged, the rest of the pilots prepared for their turn.

Tom Moore was next in line, piloting MB-23. He saw Mangrum's Dauntless gaining altitude just as he himself got the order to move forward to the catapult. With the same meticulous attention that Mangrum had paid, Tom followed every step that the squadron had learned at the catapult briefing. Tom's SBD was slingshotted off the deck without incident. He tucked the wheels in and began a gradual climb to Mangrum's MB-21, which was now orbiting the carrier at two thousand feet.

Larry Baldinus came next. The cool old hand who was practically hero-worshipped by the squadron's second lieutenants had done this many times before on the Navy's fleet carriers. He was considered the best pilot in the squadron, and he made it off without issue. The sight of three birds now circling overhead was a great tonic to morale.

Danny Iverson launched next, the lead pilot for the squadron's second section. Next came Henry Hise on the catapult. The raw second lieutenant released and started a herky-jerky taxi toward the rail, the deck crew guiding him as he got into position. It wasn't pretty, but he got the aircraft over the rail.

He went through the checklist, tested the mags, then braced himself against the seat and gave the salute to the catapult officer. A second later, the SBD hurtled forward. But Hise had forgotten to tuck his right elbow into his stomach. The moment the Dauntless cleared the catapult rail and careened off the deck, its nose tipped skyward as Hise's arm and hand accidentally dragged the control column into his gut.

An SBD with a 500-pound bomb traveling at seventy knots in the face of a thirty-knot wind could not remain airborne for long with that angle of attack. Hise knew he had bare seconds to avert disaster. Fortunately, he reacted with lightning quickness. He pushed the stick forward right as the SBD approached a stall. He was just in time. Hise got the nose down, but now he was heading for the whitecaps. It was a race between the barest of altitude margins and the SBD's ability to accelerate to sustainable flight speed. The former Texas Longhorn eased the stick back gradually, getting his landing gear up at the same time. The nose rose, and he leveled off, limping along just above the water.

It was a heart-stopping moment, but Hise recovered from his error and saved the aircraft—and probably his own life and that of Walt Kalvelage, the Oregon-born mechanic riding in his rear seat that day.

The launch continued unabated. Hempstead, New York, native Don McCafferty inexplicably took off wearing an African-safari-style pith helmet, which surprised everyone who saw it when he joined the squadron formation, especially since he couldn't use his radio with it on. They were to fly with strict radio silence, however, so McCafferty figured it wouldn't matter.

Next came the executive officer Fletcher "Brownie" Brown and his section. All three made it off safely, including Arthur O'Keefe. Prosser led the final section of SBDs into the air, clearing the way for VMF-223.

Against the odds and with a little help from the weather, Mangrum's plucky squadron had pulled off a miracle that morning. Now came Lieutenant Colonel Fike in one of VMF-223's Wildcats.

The MAG-23 executive officer inched forward to the catapult, locking his brakes once he was in position. The deck crew rigged the bridle. Fike had to have been sweating bullets after missing the briefing. He didn't know the procedures and was unprepared.

On the catwalk on the edge of the flight deck, the catapult controller hit the red launch button. The F4F surged forward. Lighter than the SBDs and purpose-built for maneuverability, the Wildcat pitched off the deck, nose high. The fighter staggered upward into a nearly vertical angle of attack. The rest of 223 watched, thinking Fike's goose was cooked. No way could the Wildcat sustain that kind of climb for long.

Fike hadn't braced his arm properly, and like Henry Hise, he'd made a nearly fatal mistake when the force of the launch caused his right arm to yank the stick back.

The Wildcat staggered, wheels and flaps down, nose at an impossible angle. "We assumed he would spin in," wrote one 223 pilot later.

Fike fought to save the airplane—and himself. The nose sagged downward, the plane seemed to stall, but it didn't fall off on one wing—the entry point to a catastrophic spin. Instead, the aircraft dropped for the water, limping along a mere few feet above the surface, its wings rocking as Fike furiously hand-cranked the wheels up. Finally, he gained enough speed to start a gentle climb.

A bitter second lieutenant, with Fike's disastrous pep talk still ringing in his ears years later, wrote, "Unfortunately, the F4F, being the stable plane that it was, staggered out along the surface of the water and [Charley Fike] was finally able to get it into the air."

One by one, the Wildcats followed Fike's plane off the deck. There were some tense moments as the fledgling second lieutenants cranked their wheels up, wings rocking from the effort, in a race to gain sustainable airspeed while descending toward the water. These young Americans won the race. They formed up on Fike and John L., climbed out above Mangrum's beautifully arrayed squadron, and waited for the final aircraft to join them. After the last F4F pulled into the position, the *Long Island* catapulted an SNJ trainer off the deck, piloted by Charley Hughes. Fike had taken his plane, so he turned south for Efate and would go into Guadalcanal with the other pilots and ground crew via high-speed destroyer-transport.

The launch lasted almost exactly two hours and ran with astonishing smoothness considering that the deck crews and the flight crews had never worked together. It took less than four minutes to get each plane onto the catapult and fired off the deck.

It was time to part ways with the *Long Island*. The thirty-one Marine combat aircraft made one more circuit over their summer ride, then Fike led them northward for Guadalcanal. Below and behind them, the *Long Island* began zigzagging south for Efate, the ship's one significant contribution to the war effort in the Pacific accomplished. The *Long Island* was the great experiment, the first escort carrier of a veritable armada of carriers under construction in stateside shipyards. The flattop was awkward, barely of operational use, but the lessons learned from its design and this mission would help shape the escort carrier fleet for the rest of the war. The biggest lesson of all, of course: ditch the angled catapult.[1]

The Marines passed near the *Saratoga*, and Henry Hise saw the huge vessel cutting through the waves. The power and strength this ship represented lifted Hise's spirits and seemed to contradict the gist of Fike's pep talk. They weren't going to be left alone on Guadalcanal to buy time with their lives, not with the fleet carriers out there giving the Marines support.

Yet, if the mission began well, it soon started to go awry. Only a few minutes after leaving the *Saratoga* behind, the Dauntlesses and Wildcats began to unexpectedly diverge. As the separation between the squadrons grew, Marion Carl and the other F4F pilots began to double-check Fike's navigation.

Mangrum stayed on a steady course, despite where Fike thought he was going. His SBDs had been in the air for over two hours now; they lacked the fuel to futz around with navigation errors, even if they needed the F4Fs to escort them in.

In his cockpit, John L. slow boiled as he watched Fike lead the squadrons astray. He pulled out his kneeboard with its clipped map of the Southern Solomons, checked, and rechecked their heading. Fike's terrible navigation was sending them into the middle of nowhere while Mangrum's men made straight for Guadalcanal. The Marines had been ordered to operate under strict radio silence, so John L. couldn't just report the error and get Fike to fix it. Besides, that would have humiliated him in front of both squadrons, and Smith figured Fike was not a man to forget such a thing.

He let it ride for a few more minutes, waiting for Fike to figure it out. Their lieutenant colonel stubbornly held his course. The other men in the squadron—even some of the second lieutenants—soon clued in on what was going on. But what to do about it? John L. was a Marine captain, two ranks lower than Fike. The captain had been in command of his squadron for less than four months. Fike was their group executive officer, a war hero with an impressive chest of medals and service ribbons. He had more flight time than John L. Challenging him was not going to go over well. John L. realized there were no other choices. He either took the lead or let Fike fly the entire squadron to God knew where until they ran out of fuel and lost all nineteen planes.

Doing the right thing meant sometimes risking damage to career and future prospects. In this case, the decision was clear-cut: step up, or the men he'd come to love would end up marooned at sea or dead.

Marion Carl watched as John L.'s F4F pulled forward and took the lead spot from Fike. The Oklahoman signaled his pilots, changed course, and headed back toward the SBDs. Instinctively, every pilot in the squadron followed John L. Fike was left alone, plodding along on his errant course until he finally swung in behind the formation and trailed it all the way to Guadalcanal. Ultimately, he would be the last aircraft to land, a fact one wartime writer attributed to Fike's "covering" the rest of the squadron while they got on the ground.

It took about an hour and a half before the island rose on the horizon like a sawtooth-backed green dragon breaking the surface of the Pacific. Tom Moore spotted those sharp ridges and mountains first and thought their peaks appeared bald. They jutted out of seemingly endless emerald acres of solid jungle. It looked like a proverbial tropical paradise.

Like tourists, the Dauntless crew members goggled at the vivid colors and scenic beauty of their new home while Mangrum led the squadron along the island's northern coastline. They flew east to west until they found the airfield, which looked like a raw, loamy wound cut right through a coconut palm grove. Perhaps 3,000 feet long and 150 feet wide, it ran northeast to southwest, flanked by two rivers, the coast to the north and a series of ridges beyond one river to the south.

The two squadrons orbited the strip, the F4Fs providing high cover for the Dauntlesses, which would get on the ground first. To make sure the strip was usable—and still in American hands—Dick dropped out of the pattern and dragged the field. Low and slow, he and Dennis flew its length. On either side, they could see Marines jumping up and down, fists raised, cheering them on. As they reached the midpoint of the field, Mangrum spotted a jeep with another Marine standing on it, arms outstretched like an LSO signaling to bring it aboard.

Mangrum rolled MB-21 into a climbing turn, then approached with his gear and flaps down. The minute the SBD's wheels touched the ground, freshly laid gravel churned up by the prop pounded the underside of the wings and fuselage. It sounded like a hailstorm in a tin shack. A few seconds later, Tom Moore touched down right behind MB-21, and the same phenomenon happened to his SBD.

As the two SBDs taxied off the runway, led by a jeep that took them to the dispersal area, the four aviators watched throngs of Marines running toward them, faces alight with smiles. They were rugged-looking men, unshaven and filthy, with sweat-soaked uniforms reduced to rags covering their slender bodies. As Dick Mangrum cut the switches, he heard some of them climbing on the wings. When he opened his canopy, arms reached for him, undoing his straps, and pulled him free of the cockpit. A moment later, they steadied him on the wing, shaking his hand enthusiastically. To Dick's surprise, some of the men were unashamedly crying. Tear tracks streaked their dirt-stained cheeks as they waited their turn to welcome him to Guadalcanal.

Other Marines gathered around the aircraft. They cheered and threw helmets in the air, slapped one another's backs or raised fists skyward in an outpouring of joy. Others raised their Springfield bolt-action rifles above their heads and whistled or shouted. For two weeks, they had been abandoned, left to be bombed at will by Japanese aircraft and shelled by the Japanese navy. They had seen the cataclysmic aftermath of Savo Island and knew the Navy had suffered a massive defeat. They were short on rations, living in muddy holes in a primordial jungle, surrounded by Japanese. Bitterly, they had started to refer to themselves as the 1st Marooned Division.

None of that mattered in that moment at the airstrip. Help had arrived. These planes represented the power to strike back at their tormentors. They also proved the high command had not written them off.

Some of the Marines ran their hands reverently along wings and fuselage of the SBD as if they had never seen such a work of art. Others just stood and watched, faces haggard and covered with insect bites, but grinning ear to ear with happiness.

Dick dropped off the wing into the throng of Marines, still a bit puzzled by the reaction but loving every minute of it. It was a marvelous feeling to see the ground and air Marines come together in celebration. All too often in the interwar years, the two halves of the service were at odds with each other, fighting over meager budgetary scraps thrown to them by the Navy.

A tall, balding Marine in his midfifties stepped through the crowd, stars on his collar. Dick recognized him immediately as Maj. Gen. Alexander Archer Vandegrift, the commander of the 1st Marine Division. He was a friend of Marine Air, a man who saw its potential as far back as 1909, when he penned an article titled, "Aviation: The Cavalry of the Future" while at the Marine Corps School.

Though he had missed World War I, Vandegrift had served all over the Caribbean during the American interventions there and in Central America before going on to complete several tours in China and with the Fleet Marine Force. He was a veteran old-school Marine, leather tough and highly capable.

As he offered his hand to Dick, the Washingtonian saw that Vandegrift's eyes were wet with tears. Dick shook his hand as Vandegrift said, "Thank God you've come."

Vandegrift stepped back, and Col. Clifton Cates took his place. Anyone in the prewar Corps would recognize Cates's penetrating eyes and square jaw. He was one of the great legends of World War I, when as a young officer he pressed an assault that seized a key French village from the Germans, only to have his company nearly wiped out in a mustard gas attack. A few weeks later, at Soissons, his unit was again almost wiped out. With only two men left, he sent a message back to his headquarters that electrified the Corps and became a rallying cry: "I WILL HOLD."

After only two weeks on Guadalcanal as the commander of the 1st Marine Regiment, Cates was noticeably thinner, his face leaned out. He shook Dick's hand as if the aviator were their personal savior. After they exchanged a few words, Lt. Col. Gerald Thomas pushed his way forward. Another veteran of the furious Western Front battles of 1918, Thomas was a Missourian—and a fellow lawyer—who had worked his way up through the ranks after wearing NCO chevrons during the Battle of Belleau Wood. He served now as the 1st Marine Division's operations officer.

"Morale just went up twenty points with your arrival, Major!" Thomas exclaimed happily to Dick. Later, he would write that there was no bigger boost to the spirit of the 1st Marine Division during the Guadalcanal campaign than that afternoon alongside the airfield.

As Dick met the division's leadership, Dennis Byrd slipped off the wing and helped a group of men push the SBD back into a concealed position under some trees. When he ducked under the fuselage to secure the aircraft, he came face-to-face with an old friend from his civilian pilot training days at Tarleton College in Texas. As they enjoyed a quick mini-reunion under the MB-21, his friend, now a fighter pilot with the observation squadron VMO-251, explained he'd come up with Maj. Charles "Fog" Hayes—his squadron's executive officer—to help prepare the field for MAG-23's arrival. They had also brought along four hundred 55-gallon drums of aviation fuel and 282 bombs, both sorely needed on the island.

While Dennis talked to his old friend and Dick went off with Vandegrift and his staff to get a quick briefing on the situation, the rest of the squadron came in to land. Henry Hise very nearly clipped a stand of palm trees not yet cut down at the eastern edge of the runway. Another SBD bogged down in some mud while taxiing. Aside from these two minor incidents, VMSB-232's crews all set down safely and received a hero's welcome.

Second Lieutenant Leland "Tommy" Thomas and his gunner, Corp. Edward Eades, landed the last SBD that afternoon. Thomas was an eastern Oregon native. When he was young, the family uprooted itself from Ontario, Oregon, and jumped across the state border to Fruitland, Idaho, where his father found shop space to open his own auto mechanic business. Both men were outgoing, effervescent, and utterly devoid of pretense; Thomas and Eades bonded probably quicker than any other pilot-gunner pair in the squadron. While most of the other back-seaters referred to their pilots by rank or "Mister," Eades had a much more informal connection with Thomas and used his nickname. Both Marines had been raised in similar economic circumstances, but Thomas counted a couple of years at the College of Idaho as his ticket to a commission and a seat up front in their SBD.

Thomas touched down on the strip and followed the men guiding them to their dispersal point. The Marines had scattered the Dauntlesses all over the field, hiding them in revetments and under the palms. That meant each crew was separated from another crew by at least several hundred meters, so each plane received its own discrete greeting from the nearest part of the crowd assembled around the strip.

When Thomas killed the switches and his SBD's prop swung slowly to a halt, a pale Marine Raider—the elite of the Corps—materialized out of the woods behind his plane. He was bearded and bandaged, a Thompson submachine gun slung over one shoulder. He walked up to the SBD and waited for the two men to get out of their cockpits.

"Gee, Mac," he said to Eades, "we're glad to see you." He ran a hand along the SBD's fuselage and added, "If I had a million dollars, I would spend it all on these babies." The Raider, who had been wounded in the early days of the invasion, burst into tears.

With the bombers being pushed under the trees around the field, John L. Smith's men began to set down. They encountered the same reaction as 232 did. Marines mobbed them, shaking their hands, and smiling wildly. Someone remarked that the stubby little Grummans were the most beautiful sight seen since the Golden Gate. As John L. climbed off the wing of his F4F, a disheveled mud Marine snapped off a smart salute and welcomed him warmly. "Christ, Captain!" he said. "We're glad to see you. The guys have been praying for this day."

The final aircraft to get on the ground that afternoon belonged to Lt. Col. Charley Fike. Exactly what transpired between MAG-23's executive officer and John L. Smith after that flight has been lost to history. What Smith had done was clear insubordination. Yet, John L. saved the squadron from total disaster. There were apparently no repercussions in the aftermath—at least not in the short term—beyond Smith's growing animosity and contempt for Fike's leadership ability. That sentiment was shared overwhelmingly by the men who had been on the mission that day. Reclaiming the respect of his subordinates after his performance would be a steep challenge for Fike in the weeks to come.

When the Marines finished securing the aircraft, the squadrons gathered separately in the coconut grove astride the airfield. Somebody asked the name of the strip, and the answer came as a shot to the heart of the Midway veterans of 232: "Henderson Field, after Major Lofton Henderson."

Tom Moore absorbed that homage quietly, remembering the sight of his skipper's SBD going down that terrible day in June. Others listened and felt heartened at the name. Lofton "Joe" Henderson was a favorite of many Marine aviators who had come up through the ranks with him. To remember him this way was unique and inspiring.

Meanwhile, with the aircraft secured, the squadron returned to the default approach of military service—hurry up and wait. The gunners stood beside their pilots under the trees, chatting quietly as they looked for their skipper to return from his meeting with the brass and give them the scoop. O'Keefe limped into the squadron huddle, doing his best to conceal how debilitating the pain from his injured hip was. He wasn't fooling anyone. To a man, they admired him for refusing to be left behind. That was the kind of *never quit* they all needed.

Shortly before sunset, Dick Mangrum returned to his squadron. The 1st Marine Division's staff seemed like an all-star team of legendary warriors whose careers spanned multiple wars, large and small. With such leaders, how could they be pushed off this island?

Unfortunately, it wasn't as simple as that.

Dick brought bad news, which he began to share after he joined the squadron circle. "Men, I have just been informed that there is at the present time no way for us to receive supplies."

He paused and let the news sink in. The men, spirits buoyed by their welcome, sobered quickly.

"Or to be reinforced," Dick added. "Or to be evacuated."

They were trapped on Guadalcanal along with ten thousand mud Marines. They would have to depend on the ground pounders to hold the perimeter around the airfield while 232 tried to stop Japanese reinforcements from landing on the island by sea.

"In fact," Mangrum continued, "COMSOPAC has said, 'Hang on. You are, in effect, expendable.'"

Fike hadn't been an ass; he'd been right. His pep talk was a warning, without a coat of sugar to balm the stark honesty with which he portrayed the situation.

All eyes remained on their skipper. Mangrum knew it would take everything they had to make it through the days ahead. For now, he needed the men to not dwell. So he grinned slyly and his voice grew lighter. "We're kinda like a June bride. We know we're going to get it, but we don't know when or how much."

The squadron burst out in collective laughter. Nobody had ever heard the skipper be crude before—he was always the consummate gentleman. But the surprise off-color quip was just what the men needed. The tension evaporated. Jack Stanner, the outfit's brawling musician, saw the reaction to their skipper's uncharacteristically raw quip and knew it took the edge off the bad news. "Right then," he wrote, "every man in the squadron was ready to go to hell and back for Dick Mangrum."

Only a few hours later, the Red Devils discovered they already were in hell.

SIXTEEN

THROWN TO THE WOLVES

Henderson Field, Guadalcanal
August 21, 1942, 0200 hours

MARION CARL LAY SOUND ASLEEP UNDER A JAPANESE CANVAS FLY tied to a pair of coconut trees, his lanky frame stretched across a couple of Japanese rice straw mats and covered with two Japanese wool blankets. Had the Japanese not abandoned large caches of supplies when the Marines first landed, the Americans would have been sleeping on bare earth with nothing but the clothes on their backs. The Navy had bugged out with the division's cots, blankets, and bedrolls and even their tents.

That first night on Guadalcanal, Marion lived up to his reputation for being able to saw logs anywhere, anytime. The other men of VMF-223 struggled to get to sleep after their afternoon flight. When they bunked down on those straw mats, land crabs kept scuttling by. They made quite a racket in the brush around their squadron area, often sounding like people sneaking around them in the dark. Birds screeched. What sounded like dogs would bark from the jungle beyond the grove. Later, the men learned that the barking came from giant lizards, not canines.

After settling down under mosquito netting—also captured from the Japanese—they listened to Guadalcanal's eerie and foreign night sounds, feeling as if they had landed on an alien world. There was nothing familiar, nothing remotely similar to the night chatter of animals back home in their Middle American communities. Creatures slithered and crawled around them in the velvet darkness. Centipedes and millipedes roamed the grove's floor. So did fist-sized furry red spiders that made the arachnophobes cringe. Snakes. Scorpions. Rats. Bats. Guadalcanal was a zoologist's paradise.

The smokers in the squadron yearned for a cigarette. They had been told not to light a match, lest they attract sniper fire. The jungle around them held not just hostile native animal life but also Japanese marksmen hiding in the trees, just waiting for a chance to kill a careless Marine. Though the aviators did not know it, the Japanese around them had seen their planes land earlier in the day and had reported the development to Rabaul. Making their lives as difficult as possible using infiltrators and snipers would be a priority of the Japanese on the island from here on out.

That first night, the men learned Guadalcanal was anything but paradise. Instead, they found it a disorienting, brutally humid place filled with putrid smells and unfamiliar sounds, with an enemy lingering on the periphery. They had been given no orientation, no explanation of the situation beyond the fact that there was no escape from it. A few had heard tales from the mud Marines of a massacre by Japanese troops. A patrol led by the division's intelligence officer had gone ashore west of the perimeter to investigate rumors that the Japanese there wanted to surrender. Instead, they ran into an ambush and died almost to a man on the beach. The few survivors returned with horror stories of Japanese troops knifing wounded Americans or dismembering them with samurai swords.

Hostile island. A vicious enemy. No understanding of the situation. It was enough to keep any man awake that first night.

Nevertheless, Marion took it all in characteristic stride. While the other pilots writhed as bugs and crustaceans roamed, the Oregonian fell off into deep sleep, figuring he and his men would get a full briefing on the situation in the morning.

Their education on all things Guadalcanal began at 0200, when a green flare shot out over the jungle to the east of the airfield. Eugene

Trowbridge, bunked down not far from Marion, was awake and saw it arc over the coastline. A moment later, shots rang out, again to the east. At first, some of the aviators thought that it might have been nervous sentries firing at shadows. Then the volume of fire grew. A machine gun suddenly chattered to life, followed by a cracking boom of a small-caliber cannon.

The cacophony woke Marion from his sound repose. He opened his eyes, disoriented at first as the sounds of a growing battle filled his ears. He sat up and peered out east, seeing tracer rounds striping the darkness like bolts from a Hollywood laser gun.

Something big was happening, and it was close by. Marion guessed the fighting was only a couple hundred yards away. He pulled the blankets close around him to ward off the night's chill. In one of Guadalcanal's many ironies that he'd already discovered, although the days were humid, oppressive, and hot, the nights were actually quite cold. He was grateful for the blankets.

The battle intensified. More tracers laced back and forth, lighting the jungle at split-second intervals. The cannon continued to pound away, but now dull thuds of grenades detonating resonated across the airfield. These sounds meant the fighting had to be getting to close range.

In the darkness, the men around Marion began calling out, asking what was going on. At first, nobody knew. Then a voice delivered the bad news: the Japanese were trying to break through the Marine lines and take the airfield. The aviators hadn't even been on the island a full twelve hours yet, and now they might well be forced into a desperate last stand in the palm grove.

Marion fingered his .45-caliber automatic, snug in its holster. If the enemy breached the perimeter, its eight rounds were his only means of defense. He was glad John L. had ordered everyone to wear their sidearm before they left the *Long Island*.

Another rash of fire swelled to the east. Rifle cracks layered with machine gun fire, a bass drum of explosions keeping time.

"I sure hope the Marines can hold them," he said aloud to himself like a prayer.

Not far from Marion's meager shelter, "Doc" Everton hunkered down under his blankets, one hand clutching his shoes and a WWI-style tin helmet he'd somehow acquired, the other holding his own M1911 Colt .45 pistol. He listened to the battle intensify, unsure of what to do. The Marines had told them not to move around at night, lest jumpy sentries accidentally shoot them. Already, that had tragically happened too many times since the first day of the amphibious landing. If they needed to use the latrine, the bearded veterans told them to travel in pairs.

Escorted runs to the latrine were one thing. The sniper-inspired smoking ban was understandable too. But they had received no guidance on what to do in the event of a Japanese infantry attack through their squadron area.

Doc chose to err on the side of caution, staying flat against his straw mats, peering out at the battle through his mosquito netting. He checked his watch. Almost 0300. There would be no point in going back to sleep now, even if he could. John L. had given him the honor of leading the first flight from Henderson Field—a dawn patrol.

John L. woke up when the first string of machine gun fire echoed through the grove. Confused, half-conscious, he initially concluded somebody was celebrating the Fourth of July. He drifted back to sleep but only for a few minutes. Reality quickly set in. Something big was going on. Despite the dangers of moving around in the dark, he got up, swung out from under his mosquito net, and headed off through the night toward the one completed building near the airstrip. This was a wooden shack built by the Japanese and nicknamed the Pagoda for its shape. With the two squadrons on the field now, the Pagoda would serve as the strip's operations center.

He arrived to find Dick Mangrum already there. While John L. and his pilots had bedded down in the coconut grove, too, 232's gunners spent the night under their SBDs, doing their best to keep the mosquitoes, centipedes, and crabs at bay. There were no tents for them anywhere else so far. Plus, they needed to protect their most precious assets: their aircraft.

Charley Fike and Fog Hayes were there, too, gathering information from divisional headquarters and building a tasking plan. Division reported that part of Colonel Cates's 1st Marine Regiment had been attacked at the mouth of the Tenaru River. The Japanese were attacking in force across a narrow sandbar. The Marines held the first attacks, but now Cates reported hand-to-hand fighting in places along his second battalion's line. Vandegrift had just released the divisional reserve to go assist. The situation sounded confused and desperate.[1]

Dick Mangrum received his first assignment: a predawn takeoff and search mission, carrying the 500-pound bombs the bombers had lugged over from the *Long Island*. Part of the search would cover the east coast beyond the battle line to look for any Japanese reinforcements that were using the sea or the beach to get into the fight.

Dick departed to lead the mission, leaving John L. at the Pagoda waiting for further updates on the battle's progress. It was a little after 0300. Everton and his three pilots would be warming up their F4Fs in about an hour.

Fike and Hayes had put together a flight schedule that sent aloft a division of four F4Fs every few hours. The idea was to give Guadalcanal top cover throughout the day. Each flight would be a roughly two- to three-hour mission. Four divisions could cover the day right until dusk, around 1820.

Dick's first search patrol left Guadalcanal long before sunrise, its pilots unused to flying at night. They climbed up around the strip, then fanned out on their search vectors. It didn't take long for one of the SBDs to discover a group of small Japanese boats hugging the coastline between Taivu Point and the fighting along the river. The SBD's gunner radioed the contact report back to Guadalcanal, and the message was relayed to divisional headquarters.

Not long after, John L. received his squadron's first mission. By now, Doc Everton, Tex Hamilton, Eugene Trowbridge, and one other 223 pilot were sitting in their F4Fs warming up their engines and waiting for the order to take off. John L. grabbed a map and bolted from the Pagoda, found a jeep outside, and drove straight to Doc's Wildcat, the sounds of battle raging just off the end of the runway, to the east.

Since volunteering to come over from VMF-212, Doc had already proved to be a great addition to VMF-223. He'd soloed at age fifteen, long before he joined the Corps in 1939. Before signing up, he'd become a licensed pharmacist. Hence the nickname "Doc." Already an experienced pilot, he'd been in the South Pacific training with Bauer's VMF-212 since May. He was the kind of pilot John L. desperately needed, one of the rare prewar old salts with plenty of flight time and common sense.

Doc was watching the tracers light up the night sky to the east when he heard John L. yelling at him. He looked off one wing to find his new skipper waving a map. A moment later, the Oklahoman climbed onto the wing and stood beside him, leaning against the fuselage as he stuck the map under Doc's nose.

He pointed to a spot east of the strip near a snaking waterway labeled Four Block River.

"Hey, Doc, we just had a report that they're coming up the shoreline in landing boats and sending reinforcements to breach our line at the Tenaru."

Doc nodded, studying the map and John L.'s finger on it.

"I want you to go out and investigate," John L. said. "Use your own judgment about strafing or returning."

Doc led the four Wildcats off the strip just before dawn at around 0600. The Americans climbed above the fighting going on along the 1st Marine Regiment's river defense line. The jungle battlefield glowed with explosions, mortar round impacts, and artillery strikes from the 11th Marine Regiment's 75 mm howitzers.

At first, they found nothing as they searched along the coast. Unbeknownst to the Americans, the twenty-three-foot Type 95 collapsible boats, commanded by an NCO named Sergeant Ogasawara, had turned down Four Block River thinking they had reached the battlefield. When they realized they were in the wrong body of water, they turned around and began paddling for the ocean. But by then, the tide had gone out and the 500-pound boats had to be lifted and carried across the beach.

The boats were filled with medical packs and other supplies for the Japanese troops fighting at the Tenaru. They were also transporting some men who had been left behind for the sad task of cremating the early casualties of the offensive. Along the way back to the ocean, the boat party encountered small knots of dazed Japanese infantrymen who had escaped the fighting and who shared the news that their entire unit had been wiped out. They streamed east along the beach, a target that attracted American artillery fire around 0720.

The boats had just cleared the surf and turned east to evade the incoming 75 mm howitzer fire when Doc Everton's division detected them. He could see men on the beach and others moving into and out of the jungle. It looked to the Americans that the boats were about to land reinforcements. He saw no antiaircraft guns. Nor were there any Zeroes in the air around them.

He decided to attack.

The Japanese boat crews saw the F4Fs diving after them and turned back for shore. Everyone aboard paddled furiously—even the men without oars helped with cupped hands. One boat just managed to reach the shore when the F4Fs came into range.

The Americans let loose with their twenty-four .50-caliber machine guns. All the pilots had fired these weapons in training, but none had ever seen what a .50-caliber bullet could do to the human body. The sight was shockingly grotesque. The rounds tore apart the fleeing Japanese. The pilots could see body parts pinwheeling through the air—legs, arms, half torsos. It was a bacchanal of horror. One Japanese soldier rushing up the beach was hammered by the barrage; he collapsed at the base of a palm tree, holding on to it as blood sprayed from multiple wounds and he cried desperately for help.

Whatever visions of dashing glory the Marines held of combat were shattered by the sight of the carnage they inflicted that morning. The grim business of killing held nothing but soul-searing images that would linger for a lifetime.

The first pass was just the beginning. The beach was now dotted with wounded, dying men. Two other boats remained just out of the surf line. The attack left them bullet riddled, filled with torn and broken bodies. The remaining men aboard jumped into the ocean and swam for the beach. At the same time, the survivors on the beach either made a break for the tree line or dove back into the surf. The attack caused complete chaos among the Japanese.

Overhead, the sight of the pandemonium their pass had inflicted convinced Doc to make a second run. They could see the unarmed men in the water flailing around their sinking boats. As the F4F's bored in again, the men still on the beach dove behind the bodies of their comrades, hoping their flesh would shield them from the devastation wrought by the .50s.

Tex Hamilton, on Doc's wing, thought he spotted a machine gun shooting at the Wildcats. He eased his gunsight onto its muzzle flash and strafed it thoroughly, pulling up and away afterward, noting that it ceased to be a threat after that pass.

With two boats sinking and the third one bullet torn and covered with the bloody remains of some of its crew, the Wildcats worked over the jungle grove next to the beach. Inside, they saw a party of Japanese troops carrying wounded men on stretchers. The gun run nearly wiped them out, and the few remaining Japanese fled eastward, abandoning at least one wounded comrade whom the mud Marines later captured.

The air attack ended, leaving a scene of gory devastation. One Japanese survivor counted about a dozen corpses in the immediate area around him, all cut down by the F4Fs.

The fighting along the river line continued all day as Marine units flanked, then counterattacked, the shattered force. Light M2A1 tanks entered the fray, churning through the dead Japanese littering the sandbar and the palm groves beyond it on the east side. It was dark, macabre work clearing the last survivors, but by late afternoon, the job was done. At sunset, it was clear the Japanese had suffered a catastrophic defeat. Somewhere between seven hundred and eight hundred men lay dead on a battlefield so compact, the vast majority of the killing took place in a three-acre area.

Meanwhile, sometime after 0730, Doc's division returned to Henderson Field. The Wildcats executed a sharp, swift pass along the strip, pulled up and around, dropped their landing gear, and landed on the gravel runway, their first mission done. The four pilots were picked up by jeeps and taken to the Pagoda, where they reported what they had seen. Trowbridge guessed the group had killed or wounded some five hundred Japanese troops. John L. reported that about a thousand Japanese had tried to land, and only about eighty survived.[2]

It was a solid debut for the squadron, but the day had only just begun.

SEVENTEEN

THE WARRIOR INFLECTION POINT

Guadalcanal
August 21, 1942, 1130 hours

T
HAT FIRST MORNING ON GUADALCANAL PRESENTED JOHN L.
Smith with an avalanche of problems that needed quick solutions
if his squadron was going to remain functional at Henderson Field. The
challenges started with breakfast and went downhill from there.

The 223 pilots had no mess gear—no tin cups, no plates, no silverware with which to eat. There was no mess tent for them. The men had
to scrounge, beg, borrow, and steal from the mud Marines just to eat
the chow—what there was of it. The mess gear was the bright spot—
at least it existed on the island. The laundry list of things the squadron
needed would have filled pages (if they had pages), and almost none of it
had reached Guadalcanal. Thus, a lack of everything required to operate
and maintain a fighter squadron in combat became the overriding issue
confronting John L. that first morning at Henderson. They were starting with nothing but the planes and pilots they had brought into this
thick jungle the day before, with minimal fuel supplies, ammunition, and
bombs. They could fly a few missions, but it wouldn't take long for the
serviceability rate to plummet. Eventually it would knock the squadron
out of action.

For a squadron skipper, control and the ability to manage the outfit's needs were essential parts of the job. Circumstances robbed John L. of his ability to do the latter, as the supply situation was way beyond his pay grade. Everyone on the island was affected. That morning, the Oklahoman learned just how dire the situation was since the Navy decamped for safer southern waters two weeks before.

The Marines lacked everything, including heavy artillery, adequate ammunition supplies, rations, force-protection items (e.g., barbed wire), fuel, vehicles, medical supplies, and spare parts for their tanks, trucks, and jeeps. When the engineering equipment failed to arrive, the Marines had to finish the airfield using the existing Japanese construction vehicles captured on the first day of the invasion. The rations that did make it ashore were supplemented with captured stocks of Japanese rice, fish heads, and—surprisingly—canned macaroni. Should the Japanese attack again with the intensity of the previous night, the 1st Marine Division would burn through its available ammunition stocks in less than three days. As a desperate plan B, the division stockpiled every Japanese weapon and bullet the Marines captured, intending to use them as a last resort.

Since the Navy's bugout, the South Pacific Area commander, Vice Adm. Robert Ghormley, chose not to risk any of his cargo ships in the perilous waters around Guadalcanal. This decision ensured that the division's heavy equipment remained in ship holds somewhere to the south. Yet the Marines urgently needed basic supplies to sustain their men and the perimeter around the airfield. The bluejackets turned to fast-moving blockade runners—old WWI four-stack destroyers converted to fast, light transports. Of course, their cargo capacity was a fraction of the larger transports, but every run up to Guadalcanal's Lunga Point provided critical items that the Marines simply could not do without.

The 1st Marine Division needed a firehose of a supply line but was instead getting drips from the COMSOPAC faucet. But a drip every now and then was better than nothing. Until the situation changed, the men on the island would have to improvise, adapt, and overcome.

The macro situation the Marines faced mirrored the myriad of problems John L. awoke to on that first Guadalcanal sunrise. All he and his men could do was fight for as long as their aircraft would hold up and pray that additional fuel, food, and spare parts would come their way at some point.

Making sure the aircraft held up for as long as possible would be the overriding priority for now. Fortunately, the Wildcats the Navy gave the squadron in Hawai'i came straight from the factory. In mint condition and factory fresh, they could be flown for a while without major maintenance. This brand-new state of the F4Fs was an important asset, since most of 223's mechanics and armorers were still at Efate, waiting for a transport to run the Japanese blockade and deliver them to Guadalcanal. A small contingent of perhaps seventy was due in on the twenty-first, having boarded the USS *McFarland* the same day the *Long Island* departed Vila Harbor. That first wave, once it arrived, would be a godsend.

For the morning, the squadron's Wildcats would be fueled and serviced by the personnel already there at the field. The Navy had delivered Lt. Col. Fog Hayes for that purpose, along with CUB-1, an advanced base logistics unit, on August 16. A young ensign named George S. Polk commanded CUB-1, which consisted of 123 officers and men. The problem was, like everyone else, CUB-1 arrived with a bare minimum of gear. To maintain thirty-one planes, the unit had exactly two master toolboxes. No replacement parts existed beyond the few brought in by the SBDs. Basic necessities like oil, electrical wiring, and aluminum sheets to repair bullet damage either didn't exist on the island or remained in critically short supply.

As soon as the 223 and 232 touched down on the twentieth, CUB-1's sailors refueled the F4Fs and SBDs using fifty-five-gallon drums of avgas. Since there was not a single automatic pump on the island to assist with this job, they manhandled the drums into position, then strained the fuel with chamois while they poured it directly into the tanks. It was a dreadfully time-consuming and exhausting task.

To arm the aircraft, men from the 11th Marine Regiment—the division's artillery outfit—were pressed into service to make sure the .50-caliber machine guns were functional and ready to fight. That task proved vital, but there was still the oxygen system issue to solve. The F4Fs would need their oxygen bottles swapped out and refilled after every mission. On Guadalcanal, there was no way to refill them.

The Japanese had been building an oxygen liquefaction facility at the airfield. Somehow, on the first day of the invasion, the Marines who took the airfield destroyed the plant, which had been about 75 percent complete. With this move, the division had no way in the immediate future to refill surgical oxygen tanks or aviation ones. The machinery to create a new oxygen liquefaction plant on Guadalcanal would have to come from the United States proper. In the meantime, both squadrons would have to swap their oxygen tanks out after each mission above about fifteen thousand feet.

Except there were no filled tanks to replace the ones currently in the planes. When those tanks ran dry, VMF-223 would be unable to intercept the Japanese raids on the island. How and from where new O_2 bottles could be obtained in the South Pacific was anyone's guess. For now, they had enough oxygen to fly a couple of high-altitude missions, and that was it. Colonel Fike made sure this problem was relayed to COMSOPAC immediately and underscored the urgency: no oxygen, no fighter defense.

One final headache beset John L. that first morning on the island. CUB-1 dispersed his F4F Wildcats all over the place, hiding them under the trees and tucking them into revetments. But with the planes scattered everywhere, it would take a half hour or more to get the squadron airborne. They were short on jeeps and trucks, making transportation difficult. There was also a shortage of fuel for those vehicles, which necessitated mixing captured Japanese gasoline with American seventy-octane fuel—with poor results.

With the sudden deluges and tropical storms blowing across the island, the field and the dispersal areas quickly turned to mud. Getting the planes out of their dispersal points was already proving difficult, as some ended up mired in the muck and needed a tractor to get clear. When every second counted on a scramble mission, waiting for a tow just to be able to taxi to the runway was not going to work.

They had a decision to make: keep the aircraft dispersed and safer, or concentrate them in one location so that the squadron could effectively intercept raids. John L., Fike, and the division staff talked it over with

Ensign Polk. They decided that during the day, they would space the aircraft out in the open so that one bomb could not damage multiple planes. But they would also keep the F4Fs close enough in one area so that the 223 pilots could get to them quickly and take off together. The risk simply had to be taken for the unit to function.

A run-of-the-mill skipper would have been chained to the ground trying to find solutions to all these many problems. But John L. Smith was not a run-of-the-mill leader, and he was certainly not going to lose himself in these details while his men flew combat patrols. He intended to set the example and lead from the point of the spear. He set the tone that morning by taking the patrol with the highest probability of contact with the enemy: the noon flight.

For the mission, he selected three of the squadron's most promising new pilots. John Lindley, the enlisted NAP, would lead his second section. Scotty McLennan and Red Kendrick would perform wingmen duties. Red was another Ivy Leaguer, a child prodigy from San Francisco who had started at Stanford as a sixteen-year-old. By the time he graduated four years later and moved on to Harvard Law School, he spoke seven languages. John L. picked the most intelligent and experienced for this first mission.

Smith led his four-plane division off the gravel runway sometime between 1120 and 1140 that morning. Their stubby Wildcats climbed slowly into the mostly clear morning sky.

The Oklahoman figured if the Japanese were coming that day, they would come down through the Solomons between Santa Isabel Island and the Russells—a cluster of small islands about sixty miles northwest of Guadalcanal. On this first patrol, he navigated for the Russells, intending to sweep from there east to the Santa Isabel shoreline before turning back for Guadalcanal.[1]

Roughly twenty minutes into the mission, the Americans called out Japanese planes at their nine o'clock, coming straight at them, somewhere between five hundred and two thousand feet above them. On this first combat mission, the Marines faced one of the worst possible tactical

situations—an enemy with the high ground, noses already pointed
their way.

John L. quickly studied the onrushing aircraft and concluded they
were Zeroes. He banked sharply to port and turned his guns at the enemy
while the rest of his formation followed suit.

The Marines counted six Zeroes in two flights of three each. Down
the Japanese came at them, the pilots picking out targets. The merge
happened shockingly fast. In fact, everything happened so fast that the
Americans later had trouble deciphering what had actually happened. It
was a rookie thing—all the mock dogfights in the world couldn't prepare
a pilot for the unbelievable quickness of actual combat.

John L. picked out a diving Zero and went head-to-head with it, with
a combined speed of somewhere around seven football fields a second.
The Oklahoman opened fire about the same time the Japanese did, and
he felt his F4F shudder as bullets struck home. A split second later, the
Zero pilot pulled up sharply to avoid a collision. The sudden move gave
John L. a snap shot on the aircraft's belly, and he thought he'd scored
some solid hits.

Then he was through the merge, barreling south now in a shallow,
speed-gathering dive. He checked his tail and found two Zeroes right
behind him, muzzle barrels flashing. Tracers zipped past on either side of
his Wildcat. He took more hits. He banked for Henderson Field, arcing
to port and steepening his dive. In seconds, the F4F pulled away from its
pursuers, who broke off the chase.

It was over in mere seconds. John L. was left dry mouthed and adrenaline filled, his body coiled and tense, eyes scanning the skies for friend
and foe. Scotty McLennan appeared and linked up with him. A moment
later, Red Kendrick joined him too.

John Lindley, whose real-life *Grapes of Wrath* sort of childhood forged
him into a tough and resourceful young man, was nowhere to be seen.

Smith liked his NAP sergeant. Both Lindley and he were native sons
of Oklahoma, and Lindley's calm and steady demeanor in the air made
him a promising section leader. Losing him would be a significant blow
to the squadron.

All three Marines searched the sky for any sign of Lindley's F4F. They saw nothing at first. Then, behind them just off Savo Island, John L. made out a number of planes still maneuvering sharply. Some were diving, others turning. It looked like a full-on dogfight.

The Japanese must have trapped Lindley. To Smith, it looked as if Lindley was fighting a solo battle against five enemy fighters. John L. called out to Scotty and Red to tell them they were going back into the fight. The three Wildcats wheeled around, reversing course toward Savo, Henderson now at their backs. Again, the speed of everything astonished the rookies. In seconds, the distant blobs of maneuvering fighters materialized into Zeroes. No sign of Lindley's F4F. The Americans drove headlong into the scrum, snapping out short bursts at fleeting targets.

The Zeroes expertly flitted out of the F4Fs' way and snaked onto their tails, shooting holes in all three planes. With no sign of their missing Marine, the Americans knew that sticking around made no sense. Outnumbered and outmaneuvered, the rookies dove out of the fight and sped for Henderson Field, coaxing all the speed that their battered Wildcats would give them.

The Japanese did not pursue.

While John L. and the two Ivy Leaguers struggled home, John Lindley approached Henderson Field with a dying bird. He'd been hit in the first head-on pass, then likely shot up again and again as he tried to disengage. His aircraft was a sieve, its oil tank shattered by a likely 20 mm cannon hit that also blew a hole in the engine firewall. The tank was located just forward of the windscreen, and eleven gallons of 130-degree oil gushed under the instrument panel into the cockpit, coating the rudder pedals and spraying Lindley with the burning, viscous stuff. His face and other exposed parts of his body were burned, and oil got into his eyes, partially blinding him.

Oil starved, Lindley's engine seized in only a minute or two, transforming his Grumman into a glider.

Pain racked and barely able to see, he traded altitude for speed, dueling against gravity and praying he'd make the runway before he ran out of this equation or before his aircraft caught fire. The Wildcat trailed a thick black tail of smoke. If that smoke turned to fire, the oil in the cockpit would act as an accelerant and burn Lindley alive.

Clear of the fight, down low over Savo Sound, John Lindley fought for his life with the same tenacity he'd learned from his hardscrabble Okie family. He ignored the pain from his burns and the agony of the oil in his eyes and somehow managed to line up his crippled F4F on Henderson's single runway. He was rapidly running out of altitude and airspeed, so dropping his gear for a conventional landing was not an option. If he did that, he'd likely stall short of the strip and die. He'd have to ride the Grumman in, dead-sticking it on its belly.

Wheels up, he slammed the Wildcat onto the gravel and skidded out of control across the strip. The Wildcat finally slid to a halt in a cloud of dust and smoke. As several Marines raced to his rescue, Lindley threw back the canopy and flung himself onto the wing, covered in oil. He stood up and blindly staggered a few more steps before collapsing beside his shattered bird.

Red Kendrick limped into Henderson, his oil line shot out and his engine also starting to seize. John L. covered him protectively as the Stanford man fought to keep his mortally wounded fighter aloft. The "blinding fury" of the fight had left Red shaken, terror filled, and surprised that he was still alive.

Without oil, his engine quit, just like Lindley's. Fortunately, he'd almost gotten back to Henderson when it died, and he was able to pancake his Wildcat onto the runway, the second belly landing of the day. His F4F ground to a stop, and the quiet intellectual in the cockpit emerged physically unharmed from the ordeal.

He was so far from home. Back in San Francisco, Red used to go to the symphony with his parents, taking along the score for the evening's musical selection so that he could follow along and better understand the conductor's interpretation of it. Somehow, bare months removed from the serenity of California, he found himself at the edge of civilization, surrounded by Japanese and jungle, walking away from the smoking hulk of an overweight, pudgy Marine fighter aircraft. It was a dizzying and traumatic dichotomy that served as the transitional inflection point on his way to being a veteran. The Red Kendrick who had spent his sixteenth birthday at Stanford would soon be left behind, replaced by the warrior growing inside him at Guadalcanal.

Scotty McLennan, shot up but unharmed, was able to get his landing gear down, as did John L. They came in together, made a quick pass over the strip, and pulled up into a fighter break—a sharp climbing turn designed to shake off any Zeroes that may have been trying to flame them as they landed.

Tails clear, they dropped onto the runway. The fighting for the day was over.

Lindley had been taken to one of the division's medical dugouts— the closest thing they had to a hospital, likely with second-degree burns and eyes that needed flushing out and several days to fully heal. His F4F never flew again. Neither did Kendrick's. The two wrecks became spare parts for the remaining Wildcats on Guadalcanal, and the maintainers would gradually cannibalize them in the days to come. John L.'s F4F would be out of action for eight days, and Scotty's for ten. The Japanese had thoroughly shot them all up.

Smith tried to put lipstick on a pig and looked for the bright spots in an otherwise dismal day. He pointed out to his men that the Wildcats had brought them all home. The aircraft had taken massive amounts of damage that would have brought down any other craft. But these Grummans—for all their many faults—were as tough as the pilots who flew them. That ruggedness gave the men confidence in their machines, but it did not deflect from the raw reality that they had lost four planes and a pilot was wounded in their first fight. It was Midway all over again. There was some additional consolation when the mud Marines reported seeing a Japanese fighter go down in flames and crash on the beach at Savo Island. John L. was given credit for this first of many kills racked up by the squadron.[2]

Though they didn't know it at the time, John L. Smith's Marines were extremely lucky to have gotten away without losing anyone. The Japanese they encountered belonged to the vaunted Tainan Air Group, perhaps the best-trained and most blooded fighter unit of the Pacific War.

One of the outfit's senior leaders, Lt. Shiro Kawai, led thirteen Zeroes from Rabaul that morning to escort a Betty bomber search-and-strike operation against the USS *Saratoga*, which had been spotted while covering the *Long Island*'s launch the day before. Kawai was an experienced veteran with absolute ice water in his veins. Shortly after he reached Rabaul in early 1942, he demonstrated a level of cold-bloodedness that eluded most aviators when he ordered—then observed—the execution of a group of Allied aviators whom the Japanese had captured.[3]

The mission took off at 0807, flew south, and found no ships. The Betties, armed with torpedoes, turned for home. Escort duties done, Kawai was released to go sweep over Guadalcanal and shoot up anything he and his pilots discovered in the air.

They found Smith's Wildcats. Where the Marines thought they were fighting only six Zeroes instead of thirteen and underestimated their odds, the Japanese thought there were at least twice as many F4Fs as were actually in the air. They claimed five Wildcats destroyed plus three probables. The high scorers for the Japanese that day were Kazushi Hato and Toraichi Takutsuka, both with two F4Fs. Takutsuka was a senior petty officer first class who had been flying operationally since 1933. On one mission over China in 1940, Takutsuka shot down three Chinese interceptors over Chunking. He'd tangled with the US Army's 5th Air Force in New Guinea, where he became a double ace. His thousands of flight hours—most in combat—made him one of the Tainan Air Group's most valuable pilots.

Leading one of the flights that made the initial head-on pass on the Marines that day was Junichi Sasai, the "Prince of Rabaul," flying a Zero with a single blue diagonal stripe on its fuselage. With over twenty kills dating back to the Java Campaign in February, Sasai was one of the most capable and dangerous aces in the Tainan Air Group. Though he claimed no F4Fs that day, he'd already been credited with five US Navy Wildcats in the first days of the Guadalcanal invasion. He was one of the lug-nut pilots who held the Tainan Air Group together with his skill, example, and leadership.

The Marines would encounter Sasai again—and soon.

EIGHTEEN

A MILLION LITTLE DETAILS

Guadalcanal
August 21, 1942, afternoon

I F JOHN L. FACED MASSIVE CHALLENGES JUST TRYING TO OPERATE HIS Wildcat squadron, Dick Mangrum's pile of problems was at least as bad. Beyond suffering from the same shortages of spare parts, crews, mechanics, tools, means of fueling his thirsty Dauntlesses, VMSB-232 also faced a host of other issues that first day on Guadalcanal. The lack of bomb carts and hoists was probably the most serious. The SBD was a dedicated ship-killer, its weapon an unguided 500- or 1,000-pound bomb that was hung on a crutch under the fuselage. When the aircraft was in a dive and the pilot toggled the bomb release, the crutch would swing down and catapult the weapon clear of the SBD's propeller arc. To mount the bomb under the plane usually took a host of tools, specialized trolleys, and specially trained ground crew who knew how to fuse and move ordnance around without accidentally setting it off.

None of that support was waiting for 232 when the squadron arrived. For now, Ensign Polk's CUB-1 personnel manhandled the bombs from their storage area to the aircraft that morning. Teams of four men carried each 500-pound bomb and, through brute force, lifted it up under the fuselage and secured it in place, attaching it to the crutch. To say this was not optimal was an understatement.

When 232's planes had come home the day before, the ground crews discovered the SBD's solid rubber tail wheel, which was designed for carrier operations, cut deep tracks through the gravel runway and the taxiways to the dispersal points. These ruts were going to be a significant problem; they had to be filled up lest they cause somebody to ground-loop, with potentially fatal results. The gunners and CUB-1's sailors had worked overtime to get the solid tires swapped out with pneumatic ones, which they had fortunately brought along. So that problem had been solved—as long as nobody blew a tail-wheel tire on takeoff or landing.

Working around those issues was a key part of Dick's first day on Guadalcanal. Fortunately, most of the problems had Rube Goldberg solutions. Yet, that first morning's operations revealed a major shortfall in the squadron's training. General Vandegrift intended to husband VMSB-232 as his antiship striking arm. For now, the Wildcats would pull double duty—protecting the skies over Guadalcanal while also lending a hand to the mud Marines with strafing attacks on Japanese ground targets. Mangrum's pilots, on the other hand, would not be used in that role. Instead, they would conduct dawn and dusk search missions to locate incoming enemy ships bringing reinforcements to Guadalcanal. Once a task force was discovered, Vandegrift would make the call on whether it merited risking his tiny offensive arm against it.

The dawn and dusk patrols were the challenge. Dick's men had done very little night flying beyond what they had done back in the training pipeline before they arrived at 232. Now, they were expected to begin missions in the early-morning darkness and return home at the end of the day under the Southern Cross. Their maps were rudimentary and not very accurate. Plus, they would be navigating through scores of large and small islands, all of which were unfamiliar to the men.

These patrols were a big ask of his second lieutenants. Even more troubling, Vandegrift might send them out to strike targets at night, using the light of the moon to find Japanese ships. Dive-bombing a ship in broad daylight was tough enough. Doing so at night off a barely usable jungle field? It would be an exceptionally difficult mission for even the most veteran pilots in the 1942 Navy.

For all the issues, the squadron's first search had gone well that morning. Everyone returned home without encountering any enemy fighters, and the CUB-1 swabbies were furiously refueling the birds even as the mud Marines delivered a deadly counterblow to the Japanese who had attacked the perimeter the night before. The sounds of that battle drummed across the airfield all day long, punctuated by sudden artillery barrages from the 11th Marines' 75 mm howitzers.

Meanwhile, the squadron had gathered to await orders, most everyone already adjusted to the cacophony of the war raging only a half mile away. Some of the men played poker. Others read or talked intermittently until the sound of John L. Smith's returning fighters filled their ears over the din of battle.

As the four crippled F4Fs crash-landed on the field, triggering a flurry of activity to get Lindley to the hospital and clear the runway of the two belly-landed Wildcats, a small convoy of trucks rolled into the MAG-23 grove from Kukum Harbor. The vehicles lurched to a stop amid squealing brakes and clouds of exhaust smoke. The drivers dismounted, dropped the tailgates, and stepped back while a bunch of Marines jumped out. There were almost a hundred in this party, all young enlisted men, with a few NCOs sprinkled into the mix. The advanced echelon of MAG-23's ground crews had arrived.

Dick felt an immense sense of relief when he recognized his men in the mix. The senior NCO among them was Pl. Sgt. Billy Lohr, the squadron's most experienced ordnanceman. As a nineteen-year-old buck private, Lohr spent his first year out of basic training serving in the fleet aboard battleships and cruisers, mainly out of Guantánamo Bay and the Panama Canal Zone. He was a Depression-era Marine: tough, resourceful, and very talented at his job. Dick knew the squadron would need every ounce of that skill and professionalism in the days to come.

The men reached Guadalcanal just after lunch aboard the fast destroyer-transport *McFarland*. Despite the threat of air attack, the skipper made a cannonball run up into the Solomons to deliver 232's forty men. Another fifty-three from VMF-223 came ashore with them, including a number of spare pilots sent up on temporary duty from VMF-212 back at Efate. The rest of the two squadrons would come up in another blockade run toward the end of the month. For now, these hundred or so men were a godsend and would play a key role in keeping the squadrons functional through the desperate moments ahead.

Toward late afternoon, Bruce Prosser's division left the squadron area to jeep down to their awaiting SBDs. Dick gave them the sunset search on this first day of their war. Their job was to find any Japanese ships bound for Guadalcanal, report their locations, and then attack them. While John L.'s men would defend the airfield from Japanese aerial raiders, the Red Devils had a much more important—and dangerous—role. Until their arrival, the Japanese navy steamed to Guadalcanal to deliver men and supplies with impunity. If the Marine perimeter were to be held, Dick and his men had to stop those naval task forces, lest the Japanese build up the strength needed to break through to the airfield. If that happened, all the Americans would be killed or captured.

Finding those ships would be a challenge, thanks to the weather and the many avenues of approach the Japanese could use to get to Guadalcanal. The Red Devils needed three times the number of planes just to carry out thorough searches. But they worked with what they had, and Dick sent them out to cover sectors that seemed like the most likely areas to find Japanese ships.

The division included the hard-charging Leland Thomas and his gunner, Ed Eades, along with Charles McAllister with his gunner, Pvt. William Proffitt.

Prosser was the first to take off that afternoon, driving through the gravel hailstorm, 500-pound bomb slung under the fuselage, and into the air.

McAllister was next. Three-hour search mission—fly northwest for ninety minutes and roughly two hundred miles. Turn around and fly back. The last hour would be in darkness with questionable maps, no experience in the area, and minimal night flying time. Get home, land on a blacked-out strip at night with the bomb still attached. Easy day.

That was the plan. In this case, the plan did not survive first contact with Henderson Field.

Halfway down the runway, one of McAllister's tires, damaged earlier when the tractor pulled the plane from the muddied revetment, blew out. Nearly at flying speed now, the SBD snapped suddenly sideways and ground-looped. Somehow, both McAllister and Proffitt emerged from the resulting crash without serious injury. It was a minor miracle, but the SBD was a total loss. Fortunately, their bomb did not detonate during the accident, or there would have been no survivors.

The other two SBDs continued on without incident. They returned and landed successfully without encountering any Japanese.

The first day's missions was complete, but John L.'s men were down to fifteen functional F4Fs. Dick only had eleven SBDs. At this rate, both squadrons would run out of airplanes in a week. Each loss was a minor catastrophe. As far as John L. and Dick knew, these aircraft could not be replaced.

That evening, the two men learned that US Navy intel was tracking a large gathering of Japanese warships and transports. Though no carriers had been confirmed to be covering these ships, they could not be ruled out. The growing strength of the Japanese naval response strongly indicated that Japan was going to make a major push to reinforce, then recapture, Guadalcanal.

It would be a race to see who could reinforce the island first with the most men and material. Dick Mangrum's eleven SBDs would be the tip of the spear against these Japanese resupply convoys. Sink those transports before they got to Guadalcanal, and 232 could maroon thousands of Japanese soldiers and sailors in the waters around the Solomon Islands. Plus, whatever supplies and heavy weapons those ships carried would be destroyed too. If 232 failed and those Japanese reinforcements reached Guadalcanal, the thinly held perimeter would come under concentrated attack again—just as it had in the post-midnight hours of the twenty-first.

When the US Navy abandoned the Marines earlier in the month, it left them with only enough ammunition for a few sustained days of combat. The perimeter defending the airfield was thin and full of gaps. Vandegrift possessed only a small reserve force. The Americans simply could not withstand a sustained counteroffensive by fresh, well-supplied Japanese troops. The fate of the perimeter would ride with Mangrum's Red Devils.

At the same time, John L.'s pilots would play a vital role in the morning of the twenty-second, providing air cover for a vital US Navy task force due into the Guadalcanal area just after sunrise.

While the fast destroyer-transports had provided the Marines with dribs and drabs of supplies and additional men, Admiral Ghormley finally realized this effort was not enough. It was time to risk some of his cargo ships if Guadalcanal was to be held. On the twentieth, the attack transports *Alhena* and *Fomalhaut* sailed from the New Hebrides with full holds, escorted by three destroyers. The plan was to be offloading supplies and men at Guadalcanal by the morning of the twenty-second. The *Fomalhaut* carried the advanced echelon of the US Army Air Forces' 67th Fighter Squadron, whose P-400 Airacobra fighter planes would start flying into Guadalcanal later in the week.

The plan, like most plans, went awry only a day later. At 2020 hours on the twenty-first, the *Fomalhaut* was ordered to leave formation and reverse course without any explanation given. The three destroyers and the *Alhena* continued on toward Guadalcanal for another two hours until the escort force commander received new orders. There was a chance that Japanese warships were operating in Savo Sound. Instead of risking a night naval battle with the *Alhena* in tow, COMSOPAC HQ ordered destroyers *Blue* and *Henley* to steam ahead and sweep the Savo Sound to make sure it was safe.

Just shy of 0200 on the twenty-second, a patrolling Japanese destroyer surprised the *Blue* and struck it with a torpedo. The sound of the explosion rolled over the water and woke some of the Marines ashore five miles away.

Another naval skirmish ended in a lopsided Japanese victory. The *Blue*, down by the stern, drifted aimlessly in Savo Sound while the crew and the *Henley*'s tried to take the damaged destroyer in tow and drag it to Tulagi.[1]

When John L. awoke before dawn on August 22 to get the latest information and mission assignments from Fike and 1st Marine Division HQ, he learned that the convoy was fragmented. His men would have to cover the crippled destroyer in the sound and the *Henley*, which was trying to save that vessel, plus the *Alhena* and its destroyer, both of which were almost to Tulagi. The *Fomalhaut* had linked up with several other escorts somewhere south of Guadalcanal and would arrive on the morning of the twenty-third.

It was a tense, long day as the Marine fighter pilots orbited over the ships, watching the sky for any sign of Japanese bombers. With four F4Fs out of commission, the remaining fifteen had to stretch to provide all-day coverage for the Navy. In the process, the men used the last of their oxygen. This intractable problem prompted the Marines to send a desperate plea to Adm. John S. McCain for more tanks. Without them, the F4Fs were strictly a low-altitude-capable force.

As noon came and went without a Japanese attack, tensions eased toward sunset. The Japanese did not attack that day. Unbeknownst to John L. and his men, bad weather had grounded the Japanese at Rabaul. The Marines gained a little reprieve, and the flights gave the pilots a chance to get to know the area a little bit.

The next morning, the *Fomalhaut* arrived off Red Beach and the 67th's thirty-one ground crewmen clambered down cargo nets to waiting landing craft and were taken to the beach. Marine trucks then drove them to the airfield and reunited them with Maj. Dale Brannon, the squadron's commander.

The *Fomalhaut*'s arrival meant critical supplies for the Marines. The first round in the Battle of the Buildup went to the Americans. Yet, even as the landing craft and lighters made runs back and forth from ship to beach, delivering the cornucopia in the *Fomalhaut*'s hold to the embattled men of the jungle, bad news arrived. The crew of an American Consolidated PBY Catalina flying boat on a search mission radioed that they had discovered a Japanese task force of at least eight ships steaming for

Guadalcanal at seventeen knots. The ships were almost due north of the Solomons and, at their range and speed, would arrive off Guadalcanal sometime around midnight. The sighting report relayed to Henderson Field also stated that four transports had been spotted, along with two cruisers and three destroyers. The news hit General Vandegrift hard. Four transports—especially large ones—could hold thousands of men. If this convoy reached Guadalcanal, it could tip the balance against the Marines holding their fragile perimeter.

As he considered the situation, Cdr. Robert Hall Smith, the US Navy officer in charge of the destroyer force protecting the *Alhena* and *Fomalhaut*, walked into Vandegrift's headquarters at around 1430. Smith asked Vandegrift if his little air force could provide night air cover for the transports and destroyers off Guadalcanal. They wanted to keep unloading supplies, but the fear of another surface engagement with Japanese cruisers was quite real. The small American task force stood no chance against Japanese cruisers unless the Marine SBDs and F4Fs could support them.

Vandegrift told Smith that night air cover wasn't an option. Instead, he was considering launching an attack on the Japanese ships that afternoon with his available aircraft. If his little air force couldn't stop the Japanese, Vandegrift promised to warn Commander Smith ahead of time so his task force could clear the area.

Until that warning came, Vandegrift made it clear the Marines needed the *Fomalhaut* to keep offloading supplies. That was absolutely crucial.

DICK MANGRUM'S SQUADRON HAD NO SPARE PILOTS OR GUNNERS. THE men had already flown three days in a row with minimal sleep and minimal food. The weather report was not good: rain squalls and low ceilings to the north. It would take at least a couple of hours to prep the SBDs for a strike mission. The aviators would have to launch in the late afternoon and return at night. Dick's second lieutenants would have to navigate through a storm, with only a waxing gibbous moon to light the way— assuming there would even be breaks in the cloud cover.

Launching this attack risked the destruction of VMSB-232 from the operational challenges alone. Over the target area, the bombers would face intense antiaircraft fire and probably a combat air patrol of Zeroes. To keep the Japanese fighters off them, John L. and VMF-223 would have to provide escort, which would leave the ships in Savo Sound without fighter cover.

At 1630, Dick's SBDs began taking off. Vandegrift posted up at the Pagoda to watch the planes depart, sick with dread that few would return. He knew that most of these young Marines had never before flown in bad weather and that bad weather killed inexperienced pilots all the time.

As the Dauntlesses formed up on their division leaders, John L. led the escort force off the runway. Nine SBDs and twelve F4Fs soon headed north into the teeth of a South Pacific storm.

It was a weather front none of the men on the mission had ever seen before. Just as they approached Florida Island, the front loomed before them like a solid sheet of water pounding the ocean below. Above the deluge towered walls of dark, forbidding clouds.

The Marines turned perpendicular to the storm, searching for any holes they could exploit. There were none. Finally, Dick decided to swing north and fly into it.

The Dauntlesses plunged into the curtain of rain. In seconds, the formation loosened as the men lost sight of each other. Turbulence flung the bombers about as the storm's fury lashed the aircraft so harshly that their normally waterproof cockpits began to leak. Water sprayed over pilots and gunners until one gunner said it was "like we were sinking in the ocean."

Soaking wet, Dick keyed his microphone. He knew that somewhere above and behind him, John L.'s Wildcats had followed him into the storm. "How's it look up there, John?" Dick asked.

"Plenty of soup, Dick," came a quick reply, freighted with plenty of static.

Even the best prewar squadron in the Corps couldn't get through this tropical storm. Dick knew that to continue meant risking losing everyone to the weather and coming darkness. Sick at heart at the possible damage to the perimeter and the mud Marines counting on them, he aborted the mission. It was the only thing he could do without risking losing Guadalcanal's tiny air force for no gain at all.

They returned to Henderson Field, where all the aircraft landed safely just before sunset. The crews dispiritedly gathered at the Pagoda, where Hayes, Fike, and Vandegrift waited for them. Dick walked up to the trio and blurted out, "I feel like hell about it, but we just couldn't get in there."

Behind him, one of his pilots exclaimed, "I came back from Tulagi two feet over the water, trying to get under the overcast. Even then I couldn't see anything."

Vandegrift tried to boost their spirits, walking among the aviators and offering words of encouragement. They read his face, noting that he had been pacing when they came in. No way to sugarcoat it: the abort was a blow, and they felt tremendous guilt. They needed to stop those ships, and no amount of kind words in the aftermath could improve the situation. They knew what was riding on their shoulders, and the failure of the mission meant that a lot of brother Marines on the perimeter would surely die once those transports made landfall somewhere on the island.

The men would sleep with their boots on that night, just in case the field got overrun.

As if to underscore the correctness of Dick's decision to abort the mission, just after sunset the sound of approaching engines rolled over the airfield. Word quickly spread that a strike group from the carrier *Saratoga* was coming in to spend the night. The planes had been launched earlier in the afternoon against the same convoy of ships, but even the more experienced Navy pilots couldn't get through the storm clouds.

To help the Navy pilots land in the dark, some of the 232 ground crew grabbed flashlights and went out to the runway to help illuminate it. Others lined the field with jeeps and flipped on their high beams. At the same time, numerous Japanese machine guns opened fire as the planes turned onto their final approaches and touched down on Henderson's rough strip. Though tracers laced the blackness around the Navy planes, none took hits. It was a hell of an introduction to Guadalcanal—flaps down, gear down, fuel tanks nearly empty, and bullets whipping past as the pilots focused on getting onto the runway in the darkness.

Altogether, thirty-one SBDs and six Grumman TBF Avengers landed that night.

Bad news begets bad news, and the chain reaction from the two failed missions spread out like ripples on a pond. With the Japanese unchecked, the unloading of the *Fomalhaut* stopped at 1900. The Marines aboard evacuated to the beach, frustrated that the ship's holds were still a third full of vital supplies.

At first, the *Fomalhaut* weighed anchor and tried to help tow the *Blue* to Tulagi. When that effort failed, the American vessels cleared out of the area a few hours before midnight to avoid the expected arrival of the Japanese task force.

The Navy crews bunked down around the Marines in the grove, listening to the disturbing sounds of the Guadalcanal jungle life. By midnight, with the Japanese a no-show, most of the aviators in the grove finally fell asleep.

Two hours later, a thunderous explosion shook the ground and woke everyone up. In the 232 area, Tom Moore's eyes flew open and he found himself eyeball to eyeball with Danny Iverson. Both men had sat up reflexively and stared at each other open-mouthed as another clap of thunder rolled across the airfield.

Curses erupted around them in the darkness. An ear-crushing whine ripped overhead followed by another tremendous explosion. Over the babble of voices, somebody shouted, "Duck! DUCK!"

Bruce Prosser, lying under layers of mosquito netting, replied laconically, "Take it easy. We'll never hear the one that gets us."

It was a terrifying experience for all, Marines and Navy, as they lay helpless under the guns of those unseen Japanese ships. As the bombardment continued, Dick Mangrum's voice rose out of the night, ordering everyone to stay low and not move around. They weren't going to risk a night takeoff under naval gunfire to attack the Japanese ships. Besides, their SBDs had not yet been fully refueled. Their ground crew, along with CUB-1's sailors, had been at it most of the night. But the arrival of three dozen extra aircraft had overwhelmed them. It would be hours before the planes were ready to fly.

The bombardment ended a short time later. Nobody in the grove had been hurt. At the time, the world seemed to be caving in around the aviators; in fact only one Marine was wounded by the shells. The Marines defending the perimeter's beaches reported that the attacker was a mere surfaced submarine, not the Japanese task force everyone had expected that night. Actually, the shells came from the five-inch guns of the destroyer *Kagerō*, which was sent ahead of the main Japanese effort to launch a hit-and-run raid on the airfield and any ships in the area.

Where was the Japanese convoy with its transports crammed with troops? Unbeknownst to the aviators, it had reversed course after being spotted by the PBY flying boat that morning. The arrival of the American flying boat delayed the Japanese attack plan by a day. But only a day. Under the light of the gibbous moon, the transports and their escorting consort of cruisers and destroyers sped south for Guadalcanal, covered by three aircraft carriers, the *Ryūjō* and the Pearl Harbor attack veterans *Shōkaku* and *Zuikaku*. The sleepless Marines were still in the crosshairs, with hundreds of planes, three aircraft carriers, and nearly fifty Japanese warships arrayed against them.[2]

NINETEEN

THE FIRST ACE

Henderson Field, Guadalcanal
August 24, 1942, 1420 hours

TWELVE THOUSAND FEET OVER SEALARK CHANNEL, MARION CARL'S sharp eyes ensured that the Japanese raiders would not escape detection. Three thousand feet below and off Marion's left wingtip at nine o'clock, they paraded along in two tight formations, clearly bound for Henderson Field. The afternoon sky was layered and dotted with clouds, so catching sight of them about ten miles away, just southeast of Tulagi, was a feat of visual acuity few pilots could match.

Marion keyed his radio microphone and called in the Japanese to both his division of Wildcats and to Henderson Field. He'd just given the Marines about eight minutes' warning to prepare for the attack.

John Lindley flew Marion's wing that day. The tough Oklahoman, half recovered from his burns, his eyesight still impacted by the searing oil thrown in his face on the squadron's first mission, refused to stay out of the cockpit. Marion trusted him. Considering him one of the better greenhorns, the squadron commander put Lindley in his division for the lunchtime standing patrol that day. Tex Hamilton from VMF-212 and Fred Gutt composed the other half of the division. Marion didn't know

Hamilton well but knew that he was an experienced pilot. He and Gutt would sink or swim now: this was gut-check time.

The tactical setup favored the Marines. Marion's four F4Fs held the high ground, perfect for an overhead attack: John L.'s favored method, which he'd drilled into everyone during their training the previous month. Marion banked his Wildcat, opened the throttle, and arrowed toward the Japanese to intercept.

The cloud cover worked in the Marines' favor. Flying along in two tight formations of six planes each, the Japanese seemed unaware of the Americans' presence. The closest formation to Marion's division flew in an arrowhead formation—five bombers in a tight vee, with a sixth behind the lead in a tail-end-Charlie sort of slot position. Marion had seen that same formation at Midway, used by the Nakajima B5N bombers ("Kates").

The other formation looked more standard—two vees of three planes each, flying just off their wingtips. The lead group of three was followed by a second vee stepped back to the left in a close echelon.

As the Marines closed on their intercept course, Marion concluded that the Japanese planes were all carrier bombers—Kates, just like the ones launched from the Kidō Butai in June. They had been coming in from the south, not from the northwest, where their base at Rabaul lay. This meant only one thing: there was at least one Japanese carrier out there somewhere close, assigned to crush the defenses at Guadalcanal. Once again, the Oregonian found himself at the center of a combined naval and air offensive.

The overhead pass John L. had made them practice required at least two thousand feet of altitude. They now had at least three thousand—and probably more, since the two Japanese formations had apparently eased into a shallow dive to pick up speed. The four Marines closed from abeam (the side), a position that allowed them to make the easier of the two overhead pass techniques. If Marion executed it properly, he could gradually bend around to the same general course as that followed by the Japanese, get into their same general vertical plane, and then launch their attack.

The Japanese reached the middle of Savo Sound now, flying at perhaps a bit over 150 knots. The Wildcats closed easily. No sign of any escorting fighters. At Midway, the Zeroes had been out of position, stacked behind the bombers. Maybe that was the same tactic here, though the four Marines could see no other planes behind the bombers. Even if the escorts lurked back there somewhere among the clouds, Marion figured he'd have time to get in among the Kates and do some damage.

The interception and setup for the attack took three minutes. Hamilton and Gutt trailed the lead section by a minute or two, which meant that a simultaneous attack by all four F4Fs wouldn't happen. With luck, the Marines would achieve surprise, anyway.

Marion passed over the bombers in the arrowhead formation. A half kilometer off that formation's starboard wing was the second vee of vees. Marion wanted the lead of that group. He kept his eyes on his target, pitched his nose up, and rolled into a 180-degree turn that ended with him inverted, hanging in his seat straps, head up so he could look out through the top of the canopy and keep eyes on his target. John Lindley stayed with him through the maneuver, and now, as the Japanese skated along below them, still heading south for Guadalcanal, Marion tucked the stick into his stomach. The Wildcat reversed course in a half loop, Marion's quarry directly ahead, visible just above the F4F's engine cowling.

Marion dropped on the unsuspecting Japanese from sixty degrees above, his Wildcat's altimeter spinning even as his air speed indicator nosed past three hundred knots. In seconds, the altitude difference evaporated. Two hundred and fifty yards out, the Oregonian triggered his six machine guns. He had only a second or two before he plunged behind and below the Japanese formation, his speed making him almost invulnerable to counterattack.

It was a textbook overhead run, and Marion's aim did not disappoint. His brief second or two of fire shredded the Japanese aircraft. It burst into flames, pitched to one side, and fell toward Savo Sound.

The fight was on.[1]

At Guadalcanal, the men of VMF-223 had been lounging near their aircraft, using wooden ammunition crates as stools while they played cards or passed the time making small talk. Seconds after Marion Carl radioed his warning, the air raid siren at the Pagoda shrieked to life. The fighter pilots instantly leaped to their feet, cards dropped, magazines cast aside, as they grabbed their gear and headed to their waiting Wildcats.

It was a madhouse scramble to get the squadron's ten aircraft aloft before the bombs began to fall. The pilots that afternoon hailed from both the original cadre of 223 who had trained with John L. in July and some of the 212 pilots Doc Everton had personally selected at Efate. They had arrived aboard the *McFarland*, a welcome, if temporary, addition to the squadron.

The team captain led the way to the planes. Rivers Morrell, stepping into the moment, barked orders as he slung his chute and bolted for his waiting F4F. From the gridiron at Annapolis not so many years ago to this life-and-death moment, Rivers proved himself a born leader. The men followed their executive officer out into the afternoon heat even as the sound of approaching aircraft engines filled their ears.

Forget the preflight. Forget checking the magnetos at the edge of the runway. This was a pell-mell charge to get airborne before bombs struck the runway. The Marines of 223 strapped themselves into their cockpits and released the brakes. Two at a time, they buzzed and bounced down the runway and into the air. In normal situations, they would have circled back over the field, waiting for the rest of the squadron to join them so they could go out with strength in numbers. Not this time. They flung themselves skyward into the overcast, searching for the source of those inbound engine sounds they had heard before reaching their own fighters.

A string of bombs pummeled one side of the airfield, blowing a truck on its side and sending the gunners of the 3rd Defense Battalion into headlong dives for cover. More bombs fell. The Wildcats never wavered. Even as smoke mushroomed over the perimeter, they darted along the runway and bounded into the air.

John L. watched them go, silently cursing that he hadn't reached a cockpit before his men. "Lead from the front" was his mantra. He lived it, embodied it. He'd been away from the squadron at the moment the air raid siren had shrieked. Too late to lead, he stood in the grove, squinting into the gray afternoon as one by one, his men vanished into the clouds.

Not far from the airfield, a Zero suddenly zoomed over Associated Press reporter Richard Tregaskis. He ducked as the Japanese plane practically trimmed the treetops with its whirring propeller, going flat-out inland from the coast, arcing toward Henderson Field. A split second later, a Wildcat roared past in hot pursuit. Unbeknownst to the journalist, three formations of Zeroes reached the perimeter simultaneously from three different directions. On the deck, speeding along at over three hundred miles an hour, their cannons spewed explosive shells into gun positions, vehicles, and groups of men dashing to slit trenches. One unloaded on a fuel dump, its cannons triggering a massive blast that the Zero practically flew through. Its pilot, unfazed by the near miss, leveled out and swept in for the runway, guns flaying everything in his path.

Meanwhile, back at Henderson, Robert "Rapid Robert" Read sat on the runway, waiting impatiently for the two birds in front of him to get aloft so he could start his own run. Ken Frazier got aloft. So did 212's golden child, 2nd Lt. Robert S. MacLeod, the former all-American from Dartmouth and a former Chicago Bear. Behind them Elwood Bailey and Zen Pond pulled themselves into the air. But there were still others on the runaway. Every second counted, and Read could hear the clock ticking in his head even as the tree-skimming Zeroes closed on the strip. Altitude was life. So was being in the air when bombs were falling on both sides of the airfield. Seeing the flames and smoke curling up from each impact, he knew that on the ground, his Wildcat was an easy target. All he could do was wait.

Rapid Robert Read was an underdog, a John L. favorite in part because he was a fellow Oklahoman. He'd been swapped into the squadron from 224 just before 223 left Hawai'i aboard the *Long Island*. He was, at first, an enigma. Quiet. Resolved. He didn't brag and he didn't talk big. He was an orphan whose dad had tried to kill him before he was six. Adopted later in his childhood, he bootstrapped himself through college, working as a florist to maintain his status as a University of Oklahoma

Sooner. Despite his desperately grim childhood, he fought his way through to graduation and earned a degree in chemical engineering. He joined the Navy as soon as he discarded his cap and gown.

The runway had now cleared. Read's was the last Wildcat left. As he opened the throttle, his fighter bounded forward, eager to get aloft.

The Zeroes swarmed over the field, chopping out short bursts with their machine guns and cannon. Read firewalled the throttle, fighting the engine's torque with opposite rudder.

A Zero flashed past above him, shooting at other quarry. Seventy knots now. A bit more, and he'd be airborne. He checked his six—the spot directly astern beyond his rudder. Zeroes everywhere. It was the worst possible way to start his first engagement with the Japanese. Not even airborne yet, and he was already a target.

A Wildcat came spiraling out of the overcast, flames skirting its fuselage. It went straight into the jungle, somehow unseen by the majority of the Marines cheering on John L.'s men from trenches and foxholes.

Read's wheels left the ground. He began the tedious, desperate job of hand-cranking the gear into the fuselage. Zeroes snapped at his heels. Bullets struck home. He stayed low, gaining speed, wings wobbling as he worked furiously to get the gear retracted.

Another Zero cut behind him and spewed lead and shells before breaking off and swanning into a high, arcing turn.

His gear locked home. He released the crank and got his hands on throttle and stick, keeping his composure even as he heard lead tearing metal along his wings and fuselage. All he could do now was run, gain speed, and pray while hunkering down behind the slab of armor behind his seat. He rocketed out over the coast, heading north out to Savo Sound even as the battle overhead sprawled above and below the scud layer. Zeroes flashed. Wildcats climbed through them, clawing for altitude and a chance to get at the bombers.

Around him, six Zeroes chased three Wildcats and two of the Army's sleek-nosed P-400s. A Zero exploded in flames and plunged onto the north coast of Guadalcanal. The other Wildcats raced north, trying to shake the Zeroes and get enough speed to have a hope in this fight. But be careful what is wished for. Even as the low-level fight played out over the water, another one raged in and above the clouds, a reality driven home when an F4F twisted down through the scud layer in a death plunge, its pilot leaping clear. His chute opened somewhere south of Tulagi.

The Oklahoman, multiple Zeroes behind him giving chase. Expertly they shot him up. As he closed on Florida Island now, more bullets raked Read's Wildcat. A 20 mm cannon shell exploded behind and to his left, spraying shrapnel through the cockpit. A white-hot metal sliver scythed into his neck; another embedded itself in his shoulder. Blood smeared his flight jacket, sprayed across the canopy and instrument panel. He refused to give up. Equally stubborn was his battered Grumman. For eight minutes, bleeding from both wounds, he dragged those Zeroes across the sound before the fusillade finally proved too much.

Read's Double Wasp engine choked and gagged, puking gray-black smoke as round after round hit home. A moment later, the Wildcat smacked into the wave tops, its nose digging into the water and throwing Read hard against his shoulder straps.

He opened the canopy as water filled the cockpit, and he pulled himself clear of the sinking fighter. In seconds, the orphan from Oklahoma found himself alone, weak from blood loss and in considerable pain, bobbing on the surface of the waves just off the Florida Island coast.

Above him, the fight raged as Rivers Morrell climbed through the scud layer and tore into the fleeing Japanese bombers, Ken Frazier and Zen Pond right along with their executive officer.

A swirling, chaotic fight inside, above, and below the clouds splayed out from Henderson Field to beyond Florida Island. Atop it all, Marion Carl and his division made textbook overhead runs on the tight formation of Japanese bombers. At one point, a Zero latched on to John Lindley's tail, but Marion swept in from astern and shot the A6M off his wingman's six. Lindley exacted revenge, shooting a bomber down as he stayed with Marion and remained in the vertical plane, diving into the bomber formation, then zoom-climbing above to maneuver into another attack position.

The Zero pilots grew frantic to defend their charges. Even as Marion's division carved them up, Rivers Morrell and the rest of the squadron punched into the fight, climbing into the attack.

Two Japanese bombers remained in formation as a third, belching smoke, fell farther and farther behind. The Zeroes slashed and hammered at the Wildcats. Marion pulled out of another overhead pass and zoomed above the melee, his aircraft undamaged, his guns almost drained of ammunition. He thought he'd scored four kills.

Rivers chased a Japanese plane down to the water. Twisting and turning, its pilot pulled every trick in the book to throw off the American's aim. For twenty-five miles, Rivers couldn't get into position for a killing shot. Finally, he connected, stitching the craft with a solid burst. The aircraft fell into the ocean.

Fred Gutt, the number four in Marion's division, found himself in deep trouble. He'd shot a Zero down, but three others quickly tacked onto his tail. He dove away, trying to outrun them, but they stubbornly clung to his six, snapping out deadly accurate bursts. These were pros; Gutt was a year removed from being a Wisconsin Badger, barely a Marine.

They closed on him even as he leveled off just above the waters of Savo Sound. He couldn't turn. He couldn't climb. He couldn't outrun these Zeroes. All he could do was take it. He slumped in his cockpit seat, maximizing the protection that the armored slab behind him would afford, and prayed they would run out of ammunition or fuel for this fight.

His Wildcat staggered with every burst the Japanese scored. Bullets and shells tore into the bird's aluminum skin. The aircraft shuddered and shook, each hit sounding like a snare drum's snap. A cannon shell exploded beside him, sending fragments into his left arm and leg. He slumped even lower, prayed even harder. The Double Wasp engine kept running, and gradually the F4F pulled away from its tormentors. The Japanese finally abandoned the chase, pulling up into a long, climbing turn to the north and toward their carrier, steaming somewhere well off the horizon.

Fred, who had elected to join the Marines over his dream of going to law school in the summer of 1941, limped back to Henderson Field and piled onto the runway. The tough Grumman had saved his life.

From the ground, little of the fight could be seen. It played out either too far north over Savo Sound or above the cloud cover. But what could not be seen could be heard. John L. and the other pilots left behind during the pell-mell scramble to their ten remaining Wildcats heard the whine and scream of engines diving under full power. They heard the chatter of machine guns and the steady drumbeat of automatic cannon fire.

They waited tensely until the squadron began to return home. In ones and twos, the Wildcats dropped down out of the clouds, made a quick pass over the runway, then pulled up in a fighter break before coming around and settling.

Pandemonium broke out in the parking areas as engines were cut and pilots climbed out of their cockpits, flashing the number of planes they got with a show of fingers. Fike and John L. counted. It was an astronomical number. They had pasted the Japanese.

Shouting and hollering, the aviators gathered beside their aircraft even as the ground crews swarmed over the F4Fs, some checking for damage while others set to work rearming and refueling them. The plane captain wanted to know how the aircraft performed and if anything needed attention. The pilots were too excited by the fight, flying their hands and recounting the battle and chattering about their roles in it.

It was like a big win back home on a football field, with the crowd surging onto the grass to join the players. The procession moved to the Pagoda, where one by one, pilots broke from the pack to take turns detailing their side of the fight to Lieutenant Colonel Fike, who stood with a notebook and pen, scribbling down each pilot's statement.

Reporter Richard Tregaskis also recorded some of the conversation that afternoon. One of the 212 pilots, 2nd Lt. John King, described chasing a bomber, hitting it, then getting jumped by Zeroes. He ducked into the clouds to escape.

Ken Frazier, the New Jersey native, excitedly told Fike how he and Marion Carl tag-teamed the fleeing bombers. Marion took one side of the formation to make his overheads while Ken climbed up to help and attacked the opposite side. "The first plane caught fire as my first burst hit it," Ken told him. "I had time to veer to the right and catch the plane

ahead of it. My fire hit his wing, and flames ran right down into the fuselage. He hung in the air, then fell off drunkenly with smoke and flame
pouring from the plane."

When Zen Pond's turn to speak came, the mood changed. Amid the
merriment, he looked stricken. His best friend, Elwood Bailey, had yet
to return. The two of them had bonded over their love of flying back in
Michigan. They co-owned an aircraft together, joined the Navy a month
apart. The two were probably the closest friends in the squadron.

Was Bailey's F4F the one streaming fire as it fell out of the clouds?
Nobody knew for sure.

Zen told Fike about getting into a tangle with the escorting Zeroes. "I
just squeezed the triggers and let him have it as [a Zero] came up in front
of me. I blew him to bits."

Robert MacLeod reported what had happened to him down low,
below the scud layer. He was one of the 212 pilots Doc Everton had spe-
cifically chosen for this temporary gig with John L.'s men. There was an
underlying reason for his selection, and it had nothing to do with his
training level or capabilities. Doc had pegged MacLeod as a malin-
gerer. MacLeod carried into the Corps the Ivy League conceit that
McLennan and Kendrick never developed. Perhaps the root cause of his
self-important attitude wasn't his college pedigree but rather his status as
a famous all-American football halfback and cornerback who contended
for the Heisman before going on to play nine games in a Chicago Bears
uniform during the 1939 season. He'd also briefly played pro basketball with the Chicago Bruins. MacLeod never missed an opportunity
to make it clear he was a big deal, his egotism running countercurrent to
VMF-223's more egalitarian culture. Worse, though he'd only been with
the squadron for a few days, Gutt had already pegged him as a bully.

Doc picked MacLeod to go to Guadalcanal as a way to get him to put
up or shut up. To his credit, MacLeod rose to the occasion and shot down
a Japanese Zero along the Guadalcanal coast during the wild low-altitude
melee.

Later that afternoon, MacLeod described his role in the mission to
Marine Corps correspondent Sgt. James W. Hurlbut, who reported that

the all-American had led the Marine attack on the first group of nine bombers. "We dove down on them from above," MacLeod recounted. "It was just like shooting at sleeve targets. They were flying at nine thousand feet when we hit them." The tale got bigger with the retelling.

The initial excitement at what looked like a tremendous victory over the Japanese began to evaporate as their watches ticked off the minutes and the men knew that the missing pilots would be getting low on fuel. There were three men missing: Bailey, Rapid Robert Read, and Lawrence C. "Red" Taylor, one of the 212 pilots. Somebody reported seeing Bailey bail out of his F4F near Tulagi. Taylor was last seen shooting a bomber down with Rex Jeans. Nobody knew what had happened to Read, other than that he'd been chased almost from the minute he got his F4F aloft.

Three missing pilots and another wounded. Four men out of action, along with four F4Fs destroyed or crippled. Earlier in the day, another one of the attached 212 pilots had taken a Wildcat up on a test flight, only to have the life raft compartment in the fuselage pop loose and force him to bail out. This left John L. with nine planes to defend Guadalcanal and to escort Mangrum's SBDs once the patrol aircraft spotted the Japanese reinforcement task force again.

When Fike added up everyone's claims, he announced the squadron had downed ten bombers and eleven Zeroes.[2]

Marion Carl was the day's high scorer. The Oregonian was initially credited with two bombers and a fighter. Later, his fourth claim was confirmed. With his kill from Midway, that gave him five, making him the first ace in Marine Corps history.

But all was not as reported, nor as it was re-reported for decades to come. Granted, this fight was a confused, chaotic series of battles among the clouds for both sides. The Japanese later claimed fifteen F4Fs engaged and fifteen shot down. A clean sweep.

In truth, both sides totally mischaracterized what had happened. At the time, it didn't matter.[3]

Perception in the moment counted far more than reality divined later. Despite their heavy losses, the Marines believed they had turned back two waves of Japanese bombers, wiping one out and savaging the escorting fighters.

Meanwhile, word reached Henderson that Read had linked up with some local villagers, was taken to Florida Island for the night, then was delivered to the Americans at Tulagi on the twenty-fifth. Taylor and Bailey had simply vanished. Zen and the others held out hope that they were still alive somewhere out in the jungle and would find their way back to the perimeter.

That evening, as sunset approached, the squadron gathered around a few standard-issue Marine Corps folding tables, the men sitting on crude benches or wooden ammo boxes. John L. broke out a bottle of liquor. As they passed it around, their celebration of the day's victory was muted by the losses they had endured. Some prophetic words Red Taylor had uttered the night before lingered in their minds.

"There's no use thinking forward," he had mused. "There's no use worrying. When your number's up, that's the end for you."

Given the loss rate of both planes and pilots, thoughts of the future seemed pointless indeed. Dreaming of homecomings back in Wisconsin or Texas or New Jersey brought nothing but pain. They couldn't focus on tomorrow. Nor could they dwell on yesterday. These young Americans found themselves in the purest, yet most seemingly superficial method of living out of sheer survival's sake: they clung to the moment. Those seconds, those minutes, that their hearts still beat and their lungs drew air—those were the only ones certain on Guadalcanal.[4]

TWENTY

THE INVOLUNTARY TOURISTS

Henderson Field, Guadalcanal
August 24, 1942, late afternoon

W HILE JOHN L. AND THE FIGHTER PILOTS WERE SHARING THAT precious bottle of liquor, Dick Mangrum and his men were sitting around a US Navy radio that some of the enlisted men had hooked up to a twelve-volt battery pulled from one of their SBDs. The radio had come with a transmitter and generator, but neither proved functional. As the men did with everything else on Guadalcanal, they figured out a way to make it work with what they had available. The enlisted guys would pull batteries out of the SBDs, take them down to the living area in the late afternoon, use them to power the radio, and then reinstall them in the morning so they could be recharged in flight.

The squadron possessed two radios. This one they used to monitor Navy chatter from aircraft and ships talking to aircraft somewhere over the horizon. The other one was a portable shortwave owned by Don McCafferty. They used it to tune in to KNX Los Angeles for the swing shift news every evening at 1900. The Marines would get about an hour's worth of reception just after sundown, just enough to hear the latest baseball scores, some war news, and—if they were very lucky—some music.

On this evening, the men clustered around the military radio as one of the enlisted men scanned the frequencies the Navy used. They were eager to hear any scrap of information that could tell them what was going on around their island. By that evening, the Marines knew that both Japanese and American carriers were out there someplace, surely sparring as they had at Midway. But who was winning? What of Harry Donald "Don" Felt and the *Saratoga*'s air group that he commanded? Had the Navy delivered the same sort of devastating blow it had at Midway? What about the ever-elusive transport force they had been sent after the day before?

Dick watched his men closely as they huddled around the radio. They were leaning out, looking a little ragged. Their uniforms were dirty and sweat stained. Most men were growing beards. Don McCafferty was the exception there. He'd brought one of the only electric razors to the island, and the New Yorker figured out how to connect it to some captured Japanese batteries he found lying around the perimeter.

Back home, the men would be torn apart by rear-echelon martinets for their appearance. Out here, it didn't matter. Performance. Capability. How much of this could a man take? Those things mattered. Dick learned fast not to sweat the small stuff and instead to stay focused on what counted.

The radio had been parked in one corner of the communal canvas fly tied to nearby trees. The canopy served as an open-air tent for the squadron's twelve pilots. They had moved their bedding and Japanese tatami mats under it and slept side by side now, their foxholes and slit trenches only a few yards away, dug in haste as protection from artillery, naval gunfire, and falling bombs. Meanwhile, the gunners slept under the planes—some of them making nests of sorts with straw mats and cotton blankets *under* the bombs still attached to their SBDs.

Dick's Midway vets were edgy throughout the day. After the mission on the twenty-third and rumors of Japanese carriers nearby, he could see in their eyes that they were reliving their experiences in June. This state of mind wasn't good for them at all. Danny Iverson, Tom Moore, Bruce Prosser—they were solid pilots and earnest officers, but they had been traumatized by the loss of so many friends at Midway. For them, there was no respite, no time to process or recover from that ordeal. They went straight from the Midway frying pan to the whirlwind workup that cast them into the Guadalcanal fire.

Dick was worried about them. He knew he could not ask too much of them. Every man had a breaking point.

The second lieutenants still hadn't quite gotten a handle on the situation. Or maybe they had and were just keeping up a good facade. Oliver Mitchell's steady patter of jokes and celebrity impressions kept them laughing. He threw out non sequiturs so absurd they left the men rolling. Still, some of what he said came close to sounding a bit unhinged. During 232's first night on Guadalcanal, as the firefight raged along the Ilu River, Dick heard Oliver say over the chatter of machine guns, "Let's go down to the drugstore for a hot chocolate and a hamburger."

A genius for morale? Or a young man struggling to cope with what the war was doing to him? Dick wasn't sure. He just knew that everyone in the squadron liked Oliver, and the second lieutenant's shtick kept them laughing despite the magnitude of their predicament.

So far, the radio produced nothing but static and an electronic hum. Because it drained their SBD batteries quickly, they didn't have much time to scan empty frequencies. The enlisted guys quickly swapped in a new battery, setting the drained one aside. They would probably have enough power for another hour or two at most.

While they waited for anything on the radio, knots of conversations carried on quietly among the men. The connections that developed between the pilots and their back-seaters particularly gratified Dick. Those men needed to bond—needed to be a team in the air and on the ground. It meant a bit of the barrier between officer and enlisted was lowered. So be it. Back home, the enlisted men and officers would never have gathered like this after a day's flying. Here, the distinction was less important. The synergy of the team is what mattered.

Leland Thomas, the eastern Oregonian, and his gunner, Ed Eades, sat together on the straw mats, chatting quietly. Those two were as tight as any pilot-gunner pair. Eades clearly admired Thomas, who was one of Dick's favorites too. Thomas was irrepressibly optimistic, the perfect counterweight for the doom and gloom seeping into the squadron from the Midway vets. Beside them sat Don McCafferty and his gunner, Luis "Lewis" Macias.[1] Dick knew a little about Macias. He'd been a Marine since February. Six months after his swearing-in, he was covering Don's tail on search missions in the South Pacific, flying from an island he'd never heard of before. The war minted warriors at a pace that made the old hands cringe. Men like Macias were long on courage but short on experience. This combination made their life expectancy in combat brutally short.

Yet, time after time, Macias showed grit and substance. Aboard the *Long Island*, he practiced longer behind his guns than anyone else. He got so good at hitting the balloons the swabbies released as targets, Don started calling him "Deadeye." The name spread through the squadron and stuck. Macias loved the nickname, knowing it was a sign of respect from the officers and men alike.

Mirroring the childhoods of some of his officers, Macias, the son of Mexican immigrants who settled in Rawlins, Wyoming, grew up hard. His dad was a laborer at the nearby oil refinery in Parco. Before Lewis joined the Marines, he'd been working at a Civilian Conservation Corps camp, making a pittance but getting three squares a day. This was a kid who grew up poor and knew privation. He knew how to survive on a shoestring. That tough childhood taught men like Macias to be tough, flexible, and resourceful. They got things done with what they had at hand.

His pilot, Don McCafferty, came from a similar background. His stepdad was the street sweeper for the city of Hempstead, New York. His biological dad had toiled in a factory through the Depression. He grew up with three sisters in a tiny house, the family breadwinner stretching each paycheck down to the last penny.

The only thing that separated Lewis and Don was a few years of college, which had given McCafferty the path to flight school and the officer's commission that followed.

They were good men—kids, really, at least most of them. The mission they had been given here on Guadalcanal would have been beyond most of the prewar squadrons Dick had served in. With civilians-come-Marines? Dick knew they had little chance, especially with their chain of command considering them expendable. Yet, these were not easily dismissed young men; he'd seen their heart and the value they brought to the table. He would not allow them to be cannon fodder. Their lives would not be thrown away in senseless attacks if Dick could help it. They deserved that much from him. If he got overruled and ordered to attack anyway, then he'd lead them the only way he knew how: from the tip of the spear. If that was to be their lot, Dick would make sure they sold their lives for the steepest price.

The radio suddenly squawked with a gaggle of distant voices. The men leaned in closer, eagerly straining to catch the conversation. But the words overlapped and were so garbled they could not be understood.

Finally, a rush of excited words burst through the radio's tinny speaker. It was a Navy pilot, calling back to his carrier that they had badly damaged a Japanese flattop. The Red Devils of VMSB-232 let a cheer out at the news. The Navy was striking back hard.[2]

The sun was almost down now, pitching a canvas of crimson sky over the Marines. The nearby 11th Marine's chow tent served dinner only until dark, lest the cooking fires reveal positions in the night. A few of the men drifted off to grab a bite before it was too late, returning a few minutes later with their mess cups filled with soup or coffee, their plates a menagerie of weevil-filled Japanese rice and corned-beef hash.

They ate the dreadful food in silence, waiting for more transmissions in hopes they would get a better idea of what was going on out there beyond their tropical shores. Suddenly, a new voice popped up on the frequency. In a distant but clear transmission, the pilot who was leading a formation of bombers informed their carrier that they had found nothing. They were at the edge of their radius of action and were turning for home.

Silence followed, then a faint reply from their ship told them to head to Guadalcanal. The men around the radio looked at one another. There were no runway lights. The trees at the southwest edge of the runway still hadn't been cut down. Henry Hise had almost collided with them coming in on the squadron's first afternoon at Henderson. In the dark, they were extremely dangerous obstacles, hundreds of feet tall. Without illumination, somebody was bound to fly into them.

Dick stood up and turned to Baldinus, asking his old hand to get down to his SBD and call the incoming formation of Navy planes with his radio. "Tell them to orbit while we organize some lights for them."

Baldy dashed off to find a jeep and get down to the parking area with his gunner, Sgt. David "Dippy Dog" Sewell. Meanwhile, the other pilots and enlisted men scrounged for flashlights. Dick went looking for anything that might work to shine light on the runway.

Darkness fell at 1817 as the sun finally moved below the horizon. Riding the clouds overhead, a nearly full moon soon rose to shine over the island. The moonlight would help, but it wouldn't be enough to get the wayward Navy planes down.

The men found flashlights. Others scored enough oil-fueled construction flare pots to mark about a third of the runway. The rest would have to be covered with flashlights and jeeps.

The Navy planes approached, following the islands to Guadalcanal as they passed through the overhead clouds. The lead pilot called Baldy to let him know they were getting close but were low on fuel.

The men of 232 joined with others around the field to line the runway and click on their flashlights. They parked two jeeps, one vehicle at the two opposite corners of the runway, high beams spearing down the strip to give the pilots an idea of where it started and ended.

The pilots circled overhead until everyone was in place. Then the silhouettes of two SBDs appeared against the velvet sky and landed downwind, kicking up huge clouds of dust from the strip as they touched down. CUB-1 taxi crews guided them to the 232 parking area, but the drifts of dust made it exceptionally hard for the pilots to see. Nine more SBDs came in, one after another, barely clearing the treetops at the southwest edge of the strip. Small arms fire rose from the ridges and jungle beyond the perimeter, but none of the SBDs were hit.

Altogether, there were eleven Dauntlesses. As the pilots shut down in the parking area, 232 came out to greet the new arrivals. To Tom Moore's shock and happiness, Harold "Hal" Buell climbed out of one cockpit.

The two had met in training before the war and had become fast friends. Buell went Navy. Moore, Marines. Now in the darkness, they shared a brief but emotional reunion.

Led by Cdr. Turner Caldwell, the eleven SBDs came from two squadrons off the carrier USS *Enterprise*. Designated Flight 300, they had been launched right as a Japanese air strike arrived and attacked their ship. Buell had seen at least two bombs hit the carrier as the Dauntlesses cleared the area and went off to search for targets of their own. When they found nothing but empty seas, they jettisoned their bombs and headed for Henderson Field, unsure of the status of the *Enterprise* beyond knowing that the carrier was still afloat and communicating with them.

Mangrum and Caldwell huddled up to discuss the situation as 232's exhausted ground crew went about refueling the Navy planes. The crew would be stretched even thinner now to handle double the number of dive-bombers in their (temporary) care. The CUB-1 sailors could help fill the gaps, but the shortages of parts, tools, hoists, bomb carts, and more would be even more keenly felt for as long as the *Enterprise*'s aviators remained at Henderson.

While those details were being sorted out, 232's pilots and gunners led the Navy crews over to their living area and helped them scare up some food. Others found them clothing—Caldwell found the Japanese underwear that the Americans had scored when they took over the airfield so comfortable, he later wore the underclothing constantly for the rest of the war. Mats, blankets, and another canvas tarp were "requisitioned."

The food shocked the Navy crews. Used to the Big E's excellent mess, with actual china and silverware, the Navy aviators found cans of Australian bully beef and cold rice unappealing. Most barely ate, electing to bundle up under mosquito nets and blankets for what would be a long night.

Before Dick headed off to get some sleep, he ordered his ground crew to move his SBD and two others to the end of the runway. Some sixth sense told him he might need to send a section aloft on a night mission. Pre-positioning them on the strip would save the pilots from having to taxi in the dark through very rough sections of the field.

By 2000 hours, everyone had crawled into his meager sleeping gear. Only a few yards from 232's pilots, the Flight 300 guys struggled with all the unfamiliar sounds that had bedeviled the Marines during their first nights on the island.

McCafferty had just dozed off when a series of painful pinpricks in his legs woke him up. Red ants had crawled under his mosquito netting, worked their way over the rice mats, and now swarmed over his bare ankles and calves. Cursing silently, he slapped at them as they stung and crawled. At the same time, several of the Navy pilots were fighting battles of their own against creepy-crawly things. They slapped and smacked, cursed and moaned at the disgusting creatures they discovered in their bedding.

It was a typical night on Guadalcanal.

By midnight, not even the occasional distant gunshots from the Marine front lines could keep the Red Devils awake. They fell off into much-needed sleep. Flight 300's pilots weren't so lucky.

Ten minutes after midnight, a distant whine arose from the north. The sound streaked across the Marine perimeter, growing in volume until it abruptly ended with a muffled, blunt explosion. The ground quaked a split second later. By then, almost all 232's pilots had flung themselves through their mosquito netting and into the nearest slit trenches and foxholes. The Flight 300 pilots lay stunned and silent as the next whining *whoosh* screamed past the airfield. A third. A fourth. Then a torrent of tortured whines filled the night as explosions overlapped in quick succession.

The Imperial Japanese Navy had arrived.

TWENTY-ONE

THIS WAR IS YOUNG

Henderson Field, Guadalcanal
August 25, 1942, 0011 hours

A S SHELLS RAINED DOWN ON THE PERIMETER, DICK MANGRUM WAS already calculating how to strike back at the ships firing on them from somewhere off to the north in Savo Sound. His squadron wasn't properly trained for night operations. He and Baldy had flown at night and carried out simulated attacks before the war. Danny Iverson may have had some time at night as well. Dick called out to both over the din of the bombardment and told them to be ready to move to the airfield as soon as the shelling stopped. In the meantime, all they could do was hunker down in their shallow holes and battle the clouds of mosquitoes their warm flesh attracted.

All at once, a stillness fell across the Marine perimeter. The explosions around them ceased. The hellish whining of the big shells rushing overhead stopped. To be sure that this lull wasn't just temporary, Dick waited for another ten or fifteen minutes before gathering up his flight gear. Baldy and Danny Iverson joined him at a jeep, and they were driven down to the runway, where the three pre-positioned SBDs waited. The night's bombardment had been loud and nerve-racking but largely inaccurate. Two Marines had been killed, three more wounded.

The Japanese ships had missed the runway and the parking area for the aircraft.[1]

Dick found Dennis Byrd curled up under their SBD's fuselage, beneath the 500-pound bomb.

"Dennis," he called to his gunner.

"Sir?" the Texan replied as he scuttled out from under the wing to meet his skipper beside the jeep.

"Well, let's go get 'em."

"Aye, sir!" Byrd responded, and dashed off to grab the hand crank used to manually start the SBDs. Iverson's gunner Josiah Humphreys joined Byrd, since it took two men to crank the inertia starter. A moment later, Baldy's back-seater, "Dippy Dog" Sewell, came over to Dick's SBD to spot the two other men. Hand-starting an SBD took muscle power and patience. After four days on the island with inadequate food, the men were already getting winded by this process, so the three men would take turns.

Dick triggered a switch in the cockpit and fired the starter. The Wright Cyclone sputtered and coughed. The prop began to turn, and the big radial engine caught and fired up, blowing a cloud of exhaust down either side of the fuselage.

While the engines warmed up and the pilots went through their pre-flight rituals, the gunners climbed aboard. A check of their watches revealed it was just about 0200. As they prepared for takeoff, the jeep was positioned at the far end of the runway, dead in the middle so its head-lights could be used as a reference point.

One by one, the SBD pilots rolled down the runway, eyes fixed on the two blazing headlights a few thousand yards away, trusting that the strip had not taken a stray shell hit. If it had, and they careened into it, that would be the end of aircraft and crew. Fortunately, all three planes made into the night sky safely. With clouds returned and the moon now masked, it was so dark they could barely see one another's aircraft. The darkness forced them to form up by watching for the glowing blue exhaust flame that streaked along the side of the fuselage from the engine cowling.

Slowly, they climbed to attack altitude, dodging clouds as they extended out over Savo Sound. The moon had not yet set, and as the pilots were now flying above the main layer of scattered clouds, the scene below was bathed in silvery light.

The clouds thinned out as they flew north toward Florida Island, six pairs of eyes searching the opaque water below. All looked still down there. They passed over Savo Island, Tulagi Island off their starboard side, with no sign of the Japanese raiders below.

The vessels had to be down there someplace. The problem was that VMSB-232 lacked surface-search electronics. No radar sets had yet been installed on Marine dive-bombers as they would in the months to come. The men could only rely on their eyesight. A blacked-out ship moving with minimal wake on black waters under a cloudy sky was almost impossible to sight unless the aircraft crew was at just the right angle.

The mission was starting to look like a fool's errand. But as they approached the northwest tip of Florida Island, Dick saw a tiny sliver of white striping the water below. He watched it carefully, his eyes focused on the tips of the stripe. There, on the northern side, he glimpsed something dark and large, gliding through the calm sea.

They had found the bombardment force.

Signaling to Baldy and Danny, Dick led them down on what they thought was a cruiser. The Japanese heard and saw them coming. Suddenly, long fiery streaks rose up at them, tracers from the ship's antiaircraft guns. The tracers zipped past off either wing as the men steepened their dives and planted their gunsights right on the ship's bow. The antiaircraft fire illuminated the vessel, making it easier for the Marines to aim.

The Marines released their bombs at around fifteen hundred feet and then pulled up and leveled off above the water as ropes of tracers chased after them. They saw no signs of a hit.

Gradually, they pulled out of antiaircraft range, then looped around to return to Guadalcanal. Their first combat drop had been a bust.

Shortly before they got back to Henderson, Turner Caldwell launched three of his SBDs, sending them after the Japanese ships. Caldwell's bombers caught the *Uzuki* off Ndai Island just after the B5N crew had been taken aboard. The SBDs attacked the destroyer but failed to score a hit and lost a Dauntless in the process. The pilot crash-landed off the coast of Malaita Island, where he and his gunner were rescued by local villagers.[2]

Back on the ground, the aviators gathered beside their planes to talk over what they had seen. The tracers had seemed to move slowly at first, when they were at a distance. But the closer they got, the faster they seemed to move until they flashed like lightning past their aircraft. Somebody started joking about how bad the Japanese gunners were. Their aim seemed way off that morning. Then Humphreys chimed in, "Well, you know . . . for every tracer we saw, there were about four more we didn't see."

They hadn't thought of that. Tracers were usually only about a quarter to a third of their own ammo load-out with their twin .30-caliber machine guns. The thought that the pilots had only seen a fraction of the shells fired at them was a sobering realization.

A moment later, a jeep arrived and the men silently climbed aboard for the short drive to the Pagoda.

Dick led them inside to report the attack to Fike and the rest of the air staff. After he finished, Dick was told that a Japanese carrier task force had been reported coming down from the north. It was going to be within close striking distance of Guadalcanal by morning.

The *Ryūjō*'s strike on the twenty-fourth was a pinprick raid that did little damage. If this new task force included the fleet carriers that had struck Pearl Harbor, Wake, Port Darwin, and Midway, then Henderson Field would be flattened come first light. Without the airfield, there would be no way to stop Japanese reinforcements from reaching the island.

Vandegrift decided to shoot the works and send everything he could against the carrier task force at dawn in a longshot bid to save Henderson. The Kidō Butai—Japan's fleet carrier force—was one of the most heavily defended naval targets on the planet. The Americans would face clouds of Zeroes before reaching their targets and scores of antiaircraft guns of all calibers when over the ships. It was the Midway vets' worst nightmare come true. Vandegrift was setting them up for a repeat of June 4.

Dick asked for fighter escort. John L. Smith was already on that, promising ten F4Fs that he would personally lead. Whatever happened, they would go through this attack together.

It was 0400. They had two hours to prepare for the mission. Dick met with Caldwell, who pledged three SBDs for the mission. Three aircraft were all that could be readied for a dawn strike. Five Marine Dauntlesses would lead the attack, and Dick ordered his ground crew to equip them with the thousand-pound armor-piercing bombs that Don Felt's aviators had left behind on the twenty-third. Takeoffs would be trickier. They would burn more fuel with the heavier load, reducing range. Loading them by hand would be an arduous task, but the enlisted men never complained. They just figured out a way to get it done. Everyone knew the larger bombs could do catastrophic damage to an aircraft carrier and were worth the additional headaches.

Who would fly the mission? It was Dick's decision, and every name he selected meant he was likely consigning that man to death. The timeline left little opportunity to reflect on the question. Instead, Dick went with his gut: he wanted the most aggressive tigers in the squadron—the men whose eagerness to fight the Japanese would counterbalance their inexperience. That meant leaving Prosser, Iverson, and Moore behind. They had been through such a desperate attack. It was unfair to ask them to face the flak and fighters over a Japanese carrier force a second time. Besides, their hearts were scarred. He needed men willing to press the attack at all costs.

He picked Baldy and Henry Hise to fly with him, even though they had never before flown together as a section. Leland Thomas and Don McCafferty would tuck in behind them as an incomplete second section.

Eight Dauntlesses and ten F4Fs against a carrier force that could have scores of Zeroes defending it.

They would need to be airborne in less than two hours. With just enough time for a last meal before heading to their planes, the aviators walked down to the 11th Marines chow tent, where a meal line of sorts had been set up along a makeshift scrap-wood counter. At the end of it sat two corrugated steel garbage cans. One contained coffee, the other breakfast. There was little conversation as the men queued up, mess tins and cups in hand. The cooks filled their cups with coffee, then dipped their ladle into the other trash can, pouring out greasy water and a six-inch-long piece of meat onto each man's plate.

Dennis Byrd examined the meat. Whatever it was, it had been boiled. Finally, somebody asked what it was.

"Sheep tongue. Japanese sheep tongue," came the reply.

Dennis sat down with the other gunners assigned to the mission. They'd been rounded up and brought over in the dark, and now all of them looked down at their potential last meal with a mix of morbid fascination and complete disgust.

Dennis couldn't bring himself to eat it.

"Hey, Byrd," Dippy Dog Sewell asked, "if you're not going to eat your meat, can I have it?"

Byrd handed him his mess plate and left. If he was going to die that day, he was going to do so without Japanese sheep tongue in his belly. Then he remembered the Hershey almond chocolate bars he'd been given just before they launched off the *Long Island*. Chocolate seemed like a much more fitting last meal, one that wouldn't give him an upset stomach in the middle of combat. He went and retrieved the box, quickly devoured a couple of bars, then returned to the group.

At 0500, the men reached the parking area where their aircraft were still being readied for the mission. Strong-backed enlisted men worked in teams to lift the thousand-pounders into place under the SBDs while others furiously hand-pumped fuel into the three birds that had flown the morning attack. It would be a miracle to get these five planes ready in time.

Dick Mangrum was exhausted. He'd been up since the previous morning, had flown his first real combat mission, and was now about to lead the most important mission of his career. One look at his men, and he knew they were sleep-deprived as well. Their faces were grim, jaws set with the raccoon eyes born from being awake for far too long.[3]

Dick waved to his men to gather, and they quickly formed a horse-shoe around him. He laid out the mission. The Japanese carrier force had been seen sometime earlier in the night about two hundred miles north of Henderson. With the big thousand-pounders, they would be flying to the edge of their range. The Wildcats, with their shorter radius of action, would stay with the SBDs as long as they could.

"It's your first fight, boys," he said. "Remember this, fellows. While we are all expendable, we are not so expendable as to take unnecessary chances. Your mission is to sink as many of those ships as you can. But a still more important mission is for *all* of you to get back here—whole."

Dick paused, looking at their resolute faces. Good men. They would fly and fight to the best of their abilities. He wished he could lead them into battle with a full squadron, properly supported. This shoestring foolishness was not worthy of their hearts. But here they were.

Not expendable.

"This war. . . . is young yet," he told his men. "We can die later."

Instinctively, he'd struck exactly the right tone. The men responded—he could see it in their eyes. They would follow him through any fire. And he would lead them through it.

"Okay, that's all," he finished simply. "Man your planes."

TWENTY-TWO

WE CAN DIE LATER

North of Guadalcanal
August 25, 1942, 0730 hours

THE AMERICAN STRIKE PARADED ABOVE A LAYER OF BROKEN, FLUFFY clouds, the scene suffused by the Pacific sunrise's golden hour. Eight SBDs in two small formations led the way, with Dick Mangrum's Dauntless at the tip of the spear. Behind and above them, John L.'s ten Wildcats covered the bomber formation. For this mission John L. picked the best pilots in 223, including Rivers Morrell, the squadron's executive officer; Marion Carl; New Jersey native Ken Frazier; and the prodigy Charlie Kendrick. They would need every bit of talent and skill to keep the Zeroes off the SBDs—and themselves.

The mission began with a critical assumption. The Japanese carrier task force had last been reported steaming south for Guadalcanal, some two hundred miles out. That location put the task force out of range for John L.'s F4Fs, which lacked external drop tanks to extend their endurance. If the Japanese continued on course and closed the distance to Guadalcanal through the morning, VMF-223 could cover the Dauntlesses all the way to the target and back. If the Japanese changed course or doubled back, then the Wildcats would not have the fuel to search for them. Under those circumstances, Dick would have to either turn for home or press on without his fighter escort. The latter, of course, would be suicide. Midway had demonstrated that.

Below them, the scattered cloud cover ranged between two and four thousand feet, obscuring the ocean below in places. Still, the Americans had a grandstand view from above ten thousand feet, and the clouds weren't dense enough to hide a carrier task force. If it was out there where the Americans had been told it was, they would find it.

Ninety minutes into the mission, and the ocean remained empty. Dick pressed on even as John L.'s eyes grew increasingly fixed on his fuel gauges. They passed the 140-mile mark with nothing in sight beyond their two tiny formations of medium-blue and gray planes.

Another few minutes ticked by as the Wildcat pilots watched their fuel gauge needles sag a bit farther toward empty. The fighters were close to the point of no return, and John L. would soon have to make a difficult decision. He could cover Dick until his squadron ran out of fuel and ditched, sacrificing his men to protect the bomber crews, or he could turn for home and preserve his small force to fight another day. There were no other options.

He couldn't keep going. John L.'s squadron wasn't just responsible for 232's protection; they were the only force available that could keep the Japanese bombers at bay. Ten thousand–plus Marines depended on his men for that. If he kept going, and this proved to be a wild goose chase, he'd have thrown away the 1st Marine Division's only means of air defense for gain.

Besides, these men with him? They were not expendable to him. These past ten weeks had bonded them with one another and with him as closely as he'd ever experienced with any squadron he'd served with before the war. They were good, earnest kids trying to learn to be combat Marines on the fly. They deserved the best chance possible to make it through this nightmare.

John L. signaled to Dick that they were low on fuel and heading back to Henderson. The older commander understood. The dive-bomber crews watched the fighters swing around and vanish over the horizon to the south.

The SBDs were alone now, meat on the table for any Zero combat air patrol they encountered. Nevertheless, Dick decided to press on in search of the Japanese carrier force, no matter the risk to his tiny formation. Perhaps he could surprise the Japanese and inflict some damage before the Zeroes caught them. If he could save Henderson from destruction at the hands of elite Japanese carrier bomber crews, he would do it. The Red Devils and the three crew from Flight 300 stayed with him, tucked in tight for mutual defense.

They flew out to two hundred miles and saw nothing. The Japanese carrier task force must have changed course. Those ships were somewhere out here, and even though the Dauntless crews had been in the air since 0600, they still had enough gas left to conduct a limited search. Dick banked to port and began to scout westward. They would fly on this course for a few minutes—perhaps fifty or sixty miles—and then angle back for home if they found nothing.

They reached the edge of their endurance a few minutes after 0800. The clouds below had grown a little denser. Still, the water below revealed no ships.

Frustrated. Relieved. Disappointed. A tangle of emotional currents ran through 232's skipper and the rest of the men. Dick had taken a huge risk pressing on without the F4Fs. The bombers had gotten away with it, albeit with nothing to show in return. Now it was time to return to Guadalcanal and report back that there was nothing out here. They turned south for home, fuel getting low.

Seven minutes on the new course, and suddenly, wakes appeared on the water off the planes' starboard wings. Dick studied the white trails through the gaps in the clouds. A cruiser in the lead. Destroyers—at least eight, plus three or four transports. This wasn't the carrier task force. This was the reinforcement convoy they had been expecting for days. It was steaming south on a parallel course that would take the Japanese through the passage between Santa Isabel and Florida Islands, then on into Savo Sound.

In a stroke of incredible luck, the Americans found themselves perfectly placed for an attack. Dick didn't hesitate. He banked starboard, turning over ninety degrees while putting the sun to the squadron's back.

Attacking out of the sun—it was an old World War I trick he'd taught 232 back in Hawai'i. Timeless and deadly effective.

They closed on the ships, the sunlight masking their approach. The lookouts on those Japanese decks couldn't see them against the brilliance of the sun. The convoy continued to steam serenely along at about nine knots. Dick let them pass off his port wing until his planes were upsun and slightly behind the task force.

Then he turned to port and swung directly behind the convoy to attack down its double columns on their same heading. This way, when the ships started to maneuver against them, the SBDs would be well positioned to react to the vessels' movements. No better way of executing a dive-bombing run had been devised.

It was textbook.

They overflew the rear guard ships. No flak rose to greet them. The Japanese continued on course. It was amazing. They hadn't even been detected, and there was no combat air patrol of Zeroes in sight.

Dick picked out the flagship, a light cruiser he pegged as one of the *Jinstū*-class vessels built to be destroyer flotilla flagships in the aftermath of World War I. Heavily armed, fast, and capable. Dick was certain he was seeing the flagship of the task force commander. Knock it out and kill or wound their leadership, and this convoy would be thrown in disarray.

Dick initiated VMSB-232's attack with a slow barrel roll up and over Baldy's Dauntless. Inverted, he could keep his eye on the target while he corkscrewed into the proper seventy-degree diving angle of attack. Moments later, Baldy rolled into his dive, Henry Hise following closely. Don McCafferty and Leland Thomas trailed the first section.

Down they went, throttles back, their Swiss-cheese looking dive flaps popped open to slow their descent so they didn't tear the wings off their aircraft. For the pilots and gunners, it seemed like they hung there over the Japanese ships for an eternity. In reality, their dives lasted about thirty seconds.

Dick lined up on the light cruiser, putting his gunsight reticle on the vessel's bow. Still the cruiser took no evasive action; the Americans had

totally surprised the Japanese. Dick held his dive until he was below fifteen hundred feet. Then he toggled his bomb and pulled out right over the
water. Seated behind him, Dennis strafed the ship as their bird ran for it.
He didn't see where their bomb had landed.

Baldy came next, holding on to his thousand-pounder until his altimeter unwound to almost a thousand feet. He felt the Dauntless surge as he
released the bomb and pulled out after Dick, speeding along the whitecaps as Japanese counterfire finally rose after them.

Hise went into his dive, searching for a carrier to attack and unaware
that the squadron was attacking the transport force. The clouds blocked
some of the convoy from view. Of the ships he could see, the cruiser Dick
had gone after was the largest. Hise followed Baldy down after it, determined to get a hit and do some real damage before he died.

McCafferty rode Hise's coattails down toward the Japanese cruiser,
separating slightly from the others as he singled out a nearby destroyer.
He plunged through a cloud, his airspeed indicator pushing past three
hundred miles an hour. A second later, he came out of the cloud's bottom, the destroyer still below. He held on to the bomb for just a heartbeat
longer, then pulled the release handle.

As he muscled the control stick in toward his stomach, dragging the
SBD's nose up, he caught sight of Baldy releasing his bomb. A huge flash
filled his windscreen. Flames and debris spewed skyward over the cruiser.
Fixated on the incredible display of destructive power the bomb had
wrought, McCafferty failed to notice he was still heading for the ocean.

An enormous gout of water erupted off the starboard side of the
cruiser, just as Hise pulled off target. Instead of running, Hise made a
gradual turn so he could get a look-see of what his bomb had done. All he
saw was the giant water plume rising over the cruiser. A near miss often
did more damage than a direct hit, caving in hull plates with the detona-
tion's overpressure. For a first combat drop, it wasn't a bad outcome at all.
Hise banked back southward and raced to catch up with Dick and Baldy.

At the same moment, McCafferty awoke to the danger he was in.
Still diving at over three hundred miles an hour, the stick forces were
supremely heavy. To pull it back even farther, he had to brace his legs and

heave. The nose climbed for the horizon with agonizing sluggishness. Something flashed nearby. The SBD shook. The Japanese had found the range. In back, Lewis "Deadeye" Macias called to his pilot, "Lieutenant, let's get the hell out of here!"

Still pulling back on the stick with all his might, the water rushing toward them, McCafferty fought the *g*-forces and tried not to black out. Then he realized he was out of altitude and had no choice: he pushed his body beyond its limits to save the aircraft. As he pulled back even harder, his vision narrowed and he grayed out for a second or two.

They made it. Just barely. McCafferty's plane captain later reported finding seaweed wrapped along the SBD's fuselage. Overstated? Probably. The fact was, McCafferty saved the aircraft with barely twenty feet to spare.

As he leveled off and started zigzagging to spoil the aim of the anti-aircraft gunners behind them now, he keyed the intercom to Macias and asked, "Deadeye, are you all right?"

"I'm okay, Lieutenant, but we got a few pieces of scrap metal in the tail section" came his reply.

"Can we get back?" McCafferty asked.

"Yes. If we keep going like hell. But I thought we were done for, back there."

McCafferty asked his gunner how the squadron had done. Macias saw the hit on the cruiser, reported that a transport the Flight 300 guys had attacked was in flames, and noted a hit on the destroyer. When he finished the quick summary, he added laconically, "Gee, but that was fun!"

They cleared the antiaircraft fire and caught up with the rest of the squadron, which was now starting a slow climb toward the cloud layer, with Dick on point again. A few minutes later, Leland Thomas and Ed Eades regained their position in the formation. The Flight 300 guys were nowhere to be seen.

Baldy suddenly waggled his wings. Dick looked over and saw him in the cockpit, holding his nose and pointing at Dick's SBD.

Dick's bomb had failed to release. The thousand-pounder was still slung under his fuselage. He'd dived on that cruiser for nothing.

The squadron was intact. Everyone alive. The Flight 300 trio had bombed the largest transport at the back of the column and were making their way south behind them. The Americans had inflicted heavy damage and suffered no losses. It was a huge victory for the squadron. They could get back to Henderson, rearm, refuel, and then hit the Japanese again before 1400. If they were quick, they might even get two more strikes in before dusk. The prudent way to go was to jettison the bomb and get the men home.

But that was not Dick Mangrum's mentality. He had a weapon, and behind him, there were targets that needed to be destroyed. He wasn't going to play it safe, not after he had risked the squadron to keep searching for the Japanese carrier force.

Dick signaled to Baldy to take the lead and get the boys home. Then, he rolled into a climbing 180-degree turn and headed back toward the Japanese task force.

The rest of the squadron watched him go, astonished that their skipper chose to go back into the fight alone. The Japanese were alerted now. They had been badly hurt and would be thirsting for revenge.

True leaders set the example. They're the first up and the last to call it a day. Their courage must be exemplary, their devotion to mission and men unmatched. Richard Mangrum set a new standard for 232 that morning as the crews watched him climb into the cloud layer behind them and disappear.

Moments later, the remaining SBDs arrowed into the scud. As they pulled through it, flying through canyons of blue sky and into the next cumulous, the squadron formation loosened. They flew on, facing heavier weather as they closed on Guadalcanal. Halfway back, McCafferty looked up at a towering cloud ahead of them. Three dots suddenly materialized out of it above them. It took only a second or two to register they were Japanese floatplanes—single-engine aircraft equipped with pontoons instead of wheels for water operations.[1]

The Japanese planes moved upsun from the SBDs before diving down after the Marines from about McCafferty's eight o'clock. The New York man juked away from one floatplane as it came into range. Macias swung his guns out, tracking the incoming aircraft with his eyes set on his primitive iron sight between the two .30-caliber guns. He kept his profile low and close to the single slab of armor that offered meager protection in his open cockpit. The enemy came into range, closing fast now. Both Marine and Japanese pilots opened fire. McCafferty flung his SBD into evasive maneuvers. The enemy plane whipped past, kept diving, and then rolled into a climb to set up another run on them.

Another plane swooped in on them. Macias snapped out bursts, his Brownings chewing through their ammo belts at an alarming pace. Again, they avoided getting hit.

The cat-and-mouse game continued even as Thomas and Eades came under attack. The Japanese held all the advantages. The SBDs could only react and dodge each incoming gun run.

Another Japanese plane made a pass on McCafferty and Macias. In the back seat, the Wyoming native steadied his guns on the craft, even as he saw tracers pouring out its nose heading seemingly straight for him. The SBD's .30-caliber mount included a small plate of armor designed to cover the gunner's face. Macias ducked under it, keeping his eyes on the Japanese plane. It kept coming, its bullets zipping around the SBD.

Lewis Macias pressed his triggers, holding them down in a long, desperate burst. His teeth chattered from fear, knees trembling under the turret combing. He pushed through the fear and kept the ring sight on his target until his counterfire chewed pieces of metal off the enemy plane's cowling. The floatplane suddenly pitched up and over into a steep dive, and Macias caught sight of a burst of flames and smoke, which he thought was his target exploding.

The entire fight lasted less than five surreal, never-ending minutes. A lifetime in five hundred heartbeats.

Macias looked over at Leland Thomas and Ed Eades. Their SBD was still there in formation, Eades blazing away at the two remaining Japanese. When he hit one of them, it belched a long tail of black smoke before diving into a cloud.

The last enemy craft broke off and disengaged, diving away to the west.

McCafferty called back to his gunner, "Deadeye, you okay?"

Macias tried to reply, but his teeth chattered so badly he couldn't make any words come out. His body shook violently from the parasympathetic backlash from adrenaline and sheer terror.

"Macias?" McCafferty tried again. "You okay?"

"Gee," he managed to croak out this time, "that was fun."

They had survived their first encounter with Japanese aircraft; now they needed to get home fast. They were quickly running out of fuel. The formation passed the southern end of Santa Isabel Island and reached Savo Sound. Baldy started them down in a descent to Henderson, and when they passed over the strip, they could see it had not been attacked while they were gone. After a 4½-hour flight, the Marines started to land a little after 1030 hours. All three of the Flight 300 SBDs set down a short time later. They reported their targeted transport was left burning and dead in the water.

The 232 pilots and crews who had been left on the ground rushed to their friends as they shut down their SBDs in the parking area. Eager conversations broke out around every Dauntless. Capt. Fletcher Brown, the squadron executive officer, quickly realized that Dick Mangrum was not with the squadron. The returning pilots explained what their skipper had done, to the astonishment of everyone.

Without him, Brown was in charge until Mangrum got back. He ordered the planes refueled and rearmed as quickly as possible. They would be going out as soon as the ground crews could get them prepped. A mad scramble ensued as the CUB-1 swabbies and 232's exhausted skeleton crew of maintainers swarmed over the Dauntlesses. Stripped to the waist, wearing filthy shorts and boots, they started hand-pumping gas into the main tanks. Sweat poured off them in the midmorning heat and swamplike humidity. Bombs were hauled into position and lifted onto the fuselage racks. The rear guns were given fresh belts of ammunition. It was backbreaking, infuriatingly slow work without any of the proper gear.

Meanwhile, the pilots and gunners gathered, waiting for their missing skipper to return. The tension grew as the wait continued. Mangrum was the one man who, they knew, could get them through this nightmare. Brownie Brown was a great administrator and logistics guy. He was organized and affable; the men liked him a great deal. Mangrum leaned on him for much of the heavy lifting in the day-to-day squadron duties. But for all those assets, Brownie wasn't the combat leader Mangrum was. He'd been an honors student at the University of Florida, where he'd been exceptionally hardworking and focused. He graduated with honors in 1937 with a degree in civil engineering. His background made him an ideal right-hand man for Mangrum. On the ground, Brownie helped solve countless issues the squadron faced, balancing Dick's combat leadership with his own lynchpin level of support for the unit's functionality.

Still, the Red Devils would be lost without Mangrum. Officers and enlisted men alike trusted him, and he repaid that trust with utter loyalty. He shouldn't have gone back to attack that task force alone. He should have jettisoned the damned bomb and stayed with the formation, bringing it home with everyone safe.

But that was not the kind of man Dick Mangrum was. His men understood that. Hise in particular was struck by the courage required to go back alone against the Japanese. He saw it as an exemplary act of courage to be lived up to in the many fights to come.

The minutes dragged toward 1100. Quiet prayers were uttered, their eyes scanning the sky, ears straining for the welcome sound of a healthy Pratt & Whitney.

The sky remained silent and empty.

TWENTY-THREE

AGAINST A RISING TIDE

150 miles north of Guadalcanal
August 25, 1942

SKIMMING THE CLOUDS, DICK MANGRUM LACKED THE TIME OR FUEL to get back to the normal attack altitude of above ten thousand feet. Because he'd have to attack the Japanese from half that, his dive-bombing run would give him only a few seconds to get lined up on a target. It wasn't optimal, but it was the best he could do, given the circumstances.

A check of the fuel gauges revealed the situation was getting critical. He didn't have much time to set up the attack. There'd be no swinging wide to the east to attack out of the sun again, no attack down the column. He needed to find, dive, drop, and run if he were going to get back to Henderson.

"Zero! Zero! Nine o'clock, Skipper!" Dennis Byrd suddenly called out over the intercom.

Dick saw it off the port wing, a single speck trolling through a canyon of blue sky between clouds. Instinctively, he banked toward it, pointing his two forward-firing .50-caliber machine guns at the Japanese aircraft. It looked like a Zero on floats. The two aircraft closed on each other swiftly. Dick opened fire, then shot past the float Zero. A moment later, he rolled the SBD and dove into a bank of clouds.

The reality of their situation hit Dennis as they were flying through the cloud. Vision down to a few meters, nothing but soupy white around them, he felt their isolation keenly. It triggered a profound sense of loneliness. If they went down, nobody would ever know what happened to them. His family, his friends: they would just know that he and Dick went missing in action somewhere over the Pacific. He was a twentysomething from Texas, carting around the clouds in an open cockpit, a pair of guns under his chin. It all seemed unreal, like a bizarre dream unfolding in real time, and no matter what he tried, he wasn't going to wake.

They ran out of cloud a few seconds later, the SBD breaking into clear sky. In a wild moment of serendipity, a Japanese transport sat on the water directly ahead and below them. Not far from it, another, larger transport lay burning. Explosions rippled amidships, and clouds of smoke boiled hundreds of feet over the doomed ship. The Flight 300 guys had really pounded it.

The other transport below steamed along unhurt. It looked to be about a 5,000-tonner with a single stack amidships and a high bridge just forward of it. When nearby destroyers saw the SBD, their antiaircraft gunners opened fire. Tracers and black puffs of exploding shells dotted the sky around them.

Dick rolled into an attack dive, popping the flaps and retarding the throttle. The SBD hung on its tail. The ship started to tuck under Dick's cowling as it steamed along southward. He corkscrewed quickly to stay on the target but had no time to swing the gunsight's pipper onto the ship's bow. Passing through fifteen hundred feet now, he was out of time and had to pull up or go straight into the water. He had only a second or two left. The skipper used the manual release to dump the bomb. This time, it worked. The thousand-pounder swung on its trapeze and sailed under the propeller arc. It landed just astern of the transport, exploding with a sudden swell of smoke and water that rose high over the target vessel.

Mangrum waited so long that he almost clipped the ship's masts as he pulled out. The minute the tail dropped to the horizon, Dennis could see their bomb and its near miss right off the ship's fantail. Then he saw the transport's main deck. It was full of men scrambling about. A perfect strafing target. He swung his guns on them and hammered away as Dick dodged and juked, heading south for home as antiaircraft fire rained around them.

It was over in only a couple of minutes. The stillness was jarring. From flak and float Zeroes, men being bowled over by the Brownings, flaming ships, and the overwhelming sounds of explosions and gunfire, all overwritten by the gravelly roar of their Wright Cyclone, they suddenly found themselves on the water with nothing in sight.

Just before 1100, Mangrum's SBD appeared in the sky over Henderson Field. The men of 232 breathed an enormous sigh of relief as their skipper set down and taxied to the ramp. He'd returned thirty minutes after the rest of the squadron, having been airborne for almost five hours. There was little but fumes left in his fuel tanks.

As soon as he shut the SBD down, the squadron gathered around him. But the reunion was suddenly derailed. An Australian member of the Coastwatchers observing Japanese activity from hiding places in New Georgia, in the Central Solomons jungle, radioed a warning that an incoming bombing raid was heading to Guadalcanal. Twenty plus, somewhere north of twenty-five thousand feet.

The boys from Rabaul were on their way.

They had to get the Dauntlesses off the field. After a quick calculation, they realized the bombers would be overhead in less than thirty minutes.

Across the runway, John L. and his pilots scampered to their aircraft. The Wildcats were half-fueled, and there was no way they could reach twenty-five thousand feet in the thirty minutes they had. Best to get them off the runway and out of harm's way. This was one strike that would have to go unintercepted.

A mad dash to escape falling bombs was the last thing Dick and Dennis expected when they returned to Henderson, but reality swept away their exhaustion. Mangrum quickly conferred with Brown. Baldy and the other crews were exhausted and needed a break. They had six SBDs with bombs already hooked up and tanks half-filled. The Flight 300 element had another three SBDs ready to go. The Red Devil pilots Danny

Iverson, Don Rose, Robert Fleener, and Arthur O'Keefe would fly the next mission with the skipper and Fletcher Brown. They were going back to sink the remaining transports.

Mangrum ordered the ground crews to just finish topping off the main tanks. The 150 gallons would have to do. None of the wing tanks had been filled yet. The incomplete fueling would severely limit the SBDs' range, but it was better than being caught in the open on the ground as Japanese bombs fell.

The Wildcats sped aloft, disappearing into the late-morning sky. The SBDs followed soon after, Dick Mangrum leading the way again with Brownie Brown at the head of the second section.

As they climbed steadily to the north toward Tulagi, the air raid siren wailed to life at Henderson. The Marines dashed to their nearest slit trenches and foxholes while the Japanese G4M twin-engine bombers appeared overhead. They were barely fly specks against the sky, gray against the blue, easily above twenty-seven thousand feet. How would the Marines ever get the Wildcats up that high in time to stop these raids?

A problem for another day, for sure. In the meantime, the raiders overflew Henderson in precise, tight vee-of-vee formation and rained some forty bombs down on the Americans below. They fell into the parking area, around the Pagoda, and a few cratered the runway. It was a remarkable display of accuracy from a ridiculously high altitude—a reminder that the Japanese were not just good at the game of aerial warfare; they were masters of it.

The attack killed four Marines and wounded five others. Fortunately, no aircraft left behind on the ground that day were hit.

Without the fuel for a proper search, the unescorted SBDs followed Dick Mangrum straight back to the scene of the morning attack. Off the coast of Santa Isabel, they encountered debris fields on the water, along with long oil slicks—wounds left over from the first attack.

The convoy was nowhere to be found. Certainly, it was not still heading for Guadalcanal; otherwise, the Americans would have found it. They pushed northward and did spot a small vessel, like a sliver on the water, just beyond the debris field. It looked like an old WWI-era destroyer, similar to the US Navy's destroyer-transports. The lone vessel hardly seemed worth the effort of an attack.

But twenty minutes of searching brought no other targets. With fuel low, Dick turned the formation around, and the pilots went looking for that sliver on the sea again.

They found it, speeding along at twenty knots and very aware of their presence. One by one, the SBD pilots rolled into the attack, thundering down on the hapless Japanese auxiliary. The canny Japanese crew dodged every bomb. All six pilots missed.[1]

Bone weary, Dick led his Dauntlesses back to Henderson, where they landed in midafternoon while teams of engineers filled in the bomb craters around the airfield.

Three combat missions in twelve hours. Dick couldn't remember the last time he'd slept. Still, he had a squadron to run, and once he and the others parked their aircraft, he headed over to the Pagoda to report the events of the day to Fike and the rest of the air staff.

Meanwhile, the gunners and pilots dragged their gear over to their living space under their canvas canopy and flung themselves onto their sleeping mats. That's where Richard Tregaskis found them later that afternoon. The war correspondent's exhaustion matched that of the men he'd come to interview. As haggard and as filthy as they were, he'd narrowly avoided getting hurt in the midnight bombardment. After the attack, he'd seen the casualties being treated and watched two Marines bleed out, crying as their lives ebbed away. Later that morning, when the Japanese air raid hit Henderson, a bomb landed two hundred yards away from his dugout, throwing chunks of earth all over the area.

A reporter willing to endure all that just to tell the men's stories engendered respect. As Tregaskis asked questions, the men began to talk. Don McCafferty was the most animated. He described the awe he felt when he saw Baldy's bomb hit that light cruiser. "The bomb hit right by the bridge," he began. "And everything came up as if it were made of wood—like a model in the movies. I veered over to watch it. I was so fascinated, just everything spraying up and coming down. The explosion blew up the front stacks."

Dick arrived and sat down with the men. When prompted by Tregaskis, he matter-of-factly recounted the mission from his vantage point. As he returned to the Japanese convoy, he said, he saw both the cruiser and the other transport on fire, "and little boats all over the water, picking up survivors." Dennis Byrd chimed in with some details on where their bomb had hit.

Ens. Christian "Chris" Fink and Milo Kimberlin, the Flight 300 crew that hit the biggest transport, told their story. After Fink's pullout, Kimberlin saw their bomb "hit right on the bridge and a sheet of flame and black smoke went to the clouds. . . . We could see the . . . smoke and flames for forty miles."

It had been a landmark day for VMSB-232. As exhausted as all the aviators were, they had come through their first day of strikes without losing a man or an airplane. Given the circumstances, it was a remarkable achievement. Though they never found the Japanese carrier force, they stopped the reinforcement convoy from reaching Guadalcanal. Where the enemy convoy went after the morning attack was anyone's guess, but it certainly wasn't heading for them anymore.

They had given the mud Marines some breathing space to prepare for another Japanese attack on the perimeter. They had also bought the Navy a few days to get more men and supplies to the island. One thing they all knew though: this wasn't the end of it. It was just the start. The Japanese would be back, sooner rather than later.

JUST HOW SIGNIFICANT MANGRUM'S STRIKE ON AUGUST 25 PROVED TO be emerged only after the war and after a thorough study of the Japanese side of the Battle of the Eastern Solomons, as the two-day action around Guadalcanal would later be called. On the twenty-fourth, the carriers from both sides launched attacks against each other. The American crews sank the light carrier *Ryūjō*. In return, the fleet carrier *Enterprise* suffered heavy damage from three bomb hits and four near misses. It was knocked out of the fight until mid-October 1942.

The carrier task force that Mangrum was sent against had turned north. It was composed of the *Shōkaku* and *Zuikaku*—the last two veteran fleet carriers that had attacked Pearl Harbor. Had VMSB-232 and the added trio from Flight 300 encountered that task force, they would have stood little chance of survival. Fortunately for the Marines, they instead found Rear Adm. Raizo "Tenacious" Tanaka's reinforcement group bound for Guadalcanal. Over the previous few days, Tanaka had bored circles in the waters north of Guadalcanal, enduring conflicting orders from his overly complex chain of command. On August 25, he decided unilaterally to race to Guadalcanal and unload his fifteen hundred troops and their heavy weapons and supplies that night. He had based his decision on an earlier report that two American carriers had been left burning after the attacks on the twenty-fourth.

But Tanaka had not counted on Henderson Field's tiny air force being so effective. Because Mangrum arrived from the north, the Japanese crew who saw his planes approaching assumed they must be friendly. Tanaka later admitted that his force was caught by surprise.

Tanaka's flagship at the head of the convoy was the *Jinstū*, a Sendai-class light cruiser. Baldy's bomb struck right between the forward two main gun turrets and exploded belowdecks in the communications compartments. The blast killed twenty-four men and sprayed the bridge with shrapnel. Tanaka was blown off his feet and knocked unconscious.

McCafferty missed the destroyer steaming nearby. Hise and Thomas scored near misses on the *Jinstū*. Toward the back of the column, which totaled eight destroyers and three transports, Flight 300's Chris Fink did indeed hit the *Kinryu Maru* with his thousand-pounder. The explosion set off a chain reaction in the transport's holds as the 5th Special Naval Landing Force's heavy weapons and ammunition caught fire and blew up.

Tanaka regained consciousness to find the *Jinstū*'s bridge wreathed in smoke. With the ship's radio room destroyed, he transferred his flag to the destroyer *Kagerō* and ordered two patrol boats plus the destroyers *Yayoi* and *Mutsuki* to save as many men from the *Kinryu Maru* as possible. Moments later, Mangrum launched his solo attack on the 5,500-ton transport *Boston Maru*, inflicting some damage with his near miss off the stern and Dennis Byrd's strafing. That was the final straw for Tanaka. He abandoned the resupply mission to Guadalcanal and split his forces up. He ordered the *Jinstū* to head for Truk Atoll to be repaired, with one destroyer providing escort. The rest of the force steamed clear of air range from Guadalcanal, then made its way to the Shortland Islands in the Northern Solomon Islands. The Shortlands served as a forward naval base for runs to Guadalcanal.

A couple of hours later, a B-17 strike force attacked Tanaka's ships busily rescuing the crew of the *Kinryu Maru* and the thousand-man detachment from the 5th Special Naval Landing Force. The raid smashed the destroyer *Mutsuki*, sinking it alongside the *Kinryu Maru* in a matter of minutes.

Two bomb hits changed the dynamic of the Guadalcanal campaign that morning. Had Tanaka succeeded in getting those desperately needed troops, heavy weapons, and supplies to Guadalcanal, the Marine perimeter would have been imperiled. More important, Mangrum's crews imparted an indelible lesson on the Japanese: from this point on, daylight reinforcement missions with slow-moving transports would be exceptionally vulnerable to air attack from Henderson Field. The Japanese had to change their strategy and employ other means to get men and supplies to Guadalcanal. None were as effective as cargo ships with full combat loads of munitions and food.

In the coming weeks, the Japanese would start calling Guadalcanal Starvation Island, for obvious reasons. And they were starving because of the threat Mangrum's dive-bombers presented to any ships trying to reach Savo Sound in daylight. In fact, the August 25 mission ensured that the Japanese troops on Guadalcanal would never be properly supplied and set the tone for the rest of the campaign through the end of 1942.

The mission proved one other thing: the fighter pilots might get all the headlines, but the bomber crews made history.

TWENTY-FOUR
THE PRESENCE-OF-MIND DEFICIT

Henderson Field, Guadalcanal
August 26, 1942

JOHN LUCIAN SMITH LAY UNDER HIS MOSQUITO NETTING, LISTENING to Guadalcanal's eerie night sounds.

When he had served in the 10th Marines as an artillery officer in Puerto Rico, they had conducted field exercises in the island's jungle-covered mountains. That experience taught him how to survive in the heat amid the insects and wildlife. Already, some of the men on Guadalcanal were getting sick. Most of the illnesses so far were gastrointestinal—diarrhea was the main affliction. Bad food. Bad water. Lots of bloodsucking bugs. It was a recipe for a lot of stricken Marines. The line units that had been out in the jungle for weeks now were seeing a surge of malaria and dysentery cases. His squadron had only been on the island for six days. What would life be like by mid-September?

This was just one of a million worries keeping him awake that night. How ironic that on the one night with no Japanese attacks, his preoccupation with the stresses of command ensured that sleep wouldn't come easily.

He'd always excelled. He studied harder and worked harder, with a dogged sense of *no quit*, than most of his peers. Yet he was never the best.

Back at the University of Oklahoma, when he graduated with a class of 129 ROTC students in 1936, he was not among the 22 singled out with awards of cups and sabers for their performance. Nor was he awarded any of the leadership positions in the ROTC program. Yet, his academic achievement and his athleticism earned him a recommendation from the military science department and opened the door to his Marine Corps career.

John L. and his ROTC comrades graduated in May 1936. The ceremony for the ROTC class was held in front of the university's fine arts building as the school's fifteen hundred other students looked on. Henry McConnell earned top honors in the field artillery program. He went into the Corps along with John L., James Mills, and Preston Wood. Somewhere out in this chilly August night, Preston and James were sleeping under the same stars. James had taken part in the battle to clear Tulagi. Preston was somewhere in the perimeter, with his artillery battery.

They were his peers. His friends. His competitors. Perhaps in his mind, John L. never quite measured up, and that insecurity, layered under thick defensive walls, left him a little unsure of his own leadership ability.

With cause too. His commanding officers had had their doubts in the past. He breezed through the Basic School, graduating in 1937 before joining the 10th Marines. Once he was out in a line unit, his fitness reports contained a common theme. John L. was emotional. He lacked presence of mind.

What did these comments even mean? Some of his former skippers had studied him under stress and during tense moments. They concluded that John L. had a problem keeping calm in a storm. He needed self-control. He needed to learn to think and act clearly when things were going to hell, so that he could take sensible, decisive action.

In his heart, he lived in the shadow of those fitness reports, even as his peers from back home apparently thrived and earned quick promotions.

This squadron, this command? It was his redemptive moment, his opportunity to get this monkey off his back and prove to his superiors and to himself that he had the measure of the task. He could lead men into battle and make tough calls in the midst of the fray. He'd already shown this ability in the past week. Yet, he knew that the real tests remained on the horizon and that, to carry the squadron forward effectively, he would have to exercise self-control and suppress his natural emotional nature. In truth, his superiors were right about his emotions. At times, he was too quick-tempered, too quick to dig his heels in and fight stubbornly whatever admin battle came his way. If he thought he was right, he didn't know how to retreat. Every hill was the hill to die on. This attitude gave him a reputation for being a black-and-white kind of officer, one who was loyal to his people but who lacked the subtlety required to negotiate the politics resident in any level of command, especially prewar. That intractability made him enemies, sometimes powerful ones.

So he'd arrived on Guadalcanal at the head of a squadron that his command considered expendable. That made him expendable too. He was the skipper with a lot of lingering questions about his capabilities. Certainly, some people would consider his leadership style with VMF-223 way too informal. Let them judge. His pilots were good kids. Young, inexperienced, in need of that informal connection to their skipper. If they were all damned to be meat shields until the Corps and country could properly sustain this "offensive," then blurring the barriers between ranks hardly mattered. At very least, they would die together on a first-name basis.

When the *Long Island* stopped in Suva Bay, John L. slipped off the ship long enough to send a letter home to his father, Robert Owen. Everyone in Lexington called him R. O. and knew him well, since he'd been their mailman for three decades. He was a local icon, a good man, and John L. was very close to him. In fact, his father remained John L.'s primary next of kin even after he got married in 1941.

Dear Dad,

. . . This has been a pleasure cruise so far since we are passengers mainly. Certainly will be no vacation after we land, however. Don't expect any more trouble than we can handle.

That last line made him grimace now. Each of these six days on Guadalcanal had been a test to see exactly how much he could handle on every front: personnel, logistic, combat, and basic living conditions. Each day, he fought those multifront battles both in and out of his F4F's cockpit, only to find no respite after dark, like all the other sleep-deprived Marines on this island, thanks to the bombardments and the night raiders who dropped nuisance bombs to keep them awake.

The logistic situation for the two squadrons had grown extreme. In desperation, on August 25, Vandegrift told COMSOPAC HQ that he needed the rest of MAG-23 on Guadalcanal as soon as possible. He and the squadrons needed more aircraft, more aircrew, more spare parts, more oxygen bottles. Even more fuel.

With everything in extremely short supply, operations were forced to change on the twenty-sixth. No longer could the squadrons sustain their standing patrols. Instead, the F4Fs would be sent aloft as a full squadron—every available plane and pilot—only after Henderson received warning of an impending bombing raid. This new plan in itself was a little problematic. A team of radar operators and technicians had come ashore earlier in the month, but their radar sets never got unloaded before the Navy pulled out and retreated after the Savo Island disaster. They tried to get a captured Japanese radar system up and running, but they simply couldn't figure it out. These problems left the Americans totally reliant on a small group of Australian, New Zealander, and British officers operating as Coastwatchers behind the lines in the Central and Northern Solomons. They could tip off Guadalcanal via radio whenever they saw an outbound Japanese air raid heading their way. There would be no time to send coded messages. It took too long to encode and decode such traffic. Instead, the Coastwatchers broadcast by voice, in the clear and with no code, to give Henderson Field maximum time to prepare for the incoming raid.

The Coastwatchers would prove extremely reliable. But with no backup should the observers miss a raid because of weather or other issues, this plan, which kept the F4Fs on the ground until warned, entailed a measure of risk. A raid might sneak through, riding above a cloud front that masked it from prying eyes below. Or a Japanese carrier might slip through again and try its hand at knocking Henderson out. In a worst-case scenario, the Japanese might triangulate the radio broadcasts and take out the Coastwatchers.

Everything on Guadalcanal required balancing the squadron's practical and logistic limitations with the risks they had to take to operate within those bounds. Such a balancing act would make any squadron leader lose sleep.

The squadron would have to spend dawn to dusk close to their F4Fs at the parking area, waiting for the word to scramble. The men would have to trust they'd get more warning than they had on the twenty-fifth. The F4F was no vertical rocket ship. The aircraft needed time to claw their way up to twenty-five thousand feet, get upsun, and wait in ambush for the incoming raiders. It meant burning through the squadron's very limited supply of oxygen bottles. And it meant hour after hour of tension for the men assigned to fly that day.

The demands of each day would be hard on his pilots, and he would have to rotate them to keep them from burning out or reaching their breaking point. Yet, VMF-223 simply did not have the flyers to do rotations effectively, especially after the last few days of combat. Already they were down Elwood Bailey and Red Taylor. John L. had received word that Rapid Robert Read was safe at Tulagi yesterday, but it would be days before the second lieutenant would be back and ready to fly. After being wounded twice, he had swum two miles to shore before the locals rescued him.

John L. knew Fred Gutt's wounds needed better hospital care than existed on Guadalcanal, so he'd secured him space on a B-17 that came in on the twenty-fifth. It would go out at dawn with Fred Gutt, Freeman, and Robert MacLeod. Freeman's bell had been rung when he crashed on a test flight on the twenty-fourth. His F4F had gone into a flat spin and flung him around before he could hit the silk. He landed hard in Savo Sound. Since he was a VMF-212 pilot on temporary duty, it was best to send him back to Efate to recover with Gutt.

MacLeod was a locker-room cancer whom the other pilots couldn't stand. Since he was also from VMF-212, John L. used the B-17's availability to get rid of him. As skipper of 212, Joe Bauer probably knew the guy was a bully and a talker. MacLeod was Joe's problem, not John L.'s.[1]

By 0700, VMF-223 would be down six pilots. With four from 212 still on temporary duty with the squadron, John L. had nineteen aviators to crew his twelve remaining F4F Wildcats. No matter how they put the morning flight roster together, some of his kids would have to fly at least a couple of days in a row. Optimally, they would fly every other day or, even better, one day for every two days off. Again, the practical realities of Guadalcanal threatened to burn out his young aviators very quickly. They would just have to tough it out, with Rivers, Marion, and John L. himself setting the example and shouldering as much of the load as they could.

John L. was already worried about Zen Pond. While there was still hope that Bailey might show up as Rapid Robert Read had, each day eroded the chances that Bailey would return. Zen started to take the loss of his best friend harder and harder as hope waned. Still, the young pilot kept himself on flight status and, in front of the other men, refused to show how much he was hurting. This was a test of emotional, as well as physical, endurance. And he was measuring up.

There would be more tests like that one for every man in the squadron in the days ahead. John L. suspected the enemy had only been testing them, sizing them up for the big blows to follow. If that was true, his men would need steady, capable, and inspiring leadership to hold themselves together, to do some real damage to the Japanese, and to take the punishment sure to come. And that's where those dark clouds of administrative judgment—his fitness reports—played on his mind. His superiors questioned his decision-making in a crisis. He would have to prove them wrong. And when the time came, John L. would shove that searing judgment right down their throats.

Just as important, John L. would need to lead the way through the trials ahead with a steel-tough heart. He'd need all his stubbornness to show his men how to take the hits and stay in the fight, no matter how hard the blows landed. He'd have to set the example by showing that his spirit was unbreakable.

But was it?

TWENTY-FIVE

THE JAPANESE FLYING DUTCHMAN

Henderson Field, Guadalcanal
August 26, 1942, 1124 hours

TWELVE MINUTES AFTER A COASTWATCHER ON NEW GEORGIA
spotted the day's incoming Japanese raid, the news reached
VMF-223 at Henderson Field. The air raid warning screamed to life.
The duty pilots lounging beside their F4Fs grabbed their gear and piled
into their cockpits. Across the runway, Dick Mangrum's SBD crews fired
up their birds and prepared to clear the airfield so that they wouldn't be
caught by bombs on the ground.

Taking off two at a time, the pilots got all twelve Wildcats into the
air in a matter of minutes. They formed up into divisions while climbing furiously. John L. led the way with Doc Everton on his wing and
Tex Hamilton and Midway vet Roy Corry as his second section. Behind
them came Rivers Morrell with Zen Pond, and Willis Lees with Scotty
McLennan. Last off the strip, Marion Carl brought up the rear of the
strung-out squadron formation with Eugene Trowbridge, Ken Frazier,
and 212's John King.

Below 223, Dick Mangrum's pilots sped off the field and made themselves scarce. Day six of operations on Guadalcanal, and the Marines
had locked down full-squadron scrambles. It took just over ten minutes

to empty Henderson of all flyable aircraft. Left behind were a couple of F4Fs and an SBD, all nonoperational for want of parts.

The enemy bombers came in at twenty-five thousand feet, moving fast in a tight vee-of-vee formation. Because their steady course required minimal changes to fly over Henderson and drop their bombs, they were able to keep up their speed. Sixteen strong, they hit their initial point at almost noon sharp, opening their bomb bay doors while their bombardiers hunched over their sights. Three minutes later, a torrent of bombs plummeted down on the airfield. A string of 500-pounders struck the runway, digging deep craters out of the gravel and soil. Incendiaries and fragmentation bombs struck the parking area, peppering the unserviceable aircraft with shrapnel.

Then a bomb scored a direct hit on one of the avgas dumps stashed around the field. This site included about forty 55-gallon drums, all of which went off with an enormous *whoosh* and blast. The flames and explosion detonated two of the thousand-pound bombs acquired from the *Saratoga*'s air group. Their two massive detonations blew more than a dozen other thousand-pound bombs all over the area. They landed around the original blast site in various states of damage—though none of them cooked off. Clearing those bombs would be a nightmare for the engineers.

The Mitsubishi G4Ms held their course, passing the airfield as they escaped initially to the east. They were at about twenty-four thousand feet now. That's when John L. and seven of his Wildcats pounced. Using almost the last of their oxygen stocks, the Marines managed to get to twenty-six thousand feet, missing the chance to intercept the bombers before they reached the target. But better late than never. Lacking the altitude for a proper overhead run on the formation, John L. led his division down in a high side pass on the portside vee of three Betties. The idea was to force the Japanese gunners to use a lot of deflection to minimize the Wildcats' chance of being hit during their runs. The Americans also believed that the Betties had a blind spot off each wing, making their high deflection runs almost impervious to return fire.

The Wildcats dove at the big green Betties, the F4F pilots noting that the Japanese planes looked similar to the Army Air Forces B-26

Marauder. The consummate professional, John L. held his fire, angling his run to stay out of the line of return fire as much as possible. A sharp, quick series of bursts from his six guns, and he rolled skyward and to port, climbing above the bombers to set up another pass. He quickly checked his six, maintaining his situational awareness. No Zeroes. In fact, there didn't even seem to be a fighter escort. That was simply too good to be true.

Behind him, Doc Everton's hands shook on the stick and throttle as he tried to line up on one of the bombers. Filled with nerves and fear, he'd lost some of his small motor coordination. He could feel the F4F mirroring his nervousness as he translated it through the controls. When he opened fire at four hundred yards, his bullets sprayed out in a useless fan behind his targeted G4M.

He hadn't used enough lead. With only a couple of seconds left before he'd have to break off the attack, he pulled his nose forward of the G4M and tried again. This time, he saw pieces of debris tumble backward from the Betty. He held his trigger down, hammering the G4M until smoke started to pour from its right engine. A second later, he barreled right over the front of the bomber formation, using the speed he'd accumulated in his dive to zoom back up above them to get into position for a second run.

Tex Hamilton and Roy Corry entered the fray at almost the same time as the rest of the division. Hamilton, perhaps the most experienced Marine in the air that day, executed a precise high side pass, mirroring John L.'s attack. But Corry ignored the standing squadron policy: never attack a bomber from dead astern. At Midway, he'd concluded that the best way to shoot planes down was to get dead astern of them and then to nearly point-blank range before unloading a fusillade of .50-caliber bullets on the Japanese.

He did just that, eschewing the high side pass the other three pilots made and diving down directly behind one vee of bombers. The three Japanese tail gunners unleased a cross fire on him. He hurtled his plane into it in a bid to get even closer. The Japanese gunners, shooting without deflection, scored hit after hit. Corry held his course, but the Wildcat took too much damage. It suddenly snapped into a spin and dropped out of the fight. Doc Everton thought he saw the Wildcat explode on the water a few minutes later.

Corry bailed out, and at Henderson, a keen-eyed observer on the ground saw his aircraft fall out of the sky and Corry's chute trailing behind it. The parachute never fully deployed. Corry fell twenty-four thousand feet with a half-opened chute. Nobody saw where he landed. His premonition of death had become a grim and terrible reality.

Rivers Morrell and his pilots joined the fight as the Betties made a shallow left turn that took them out over Savo Sound toward Florida Island. The American pilots attacking from the starboard side of the formation suddenly found themselves on the outside of their turn, a position that made catching the Japanese much more problematic. The Betties porpoised up and down, climbing five hundred feet, diving five hundred feet, in hopes of spoiling the Marines' gunnery.

The second lieutenants had never seen anything like this before: the sixteen Betties in tight vees spread across about three-quarters of a mile of airspace. There were targets everywhere. The Marines made their runs without focus or discipline, spraying at the formations rather than staying on one target. It was a rookie mistake, and Zen, Willis, and Scotty failed to shoot any of the bombers down.

John L. and Doc started down into their second passes at almost the exact same time, sweeping into the bomber formation from opposite sides. Doc was settled now, the fear and nerves replaced by a strange calm in the presence of so much speeding danger around him. His hands stopped shaking on the controls as he winged over and roared down on the starboard side of the formation. He spotted the Betty he'd hit on the first run. Its engine smoking, the aircraft was slowly dropping behind its comrades. Doc arrowed after it, snapping out long bursts as he closed the distance. His bullets threshed their way across the Betty's fuselage and wing root, detonating the starboard-side fuel tank. Spewing flames and debris, the big bomber rolled left and fell into a steep dive.

John L. raced past Doc, shooting up another bomber while cutting across the formation in the opposite direction. Once again, as he pulled out, the Oklahoman checked the sky around them for Zeroes. Still none in sight. It seemed almost too good to be true.

The Betties finished their left-hand turn near the north tip of Malaita. They were on their homebound course now, throttles wide as they tried to run from the savage Marine attacks. The F4Fs dove again and again after them from either side of the formation. Another Betty caught fire and turned back toward Guadalcanal, Doc in hot pursuit. Others limped along, shot up and streaming tails of smoke, advertising their crippled status to the eager Marines.

The green-brown planes, not the men inside them, were the targets to be destroyed. The distance and nature of air combat provided a barrier to the killing that their .50-calibers inflicted that morning. For young men unused to the violence of combat, the focus on the hardware, not the men inside, provided a safe mental cushion. As Doc Everton later said, "What made me feel good was not the thought of those Japs with smoke choking them and fire jumping in their faces. Their number was up, and of course they knew it. But a pilot doesn't think about that. He shoots at the planes, not the men."

As the Betties fled, some of the Marines ran out of ammunition and dove out of the fight, heading back to Henderson. Tex thought he'd knocked down two bombers before his guns went dry. He radioed to John L. and Doc that he was done and turned for home. Rivers Morrell and his three second lieutenants soon followed.

Now it was just John L. and Doc against the battered formation. They counted twelve bombers left at this point. They still had ammo and enough fuel for a few more runs. As both pilots climbed on either side of the Betties, the Japanese did something totally unexpected. Instead of staying in their tight, protective vees, they fanned out into line-abreast formations, three or four bombers in each section. There seemed to be no reason for this formation, which mitigated the power of their collective defensive firepower.

John L. called out over the radio, "There's the table spread. Help yourself, Doc."

Into the attack they went, guns chattering, eyes fixed on their gunsight reticles as they calculated lead and dragged their bullet streams

John L. Smith was a young captain without much time in fighters when he was given command of newly formed VMF-223 shortly before the Battle of Midway. In the months that followed, his squadron's ranks were filled with hastily trained pilots with little experience flying fighters. The Corps gave him less than a month to forge these raw citizen-warriors into an effective combat force. (National Archives)

Marion Carl, seen here at Pearl Harbor after VMF-223's fifty-three days on Guadalcanal. Young, even-keeled, and deadly in air combat, he was John L. Smith's best combat aviator. Carl joined VMF-223 shortly after surviving the Battle of Midway, where most of his squadron had been wiped out in a single dogfight with the Japanese. (National Archives)

The hero tour photo op, November 10, 1942. L-R: John L. Smith, Richard Mangrum, Marion Carl, seen at NAS Anacostia before a *Life* magazine photographer captured John L.'s ruggedness while in the cockpit of an F4F Wildcat. That photo made the cover of *Life* and forever enshrined the Oklahoma native as one of the greatest early war heroes to emerge from the Pacific. (National Archives)

John L. Smith in the cockpit of an F4F during the photo shoot at NAS Anacostia. For a brief few weeks that fall of 1942, John L. was the leading American ace with nineteen planes to his credit. He would be awarded the Medal of Honor in February 1943. The award, and his time on Guadalcanal, lingered like a shadow over the rest of his life. (National Archives)

LTC Richard "Dick" Mangrum, the statesman of the three Marine aviators who came home to be thrown into the hero tour. Born in Washington State, he graduated from the University of Washington's law school while serving as a Marine reservist. By 1942, he was one of the most experienced pilots in the Corps. He commanded dive-bomber squadron VMSB-232 on Guadalcanal, the first offensive air power to reach the island. (author's collection)

The dreadful Brewster F2A Buffalo was the aircraft most of the VMF-223 pilots flew before joining John L. Smith. Marion Carl's squadron on Midway was largely equipped with F2As. The lack of armor plating behind the pilot's head probably served as a key reason why the squadron lost nineteen of its twenty-six pilots in less than an hour and a half of combat. (National Archives)

Lt. Tom Hamilton (left), coach of Navy's football team, talks to Cadet Rivers Morrell, Navy's captain, shortly before the 1936 game against Army. Rivers served as John L. Smith's executive officer in VMF-223. He distinguished himself in combat and proved an outstanding leader. For his time with 223, he was awarded a Navy Cross, a Distinguished Flying Cross, and a Purple Heart. (author's collection)

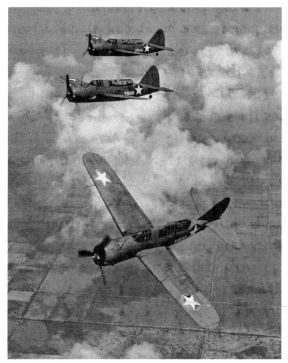

Dick Mangrum test-flew the Brewster SB2A Buccaneer during the New York City leg of the hero tour. The Navy counted on Brewster to replace the aging SBD Dauntless VMSB-232 took into combat at Guadalcanal. One flight convinced Dick the SB2A was a dog. The Navy ultimately relegated it to training duties only, and the Curtiss SB2C Helldiver would eventually take the SBD's place during the final year of the Pacific War. (author's collection)

The first escort carrier, CVE-1, USS *Long Island*. She and her sister ships were rush jobs all the way, quickly converted from merchant ships to carriers in ninety days. Many corners were cut along the way, making the *Long Island* of minimal use in combat. However, the lessons learned from her reconstruction were applied to later generations of escort carriers, which would go on to play crucial roles in the Atlantic and Pacific campaigns. For the *Long Island* and her crew, rushing Smith's and Mangrum's men to Guadalcanal became their closest brush with combat. (National Archives)

An F4F Wildcat is catapulted off the *Long Island*. The hasty conversion from merchant ship to aircraft carrier necessitated placing the ship's catapult at a steep angle to port. Shortly after she was completed, she returned to the yard and had her flight deck lengthened. That modification put the catapult dozens of yards back from the end of the flight deck. The result was a very dangerous and marginally useful system that nearly caused several of Smith's and Mangrum's pilots to crash when launched off Guadalcanal. (National Archives)

Henderson Field, Guadalcanal, as seen from one of Dick Mangrum's SBDs on August 22, 1942, the first day of flight operations for VMF-223 and VMSB-232. The field was primitive, dangerous, and, more often than not, taking fire from the nearby jungle, where Japanese snipers and machine gunners lurked. (National Archives)

One of VMSB-232's battered SBDs being readied for another mission at Henderson Field. By day two, the underside of their wings and fuselages were peppered with dents, their dive flaps damaged, and their props chipped from the gravel the engineers laid down on the runway. (National Archives)

Dick Mangrum stands in front of VMSB-232's operations headquarters tent. In the first days at Henderson Field, the aviators didn't even have tents. The ground crews and gunners slept under the SBDs, and the pilots bunked down under tarps. Getting a tent for the squadron HQ was a big step up on Starvation Island. (USMC)

An SBD over Henderson Field armed with a 500-pound bomb, the standard load for a ship-search mission. At the start of the fifty-three days, the squadron only had these bombs. Later, thanks to a passing Navy strike group that refueled at Henderson, then left their ordnance behind, 232 was able to acquire some heavier, ship-busting 1,000-pound bombs. (National Archives)

The ground crews at Henderson Field established themselves as some of the most devoted, selfless men on the island. They worked under miserable conditions with virtually no equipment, sometimes taking artillery or small arms fire, to keep the available aircraft flying. Most had been in the military for less than a year. These men of the 67th Fighter Squadron worked under the added burden of not having any tech manuals for their unit's Bell P-400 Airacobras. (USMC)

Marine engineers tried to improve Henderson Field by laying pierced steel planking down (PSP) atop the gravel as succeeding transport runs brought the material to Guadalcanal. It helped but came at a price. Bombs and heavy artillery shells tore the PSP up, creating deadly obstacles for the aviators that slashed open tires and caused landing and takeoff accidents. (National Archives)

The burnt remains of a Marine SBD Dauntless destroyed by a Japanese attack. By mid-September, VMSB-232 was down to only a few operational planes out of the twelve they brought to Henderson on August 21. (National Archives)

The Japanese Mitsubishi G4M "Betty" bomber was the standard aircraft used to strike the Marines at Guadalcanal. Their destruction became John L. Smith's top priority, and most of the battles VMF-223 fought centered on trying to penetrate the A6M Zero fighter screen to destroy the G4Ms before they could bomb Henderson Field. (National Archives)

Cactus Air Force's nerve center, the "Pagoda." It sat atop a hill overlooking Henderson Field and served as the heart of operations there until mid-October. It was finally demolished by the Marines themselves, who began to suspect it could be seen by Japanese ships offshore and served as their aiming point during the night bombardment attacks. (USMC)

John L. Smith sits at the wheel of a jeep, the exhaustion, tension, and grief evident on his face. This photo, taken late in their fifty-three-day deployment, shows the psychological toll defending Guadalcanal from bombing raids took on the young Marine pilots. L-R: Marion Carl, Rapid Robert Read, John L. Smith. Back row: Jack Conger (from VMF-212) and Cloyd "Rex" Jeans. (USMC)

The destruction wrought on VMSB-232's living area by the mid-September bombardments. Mangrum's men emerged from the Battle of Bloody Ridge traumatized by the naval gunfire and artillery that demolished their camp and killed key members of the squadron. (USMC)

The aftermath of the Battle of Edson's Ridge. Japanese and Marine Raiders lay dead and intermingled as the fighting over those two brutal nights devolved into desperate hand-to-hand combat. The fate of the Marine perimeter hinged on the 800 Raiders who held firm and blunted General Kawaguchi's 3,500-man assault force. (USMC)

Arthur O'Keefe poses with one of his beloved cameras in Hawai'i before Guadalcanal. He was VMSB-232's seriously injured pilot who pleaded with Mangrum not to be left behind on the *Long Island* the morning of the launch off Guadalcanal. He was evacuated from Henderson in mid-September, stricken with malaria and nearly broken after witnessing the deaths of two close friends. He returned to combat flying on Iwo Jima, where he earned a second Distinguished Flying Cross for his bravery under fire. In 1947, he took command of VMF-223, one of the last MAG-23 vets to lead John L. Smith's beloved squadron. (Mike O'Keefe)

John L. Smith and the men of 223 on October 10, 1942, shortly before they left Starvation Island. The pilots were celebrating their last combat mission and Fred Gutt's twenty-third birthday. (USMC)

October 1, 1942, Admiral Chester Nimitz presented awards to some of Guadalcanal's defenders during a short visit to the island. At far right is John L. Smith, who received a Navy Cross along with Marion Carl and VMF-224's skipper, Robert Galer. To the shock of these men, Dick Mangrum received a DFC, a lower award. Nimitz had run out of Navy Crosses to give. The apparent snub affected morale and the ceremony was not well remembered. Within days, several of the men honored that day would be killed in action. (USMC)

John L. Smith, Bob Galer, and Marion Carl wear their freshly awarded Navy Crosses on October 1, shortly after Nimitz's departure. Galer complained bitterly in his diary that so many deserving men were overlooked by the short, impromptu gathering. He, John L., and Dick Mangrum vowed to ensure their men would receive the awards their courage and devotion deserved no matter how long it took. (National Archives)

Back in the States, after a whirlwind romance that lasted only a few weeks, Marion Carl married Edna Kirvin. Their wedding and honeymoon in Oregon made national news. They stayed together for over half a century as Marion shattered records, returned to combat twice, and rose to the rank of major general before he finally retired in the early 1970s. (author's collection)

Bruce Prosser, the operations officer for VMSB-232, grew up in Oregon and first saw combat at the Battle of Midway. He was wounded in the bombardment during Edson's Ridge and evacuated from Guadalcanal shortly after the battle. He returned to battle later in the war, serving in the Central Pacific, the Philippines, and Okinawa while racking up 114 total combat dives, more than any other Marine dive-bomber pilot. (Jack Cook collection via Bruce Prosser)

A6M5 Zero fighters captured on Saipan head for the US for testing aboard the escort carrier USS *Copahee*. The A6M5 tried to address some of the weaknesses in the A6M2 that the air war over Guadalcanal and New Guinea exposed, including better armor plate protection for the pilot and self-sealing fuel tanks. Still, by 1944, the Zero was an aging design long surpassed by the planes John L. and Marion Carl flew that day on *Long Island*—the F4U Corsair and the F6F Hellcat. Incidentally, one of the Zeroes in this photo continues to fly to this day with the Planes of Fame Museum in Chino, California. (National Archives)

The captured wreck of a downed Tainan Air Group A6M Zero, seen at Port Moresby, New Guinea, in the fall of 1942. The Tainan Air Group faced a difficult double mission: help destroy the Fifth Air Force defending Moresby while simultaneously trying to defeat the Cactus Air Force on Guadalcanal. The grinding long-range escort missions wore the unit out and cost Japan the core of its most elite fighter pilots. (author's collection)

across their targets. It was pure mayhem, these two aggressive Americans against a shot-up and demoralized formation of unescorted bombers. Doc saw another of his targets drop out of formation. John L. jumped on it, chasing it as the Betty dropped below and behind the safety of the bomber herd.

Doc pulled up into a steep climb. He had perhaps a couple of bursts' worth of ammunition for his guns. Leveling out at twenty-eight thousand feet, he looked down at the long line of Betties. He picked out a new target and rolled into a steep overhead pass. Just as he got off one long burst that caused the Betty to start smoking, his guns jammed. He was eighty miles from Guadalcanal now, his fuel tanks nearly empty. He called to John L. and broke for home.

The skipper was alone now.

Down he went after the crippled Betty, setting up another high side run on it as the bomber continued its shallow descent. Though the G4M was fast and even faster in a dive, the F4F ran it down without serious trouble. John L. winged over and started his curving attack, pulling his nose across the target and gauging the lead he'd need to do it.

He'd drilled into his men that it wasn't enough just to aim at an airplane. As in deer hunting, you didn't want to hit just anywhere. Bullet placement was key. There were three areas of vulnerability to aim for in a bomber: the cockpit, the engines, and the fuel tanks. The tanks were assumed to be in the wing roots, right alongside the fuselage, and gave the largest target area. The Betty's greenhouse cockpit was the hardest of the three vital spots to hit—like scoring a head shot on a deer.

Closing fast now, he triggered his guns and raked the Betty. He had it dead to rights; another second or two, and his guns would finish it off. But his guns suddenly fell silent. Out of ammunition.

The Betty didn't waver. It simply continued its shallow dive with its wings level. John L. kept on course, watching the aircraft closely. He noticed that none of the gun positions were sending tracers his way. He rolled level and matched the Betty's course and speed, just behind and off its left wing.

He could see plenty of battle damage across the fuselage and wings. Smoke poured from the starboard engine. A fire burned inside the fuselage. The bomber's metal skin was ripped and holed. Fifty-caliber bullets did terrible things to metal and flesh. The squadron's armorers linked their ammunition belts with a one-for-one mix of tracers for aiming, AP for maximum damage, and incendiary bullets to spark fires. A single burst could pulverize metal, penetrate armor, and ignite anything flammable. In this moment, John L. received an object lesson on just what that looked like. The Japanese bomber was a flying wreck.

The blister gunner in the side fuselage waist position would have had an excellent shot at him, but there was nobody there to shoot the gun. The dorsal blister gun was cocked at an odd angle away from him. Not a threat.

He inched closer, fascinated, fixated on the enemy plane. The Marines did not know much about Japanese bombers, so the professional in him studied its armament. He could tell that the dorsal gun and the waist blister guns were light machine guns, but the tail stinger was something different. John L. could see it through the greenhouse: a heavier, longer weapon than the others. It was a 20 mm cannon for sure. No wonder why Roy Corry had been shot down so quickly. He'd been caught in a cross fire of three autocannons. No Wildcat could survive that kind of punishment for long.

He checked the sky. No Zeroes. Still no counterfire from the Betty. As he edged even closer, the details of the aircraft came into view. The waist blister was empty for sure. No crewman. His eyes roamed forward to the dorsal position. It was shot up, the gunner in there struck by .50-caliber bullets. John L. could see what was left of him in the blood-soaked ruins of his turret. A single .50-caliber round possesses the kinetic energy to turn a man into shredded flesh. It will rip limbs from bodies and blow chunks from midsections. It remains to this day one of the most destructive and powerful machine guns ever built.

The Marine inched forward until he was even with the bomber's wings. He peered at the cockpit, looking for the pilots. Nothing. He moved forward to get a better view. The shattered cockpit looked empty. Nobody was at the bomber's controls. The pilots had been torn apart. The Betty was a ghost craft now, crewless, smoke wreathed, and doomed. Like an aerial Flying Dutchman.

John L. eased off the throttle just a bit, dropping back along the bomber's fuselage. Movement caught his eye, and he turned his head to get a better view of the tail stinger. The gunner there was still alive, frantically moving around in the smoke. Did he have a parachute? Was he trapped? John L. couldn't tell. He looked to be the only man alive inside the aircraft.

They passed through three thousand feet now. The other bombers were far overhead and to the north, approaching Santa Isabel. It was just the Marine pilot and Japanese gunner now, the water below seemingly rising to them as the G4M continued its uncontrolled descent. Flames licked through the fuselage, illuminating the interior through the windows and bullet tears. If the gunner couldn't get out, he faced burning alive before the aircraft impacted on the water. John L. could not take his eyes off him.

Suddenly, a chunk of the tail's greenhouse broke away and spun off in the slipstream. The gunner fell out, tumbling downward behind his dying bomber. John L. watched him writhing and spinning in free fall, waiting for his chute to open.

He didn't have one. He chose a terrifying death by free fall over burning alive in the charnel house the Betty had become.

John L. followed the bomber and watched it strike the water a minute or so after the gunner's death. In seconds, the bright blue Pacific swallowed all signs that the Betty had ever existed.

There were men inside these machines. Their brethren on the ground were vicious and savage; stories of their atrocities circulated through the Marine ranks every day. Yet, a man is still a man. In that moment, as John L. flew home alone, the image of that gunner plunging to his death lingered in his mind. The cushion between deeds and the reality of the killing they inflicted with those deeds ceased to exist. There was no glory here, just the ugliness produced by violence and war.

TWENTY-SIX

ONE CHANCE TO LIVE

Guadalcanal
August 26, 1942, noon

MARION CARL'S DIVISION NEVER MADE IT TO THE BETTIES. LAST to take off, the squadron was thousands of feet below the other eight F4Fs. In a weird twist, its positioning helped alter the balance of power between the Japanese at Rabaul and the Marines defending Guadalcanal.

Marion was climbing after the rest of the squadron—Eugene Trow-bridge, Ken Frazier, and John King right with him—when he and the others spotted a formation of Zeroes at fourteen thousand feet, heading back toward Guadalcanal. In all likelihood, the A6M pilots had assumed that their escort duties were done after the Marines had failed to materi-alize before the bombers hit the field. Figuring the Betties were safely on their way home, the Zeroes turned back for Henderson and started losing altitude in preparation to give the field a thorough strafing-up.

It was a tactically perfect situation for Marion. He was far above the Zeroes for a change, and they clearly hadn't seen his four Wildcats. He called out the Mitsubishis to the rest of his division, then rolled down on the unsuspecting Japanese. To his surprise, he saw that the A6Ms still retained their external fuel tanks tucked under their centerlines. That would make their fighters slower and less maneuverable, at least until they could be jettisoned.

The Zero pilots never saw the Marines coming. In the first pass, the stubby American flyers cut down two fighters, one of which was the lead in a three-plane section. The other was the lead's wingman.

The fight was quick and one-sided. Eugene, Ken, and Marion all thought they had destroyed a Zero. Through that first run, though, the Marines became separated as they maneuvered for the high ground, the Zeroes giving chase. Down the Americans went again, guns flashing. The Zeroes dodged and fired back whenever they got an opportunity.

At some point, Marion dove out of the fight. Enough was enough— he'd done some damage, and tangling with those Mitsubishis for long drained energy and altitude. Those were the only things that evened the odds against such a supremely maneuverable and fast-climbing aircraft like the A6M.

Marion reached Henderson and swung into the pattern, heading along the north side of the strip toward the hills. He looped back onto the downwind leg and dropped his landing gear. He would land from the coast-side end of the runway, his fourth mission since August 23 complete. His Wildcat, "Black Thirteen," had carried him through every engagement without major damage. It was a near miracle and a testament to how smart Marion fought.

Just as he was about to turn onto base leg and run across the beach to the edge of the strip, a flurry of tracers suddenly filled the sky around his Wildcat. He immediately knew this wasn't ground fire from Japanese in the jungle beyond the perimeter taking potshots at him. A quick look over his shoulder confirmed that a Zero was back there, diving on him and closing fast. Muzzle flashes lit the leading edge of its wings, and two more shots flared from atop the cowling. Under the fuselage, the Zero still had its belly tank. That was a crucial mistake. That Zero would be sluggish and slower than usual. Marion realized it might just give him the edge to survive this aerial ambush.

Marion was only at a few hundred feet, but he jerked the stick forward and right, diving and turning sharply toward an antiaircraft gun position near the end of the runway. The gunners saw him coming, saw the Zero behind him, and realized it was a life-and-death moment. They unloaded on the Japanese plane, which broke off and sped over Marion, making for Savo Sound.

The Marine leveled off, pushed his throttle to full power, then started cranking up his landing gear. He couldn't continue to land. The Zero might come back and finish him off. The Wildcat was too slow to run away. All Marion could do was fight.

The Zero pilot ran for it, Marion in slow pursuit. The Oregonian realized that trying to catch him would be impossible—even with its belly tank, the Zero was probably going twice as fast as the Wildcat. Yet the Marine kept his guns and nose pointed at the threat in case the Japanese came back.

Captain Carl passed over the beach, his wings wobbling as he furiously worked the landing gear's hand crank. Finally, he heard the wheels clunk into place and lock. Just in time too. The Zero pilot was turning around for another pass.

Challenge accepted.

A single Wildcat down low against a Zero stood little chance. The F4F's best play against the A6M was a high-speed diving attack. One pass, haul ass. Turning with a Zero was a death sentence. So was climbing with one. Down low, there was no realm where the F4F reigned superior to the Mitsubishi. The Japanese held every advantage but one: durability went to the Grumman.

The Japanese was almost through his turn. The American struggled to get his speed up; the heavy and underpowered Grumman was never going to win a drag race. Still, Marion coaxed every ounce of speed out of Black Thirteen.

The Zero completed its 180-degree turn. It came straight at Marion, head-to-head like an aerial version of a medieval joust. Now they were on a collision course, neither pilot wavering. Below them, thousands of Marines who had just undergone the bombing attack climbed out of their slit trenches and dugouts to watch this one-on-one aerial duel.

The Japanese pilot had just handed Marion the one fight he could win. Head-to-head, he could rake the Zero with the incredible destructive power of his six .50-caliber Brownings. At the last second, the Japanese pilot seemed to realize his mistake. He should have kept heading north, climbing to establish a superior position. But he still had a chance. A quick zoom-climb, half loop, and roll would put him above and behind the F4F.

He pulled up too soon, thinking Marion could never follow him. The Oregonian saw the Zero stand on its tail, suddenly zooming for altitude just as he got into effective range. In past dogfights, a P-40, P-39, or Wildcat that tried to follow a Zero through a maneuver like this would have never been able to catch the Japanese plane. The Americans would have bled off their speed and their ability to maneuver, leaving themselves ripe for a killing blow.

If Marion ducked under the Zero and kept going, to build his speed up, the Zero pilot would have simply dropped behind him and killed him. That was a consequence of not having the energy for the fight. He only had one chance, a snap shot at the skyward-fleeing Zero. To do that required pulling nearly vertical after the A6M. If he missed, he'd be dead: low, slow, and out of options.

Marion committed, depending on his marksmanship to keep him alive. He pulled up into a steep climb, dragging his gunsight reticle across the Zero's belly to a point ahead of its nose. It was a ninety-degree deflection shot, the hardest kind to make in air combat, and one that only a handful of pilots were ever good at.

Marion Carl was one of those, and he didn't miss. His bullets lashed out, tracers seemingly linking the two aircraft for a split second. The Zero exploded in a brilliant red and yellow ball of fire. Its remains tumbled into the coconut grove just in from the beach, filling the area with flaming debris and fuel.

The pilots of VMSB-232 watching the fight from the ground saw the stunning gambit, saw Marion's deadly accuracy and the guts game he'd played to get the shot. They cheered along with countless other Marines as the remains of the Japanese aircraft smashed into the trees, the beach, and the surf. It was a morale moment never to be forgotten—one of their tormentors had been sent to his grave in an epic man-against-man duel.

Marion circled the wreck and then swung back over the airfield, dropping his gear again and landing. Behind him, the rest of the squadron straggled in and set down. They met in the parking area, slapping one another on the back, flying with their hands, and checking out the bullet holes in their F4Fs. The mood was light and happy. They had inflicted considerable damage and were eager to celebrate.

When John L. finally arrived to join them, though, his eyes were stern and his lips tight. He said little as the men let off steam and gathered to debrief the fight. Reporters Bob Miller and Richard Tregaskis arrived to observe the scene just as the pilots entered a half-built, damaged Japanese hangar beside the parking area, where Dick Mangrum waited with a notebook in hand. Apparently, he was filling in for Lieutenant Colonel Fike that day, and he began to document the mission.

The other pilots dubbed Marion Carl "the Zero Man," a name he took in quiet stride, offering a hint of a smile to indicate he didn't mind the moniker. While he related his mission to Mangrum, some of the 223 pilots sidled up to Tregaskis and whispered high praise about Carl. "He's a natural. Always relaxed" was a familiar refrain.

When he finished up with Dick Mangrum, Tregaskis approached Marion and asked him how the Zeroes here compared with those he faced at Midway.

"I dunno why," Marion replied, "but we got shot up a lot more there than we do here. Maybe the pilots were better than these."

The cheerful atmosphere suddenly vanished when Dick asked if anyone was missing. John L. replied, "One. Roy Corry."

A sudden swell of guilt swept the room. Faces went from happy excitement to stoic and silent. Corry wasn't particularly close to anyone, and his fixation on his own death made the men uncomfortable. Still, it seemed inappropriate to be euphoric when one of their own was gone.

Somebody broke the silence. "Maybe he'll turn up."

Echoing the sentiment, somebody else said, "Yeah, like Read did yesterday."

Zen Pond, perhaps thinking of Bailey again, looked stricken.

The pilots drifted back to their aircraft in small groups to talk with their plane captain. Mangrum finished his interviews. As some of the men walked over to one of the squadron's jeeps and piled in, John L. took Rivers Morrell and Marion Carl aside. He'd listened to everyone's descriptions of their attacks. The second lieutenants had underperformed. This had been their first real bomber intercept, and they had sprayed and prayed at the Betty formations. Rivers concurred. His three claimed no kills. Opportunities to hit unescorted bombers were not going to happen often. The squadron would have to make the most of these opportunities and inflict maximum damage on the Japanese. Later in the day, John L. decided he would have to pull his pilots together to go over tactics, gunnery, and target selection again.

Meanwhile, inside the hangar, Dick Mangrum carefully noted the kill tally for the day. The count came to eight bombers, four fighters. Half the Japanese Betties never made it home, by that count. John L. got two, Doc three, Tex two, Rivers one. Dick gave Marion two Zeroes, Ken a third, and Eugene a fourth.

Still, it seemed an uneven trade for one of their own.

That night, John L. pulled Doc aside. He told him about the crippled Betty he'd followed down, the pilots dead, the dorsal gun position a horror. "The tail gunner. . . . he was like a rat in a trap, scrabbling around trying to get out." He told Doc how he saw him tumble into the sea.

John L. had seen men die before. In 1940, an F3F biplane had crashed when he was stationed at Cuba, killing the pilot instantly. Death, though, was always at a distance and seen through that cushion of the machinery that claimed their lives. The only closer experience he'd had with death as an adult came in April 1941, when his dad summoned him home. John L. had secured emergency leave and flew from Quantico to Oklahoma, arriving back in Lexington just in time to be with his mother through her final hours. She was only sixty, but a bout with influenza had left her in heart failure.

That Japanese Flying Dutchman was something entirely different from the tragic and painful loss of his mom. It was gory, violent, horrific. John L. had watched a man die. It was the first major traumatic event of his combat experience, one that would linger in his mind long after he made it home to cheering crowds and public accolades. There would be many more such moments to come.

THE SQUADRON'S ATTACK ON THE BOMBERS ACTUALLY NETTED THREE kills over Savo. The mission leader's G4M was so badly shot up that he crash-landed along a beach on Buka Island in the Northern Solomons with dead and wounded crewmen aboard. Four of sixteen Betties was a catastrophic loss rate of 25 percent for the Japanese. It was made worse by all the spraying and praying the second lieutenants had done. No fewer than nine of the remaining G4Ms returned to Rabaul thoroughly shot up. Only three went through the mission unscathed.

Marion Carl's diving attack on the Zero escort on the twenty-sixth killed two veteran pilots. Who got whom will never be known for sure. Lieutenant Yuki Kunisuke led the second section, or *shotai*, of Zeroes that day. He failed to return, along with his wingman, Kumagaya Keni-chi. An August 1940 graduate of the Imperial Japanese Naval Academy at Etajima, Kunisuke was one of the young up-and-coming leaders of the Tainan Air Group. His loss was keenly felt.

In return, the Japanese Zero pilots claimed nine Wildcats destroyed and one probable. While several of the F4Fs were shot up, only Corry was lost. Again, the reality of air combat was so confusing and fast-moving that figuring out what happened after the fact was simply impossible.

Lieutenant Junichi Sasai led the escort mission that day. He'd just written to his parents that he'd scored his fifty-fourth kill and intended to best Manfred "the Red Baron" von Richthofen's WWI total of eighty. Japanese records credited him with twenty-seven by August 26, but whatever the score, Sasai was one of the key veterans holding the Tainan Air Group together. Charismatic though stubborn, he was a natural leader his pilots admired and followed without question. He loved the nickname they had given him: "the Richthofen of Rabaul."

Marion Carl's division killed Sasai. Whether he died in the initial engagement at fourteen thousand feet or it was Sasai whom Marion went head-to-head with over Guadalcanal will never be known for certain. After the war, the Zero Fighter Pilots Association credited Marion with shooting down their great leader, for only a superb pilot and leader in his own right was truly worthy of besting one of their own.[1]

TWENTY-SEVEN

THE BUTCHER'S SON

Henderson Field, Guadalcanal
August 27, 1942

ONE OF THE COASTWATCHERS ON NEW GEORGIA SQUAWKED A warning at 1035, setting off a mad dash to get every flyable bird off Henderson Field.

It took ten minutes to get everyone airborne this time and to clear the field. Those left behind at Henderson girded themselves for another rain of bombs, moving into slit trenches and dugouts. One man did not. Richard Tregaskis, the war correspondent, lay on his cot, too sick to move. The docs had diagnosed him with gastroenteritis. Probably triggered by a combination of bad food, bad water, and circumstance-induced bad hygiene, Tregaskis had spent the night in extreme distress. He turned face down on his cot and told everyone who came to get him to go away. He'd risk the bombs.

Thirty minutes passed with no sign of the bombers. The sound of John L.'s Grummans faded in the distance as they climbed out over Savo and vanished among the scattered clouds. For fifteen minutes, those around Henderson held their collective breaths. The antiaircraft gunners scanned the sky, tense with anticipation.

Finally, a swell of engines rose in the distance. Incoming aircraft. The closer they came, the more the tension built. The gunners could hear them, yet there was no visual sign. At 1130, the first dots appeared on the horizon. The antiaircraft crews trained the weapons on them and were about to open fire when word came that these were friendlies. It was a near-miss blue-on-blue incident, averted at the last minute.

A single B-17 leading nine P-400s made a quick circuit of the field and then touched down, the fighter planes following, one at a time. The bomber brought in three pilots John L. had left back at Efate with Joe Bauer's VMF-212. Clayton Canfield, Conrad Winter, and Charley Hughes stepped out of the bird and went to report at the Pagoda while the P-400s taxied into the parking area. The Flying Fortress had guided the men and their fighter planes from Efate up to Guadalcanal as reinforcements for Dale Brannon's advanced echelon of the 67th. The pilots had arrived on the dregs of their fuel supply, grateful there were no delays on getting down.

The Japanese failed to materialize that morning. Unbeknownst to the Marines, the badly shot-up G4M units at Rabaul were ordered to hit Port Moresby, in Papua New Guinea, that day. What Coastwatcher Donald Kennedy had heard passing over New Georgia was an "Emily," a four-engine Kawanishi H8K seaplane, on a long-range scouting mission, accompanied by eight Betties, also fanning out to search for US Navy warships.

By 1215, the all clear sounded and the Marines relaxed. Don McCafferty jumped off the wing of his SBD and saw Oliver Mitchell clowning around as usual, this time with Tom Moore.

"Hey, Tom?" Mitchell called out to Moore, who was also dismounting from his SBD.

"Yeah, Archie," Tom replied, using the squadron's nickname for Mitchell.

"So, this is what twenty-five feels like."

"Wonder if we'll see twenty-six," Moore answered with a grin.

Oliver didn't laugh.

The men drifted back to their living area in the coconut grove to enjoy a rare day off. Some grabbed bars of Japanese soap and headed down to a nearby creek to get cleaned up. Along the way, they had to pass the POW enclosure, where some of the VMSB-232 pilots stopped to chat with the Marines guarding them.

Most of the POWs were Korean laborers forced to serve the Japanese military. They were not very upset that they had fallen into American hands. The Yanks treated them better than the Japanese ever had. The Marine guard explained that they were even paying the POWs out of stacks of Japanese yen captured at the airfield on the first day of the campaign.

"They ever give you any trouble?" McCafferty asked the guard.

"Hell no," answered the mud Marine. They were getting paid ten times what the Japanese Army paid. "They got a job to do—to bury dead [Japanese] so they don't stink up the place too much. We figured we'd get more work out of 'em if we paid 'em."

The guard produced a roll of Japanese bills. He peeled off a few and handed them around to the pilots as souvenirs. As the Red Devils walked away, Fletcher Brown remarked, "Boys, remind me to mention this to my wife the next time I send her a letter."

At the creek, Brownie went on about his wife, Elynor, who was one of his favorite topics of discussion. Her photo had long since made the rounds among the pilots. Gorgeous, with wide-set, intelligent eyes and a genuine smile, she had curly dark hair and a photogenic nature that made eyes pop throughout the squadron. Brownie's stories underscored her brilliant intellect. She was a Navy brat, raised throughout the Pacific Rim during the interwar era. This upbringing gave her a worldly quality few people embodied in that era, when world travel was largely the province of the wealthy. She'd gone to school in China, the Philippines, and France as her family followed her father's naval career from posting to posting. That exposure to different countries and cultures propelled her toward a career as a writer, and Brownie met her while she was working on a journalism degree at the University of Washington.

While the pilots scrubbed themselves in the creek, chatting about girlfriends, wives, or other family back home, they kept a steady lookout for crocs and snakes. A bit of captured Japanese soap, a long dip in the lukewarm tropical waters, and the men almost felt human again, at least until they had to put their filthy khakis back on.

While the pilots bathed, Dick Mangrum remained with the aircraft, getting feedback from his plane captains (crew chiefs in USAAF lingo), and working through a myriad of issues needing attention. At the top of the list were the squadron's forward-firing guns. The SBDs carried two .50-caliber Brownings over the engine cowling; these machine guns were synchronized to fire through the propeller arc. After only a couple of missions that used the guns, the synchronizers filled with oil, which upset their timing. So far, nobody had shot a propeller blade off, but a blade had been hit by a hang fire that discharged when the pilot landed back at Henderson.

The synchronizers were a complete headache for the mechanics and took inordinate manpower time to remain functional. Their maintenance kept the ground crew from getting to other critical tasks that had to be addressed before the SBDs could be flown again. With the crew so badly stretched trying to handle both 232's and Flight 300's aircraft, the mechanics had two options: They could fuss with the synchronizing gear and slow the other work each aircraft needed, consequently lowering the in-service rate for both squadrons. Or they could give up maintaining the guns until the rest of the squadron finally arrived.

Not having forward-firing guns in a fight would be a problem. The Red Devils needed them to strafe the ships the squadron dive-bombed. Dick himself had turned to attack a Japanese floatplane, relying on those forward-firing guns. Losing them to maintenance issues would halve their firepower and leave the SBDs defenseless to head-on attacks. Yet if Dick had to choose between a dozen SBDs flyable without their forward .50s and only six or seven SBDs with everything working, he had to go with the numbers. The number of bombs that could be put on a Japanese convoy mattered far more than the rounds the bombers could fire at them.

He told his plane captains to stop working on the synchronizing problem. The pilots would use the forward-facing guns until they stopped working and then manage without them.

The gravel that blasted each plane at takeoff and landing was causing a host of issues too. Among other problems, the blast battered the
propeller blades, reduced their effectiveness in the air, and tore up the
center-section flaps under the fuselage. The constant gravel strikes
cracked the flaps and tore pieces from them. The mechanics were finding others with the metal twisted and abused. Because the flaps were
made of perforated aluminum in the first place, the damage was made
worse as the cracks between the perforations ruptured. The only thing the
mechanics could do was cut out the damaged sections since there were
no replacement flaps available. As a result, the flaps were being slowly
chewed apart with each takeoff roll and landing, degrading the vital
additional lift they provided.

Without any hoists or stands, the mechanics couldn't do any serious
work on the engines. The Wright Cyclones were already showing signs
of wear from the hard flying the pilots put the SBDs through every day.
With minimal tools, about all the ground crew could do was clean the
fuel strainers. Anything else would have been too time-consuming, anyway, until the rest of the squadron arrived.

On the third mission of August 24, several of the SBDs had lost
their bombs because of electrical failures. Something triggered their
inadvertent release long before the remaining Dauntlesses attacked the
lone Japanese warship they found on this mission. Similar problems
afflicted the Navy's SBDs at Midway, when Lt. Cmd. Maxwell Leslie's pilots off the USS *Yorktown* tried to electrically arm their bombs.
This Midway problem seemed like a different issue, which the Navy
mechanics had yet to figure out. Given the high humidity, constant rain
squalls, mud, dust, and heat, the Red Devils resigned themselves to the
intermittent issue. Electrical system malfunctions would just have to be
part of the game.

Dick rejoined the squadron's pilots late that afternoon. They were sitting on their rice straw mats under the broad canvas fly. Some were eating; others played cards. It was almost 1800 hours, their chance to get
news and music from the States, so somebody flipped on Don McCafferty's radio and started tuning it.

Don was sitting with a pen and some captured Imperial Japanese Navy stationery, writing a letter to James Watkins, the program director at WCKY Cincinnati. This was the only other station they could get from the States during their short, hour-long window of reception every evening, but it never played anything interesting for the Marines. Don was determined to fix that and asked that the station include some music and news.

He read back part of the letter to the men:

Half the squadron is clustered around the small, portable radio, we have to hear some of that good old American Jive. You don't realize how much you miss it until you are in a position such as ours, where it is almost impossible to hear any of it.

Somebody suggested he ask for some news too. Somebody else added, "Like baseball scores."

Don went back to work as the guys started discussing the pennant race between the St. Louis Cardinals and the Brooklyn Dodgers. A moment later, he read his additions to the approval of the squadron, then signed off with this:

Hope your morale is as good as ours is. I remain as ever, as all the Marines out here, still fighting. So keep your chin up, ours is out.

Mangrum settled down next to Brownie Brown and quietly gave him an update on the aircraft situation. As the two men exchanged information, Brownie told the skipper that snipers were getting worse. One of the enlisted gunners nearly got shot earlier in the morning. The Japanese had been infiltrating these crack shots through the Marine perimeter, apparently with orders to target aviators. They lurked in the trees and the dense jungle around the airfield and their living quarters, taking shots at the men as they moved around, especially at night.

Word from 223 had it that a few nights before, a mud Marine had spotted one of these snipers and put a round through his head. When the Marine went to search the body for intelligence, he discovered his brother's wallet in the dead man's pocket. His brother had been on Wake Island in December 1941. When the Marine recognized his brother's photo inside the wallet, he went berserk and bludgeoned the corpse to a pulp with his rifle butt.

IT WAS NOW 1800 AS THE MEN GATHERED AROUND THE RADIO. IT played nothing for a few more minutes, but at last they heard the distant sounds of music beneath the hiss of static. The men recognized it at once: Harry James's "Sleepy Lagoon." It had climbed to the top of the hit parade in July while they were in Hawai'i training, and its soft, wind-through-the-palms rhythm reminded them of the few nights of liberty they had enjoyed in Honolulu. James's treatment was instrumental, but some of the pilots knew the lyrics other bands had played with it.

> *A sleepy lagoon, a tropical moon and two on*
> *an island*
> *A sleepy lagoon and two hearts in tune in*
> *some lullabyland*

Love in the tropics. A very few of the men had experienced that in Hawai'i. Dick had. Virginia and the kids lived with him in Hawai'i until early 1942, when the Navy evacuated them. He and Virginia had been college sweethearts, having met at the University of Washington. Never one with a wandering eye, Dick loved her intensely. When she boarded the steamer for the States, he felt as if half his life were sailing away.

It was dark now. A voice rose from around them. "Some tropical paradise for two," he grumbled. "I gotta sleep with you ugly sons of bitches."

That provoked a round of ribald comments until the next song was introduced. They recognized the voice as one of the KNX announcers. It was after 0100 in Los Angeles, music for the swing and night shifts in the war factories around the county. It comforted the pilots to know they were listening to the same songs the Rosies were listening to at the very factory in El Segundo where the Douglas Aircraft Company built its

SBDs. They groaned when they lost the signal all too soon as an Aussie station drowned out the distant station.

Henry Hise and Bruce Prosser showed up as the others were listening to the Aussie station describing the Russian defense of Stalingrad and Rzhev. Nobody in the squadron had any idea where either city was on a map, but it sounded as if the Russians were making an epic stand. The Germans had launched eleven consecutive assaults on the Soviet defenders, who repelled every attack. The fighting in Rzhev was not just street to street but also building to building and, in some cases, room to room.

Dick Mangrum listened to the announcer detail those desperate battles and felt a surge of respect for the Russians. Here he and the other Americans were, a tiny force on a distant island, thousands of miles from home. The Russians were fighting *from* their own homes and factories. Millions of men, thousands of tanks and aircraft, all arrayed against one another in a titanic clash whose outcome no doubt would affect the course of the war and the future of the world.

The broadcast moved to the Pacific. The aerial defenders of New Guinea claimed twelve Japanese planes downed. Hopefully, some of those would have been from Rabaul so the numbers against them were thinned out a bit. The news provoked a rash of conversation over pilot quality and who was better, the guys at Port Moresby or Henderson's defenders. In the darkness, Dick heard Henry Hise's weary voice penetrate the hubbub. "You know, one pilot is pretty much like any other. Except for Marion Carl."

That silenced the discussion. Everyone agreed. Half the squadron had seen Marion shoot down the Zero over the beach the day before, and they knew it took a special kind of aviator to have pulled that off.

The radio shifted attention to their neck of the woods. The men grew still, hanging on every word. "A decisive American victory over Japanese counterinvasion forces in the Solomon Islands was announced today by the United States Navy Department. The Navy Communiqué number one hundred and thirteen declares two aircraft carriers and a battleship were bombed, eight vessels sunk, and twenty-five warships and barges sunk in the Solomons and at Milne Bay. The Communiqué reads, 'Japanese surface forces have appeared to have withdrawn from the vicinity of our positions in the Tulagi area.'" The report made no mention of the Marines defending the island or the aviators fighting above it, a fact that provoked some grumbling. It did go on to state that aerial reinforcements were on their way to the Pacific from the United States.

Could the squadrons even hope this was true? Something beyond a handful of P-400s, like the ones that arrived earlier in the day?

The broadcast ended, and Dick ordered the radio turned off for the night. There would be plenty of flying to do in the morning.

BEFORE DAWN, AS THE SQUADRON MEMBERS AWOKE AND WENT ABOUT their now-routine duties, Oliver Mitchell approached Don McCafferty. Oliver's normally round and jovial face looked deadly serious, and Don could tell he had something on his mind. Don stopped and greeted his friend. He and Oliver had been chums since flight school the year before, and they knew each other better than anyone else in the squadron.

Oliver did not waste time with pleasantries. "Mac," he said, "I'm never going to leave this place alive."

The words shocked Don. Oliver had never been one of the hard-charging second lieutenants, but his levity and wisecracking always made the squadron feel better about their circumstances. Now, he sounded and looked like one of the Midway vets.

"That's no way to talk, Mitch."

Oliver looked straight into Don's eyes and quietly answered, "Don't get me wrong. I don't mind dying. But this whole thing never should have happened."

Oliver's dad had immigrated from Greece in 1903, settling in South Carolina briefly before making his way to California. He cut meat at a Quality Market to pay the bills until America joined World War I. The Greek immigrant had served in the "war to end all wars," leaving his wife, Margaret, with their three-year-old son, James, and newborn, Don, who had entered the world almost the same day their adopted country entered the war.

His father loved America and the opportunities it afforded him. He went from cutting meat in a little market to owning his own grocery store in a decade. The family had survived the Depression, the store providing a good living. His father was a devoted patriot who even registered for the draft again at age fifty-two.

"The last war was fought to prevent this one," Oliver said. "This war is being fought to prevent another one. I wonder if it will."

Don tried to cheer him up. "Sure it will, Mitch. This is really a fight to the finish."

"I hate war, Mac. The killing. Even the idea of killing."

In their barracks at Pensacola, Florida, in 1941, they had talked over the same issue. Oliver saw the writing on the wall back then, knew the war was coming. He had volunteered to serve straight out of Whittier College because it was the right thing to do.

Oliver was his father's son.

Don knew the measure of his friend. He knew he wasn't yellow or broken by the experiences since the squadron had reached the island. Yet he could see how much Oliver despised all this and despaired over the direction the war had flung his life.

"It is a fight to the finish," Don repeated.

Oliver replied, "I wish I could convince myself of that. Then I could go over happy."

Before Don could say another word, Oliver saw three more of the squadron's pilots heading their way. The transformation on his face was instant. The serious world-weariness vanished and was replaced with a broad, comedic grin. He waved at the trio and, using his Jerry Colonna voice, shouted, "Hello there, Hope! Let's go down to the Owl Drugstore and line up a couple of blondes!"

The three burst out laughing.

Oliver looked back at Don, then walked away with the other pilots, a man with a troubled heart wrapped in a cloak of humor.

TWENTY-EIGHT

A SINGLE SHOT OF BRANDY

Henderson Field, Guadalcanal
Friday, August 28, 1942, afternoon

MORNING BAD WEATHER THROUGHOUT THE SOLOMONS CHAIN scrubbed the Japanese raid against Guadalcanal, a blessed reprieve at a time when men from both squadrons were starting to get sick. Most had developed whatever had knocked Tregaskis off his feet—gastroenteritis. After the reporter had refused to get out of his cot during the previous day's air raid alert, corpsmen had taken him to the local medical tent, where he stayed throughout the twenty-eighth.

The aviators and ground crew afflicted by the same virus fell out with vomiting and diarrhea. In the heat and humidity of Guadalcanal, they quickly became dehydrated, which made them weak and listless. With the Marines already shorthanded, any illness spreading through the ranks threatened to reduce the squadrons to skeleton crews.

Dick Mangrum could not afford to lose any of his aircrew to disease. He had twelve pilots and gunners and nine planes, all currently overtasked.

Dick also loved building structures and systems. He was a methodical thinker and had been this way since his youth, when he'd been an honors student at Franklin High School in Seattle. His father worked as a carpenter and contractor. From him, Dick had inherited the vision and ability to manage the creation of something complex, like a building.

In school, Dick had not been a spectacular athlete. Second string on both the football and the basketball junior varsity squads. Instead, he was the architect behind the scenes and out of the limelight, making sure things ran smoothly. He'd been the manager for the track team, where his meticulous attention to detail shone. Same with the school plays and operettas, where he never performed onstage but coordinated all the ushers.

On Guadalcanal, with Lt. Col. Charles Fike's input and blessing, Dick Mangrum built the search-and-strike system that both 232 and Flight 300 used. Each squadron dedicated part of its available pilots and planes to the two searches a day. The first search would go out before dawn, looking for any ships either running up the Solomons after debarking troops at night or coming down in daylight as had happened on August 25. A late afternoon search would seek incoming Japanese task forces intent on unloading under the cover of darkness. Each crew had orders to go out to 250 miles.

Meanwhile, Dick kept a reserve strike force sitting on the runway at Henderson, armed with thousand-pound bombs and capable of taking off to hit a target within minutes. Because these aircraft would also have to be cleared off the field if there was a Japanese air raid, the ground crews had to refuel and service them every afternoon after those scrambles.

Every aircraft was dedicated to one or the other role; there was no ready reserve. With only three extra crews for the nine SBDs, some of the men would have to fly every day.

This strike and search system was fine with Henry Hise, whose first week on Guadalcanal proved the axiom that in a crisis, the best characters emerge. He volunteered for every flight, every mission. He was up for anything and wanted to fight. He thirsted for it. Mangrum knew to be careful not to burn out his hard charger. In the meantime, the skipper gave Hise a long leash to get out and get in the air often.

On August 28, Henry flew both the morning search and the afternoon one. In the first days after 232 had arrived, the squadron had been able to commit only a few planes for a token search. With Flight 300 helping out, Mangrum could afford to be more thorough. On the runway that day, his strike element consisted of four SBDs from 232 (Mangrum, Tom Moore, Oliver Mitchell, and Don Rose) plus another five from Flight 300. The afternoon search element started taking off around 1400 and consisted of two Flight 300 SBDs and five more, piloted by Danny Iverson, Henry Hise, Don McCafferty, Fletcher Brown, and Bruce Prosser. With seven SBDs, the group could fan out from the Russell Islands in the northwest across Santa Isabel and all the way to the north beyond Ramos Island near where they had destroyed the August 25 convoy.

Iverson and Hise flew the left flank of the pie, running up toward the Russells along the west side of the New Georgia Sound, called the Slot, the long body of water between islands in the Solomon chain. The two Flight 300 crews and McCafferty, Prosser, and Brown flew the middle and northernmost wedges of the search fan, spread out across the Slot almost due north up between Santa Isabel and Malaita.

About two hours into the mission, Don McCafferty heard a distant voice in his radio headphones reporting four large Japanese destroyers heading south for Guadalcanal. The voice gave their position, and Don pulled out his kneeboard to plot it on his map. They were close, somewhere behind and north of him. The scattered layers of clouds must have shielded them from his view when he passed them.

The voice, probably Brownie's, ordered everyone to converge on the target and sink those ships. Don turned to the northeast. In only a few minutes, he spied them through a break in the clouds: four dots riding the horizon. The sun hung low in the west, dusk only about ninety minutes away now. Still, attacking from upsun would help shield his SBD from the Japanese. He positioned himself just as Dick Mangrum had taught the aviators, then called to his gunner, Lewis Macias, "Here we go."

A wingover and steep dive later, his nose was pointed right at a twisting, turning destroyer busily working up to flank speed. Don stayed on the vessel, passing through a thousand feet before pushing the bomb release lever. His bomb swung clear of the propeller arc and speared down at his target. As he pulled out on the wave tops, Lewis called out, "You laid that one right off his beam, Lieutenant. Gee, but this is fun."

Don stayed low and pulled out of antiaircraft range. As he did, he heard Danny Iverson's genteel Southern accent call over the radio, asking if the ships were friend or foe. The atmospherics in the Solomons were terrible, and radio communications frequently failed, especially with the frequencies the SBDs used. Don assumed Danny hadn't heard the initial contact report or the order to converge on the target and sink it. He checked his gas situation and found he had plenty left, especially since they were only about sixty miles from home. He decided to climb back up, turn around, and keep an eye on the task force while reporting their movements over the radio.

As Don found a good cloud to loiter in, outside antiaircraft range, Danny Iverson dropped through the scud and ordered his gunner to flash a recognition signal at the ships below to confirm if they were friendly or not. They replied by sending a barrage of flak up their way. Most certainly not friendly. Danny pulled back up into the clouds and reunited with Hise. They flew on for a minute or two longer when, without warning, Danny suddenly rolled up and over into a steep dive through a hole in the clouds. Hise hastily followed. It was a fouled-up run from the get-go. The bad weather made it even harder to stay on the targets while the ships maneuvered furiously. Plus, the dive was quick and not well planned. Danny never got properly lined up and abandoned his run without dropping his bomb. Hise did the dive-bomber equivalent of a spray and pray—launching his weapon at twenty-five hundred feet. The only things he killed were fish.

Furious that he'd blown the run, Hise raced back to Henderson Field with Danny. Both Brownie and Bruce attacked the ships and also raced home while the two Flight 300 crews made attacks of their own. Ens. J. T. "Dog" Barker thought he'd scored a hit on the fantail of the trail destroyer.

Around 1645, Henry blazed over Henderson, made a quick circuit as he dropped gear and flaps, and then planted his SBD on the runway. Instead of taxiing to the parking area, he drove his dive-bomber straight to the Pagoda to save time. He cut the switches, jumped out, and ran inside to report the contact while his gunner busily went after the ground crew to get their aircraft refueled and rearmed.

Henderson Field did not have a radio system that could communicate with the search planes beyond twenty or thirty miles, so Mangrum hadn't heard the contact reports or Don McCafferty's ongoing commentary on their position.[1] He quickly plotted the ships' locations, briefed the crews, and headed out to get their birds off the ground. Flight 300's strike element was parked closest to the runway and would take off first, led by their commander, Lt. Turner Caldwell. Mangrum decided to give Brownie and Hise enough time to get their planes rearmed with a bit of extra fuel for the mission. Since they were only seventy miles from Henderson, they wouldn't need to waste time filling all their fuel tanks.

Over at Vandegrift's headquarters, Bob Miller, one of the only other reporters on the island, sat beside one of the most treasured captures of the campaign, a Japanese radio set that could hear the SBDs quite clearly. The division staff clustered around the radio, listening to the 232 crew's chatter. For whatever reason, the initial contact reports had not been passed to the flight line and the waiting strike force. The delay ensured that Mangrum's men would go in right at sunset and wouldn't have time for a second strike.

Four large destroyers could carry a significant number of troops—150 to 200—plus heavy weapons like anti-guns or light artillery, and around 30 to 40 tons of supplies. If the Japanese reached the island, this task force would put ashore at least 600 fresh troops and up to 160 tons of ammo, food, medical gear, and so forth. That amount of men and material presented a significant threat to the Marine perimeter.

The Navy's Dauntlesses rose off the gravel runway first, forming up as they flew north with thousand-pound bombs on their centerline racks. It took about twenty extra minutes to get Henry and Brownie ready to fly. Bruce Prosser and Danny Iverson were out. Henry had already flown two missions that day, spending over seven hours in the air, but he wasn't feeling it. He wanted a second crack at this Japanese task force and wasn't about to be left behind. Brownie felt the same way. The executive officer had missed the attack on August 25. This was his chance to make up for that.

Second Lieutenant Don Rose also missed the action on the twenty-fifth, as he was assigned to patrol duties. Mangrum liked this young Minnesotan, who at five feet ten and 150 pounds was one of the taller pilots in the squadron. He was an earnest and intense farm kid from the tiny town of Lanesboro, where he'd been the valedictorian of his high school class. He'd graduated with honors from St. Olaf College before enlisting in the Navy in April 1941.

Shortly after arriving at Henderson, Rose discovered that Angsar South, one of his favorite professors at St. Olaf, was serving as a chaplain in the 1st Marine Division. The two shared a what-a-small-world reunion and stayed in contact whenever they could around missions and duties.

Sometime after 1730 on August 28, Mangrum's little force went wheels up and feet wet over Savo Sound, rushing north as they climbed to attack altitude through the scattered clouds. Dick led the way, with Tom Moore, Don Rose, Fletcher Brown, Henry Hise, and the butcher's son, Oliver Mitchell, fanned out in line abreast on either side of him.

Caldwell didn't wait for Mangrum's six planes. His five were many miles in front of the Marines and off their starboard wings. They would reach the enemy first and make their attacks without Dick's group. Though going in piecemeal was far from optimal, having daylight overrode any other consideration.

Meanwhile, Don McCafferty continued to duck in and out of the clouds near the Japanese ships, reporting that they had turned north away from Guadalcanal. Dick was able to talk to him as they closed on the target area. "Okay, Don, we're going in where you left off."

Don had been loitering for over half an hour. It was time to get his bird on the ground. He swung his nose south and headed for Henderson as the two small strike groups reached the target area.

Sure enough, Caldwell's bombers rolled into the attack first, coming in from the east. Dropping down between the clouds, Caldwell scored a near miss on one of the destroyers while Ens. Chris Fink dropped his bomb dead amidships on another, the thousand-pounder landing directly atop one of the ship's torpedo mounts. The bomb touched off the torpedoes and created a massive explosion that blew the destroyer in half. Hal Buell, a veteran of all three 1942 carrier battles, dove fourth out of the five Flight 300 aircraft. He blew through a cloud and, from less than two thousand feet, released his weapon on a hard-turning destroyer. His gunner reported that their bomb struck almost amidships, but they had no time to stick around and observe. The two trailing destroyers opened on them with rapid-fire 25 mm guns, spraying the sky around them with tracers. Buell hugged the water and raced for home.

As the Marines closed from the southwest, Dick called out, "Four ships sighted, fifteen miles north of Ramos Island. One seems to be afire."

The radio remained silent for a couple of minutes as Dick worked them into attack position. The sun sagged right on the water, casting the ships in twilight-gray shadows. Between the clouds and the gathering darkness, they were hard to see now.

Dick watched the ships below, their antiaircraft guns striping the sky as dozens of muzzle flashes illuminated their decks. Though the flak remained a serious threat, the fact that they were firing gave the Marines an unexpected advantage. As long as the Japanese kept shooting like that, his pilots would have well-defined aiming points, thanks to those muzzle flashes.

Just follow the tracers back to their sources.

One of the destroyers completed a 360-degree turn, inscribing a lopsided white circle in the calm sea with its wake. Another destroyer had snaked past it, its wake carving an *S*. There seemed to be no base course for the remaining ships anymore. One appeared dead in the water. Another was little more than a bit of bow and stern protruding from the waves with a rash of debris and fire in between. The remaining two maneuvered radically, sending up shocking amounts of flak at the SBDs.

About ten thousand feet over the Japanese ships, Dick keyed his mic and assigned targets to his men. The Japanese suddenly found the range, and bursting red-black puffs of high-explosive shells scarred the air around them. Were these five-inch blasts from their main batteries? The Marines didn't know, but they threw the Dauntlesses around with violent fury.

In the open gunner's cockpit of Dick's SBD, Dennis Byrd could smell the cordite and gunpowder from the nearest bursts. The stench reminded him of the fireworks he used to set off as a kid in Texas during the Fourth of July. A fond memory, one that contrasted sharply with the terror of the moment. The flak seemed to inch closer and closer to their SBDs, and Dennis wondered how any of them flew through it and survived. Concussive waves from the exploding shells buffeted their aircraft, and shrapnel whirred through their formation.

Mangrum's voice broke the static back at Vandegrift's HQ, where the staff and Miller heard him say, "We'll rendezvous after the attack."

Dick chopped his throttle, popped his dive flaps, and pushed his stick forward. The Dauntless's nose dropped into a seventy-degree dive from ten thousand feet. Tracers streamed by. Flak burst above and behind their bomber now. The sun was gone, the water nothing but a sheet of blackness on which the destroyers glowed red-orange as all their guns blazed away at 232's Dauntlesses, which had dived at one-second intervals after their skipper.

Dick's target turned hard to port, its wake broad and long, signaling it was doing probably thirty knots or better. The destroyer skittered out of his gunsight, forcing him to roll left. He passed eight thousand feet now, clouds zipping by on either side of the aircraft. Suddenly, the destroyer heeled over and turned sharply to starboard, throwing Dick's aim off again. The skipper rolled hard right to get back on target. Dennis looked up and realized they were inverted now, the destroyer and black sheet of ocean stretched *over* his head.

The terrifying dive continued as fireballs of flak lit the night and shook their plummeting SBD. Dick worked back onto the target and released while pulling through the dive. They leveled off at less than a hundred feet, racing past the broken, sinking bow of the destroyer Ensign Fink had blown up.

Tom Moore was probably the second Marine to dive that evening, following his skipper down through the rising tide of antiaircraft fire. He muffed the run and, on pullout, heard his gunner say laconically, "Miss."

Don Rose went in after Tom did, the wind shrieking like a siren through his butterfly flaps. Again, the destroyer skippers proved canny and skilled. His target twisted out of the way, and Don's bomb scored only a near miss.

Brownie went next, closely followed by Oliver and then Henry, who had forgotten to shift his supercharger to high blower and was lagging behind. Brownie thought he scored a hit and pulled out just above the surface, which he could see was strewn with flaming debris and bodies. He sped after Dick's SBD, which was just visible as a black silhouette in the distance with a blue exhaust flame streaming back from the cowling on either side of its fuselage.

Henry thought he'd executed a perfect dive. He had that sense he used to get when staring down a pitcher on a baseball diamond. That instinct told him his swing was going to connect. He led his target, held the bomb until he passed well below fifteen hundred feet, then cut it loose. By the time he'd closed his flaps and pulled out so low that his own tail wheel left a bright wake in the water, his gunner reported their bomb had exploded just forward of the destroyer's bow. Another goddamned miss.

As Henry made his attack, Dennis Byrd and the other gunners saw Oliver Mitchell's SBD arrow straight after one of the remaining ships. The destroyer flung a wall of flak up at Oliver's diving Dauntless, but that didn't deter him. Oliver Mitchell stayed on target, his forward guns spraying long ropes of tracers as he dove, strafing the destroyer in a desperate bid to kill the gunners shooting at him. At the last possible second, he dropped his bomb.

Oliver's SBD went straight into the water. Dennis Byrd saw it impact the water's surface and vanish in the darkness.

ABOUT TWENTY MILES OUT FROM HENDERSON FIELD, DON McCAF-ferty heard Dick Mangrum's voice come over his radio. "Three destroyers down. My apologies to General Vandegrift. One got away."

Elated by the news but unaware of any losses, Don and Macias got on the ground as quickly as they could, reaching the runway well after sunset. Don rushed over to the Pagoda and reported to Lieutenant Colonel Fike, who hadn't heard any of the radio chatter. The operations section at Henderson relied on a radio pulled out of one of the wrecked F4Fs and mounted on a truck, a field expedience that proved woefully inadequate, as even the receiver Dennis Byrd had brought along and set up at 232's encampment possessed better range.

When Don discovered Fike was still in the dark, he repeated Mangrum's message that three of four destroyers had been hammered. Then he added, "May I express apologies, sir, on behalf of Colonel Mangrum for not getting all four?"

Fike broke out in a rare smile. Don saluted and left to await the return of his squadron.

Over at Vandegrift's HQ, Bob Miller heard Mangrum's report on the radio and knew he had the hook for a terrific article. As it took shape in his mind, he knew the "apologies to General Vandegrift" line would feature prominently. He tucked his notebook and pen away and rushed out to interview the aviators.

They started landing a little after 1900, eight SBDs in total. The men gathered around the planes to figure out who was missing. When they realized it was their morale-lifting Southern California kid with the knack for impressions, the celebratory mood evaporated. Oliver Mitchell and his gunner, Frank O. Schackman, would be listed officially as missing in action. But those who saw their SBD go in knew the chances that either man was still alive were slim to none.

Don walked among the crews and learned that his closest friend in the Marine Corps had not returned. The lighthearted mood he'd exhibited in the Pagoda seemed hopelessly inappropriate now. He went silent. Oliver's folks would be sleeping back in Los Angeles right now. His father always woke up early to be at the market several hours before it opened. They would receive the dreaded yellow telegram from the War Department in a matter of days, and their world would change forever.

Don would have to write them, but he had no idea what to say. All he felt was a combination of guilt for his earlier mood and despair that Mitch's prophecy of doom had come true.

Mangrum told everyone to go get debriefed at the Pagoda, that Fike was waiting for them. So was Miller, pen and notebook out, eager to hear the story of the raid.

Tom Moore mentioned how odd it was to see so much chaos and death below them without any sounds accompanying it. Like a silent film. He stood lost in thought as the men each told their side of the mission. All he could think of was Oliver Mitchell greeting him.

This is what twenty-five feels like.

Wonder if we'll see twenty-six.

Turner Caldwell was last to arrive. He'd stayed over the target area to observe what the Japanese did. He watched as the one undamaged destroyer circled the area, picking up survivors. A follow-up strike could have wiped out the whole force; nightfall saved the Japanese from that fate.

When the debriefing ended, Mangrum pulled his crews together and told them to meet at their camp in the coconut grove. He showed up a few minutes after everyone else, holding a bottle of brandy. The men scrambled to find mess cups as Mangrum took turns pouring a bit for each man.

When everyone held a cup with a shot in it, Dick raised the bottle and said, "To Lieutenant Mitchell."

The men repeated the words, hoisting their tin cups high. Then the squadron quaffed their shots together, an aviator's farewell salute in the black jungle night at the nexus of a combat zone. The brief moment was all they could afford. The true grieving for lost friends would have to come later. For now, each man needed to keep his head in his job.

A similar ritual played out at the flight line among the enlisted gunners. Frank Schackman had been a late addition to the squadron, so he wasn't known well by most of the men. Still, the loss cast a pall over their evening victory, and the men were subdued. Dennis Byrd tried to look at it dispassionately. Flying was a dangerous game. Combat flying even more so. Losses were common in the service, and they had to be expected. Managed. Oliver's and Frank's friends would suffer their losses in silence.

THE AUGUST 28 TASK FORCE CONSISTED OF FOUR OF JAPAN'S LARGEST destroyers, *Fubuki*-class veterans of the 20th Destroyer Division. The *Yugiri*, *Amagiri*, *Shirakuma*, and *Asagiri* each carried six 5-inch dual-purpose guns, a number of 13 mm antiaircraft machine guns, and up to twenty-two rapid-fire 25 mm antiaircraft cannon. At 370 feet long and displacing seventeen hundred tons, these four ships were part of the first truly modern destroyers built by any navy in the interwar period. They were exceptionally formidable opponents, with a balance of armament that made them capable of filling nearly any role.

The 20th Destroyer Division was originally assigned to commerce raiding duties in the Indian Ocean in late July. After Guadalcanal was invaded, the Combined Fleet canceled that operation and sent them to Truk. The four destroyers, under the command of Capt. Yuji Yamada, reached Truk on August 23. Already loaded with about forty tons of supplies each, the quartet set sail for Guadalcanal the next day. En route, they rendezvoused at sea with some transports carrying about six hundred Imperial Japanese Army soldiers of the 2nd Battalion, 124th Infantry Regiment—the advanced element of Gen. Kiyotake Kawaguchi's crack 35th Brigade, which the Japanese planned to deploy to Guadalcanal over the next few weeks. These soldiers would represent almost five thousand additional troops for the island, giving the Japanese an offensive force that, if concentrated against one part of the Marine lines, could overwhelm the sixteen thousand Americans strung out thinly in an arc around the airfield.

Along with these four destroyers sent directly from Truk, the Imperial Japanese Navy was also running destroyers down from Rabaul and the Shortlands. The hasty plan called for two destroyer task forces to land about twelve hundred troops on the night of August 28—troops carried by the four destroyers that Mangrum's squadron had attacked—plus three more task forces running down the Slot from the Shortlands.

The American attack totally derailed this reinforcement effort. The search element succeeded in slightly damaging the *Amagiri* about twenty minutes before Flight 300's five SBDs went into their dives. Ensign Fink's thousand-pounder sank the *Asagiri* in a matter of seconds, blowing it in half. One hundred and twenty-two men died almost instantly, sixty of whom were Kawaguchi's soldiers. Either Hal Buell or another member of the squadron put a bomb into the *Shirakuma*'s engine room, flooding it and leaving the destroyer dead in the water while killing scores of soldiers. Twenty-seven minutes later, Mangrum's Marines planted a thousand-pound bomb on the bridge of the *Yugiri*, killing Captain Yamada and thirty-two others. Another forty were wounded in the blast and ensuing fires.[2]

Near misses and another possible hit added to the Japanese misery and increased the number of casualties. When the Americans turned for home, the *Amagiri* was the only functioning warship remaining. Its crew rescued survivors, then took the *Shirakuma* in tow. Together, the three ships limped slowly to the Shortlands, Japan's nearest naval base, arriving on August 30.

When the Japanese reported the disaster in the immediate aftermath of the attack, the other task force heading down the Slot for Guadalcanal turned around and returned to base. Nine Dauntless dive-bomber crews had spared the mud Marines from facing over a thousand fresh troops. The disaster sent shock waves through the Japanese navy's high command in the area. It had lost face in front of the Japanese army, a humiliation made exceedingly painful given the hypercompetitive and contentious relationship between the two services. The chewing-out Admiral Tanaka and his subordinate commanders received from their superiors worsened an already-toxic relationship between the multiple layers of command in the South Pacific.

August 28 represented an outsized victory the Marines would not fully understand until years after the war. Nevertheless, it did not deter the Japanese. Instead, the disaster had the opposite effect. More determined than ever to recapture Guadalcanal, the Japanese worked overtime to find ways to get men onto the island in the face of Mangrum's dive-bombers. The coming days would determine the fate of the island.

TWENTY-NINE
A CAVALCADE OF INCOMPETENCE

Henderson Field, Guadalcanal
Sunday, August 29, 1942, dawn

T HE MEN IN LINE AT THE IITH MARINE'S CHOW TENT STOOD IN silence as a new day greeted Henderson's defenders. Ninety minutes before, three Japanese G4M bombers from Rabaul had swept in low, waking everyone up as they unloaded strings of antipersonnel bombs. The ordnance missed the runway and the aviation personnel, falling instead to the east of the strip in the 11th Marine's cantonment area. The artillerymen lost three men killed and many more wounded. The rest of the perimeter lost vitally needed sleep.

After the attack, nobody was in the mood to talk.

Marion Carl and the other VMF-223 pilots now stood in line with the mud Marines and the pilots from the 67th Fighter Squadron before they headed down to their aircraft to await the scramble order. The men looked gaunt. Their filthy uniforms draped loosely, thanks to the weight loss their crash diet over the last week had triggered. None of the men had much weight to lose in the first place, but the scant rations had already caused them to drop four or five pounds each. The lack of calories meant they spent their days perpetually hungry as they swatted mosquitoes and lounged by their planes, ready to scramble at a moment's notice.

Their nights passed with fitful catnaps between firefights on the perimeter. Tracers that lit the sky, the sounds of automatic weapons booming through the night, and the crack of sniper rounds became as routine as the squawking birds and barking lizards. Twice in the last seven days, the Americans had been shelled by Japanese ships during the night. The shellings prompted mad rushes to dugouts and slit trenches. Between those attacks, the enemy made a point of slaughtering the men's sleep with the persistent sounds of aircraft engines overhead—Japanese bombers dubbed "Washing Machine Charlie" and "Louie the Louse."

No wonder the men in that line on the morning of August 29 felt worn-out. Yet they knew the real fighting lay ahead, as the enemy was nothing if not stubborn. The Japanese had come for their seven-by-four-mile corner of the Pacific—of that nobody had any doubt. Mangrum's boys had just bought the Marines a little time.

Dehydrated potatoes, canned fruit, and weevil-ridden rice awaited them as they reached the front of the line. The cooks from the 11th Marines scooped a bit of each onto the waiting mess plates, a few of the servers admonishing their customers to be sure to eat the weevils since they were high in protein.

The men ate their food standing up, with little conversation between them. Dawn streaked the sky with reds and oranges, making for a beautiful scene above the coconut trees. The fighter pilots gave it a gimlet eye, knowing the weather meant they would probably be seeing the Rabaul crowd at lunchtime. Another pell-mell scramble to twenty-five thousand feet, engines protesting the abuse such combat climbs required. At fifteen thousand, the aviators would have to go on oxygen. Already, their lungs ached with the effort from prior missions since the F4F Wildcats had no pressurized system. Instead, the pilots had to suck in air through their fragile masks. The higher they went, the more effort their breathing took. By the time they got back on the ground, the sheer effort required to breathe left them fatigued and achy.

The 67th pilots had no ability to operate above about fifteen thousand feet. Their P-400 Airacobras, destined originally for service with the British, came equipped with the Royal Air Force's pressurized oxygen system, which was completely different from what the Marines used. The setup was great, except the pilots had no way to use it since the US Army Air Forces didn't see fit to send along any of the equipment needed to make those systems functional. Not that it mattered. The P-400s lacked a multistage high-altitude supercharger. It climbed like a lead brick, and its performance above twenty thousand feet was so bad it was virtually useless as a bomber interceptor.

Some of the pilots took the cooks' advice and ladled the rice—weevils and all—into their mouths. In a place where calories were hard to come by, everything, even the vermin, counted. Others couldn't bring themselves to do it, and by the time they finished their meals, a small pile of picked-out weevils lay scattered around their boots. The men stowed their mess gear and tramped down to the waiting jeeps and trucks to get to the flight line. Day nine of combat operations on Guadalcanal had begun.

Spread out in a line abreast in the parking area, the Wildcats waited for their pilots as the mechanics and CUB-1 sailors fussed over them with last-minute tweaks. The humidity was already so high, some felt as if they were trying to breathe underwater. The higher the sun rose, the higher the temperature spiked. The rain squalls from the previous night left the field a boggy mess. Now the top layer had dried and turned the mud to powdery dust. Jeeps, trucks, and aircraft all kicked up clouds of dust as they moved around. The stuff clung to everything and everyone, making bathing in the local river at best a momentary reprieve from grime.

On the southwest edge of the airfield, down by the Lunga River, Japanese snipers continued to infiltrate the nearby jungle. They climbed trees and tied themselves to the trunks, then patiently waited to take a shot at the mechanics laboring away on the aircraft. The ground crews, weary of these sudden attacks, kept rifles or tommy guns close at hand. When a sniper opened up, the ground crew would grab their weapons and spray the tree line. Day after day since August 21, this cat-and-mouse game played out. A few Americans were hit, but the snipers paid a hefty price. The return fire caused more than one sniper to drop his rifle and dangle, still attached to the tree, as he bled out from the bullet wounds the Americans had inflicted. They hung there, rotting in the sun until mud Marines with the unenviable task of clearing the jungle cut them down and searched them for intel. The Korean POWs would then dispose of their corpses.

It was a macabre way to work on aircraft. Yet, the men somehow managed to get ten Wildcats in fighting shape for the day's mission. Had there been spare parts and more maintainers, the remaining F4Fs might have been returned to service too. Fortunately, help on that front would arrive that very morning. The ground echelons for both VMF-223 and VMSB-232, embarked aboard the USS *William Ward Burrows*, reportedly would arrive that morning before lunch. The *Burrows* was a 4,500-ton converted attack transport that originally had been a passenger liner before the war. Built in Denmark at the start of the Great Depression, the vessel now sported a wartime paint job and four 3-inch antiaircraft guns.

With a small convoy, the *Burrows* arrived off Kukum shortly after breakfast, dropped anchor, and sent ashore well over a hundred enlisted maintainers from both squadrons. Its holds contained the most vital aviation supplies imaginable—spare parts for the Wildcats and Dauntlesses, a futuristic SCR-270 radar set to assist in detecting and intercepting incoming raids, hoists, tools, and logistic gear the men at Henderson desperately needed. The ship's crew began the hard work of getting this precious cargo offloaded while the men from both squadrons rode in trucks over to the airfield.

The Japanese ruined the reunion. Three times that morning, the air raid siren wailed to life, sending the men around the strip into the shelters. They huddled together, waiting either for a rain of bombs to fall or the all clear to sound, stuck shoulder to shoulder in their muddy holes. Some hunkered down inside bombproof dugouts—pits reinforced with lumber, covered in palm logs, sandbags, and dirt. Others lay in slit trenches. Though getting belowground offered the best possible protection against air attack, the covered shelters in particular were nexus points for disease transmission. Gastroenteritis was still going through the ranks at a blistering pace. Men, weakened from the virus, vomited or lost control of their bowels. Others slumped against one another listlessly, their faces waxen and wan.

Huddling in the shelters was sheer torment for the sick and a near-guaranteed ticket to pass the virus to the healthy. Richard Tregaskis, still recovering from his own bout with the disease, described the scene in one dugout: "The feverish, emaciated wrecks, most of them suffering from gastroenteritis, were a pitiful sight."

The cause of the frequent alarms stemmed from both the jumpiness triggered by the predawn surprise attack plus the warnings from the Coastwatchers up the Solomon chain. The first alarm, from a Coastwatcher on Bougainville at 0940, reported at least eighteen bombers heading south. New Georgia confirmed this sighting at 1105, triggering a scramble to get all flyable aircraft clear of Henderson.

John L. Smith led his ten Wildcats off the ground first, followed by the P-400s of the 67th Fighter Squadron. Once airborne, the SBDs made themselves scarce. Everyone was off Henderson Field by 1115, an incredible achievement, given the rough condition of the runway.

The air raid warning reached the *William Ward Burrows* only minutes after the scramble order went out to the fighter units. The ship's skipper, Lt. Cdr. Edward I. McQuiston, suspended unloading operations and weighed anchor. He steamed out into Savo Sound with the rest of the convoy, where the wider waters afforded them the ability to maneuver should they come under attack.

The raid arrived five minutes before noon, Tojo Time, as the lunch hour had become known to the Marines. The Betties hit their initial point, opened their bomb bay doors from twenty-five thousand feet, and released tight strings of bombs on Henderson. Some fell across the runway, blowing huge craters in the gravel and dirt. Other sticks battered the fighter parking area, striking the half-completed Japanese hangar the 67th used to refuel its fighters. Two out-of-commission F4Fs took shrapnel damage and burst into flames. An SBD also caught fire. Moments later, the 67th's cache of fuel drums suffered a direct hit, spraying flaming aviation fuel all over the area.

The ground crews and CUB-1 sailors swarmed over the fires, using shovels, blankets, buckets, and even bare hands to try to extinguish the blazes. As the men, covered in dirt, grime, and blood, fought to contain the destruction, VMF-223 swooped down on the bombers from twenty-eight thousand feet. A stricken Betty spiraled out of the fleeing formation, engines ablaze, its crew either dead or incapacitated by the g-forces of its death plunge. It went straight into the jungle not far from the airfield, where it exploded with such force that barely any part of it survived. Marines sent to examine the wreck discovered only bits of aluminum, with nothing of intelligence value to be gleaned.

The freshly arrived MAG-23 ground crews had been on Guadalcanal for less than a morning, and already they were thrown to the deep end of life within the perimeter. They emerged from bomb shelters, slit trenches, and foxholes to experience rivers of flame, destroyed aircraft, and the sounds of a dogfight swirling overhead. They pitched in to save what could be saved, even as their aviators fought for their lives almost five miles above their heads.

Engineers pre-positioned around the runway in trucks filled with gravel and dirt sped to the bomb craters. They quickly found more craters than they had material to fill them with, so they extemporized warnings for the aircrew by placing piles of tree branches or bushes beside the craters to mark their locations. Even with their quick work, it would be hours at the minimum before the airstrip was usable without unacceptable risk.

In the middle of the effort to fill the holes, an F4F carving a black stripe of smoke out of the clear blue sky glided over Savo, engine dead, props still. With the aircraft's wheels still up, the pilot barely made the runway. He smacked down on the strip and skidded out of control, straight into an unfilled bomb crater. Nearby Marines ran to the wreck, intending to pull the pilot out. The Grumman was studded with bullet and 20 mm shell holes. The cowling was torn open; black oil slicked across its windscreen and canopy.

Inside, the pilot lay still, chin on his chest, blood spattered all over the cockpit and canopy. One of the would-be rescuers called out, "That guy has had it. His watch is mine."

Eugene Trowbridge, the musician from Minnesota, stirred. The Marines recoiled, surprised that he was still alive. They recovered from their shock to quickly pry open the canopy and pull him clear. Concussed and covered in hot oil and blood, Eugene appeared to be in bad shape as the Marines laid him gently on the runway until a vehicle arrived to take him to the nearest aid station. He drifted in and out of consciousness but miraculously suffered no mortal wounds. Moments before, his F4F had caught the attention of two escorting Zeroes. They had followed him into a steep dive, raking his plane over and over with cannon and machine gun fire. His survival was nothing short of an act of God.

Other Wildcats appeared overhead now, turning into the pattern in preparation to get down on the runway. But Trowbridge's F4F wreck made landings impossible, so the engineers hooked towlines to the aircraft and used a vehicle to drag it to the side of the strip.

Still, Henderson was barely functional. The runway was stippled with bush-marked bomb craters, which forced the returning pilots to touch down and use their brakes and rudders to swerve around them in a ghastly sort of obstacle course. Somehow, nobody cracked up, including Zen Pond, who got back to the strip with a badly crippled fighter. Shot full of holes, engine on its last legs, the Wildcat executed a textbook landing in the worst possible conditions, thanks to the young second lieutenant, whose skill saved his aircraft for the mechanics to repair.

Trowbridge's F4F was a total write-off, fit only to be cannibalized for parts. Pond's fighter would be out of action for days. The two Wildcats destroyed on the ground left John L. with a total of eight functional aircraft, a mere two divisions. When Fike sent that information to Vandegrift, the general hit the panic button, writing to COMSOPAC HQ, "The steady deterioration of fighter strength is alarming." He asked for all available reinforcements to be sent immediately before Guadalcanal lost its tiny fighter force completely.

The day still seemed like a victory to John L.'s men. Nobody had been killed. Eugene would recover. Though they lost three fighters, the other pilots claimed four Betties and four escorting Zeroes. Both the Ivy Leaguers Red Kendrick and Scotty McLennan came into their own during that fight. Red claimed a Betty and a Zero while Scotty assisted Marion Carl in shooting down one of the bombers. John L. claimed two

Betties, Zen Pond got a Zero before he was shot up, and Ken Frazier claimed a bomber. Hyde Phillips, on his first mission, was credited with a Zero.

The Japanese reported losing a Betty and a Zero over the target area, and another battle-damaged Betty crash-landed at Buka Island in Papua New Guinea and was destroyed.

As the cleanup continued at Henderson, the *Burrows* made its way to Tulagi that afternoon, the skipper intending to spend the night in its harbor before returning to Guadalcanal to offload all the aviation gear. Less than five minutes after entering the channel that led to the main harbor, the ship ran hard aground on Sylvia Reef. For the next ninety minutes, every effort failed to dislodge her. The ship was stuck hard, and when darkness fell, efforts to get it clear were abandoned for the night. The spare parts the Marine squadrons needed more than ever would stay aboard ship at least until the morning.

Just before sundown, an Allied patrol plane spotted a task force of Japanese ships speeding down the Slot for Guadalcanal. The crew identified five cruisers, a deadly powerful squadron with heavy eight-inch guns. This could only mean two things: First, Henderson was going to get shelled again. Second, any American ship in the area was sure to take a pounding. At their current speed, the cruisers would reach Savo Sound sometime around midnight.

Communications being what they were, Henderson didn't get the warning until well after dark. At 2300, Dick Mangrum received orders to make a maximum effort to stop these cruisers, which could easily find the *Burrows* stuck on the reef. Hastily, he and Turner Caldwell assembled fourteen SBD crews and led them aloft.

A waning gibbous moon dimly lit Savo Sound while clouds periodically obscured everything. The Marine and Navy pilots patrolled, determined to find the Japanese ships before the enemy could attack the transport carrying all the aviation supplies the Americans desperately needed.

The aircraft ranged back and forth along the coast, from Taivu Point west to Cape Esperance, then across Savo Island to patrol Sealark

Channel. They found nothing. Dispirited, they returned to Henderson where miraculously all planes landed safely.

Those twenty-eight American eyes in the sky that night missed the Japanese task force as it lay off Taivu Point. The patrol plane had been wrong. There weren't five cruisers; there were seven large destroyers plus a couple of patrol boats. Admiral Tanaka had ordered them to deliver the 1st Battalion, 124th Infantry, along with the rest of Ichiki's battalion, some of which had been aboard the ships attacked on August 25. Altogether, they offloaded about a thousand imperial soldiers, supplies, and four antitank guns. It was the first successful landing of troops at this scale since VMSB-232 had arrived at Guadalcanal.

But the operation proved only half successful. Tanaka had given the destroyer commander, Captain Murakami, explicit orders to sweep Savo for Allied ships once the crew finished unloading. Instead, on hearing the engine sounds of Mangrum's strike force pass nearby, the commander got cold feet and retreated up the Slot. Thus, the *Burrows* and the other ships in the area were spared from near-certain destruction. Murakami had been the skipper who turned around in violation of his orders on August 28 after Mangrum's planes attacked Destroyer Squadron 20. This earlier retreat had earned him a royal ass-chewing from Tanaka. This time, when Murakami returned to the Shortlands, Tanaka relieved him on the spot for ignoring his orders.

The Marine dive-bombers were directly responsible for wounding Admiral Tanaka, killing a destroyer division commander, and getting another one relieved—all in nine days of operations. It was a remarkable ancillary effect to their arrival on Guadalcanal.

Though the *Burrows* avoided Japanese gunfire that night, Lieutenant Commander McQuiston's crew could not get the vessel off the reef the following morning. They pumped out oil storage tanks, passed towlines to other ships, and strained the ship's engines to their limit and beyond. Nothing worked. The towlines broke again and again. Draining some of their fuel oil also failed to lighten the ship, which remained stuck fast in about fifteen feet of water. The *Burrows* stayed trapped on the reef until midafternoon on September 2. Finally, on either September 1 or 2, the

SCR-270 radar set was offloaded to a small boat and shipped across to Guadalcanal. That piece of equipment proved to be about the only significant *Burrows* cargo that reached the Marines.

In his desperation to get his ship off the reef, McQuiston ordered his crew to toss much of MAG-23's gear overboard in an effort to free the transport vessel. The desperately needed spare parts, hoists, spark plugs, oil filters, crated engines, and other material the squadrons had loaded aboard ship in Oahu ended up underwater, unused, scattered around Sylvia Reef, where they remain to this day.

Finally, in the late afternoon of September 2, the transport finally pulled off the reef and got underway again. McQuiston guided the *Burrows* into the inner harbor, where he promptly ran the ship aground again on Southern Cross Reef less than two hours later. It took until sundown the next day to get off this reef. The *Burrows* sporadically unloaded what was left of the cargo, some at Tulagi and some at Kukum, before departing the area for the New Hebrides on September 5.

Bottom line: most of the aviation gear never reached Henderson. It was a logistic disaster for MAG-23, one which McQuiston failed to mention in his ship's war diary. But Dick Mangrum did. He made a point of calling the ship out for what had to have been one of the worst and most consequential series of blunders of the campaign to date.[1]

Hamstrung without their logistic tail, John L. and Dick Mangrum's men faced the worst trials of their lives in the days to come.

THIRTY

NINETY SECONDS TO FAME

Henderson Field, Guadalcanal
August 30, 1942, morning

THE PILOTS OF VMF-223 SAT IN THE PAGODA, PLAYING CARDS AND smoking. The clock, recently installed, ticked past 0900. None of them had slept much the night before as everyone assumed the task force that Mangrum's men went searching for would soon bombard the field. Instead of sleeping, they passed midnight sitting atop overturned ammo boxes, talking quietly, and waiting for the distant sound of naval guns that would send them rushing to the nearest dugout or slit trench.

The rest of the night was interrupted with frequent false alarms that denied the pilots any consistent sleep. They finally rose around 0430 to warm up their engines and grab a little chow before heading to the Pagoda for the morning's wait. John L. avoided the typical fare of rice with "protein" and snagged some Japanese vanilla wafer cookies, washing them down with coffee.

The P-400 pilots sat together in another part of the Pagoda, also awaiting word to scramble, despite the limitations of their aircraft. They were a spirited, if frustrated, bunch who wanted to contribute. Their airplanes were not the measure of their heart. The Marines felt great sympathy for them.

Marion Carl attended Oregon State with one of the pilots in the 67th. They had been good friends. Now that he was on Guadalcanal, Marion made a point of sharing his knowledge with the friend and the other P-400 pilots. The memory of those first Zeroes he'd fought at Midway never left Marion's mind. Their agility and the quickness of their turns made the Wildcat look like a bloated beast—and the P-400, only more so. The Airacobras lacked the agility to evade a surprise attack. Diving away would be their only chance.

The tactical problem was obvious: the P-400 was never going to get above any Zeroes. Not in this battle area, anyway. The P-400 pilots had talked it over at length, deciding that the best thing to do would be to create a defensive circle with the squadron if attacked from above. That way, each pilot could cover the tail of the next in the circle. In World War I, this tactic was called the Lufbery circle, after French American ace Raoul Lufbery. It was used for a while on the Western Front until the Germans figured out that fighters flying defensively were little threat. The Germans could take their time, sit above the Lufbery circles, and dive down in slashing attacks to pick off a plane or two.

The truth was, there just weren't many options for the men of the 67th.

At 0930, the Pagoda's phone rang. Paul Mason, a Coastwatcher on Bougainville, had reported seeing a large formation of single-engine aircraft heading toward Guadalcanal. No two-engine Betties though.

This situation was new. What were the Japanese up to now? A discussion at the Pagoda followed as the aviators waited for word from New Georgia that the formation was in sight. Maybe Mason had just missed the Betties, or maybe they had been obscured by cloud cover. The Americans concluded that the formation was a dive-bombing raid and that the destroyer-transport *Colhoun*, anchored off Guadalcanal, and the *Burrows* were probably the Japanese's targets.

At 1100, New Georgia reported that engine sounds could be heard somewhere above the overcast layer sitting above the island. Though nobody identified the aircraft, the Marines at least now knew the Japanese would arrive by noon. John L. Smith gathered his seven other pilots, reminding them not to repeat the mistakes of August 26. No spraying and praying. No trying to hit multiple targets. Select one, and stay with it until it burns. He told them they would climb to twenty-five thousand feet heading east, rallying about ten miles from the field. Then they would turn back and patrol over the beach, staying close to Henderson while covering the *Colhoun*.

The 67th Fighter Squadron scrambled a flight of four P-400s to perch above the *Burrows* in hopes they could pick off the Japanese dive-bombers during their attack runs. Not long after, seven more P-400s led by their commander, Maj. Dale Brannon, lifted from Henderson Field. Including John L.'s own Wildcat, eight F4Fs took off next, turning east as briefed while their props dragged them to altitude. By 1120, every flyable aircraft left the strip. Mangrum's SBDs lit out south to stay well clear of the action.

The eight F4Fs formed up into two divisions east of the field. John L., Charles Kendrick, Marion Carl, and Willis Lees composed the lead division, with Rivers Morrell, Scotty McLennan, Ken Frazier, and Zen Pond following. Brannon's P-400s struggled up to about twelve thousand feet. A weather front had moved into the area, and lots of clouds at different altitudes lay scattered before it. The two American squadrons kept losing sight of each other.

Brannon turned back for Henderson to begin his patrol. John L. and his men did the same a couple of minutes later. Running back along the coast, they flew between towering cumulous clouds that created chasms of clear sky.

A mass formation of Zeroes suddenly burst through one of the cloud walls, diving like falcons onto Brannon's seven P-400s. The A6Ms dipped just below the Airacobras and pulled up to hit their vulnerable bellies.

"Zeroes! Zeroes over us! Jumping us!" one of the P-400 pilots called out. "We're just north of the field!"

The Marines didn't hear the warning, but the other P-400 flight over the *Burrows* did. The Airacobras turned south and raced to get into the fight. Meanwhile, John L. and the other Marines saw the Zeroes go after the 67th. He swung his men upsun, then rolled right in after them, following them down at over 340 miles per hour. At that speed, the Wildcats chewed up the distance quickly. John L. keyed his mic and reminded everyone again to pick one target and stay with it on this first pass.

The P-400s broke hard into a Lufbery circle, the Zeroes zoom-climbing after them, still in tight formations of three each. John L. counted twenty-two aircraft. If his squadron didn't get there in time, it would be a slaughter.

The Marines got there just in time. The Zero pilots, totally absorbed with their P-400 targets, never saw the F4Fs screaming down on them. The Grummans spewed lead. One tracer, one armor piercing, one incendiary. That's how the 223 armorers belted the ammo. These crewmen had spent their first night on Guadalcanal rubbing oil off each round to ensure that their pilots would suffer no jams. At 1,850 bullets per F4F, it had been a long night for those men.

Their labor paid off now. The Marines decimated the Japanese formation with the one pass. Everyone scored. Flaming aircraft fell out of the sky, twisting and turning in death spirals as 223 zoomed for altitude, trading the speed they had gained for positional advantage.

The remaining Zeroes split their attention. Some went after the Marines while some stayed on Brannon's P-400s. As a pair of Airacobras exploded in flames, their pilots popped the unusual car door on the side of the fuselage and hit the silk. Their chutes blossomed among the clouds, and the spinning, dying aircraft fell earthward around them.

John L. checked his six and saw Red Kendrick tacked onto him with loyal tenacity. In such chaotic moments, it was easy to lose a wingman. Red came through the first pass, scored a kill, and clung to John L.'s tail. But as the Oklahoman scanned the sky on his starboard side, he saw a lone Wildcat climbing slower than the others, a Zero on its tail, snapping out bursts. Streaks of tracers seemed to connect them for a second or two. The Japanese pilot's aim was good. His bullets battered the Wildcat.

In the cockpit of that bird, Willis Lees juked and jinked, trying to throw the Zero's aim off. He was running out of airspeed with the Japanese closing on him fast. Another volley of cannon and machine gun fire lashed his F4F. Bits of metal flew off the cowling. Puncture wounds suddenly appeared on it, and the engine coughed.

John L. banked sharply and rolled down on the Zero. The maneuver gave him a high deflection shot. He pulled the trigger on his control stick. His six .50s roared to life. The Zero erupted in flames and fell out of its climb, tumbling earthward as Willis dropped his nose and dove into a cloud, momentarily safe.

Another Zero appeared in front of John L., slightly below and to one side. It turned toward him. He felt a trill of cold terror as he realized the Japanese pilot had targeted him. A few more seconds, and he would be in range. He clamped down on the fear, pushing the nose of his Wildcat low to get his guns on the Japanese. The two planes barreled straight at each other in a head-on pass, the Zero in a slight climb, John L. in a slight dive. The Japanese opened fire first. Laser-like streaks of tracers flashed around John L.'s speeding Wildcat. His windscreen suddenly spider-webbed as a bullet smashed into it dead in front of John L.'s nose. But the shot failed to penetrate the armored glass. He forced himself to keep his eye locked on his gunsight's reticle. The Zero swelled in his view. Only a few hundred yards away now, time for only a short burst.

John L. pulled the trigger. His six gun barrels flared as ten bullets per second poured forth. Several guns ceased firing almost immediately, out of ammunition. But those last bullets arrowed straight into the Zero's engine, shattering the propeller and blowing chunks out of the A6M's fourteen-cylinder air-cooled Sakae engine. Debris spun off the plane's cowling even as the Japanese raked the F4F's fuselage aft of the cockpit. John L. heard the hits strike home with dull, metallic thuds. The difference was, his bird could take the punishment. The Japanese was not so lucky.

The aircraft zoomed past each other less than twenty feet apart. John L. saw that the Japanese pilot had flung back his canopy, and the American caught a fleeting glimpse of his rust-brown helmet and goggles. Pieces of the Zero smacked against the Wildcat's wings, buffeting the Grumman as John L. twisted in his seat to see the Zero's ultimate fate. He saw the Japanese pilot, half in, half out of his cockpit, trying desperately to get away from his dying aircraft. Then it spun sharply, obscuring the fate of the pilot from view, and fell into a cloud, trailing flames and smoke.

The entire battle lasted ninety seconds.

Marion Carl's voice came over the radio. "Got two, heading home."

The Oklahoman decided to do the same. He rolled into a long dive, Red still with him despite battle damage of his own. The Stanford grad had taken a cannon round right into the side of his canopy. It blew a fist-sized hole through the plexiglass and studded his neck and shoulder with shrapnel wounds. Even as the slipstream whistled shrilly through the hole, he doggedly protected his skipper's tail.

While the two F4Fs dove for the beach, Marion returned to Henderson at five thousand feet, skirting the cloud banks, some of which stretched to over forty thousand feet. The weather was really closing in now. While he negotiated the clouds, he kept his head in constant motion, eyes sweeping the sky to make sure he didn't get bounced again like he had on the twenty-sixth.

His eyes caught sight of a lone Wildcat clearly in bad shape. It limped along, trading altitude for airspeed below him, a black scarf of smoke streaming behind it. It would be hit or miss if the Wildcat could make it back to Henderson before the pilot ran out of altitude. As he watched it, a black form dropped out of the bottom of a cloud and made straight for the crippled Grumman.

Marion rolled over and dove furiously after the attacker. Once again, the Japanese pilot focused on his target and failed to check his six. If he'd looked, he would have seen Marion's Wildcat dead astern, running him down, thanks to the speed gained in the dive.

Marion held his fire. No deflection, point-blank range. It was a perfect setup. He pulled the trigger. The A6M staggered and dropped into the water just off the beach, sending up a huge geyser of seawater to mark its final resting place.

Willis Lees, Marion's wingman, looked back to see his life saved a second time that day. He dragged his shattered F4F back to Henderson, barely clearing the trees at the end of the runway before crash-landing.

At the field, the fight could not be seen by those on the ground, but they could hear the whine and scream of engines under full military power and the chatter of gunfire. A few of the doomed fighters spinning under tongues of flame came into brief view as they dropped out of the clouds to crash in the water offshore.

Then a Wildcat, already badly shot up, sped over the field, dragging a Zero close behind. The Zero riddled the F4F with bullets, so close the antiaircraft machine gunners around the runway couldn't risk firing at it. Then the Wildcat turned hard, and the Zero raced past it and zoom-climbed into the clouds. The F4F swung back toward the strip and crash-landed.

The other F4Fs and P-400s started appearing over the field. Most of the Airacobras looked pretty beat up to the observing Marines on the ground. As they began to land, John L. and Red sped home on the deck just off the beach west of Henderson. Just above the trees in front of them, a Zero materialized, heading toward Savo Sound. John L. swung behind it, closed rapidly, and fired. Only one gun responded to his trigger pull, but the Zero pilot flew straight and level, giving John L. a perfect target to maximize the few rounds he had left.

His lone functional gun stopped after a short burst, but it was enough. The Zero pitched nose down and went straight into the water, right off the beach.

Red and John L. landed last after the sprawling dogfight. They taxied to a stop to find the 223 pilots celebrating. The squadron had mowed through the Zeroes that day, Fike crediting them with fourteen kills. In return, three of the F4Fs—including Willis's—were total write-offs, fit only for parts to keep the others running. Of the remaining five, only two could be returned to immediate service once they were rearmed and refueled.

What mattered, though, was that everyone had come back alive. Red Kendrick's wounds proved superficial. He'd be back in action within a couple of days. In return, the Americans had tackled the vaunted Zero and given the Japanese a severe thrashing, thanks to their surprise attack. The Japanese got sandwiched between the Marines and Air Corps pilots and suffered catastrophic losses. The myth of the Zero's invincibility had been shattered for good.

The dive-bombers never materialized. Neither had any level bombers. The Marines concluded that the weather must have forced them back while the escorting A6Ms pressed on to the target.

Dale Brannon's Airacobra pilots were in no mood to celebrate. Though they had claimed four Zeroes, two P-400s fell to these enemy fighters during their initial pass. Both pilots bailed out and survived, but the rest of Brannon's fighters all took substantial damage. Worse, when the flight of four P-400s that had patrolled over the *Burrows* turned south, they were bounced by Zeroes and half went down in flames. Neither pilot survived.

It was a hard lesson that embittered the Air Corps pilots. The squadron's history reflected that frustration and anger, pointing out that as much as the men wanted to fight, Bell Aero Corporation had saddled them with a complete clunker. As an interceptor, the P-400 was a death trap. As an air superiority fighter, it stood no chance with the Zero. The men learned that at medium altitude, the Japanese could stick with them at least partway if they tried to dive out of the fight. The Airacobras couldn't climb. They couldn't turn. They couldn't dive. And they couldn't get to the altitude the bombers usually used.

From that point on, the 67th was out of the air-to-air game. MAG-23 would use Brannon's men for ground attack and antiship missions, something the P-400 excelled at since it did possess heavy firepower, including a 20 mm cannon.

Later that afternoon, the Japanese sent another raid to Guadalcanal. Between the two squadrons, only two F4Fs could get aloft. Marion Carl grabbed Scotty McLennan, and they took the functional Grummans into the air together. Above them, about eighteen Betties and a dozen Zeroes droned over the *Colhoun* at twenty-five thousand feet. The vessel, anchored offshore and busily unloading vital supplies for the Marines, made a perfect stationary target. The Japanese crews struck it repeatedly, blowing flaming diesel oil over the aft portion of the ship, destroying the searchlight platform, and trapping the engine room crew belowdecks.

Two other bombs obliterated the aft deckhouse a moment later. The destroyer sank quickly, taking fifty-one of its crew with it.

Despite being hopelessly outnumbered, Marion and Scotty did their best to intercept the raid. They had received warning of it too late to get up to the bombers, so they never made contact. Had they done so, the twelve Zeroes would probably have made short work of them.

Still, it was a reprise of the sheer, raw courage Marion Carl had displayed at Midway, when he and Bill Humberd had done the same thing on the afternoon of June 4. At Guadalcanal, the act of bravery added to Carl's growing legend and demonstrated that Scotty McLennan held his own with the best too—at least in terms of heart and guts.

It would be decades before the surviving American pilots of this fight learned the truth of that August day in 1942. The Japanese, appalled by the losses inflicted on the Betty squadrons, had changed up tactics. Instead of sending down the typical raid at lunchtime, they redeployed the *Zuikaku*'s and *Shōkaku*'s fighters to Buka in the Northern Solomons. Nine A6Ms from each squadron executed a fighter sweep two hours before the main bombing raid of the day reached Guadalcanal.

The tactic served its purpose. The bombers suffered no losses that day, and the defenders of Guadalcanal were reduced to a handful of functional fighters. That said, the Japanese paid a catastrophic price for their success. The fighter sweep lost eleven aircraft—nine over the target and two more in crash landings back at Buka. The destruction of eleven out of eighteen A6Ms in one mission, along with the loss of eight irreplaceable veteran pilots, some of whom had been in combat since 1937, crippled the fighter squadrons of Japan's last two large fleet carriers. It was a devastating blow, made worse by the loss of the mission's leader, Lt. Hideki Shingō. A 1933 graduate of the Imperial Japanese Naval Academy at Eta Jima, Shingō had cut his teeth in combat flying the Zero's predecessor, the A5M "Claude," in China. He later served in the Tainan Air Group before joining the *Zuikaku*'s fighter squadron.

During the dogfight, he'd been badly shot up. He limped out of the fight and belly-landed his Zero on the beach at Guadalcanal. After vanishing into the jungle, he made contact with Japanese troops and eventually made his way back up to the Northern Solomons. For the moment, though, Shingō was out of action, another veteran leader downed by the Marines defending what some of the Japanese aircrews now called "Death Island."[1]

THIRTY-ONE

THE DEVILS AND KAWAGUCHI

Guadalcanal
September 1, 1942, 0130 hours

INSIDE THE COCKPIT OF MB-21, MAJ. RICHARD MANGRUM AND HIS gunner, Dennis Byrd, dozed fitfully. The two men had been flying around the clock, grabbing catnaps in the cockpit for days now, just like the rest of VMSB-232. The Japanese were up to something big, and the Dauntless crews were working overtime to put a stop to it.

Dick was beyond exhausted. The stress of command, the loss of Oliver Mitchell, and the constant missions—combined with sleep deprivation and lack of food—left him looking gaunt, hollow eyed, and haggard. Yet he possessed the self-discipline not to take his stress out on those around him, something John L. would sometimes do. Dick remained even-keeled, always appearing to be unaffected by the fury of the fray.

It did help that on August 30, just as the second Japanese raid arrived to sink the *Colhoun*, the other two MAG-23 squadrons reached Henderson Field. Maj. Robert "Bob" Galer, skipper of VMF-224, brought in nineteen Wildcats and the air group commander, Col. William J. Wallace. They jumped out of their F4Fs and ran for the nearest slit trench as the air raid siren wailed—quite the introduction to their new home. Coming in with them was Maj. Leo Smith's VMSB-231 and the squadron's twelve SBD-3 Dauntlesses. For a miraculous two days, the three SBD squadrons could count on about twenty-five operational dive-bombers. But losses would soon reduce their numbers.

Dick had hoped the reinforcements would mean the load could be shared a little more, giving his men some breaks between missions. Unfortunately, circumstances prevented this support from happening. Since August 29, his squadron had been flying more than any other time in his entire career, thanks to the sense of urgency to find and attack the Japanese reinforcement convoys that some wag had dubbed the Cactus Express, a nickname that later evolved into Tokyo Express.[1]

His men were sick, slowly starving, and being asked to do too much. Tom Moore, snoozing in the aircraft next to Dick's, had flown six hours' worth of anti-submarine patrols earlier that day. Arthur O'Keefe, still hobbling from the injury he'd suffered aboard the *Long Island*, had flown six as well. Bruce Prosser, Henry Hise, Danny Iverson—they all averaged seven to nine hours in the cockpit each day. There were no days off either. Sleeping between missions inside their SBDs while the ground crews refueled and rearmed them became standard fare.

Flight 300's crews flew with equal intensity, and Leo Smith's outfit was just ramping up to do the same. Before this deployment, nobody expected inexperienced crews fresh from the training pipeline would be flying twenty-four-hour continuous ops, day after day, but here they were, doing just that.

Mangrum glanced out the canopy into almost total darkness. The moon had long since been obscured by clouds. It had been raining on and off all night. Now it was drizzling, sending water droplets streaking down his windscreen and canopy. The ground crews were soaked and shivering as they worked to refuel and rearm the birds. The ops tempo was as hard on them, if not harder. During the daytime, the sun baked their skin while the dust from the runway clogged their noses and covered them with grit. Some fell out with the illnesses raging through the ranks. Others kept at it, doing their best to ignore the fevers, the vomiting, and the constant diarrhea. Their only break since August 29 came when their SBDs were aloft.

Dick could see their shadowy outlines moving beyond his wingtip, preparing to sling a 500-pound bomb under his aircraft. He felt a surge of pride and admiration for them. They toiled anonymously, ignored by the reporters on the island. But these kids—some of them Marines for barely six months—were rising to the occasion just like his pilots and gunners. For all they faced, the Red Devils were holding their own.

He was holding his own, too, thanks in large measure to his only true friend in the unit, his executive officer Fletcher Brown. Brownie may not have been the best pilot in the outfit, but he shouldered much of the administrative duties, proactively problem solved, and repeatedly proved himself courageous in the sky. The two men really ran the squadron together, and Dick knew his friend would be a great skipper someday soon. If they survived this.

Brownie's keen eyes made him an ideal night-flying pilot. On August 30, while John L. and his boys battled Zeroes, Dick's scouts found an inbound Japanese task force off the Russell Islands just before sunset. Leo Smith's guys had just arrived, so it fell to Flight 300 and VMSB-232 to go after the task force. Flight 300 launched Lt. Hal Buell and Lt. Elmer "Spike" Conzett, a veteran dive-bomber pilot who had seen a lot of action aboard the *Enterprise*. Dick Mangrum took Fletcher Brown and Tom Moore. Together, they fanned out and roamed the coast of Guadalcanal until after midnight. Brownie and Spike finally found the Japanese off Taivu Point, some twenty miles east of Henderson. Brownie spotted the ships first and called them out and rolled into a dive before Spike even realized they were there. A hail of flak rose to greet Brownie and Spike's SBDs just as Brownie planted his bomb about fifty meters off a patrol boat's beam.[2] Spike's 500-pounder landed on the other side of the same vessel, about an equal distance away.

The near misses rocked the vessel, caused minor damage, but inflicted terror among the Imperial Japanese Army troops aboard. The near misses came at a price—a 25 mm flak shell pierced Spike's fuselage and exploded against the cockpit deck, throwing shrapnel into the instrument panel. A sliver of shrapnel sliced through Spike's calf and lodged behind his shin bone. Bleeding profusely and dazed, Spike lost control of his SBD.

It entered a spin and plunged through the darkness. Somehow, without most of the instruments functioning, he pulled out and limped home to Henderson.

These encounters convinced the 1st Marine Division HQ that the Japanese were undertaking a massive reinforcement effort that threatened to dislodge the Marines. General Vandegrift protected the airfield with only six understrength rifle battalions whose half-starved men suffered from dysentery, malaria, and gastroenteritis. To strengthen the perimeter, he brought over the Marine parachute battalion and Col. Merritt "Red Mike" Edson's Raider Battalion from Tulagi. They had taken heavy losses capturing the islands around Tulagi Harbor, but Vandegrift needed every Marine he could get for what lay ahead.

In the meantime, it fell to the SBD crews to find and sink as many of these reinforcement convoys as they could find. On this night, reports of cruisers and destroyers in the Taivu Point area again sent the Dauntless crews aloft. Shuttle bombing, they called it. The problem was, they couldn't bomb what they couldn't see. The search-and-strike teams had failed to find the Japanese earlier in the night. Now, Mangrum would lead another effort as soon as his division's planes were ready.

At about 0200, they fired their engines up. Dick, Danny Iverson, Tom Moore, and Charley McAllister had this mission. Flight 300 would run the next one in about an hour. As the pilots taxied to their launch points, the night was lit by the engineer flare pots that marked the runway. Their red-orange glow through the mist and drizzle cast a medieval air. Beyond their little spheres of light, the darkness was total, the moon still hiding behind the clouds. The rest of the island remained blacked out, lest even the tip of a lit cigarette draw the aim of Japanese snipers.

The runway was a boggy mess. Muddy, with wheel ruts cut through it by previous missions. As Mangrum began his takeoff run, the SBD felt sluggish, its tires slopping through the muck as viscous as molasses. Mud spattered the fuselage and underbelly, whipped up by the wheels, then blown against the aircraft by SBD's prop wash. It took added runway to drag the dive-bomber aloft, but Mangrum pulled it into the air. Behind him, Tom Moore began his takeoff run. Like Mangrum's, the SBD felt mushy and slow as the bomber slogged through the mud. The bird passed the midway point of the strip, tail reluctantly coming up. A moment later, it broke free of the ground.

At a hundred feet, still over the strip, Moore's engine suddenly coughed and quit. He was barely at flying speed with only seconds to save the aircraft. He switched tanks and grabbed the fuel system's wobble pump. The bird sagged toward the end of the runway, hit the ground, and skidded into the trees. The engineers had just cut down the tallest ones only a day or two before, so the SBD careened right into a field of stumps. The impact tore the Dauntless into three pieces, sending its 500-pound bomb tumbling through the ruined jungle-scape.

Somehow, Moore and his gunner, Claude Hallyburton, found themselves outside the wreckage, standing in the damp and cold night. Both were badly injured and in shock. As Marines rushed up to the scene to effect a rescue, one turned to Moore and said, "Do you think we'll ever find the pilot?"

Both pilot and gunner collapsed a moment later.

As they were rushed to the division's field hospital, Mangrum, Iverson, and McAllister continued with the mission. They formed up on one another's blue exhaust flames and set off in search of the reported Japanese ships.

Somewhere in the darkness, eight Japanese fast destroyers lay hove to, disembarking a thousand-man force from Gen. Kiyotake Kawaguchi's 35th Infantry Brigade. Kawaguchi himself was already on Taivu Point, watching the rest of his troops come ashore in small landing craft and boats.

Overhead, the Marines could see nothing. The mission, useless. Flying in pitch darkness through bad weather in the dead of night made no sense, but the situation was so desperate it had to be done. At 0430, Mangrum finally called it quits and led the Devils back to Henderson. Frustrated and worried about Moore and Hallyburton, they splashed down on the morass of a runway and reported in at the Pagoda.

As soon as they debriefed, Dennis Byrd headed off to the field hospital with another gunner to find out the status of Moore and Hallyburton.

Claude was a good friend of his, and since the rest of the unit arrived from the *Burrows* a few days before, they had shared a tent.

Byrd and Josiah Humphreys entered through the canvas flap to find a different world. Wounded, sick men lay on narrow cots arranged so close, there was hardly any room to move between them. Some of the malarial victims moaned and hallucinated through fever dreams. Men with missing arms, missing legs, stumps bandaged, eyes dulled from morphine, stared at the tent ceiling as the medical staff circulated among them. These were the men slated to be evacuated as soon as a transport came into Henderson. They would be flown out to the New Hebrides to the naval hospital there, then sent home when stabilized.

Byrd asked a passing corpsmen where Moore and Hallyburton could be found. Harried and overworked, the medic pointed toward the back of the tent and moved on before Dennis could ask for clarification.

The two Red Devils walked down a narrow central aisle in the tent, searching for familiar faces. There were none. At this end of the tent, bandages concealed almost every man's visage. Dennis looked for a name on a chart or at least a tag of some sort at the end of the cots but could find no such markings. They wandered through the swaddled and still men, unable to find their friends. Finally, they gave up, assuming that Moore and Hallyburton were unconscious or asleep.

Meanwhile, Mangrum returned to the squadron's bivouac area. It had changed significantly in the past forty-eight hours. The communal canvas fly had been replaced by tents, brought in with the rest of the squadron's ground echelon. The enlisted men had spent Labor Day weekend busily improving the entire outfit's living conditions. Every man now had his own cot, a locker box, and a couple of tentmates. It sure beat sleeping under—or inside—the SBDs.

Mess Sgt. Al Gruenke intercepted Dick as he entered camp. Gruenke had come ashore with the main echelon only a few days before, his cooks and bakers ready to do their best for the squadron—by any means necessary. Leave it to old-hand NCOs to find ways to "acquire" things the outfit needed. Gruenke and the other NCOs took it as their personal mission to make things better for everyone, even at the expense of other outfits.

In other words, they were foragers and master thieves. They fanned out that first weekend, stealing everything they could find that might be of use. Gruenke's men quickly set up their field kitchen, painting a sign that read "Gruenke's Grill: You Can Please Some of the People Some of the Time, but You Can't Please All of the People All of the Time."

Dick stopped to talk to his mess sergeant, who cataloged some of the things his band of thieves had returned with. Chocolate, some captured Japanese noodles, Aussie rations like bully beef. Gruenke saved the best for last. His men managed to purloin several boxes of frozen steaks off the *Burrows* while helping offload some of the aviation equipment. Actual steak. Dick couldn't believe it. The whole squadron would get a steak dinner that afternoon.

It got better. The mess crew had also gotten their hands on a small amount of frozen chicken from another ship. Other units might save that treat for the aircrews or the officers. But not 232. Dick told Sergeant Gruenke to make chicken soup so that every man—enlisted or officer, ground crew or aircrew—could share in the bounty. Gruenke smiled and bounded off to get to work. It was the start of his field kitchen's reputation for the being the best on the island.

Later that morning, between air raid alerts and while Dick and Brownie worked some of the endless administrative issues, 2nd Lt. Don Rose went to see Dennis Byrd. Dick had asked the lieutenant to handle Moore's and Hallyburton's personal effects. Both men would be evacuated off the island soon. Their locker boxes would need to be sent home with them.

Dennis and Don silently packed up Claude's belongings, tucking them reverently into his trunk. They inventoried each item, noting it on a form that would go back with the gear. When they finished, each man grabbed an end and carried the box to the squadron's new admin tent. In back stood a small stack of locker boxes. Byrd saw Frank Schackman's box sitting next to Oliver Mitchell's and felt his gut tighten. They put Claude Hallyburton's on top of it, Tom Moore's atop Mitchell's. Four out of twenty-four. Two dead, two injured. The mounting cost sobered both men. Yet they couldn't dwell on these losses. Both had missions later in the day, and to dwell on the dead distracted focus from survival.

The morning search missions left Guadalcanal at dawn. The two F4F squadrons put up a morning patrol. Then Colonel Wallace ordered all available aircraft to hit Taivu Point. Clearly, the Japanese had been using it as a staging base, landing troops and supplies.

All day long, Dale Brannon's two flyable P-400s, along with a few F4Fs and SBDs from every unit on Guadalcanal, bombed and raked the jungle on Taivu Point. When the air raid alert tripped a full scramble off the strip, the dive-bombers all went to shoot up the jungle instead of boring holes in the sky south of the airfield. The attacks left General Kawaguchi with ruptured eardrums, his men shaken. By day's end, the jungle around the point was reduced to smoldering, charred ruins. Kawaguchi's men, fresh ashore, suffered a number of killed and wounded while some of the dearly needed supplies the Japanese had brought ashore went up in flames.

The ceaseless tempo in operations that day would have driven healthy men into the ground. Gruenke's steak feed did wonders for morale that afternoon. So did the arrival of the first mail bags to reach Guadalcanal. Everyone got letters from home. Between missions, the men read and reread the words their loved ones had sent across the vast Pacific expanse to their lonely tropical hell.

Charley McAllister opened a letter from his newlywed wife and read with jubilation that he was going to be a father. He spent the rest of the afternoon trying to buy up every cigar he could find to salt away for the day he received the news of his child's birth. As he wandered the bivouacs in search of tobacco to hoard, both Mangrum and John L. Smith opened official letters letting them know they had been promoted, Dick to lieutenant colonel and Smith to major. They pinned on their new insignia later that day amid hasty celebrations with their squadrons.

The afternoon search went out but failed to find the night's Cactus Express. Dusk came and went. The flight operations continued without letup. Small groups of three or four SBDs launched throughout the night, with orders to patrol the coastline on either side of the perimeter and attack any enemy force they discovered. The weather turned bad after dark, again concealing the moon. This time, however, the Americans tried a new tactic. Deploying a slow-moving Consolidated PBY Catalina flying boat over the area, its crew would drop flares above the SBDs to give them a better view of the shoreline.

Through intermittent squalls, the SBDs searched for the enemy. Finally, around 0130, they caught a break. The mud Marines reported seeing flashes at Taivu Point. Something was going down there. The PBY and three SBDs rolled in to investigate.

Four Japanese destroyers carrying the 1st Battalion, 124th Infantry Regiment, had arrived off Kawaguchi's landing site from the night before. The Japanese navy's failure to alert the general of their arrival caused a blue-on-blue, friendly-fire incident. The Japanese in the jungle, dogged all day long by American planes, had panicked on seeing landing craft heading toward their beach. They opened fire and a firefight ensued, inflicting casualties on both the landing force and Kawaguchi's men on shore. By the time they figured out what was going on, the SBDs and PBY were on their way.

Fletcher Brown, Bruce Prosser, and a third pilot, probably from Flight 300, spotted three of the destroyers just offshore. Landing craft chugged along between the ships and the beach. Brownie called it in to Henderson, and the PBY lumbered over to assist.

"To all planes from control," Henderson called to Brownie's formation, "Plane Two is in the target area; he will drop flares. He will drop flares."

A moment later, the PBY crew confirmed, "Over enemy ships. Will drop flares."

"I'm down to a thousand feet, trying to pick up the enemy," reported one of the SBD pilots. "Visibility is very poor."

The parachute flares bloomed over the Japanese, lighting the area with an ethereal white glow. Brownie, Bruce, and the third pilot rolled in under them, picking out targets in the bifurcated night. It was a scene of stark white and stark blacks, like a negative come to life. As luck would have it, the Americans hit the Japanese at their most vulnerable—right in the middle of a night amphibious landing. Kawaguchi, unaware that these ships were due in, had not prepared any landing craft or barges to assist them. As a result, the few landing craft the destroyers carried were slowly chugging back and forth, shuttling troops to the beach.

The SBDs swept in, guns lacing the blackness with streams of glowing tracers. A bomb damaged the destroyer *Shikinami*, killing five men and wounding six. Another 500-pound bomb landed right beside one of the Daihatsu landing craft, killing and wounding another eight soldiers.

Bruce, Brownie, and the Flight 300 crew swept in again and again, doing their best to find a target through the mist and rain. Every now and then, a ship or landing craft would materialize out of the night, giving them a snap shot with its machine guns. The weather, the darkness, and the flares precluded using dive-bombing tactics. Instead, they stayed low, attacking in gentle dives under the canopy of surreal light burning from beneath the parachutes.

The attacks totally disrupted the landing, forcing its suspension. The four destroyers scattered at top speed, leaving behind their landing craft and only about half the men and supplies they carried. At one point, one of the SBD pilots reported a cruiser had gone east, not west, at high speed, trying to get away. Somebody else spotted another group of landing craft just on the west side of Taivu Point.

The three American crews hunted for the landing force, strafing whatever they found, until—ammunition exhausted and fuel low—they turned for home. Even as they did, Henderson launched three more SBDs in hopes of regaining contact with the enemy force. Maj. Leo Smith led this mission, taking with him Henry Hise and Capt. Rubin Iden, another VMSB-231 pilot.

They hunted eastward toward Taivu Point in the predawn gloom. Along the way, Henry's radio went out. Somewhere over Taivu, Leo saw something, rocked his wings, and rolled into a shallow diving attack. Rubin winged over and went after him. When Henry followed the two new arrivals down, he could see nothing but beach and jungle. Nothing worth a bomb. So he pulled up and continued heading eastward, beyond Taivu. A few minutes passed. The weather remained poor, but the sky was gradually becoming lighter now. Up ahead, Henry just made out a ship, its bow pointed toward the beach. At first, he wasn't sure if it was friendly. As he thought it over, it made no sense for an American vessel to be out on this side of Japanese lines. He resolved to attack it.

The overcast layer at six thousand feet made a dive-bomb attack impossible. An SBD needed a minimum of ten thousand feet for that. For lower altitudes like this, the Marines and Navy crews used a shallower method of attack dubbed glide-bombing. It was less accurate but easier to execute.

Henry swung around until he was set up to attack the ship from stern to bow along its length, maximizing the chance for a hit. Then he pushed his nose down and dove on the vessel, determined to get a hit this time. He yanked the release level and pulled up as his gunner hosed the ship with his twin machine guns. The Japanese ship opened fire in return. Still, Henry stuck around long enough to see his bomb land just astern of his target.

So. Damn. Close.

Grumbling over the miss, he banked for home and landed back at Henderson sometime after dawn, the last one down; Smith and Iden had already come home. They reported no enemy ships or landing craft in the area, which made Hise wonder, when he showed up at the Pagoda to be debriefed, what they drove on. He detailed his sighting and the attack, then headed off to the squadron area to grab some of Gruenke's chow.

His debrief stirred up a hornet's nest. The morning duty operations officer for the day, possibly Fike, looked at the three debriefs—one from a major, one from a captain, and one from a raw second lieutenant—and questioned just what the hell Henry Hise was talking about. He ordered Hise back to the Pagoda to give a second accounting of the mission.

By now, it was almost midmorning, and Hise was tired and pissed that his word was being questioned. If Dick Mangrum had been around, he'd have protected the second lieutenant from all this. Hise returned to the Pagoda, where the duty operations officer interrogated him as if he were a POW, clearly not believing Henry's story.

The debriefing went on through an air raid alert and scramble. All the available F4Fs launched skyward while the remaining aircraft cleared the field to pound Taivu Point with bombs and bullets. Hise was finally released sometime after that. He waited around the Pagoda, looking for a ride back to the squadron area, until a truck rolled by. He hopped in the back, and they headed across the airfield for 232's bivouac.

Overhead, eighteen G4M Betty bombers in a tight vee-of-vees formation arrived even as John L.'s and Bob Galer's men raced to intercept. At 1135, bombs began falling on the airfield. As usual, the Japanese bombardiers demonstrated their superb marksmanship. Their bombs fell in a deadly accurate pattern along the runway and dispersal area, striking one of the few remaining 232 SBDs, which caught fire.

Oblivious to the danger of falling bombs and burning aircraft, Don McCafferty calmly walked through the chaos, camera in hand, to photograph the flame-wreathed SBD. He'd just come back from a search mission with Baldy Baldinus, having discovered an entirely new Japanese reinforcement method, which used the small Daihatsu landing craft to hug the shores of the islands dotting the Slot south of New Georgia. For the moment, that intel was forgotten as Don knelt, composed his shot, and focused his lens on the burning Dauntless. He snapped a couple of photos before the SBD suddenly exploded, blowing him some twenty feet across the parking area. He landed in a crumpled heap, knocked senseless by the blast. Yet, like a true photographer, he'd managed to hold on to his irreplaceable camera and kept it intact. The blast threw aviation gas onto a cache of 90 mm antiaircraft shells, which soon began cooking off, inflicting casualties and setting secondary fires all over the area.

The sudden rash of explosions panicked Henry Hise's truck driver, who floored the gas pedal in a desperate attempt to outrun the strings of ordnance detonating behind them. There was no escape. Through falling bombs, the truck swayed and slewed, towering plumes of smoke erupting in every direction around them. In the back, Henry held on desperately as concussive waves hammered them. The truck veered suddenly, and Hise lost his grip. He felt himself being catapulted out of the truck bed, striking the finder before tumbling into the muddy roadway. A moment later, he blacked out.

Henry woke up on a stretcher, unable to move. Pain racked from a crushed pelvis and two broken lumbar vertebrae, he slipped in and out of consciousness. A couple of Marines carried him to another vehicle. The air raid was over. Men moved about freely, picking through the wreckage and assisting the wounded. Waves of pain overcame Henry, and mercifully he passed out again.

He regained consciousness inside a soggy, poorly lit dugout crammed with horrifically wounded men. Amid the sea of bleeding Marines, a few overworked orderlies and exhausted doctors moved from patient to patient. An 0500 bombing raid by floatplanes—which the Americans thought was actually another bombardment by the Tokyo Express—drove the medical staff to carry these grievously wounded men to the safety of this underground shelter.

Henry couldn't move. Filled with morphine, he existed in a twilight sort of consciousness. Dimly, he became aware of another Marine beside his right elbow. The man's eyes were saucers, his face bandaged, his hands trembling. His jaw had been torn away by a Japanese bomb fragment. Now he sat on a cot, leaning against one of the dugout's vertical support beams and looking desperately afraid. When a doctor came by to check on him, the Marine, shaking hands and all, found the strength to write a note that read "Will I be all right?"

The doc replied, "Oh yeah, you'll be fine." Then he turned to an orderly and said, "Keep this man sitting up." The orderly nodded. The Marine looked a little less afraid.

As the hours passed, the Marine grew weaker. He began to slump over. Henry, unable to move, couldn't help him. The orderly was busy with other men. Night fell. The Marine began to cough and gurgle. He finally slumped down to lie on his cot, inches from Henry's elbow. Henry kept passing out and regaining consciousness. Each time he recovered his senses, the Marine beside him sounded worse and worse. Finally, the man stopped gurgling.

He drowned in his own blood, Henry helpless to do anything beside him.

In the morning, orderlies carried a traumatized and pain-ridden Henry Hise on a stretcher to a waiting B-17. Tom Moore, covered in bandages, and Claude Hallyburton, equally bandaged, joined him aboard the aircraft. Before the noon raid came in, the big bomber lumbered down the runway in one final trip down Henderson Field, carrying them south and out of the fight. Henry never scored the ship-killing bomb hit he so dearly wanted. No matter. Such things meant little now.

THIRTY-TWO

TRANSFERRED

Southern Solomon Islands
September 2, 1942, morning

S KATING ALONG ABOVE SANTA ISABEL'S COASTLINE, LAWRENCE BALD-
inus and Don McCafferty shared a grandstand view of a tropical sunrise with their gunners on the morning of September 2. Launching from
Henderson in the dark for the usual two-hour, 250-mile search, the pair
cruised through the new dawn, each with a 500-pound bomb under the
fuselage. They dodged rain squalls and layers of overcast as they scouted
through the Slot for any sign of the ships that had been offloading at
Taivu Point earlier that morning. They found nothing but empty seas.
When they reached Santa Isabel, they banked to port and followed its
southern shore up toward the island's tip, beyond which stretched a maze
of islets and reefs.[1]

Sharp-eyed as always, Baldy noticed that amid those islands was
a white stripe that looked remarkably like a wake. He studied it for a
moment, trying to figure out what it was from. Could it just be water
breaking over shoals? No way. It seemed to be coming from one of the
islets that was densely covered with jungle.

The islet moved. *What the hell?* Baldy looked closer. Sure enough, it wasn't an optical illusion. It was a camouflaged vessel of some sort, snaking its way through an aqua-blue channel.

"Mac," Baldy called over the radio, "notice anything peculiar about that little island just below us?"

It took a minute for Don to figure it out too. They stepped over each other on the radio until Don fell silent and heard Baldy say, "Let's go down and have a better look at that thing."

"Okay," Don answered, then keyed the intercom to tell Lewis Macias in the rear seat what they were doing. "Don't fire unless you have to—we don't know what we're going to do yet."

Macias acknowledged. The two SBDs wheeled around and dove to investigate. Baldinus went first; McCafferty followed a short distance behind. As they approached, the early-morning sunlight reflected off something under all that camouflage foliage.

"They've spotted us!" Baldy said. "See those helmets?"

Sure enough, as they closed, both pilots could see that the vessel was packed with Japanese troops, their steel helmets peeking out among the palm fronds used to disguise their ride. The two pilots kept going as if they had not seen anything. They climbed up into a cloud, then circled awhile. When Baldinus dropped out the bottom, the Japanese vessel had ducked into an inlet, and several small landing craft now clustered around it.

They dove into the target area, seeing perhaps fifty Japanese troops on the beach with others just coming ashore. Neither SBD's forward-firing guns functioned, so the pilots had to be content to observe while their gunners hosed the enemy as they flew by.

The Americans rolled back into several more low-level passes, the twin Brownings in the rear seats chattering as they sped over the Japanese. Dead and wounded lay scattered in the sand, and several of the small boats looked riddled with .30-caliber strikes.

Both Americans still retained their 500-pound bombs. Low on fuel now, they decided to attack the camouflaged vessel together. They gained some altitude and came back around, Don in the lead this time.

He executed an abbreviated glide-bombing run, pulled up, and heard Macias's emotionless report, "You missed, lieutenant."

Don watched as Baldy went into his dive. From what both men saw, the 500-pounder scored a direct hit. A massive explosion mushroomed over the vessel, throwing flame and smoke-wrapped debris all over the inlet. The SBDs climbed above the carnage, the men's eyes peering back at the rain of wood, bits of metal, and bodies falling into the water and along the beach. The strike reinforced Baldy's rep as a can't-miss dive-bombing sharpshooter.[2]

On the way home, the two Red Devils spotted seven more large landing craft tucked into inlets and small bays in the island hodgepodge just off Santa Isabel. The Japanese were definitely up to something. When back in range of Guadalcanal's radios, they reported the sightings and the attack. The MAG-23 staff huddled up to discuss the situation, evaluating other intel as well as Baldy's radio message. Leland "Tommy" Thomas and Ed Eades had also found and attacked a nest of barges, but they reported the watercraft 120 miles out from Guadalcanal. Could there be two groups? If so, what were the Japanese doing?

To the MAG-23 staff, the Japanese appeared to have undertaken a new operation designed to move large numbers of men and material down the northern side of the Solomon Islands, probably intending to get them to Guadalcanal. If not, it looked as if the Japanese might intend to establish some sort of forward operating base on Santa Isabel. Using the barges made sense in theory. They could hide during the day and move along the coastal waters of the Slot at night, avoiding American airpower. Except that VMSB-232's sharp-eyed crews detected them.

The Red Devils estimated the landing craft carried about fifty men each. MAG-23's leadership quickly realized that given the number of landing craft seen by the morning search planes, the Japanese troops on the move in this manner represented a significant threat to the perimeter. Colonel Wallace ordered a maximum-effort strike to take them out before they reached Guadalcanal.

* * *

THAT AFTERNOON, MANGRUM LIFTED OFF THE RUNWAY AT THE HEAD of a seventeen-plane formation, the largest attack force yet assembled from Guadalcanal. The fact that the dive-bomber squadrons could muster this many SBDs was a testament to the ground crews and their relentless devotion to repairing the battered planes. Fletcher Brown, Danny Iverson, Baldy Baldinus, Don Rose, Arthur O'Keefe, and Robert Fleener represented 232. Hal Buell, who had been badly hurt in a night takeoff crash a few days before, hobbled to his aircraft and joined the mission with nine other Flight 300 pilots, including half-healed Spike Conzett. Several of the crew members suffered from dysentery or gastroenteritis, but they flew anyway. They knew the importance of this mission. The Japanese could not be allowed to get on the island.

The Americans found dozens of Japanese landing craft in little coves and other hideaways in the same area where Baldy and Don had carried out their attacks. Some of the watercraft were pulled ashore and covered with foliage; others peeked out from under the jungle canopy at the edge of the beaches. None were in the water. Either the Japanese had come to stay in this area, or they were hiding in daylight and planned to move under the cover of darkness.

The SBDs wheeled in, dropping bombs among the square-bowed vessels, the gunners raking the targets as the planes pulled out of their dives. The pilots who had working forward-firing guns used them to maximum effect while those without this capability positioned their planes to give their gunners the best possible shots. The strike group pulled off target only after running out of both bombs and ammo, unsure of how much damage they had inflicted. They thought the damage looked extensive, but the SBDs were uniquely unsuited for attacking such small targets. Their 500-pound bombs were designed to sink warships, not sixty-foot landing craft. Their heaviest guns—the .50-calibers in their noses—more often than not proved nonfunctional. That left the onus of the strafing on the backward-facing gunners. Rifle-caliber bullets didn't have the punch to fatally damage these landing craft.

So began Mangrum's war on General Kawaguchi's so-called Ant Freight, a massive logistic effort to bring an entire reinforced infantry battalion—with its heavy weapons, supplies, and vehicles—to Guadal-canal via landing craft. The outlandish idea was proposed by Kawagu-chi after 232 and Flight 300 savaged the August 28 destroyer task force. He'd used landing barges to move along the coast of Borneo to capture key positions from the Dutch earlier in the year, and he saw no issues with doing the same thing in the Solomons. He seemed to forget that the skies over the Dutch East Indies had been dominated by the Japanese, whereas here, they had to contend with the Americans. Also, the landing craft would have to travel hundreds of miles along island coastlines before making the final jump to Guadalcanal. These were treacherous waters, even for shallow craft, and the final leg to Death Island would require traveling through rough open ocean, something the landing barges were not designed to do.

While Kawaguchi rode a destroyer to Guadalcanal, his subordinate, Colonel Oka assembled the barge convoy. Dubbed Ant Freight by the Imperial Japanese Army soldiers, it included sixty-one landing craft of various sizes. The largest could carry a hundred men or a vehicle. Alto-gether, the convoy carried eleven hundred men and their supplies, equip-ment, and battalion trucks.

The two transport crews loaded the men and barges aboard ship in the Shortlands, then set sail on September 1. By 0300 the next day, they had reached the maze of islands at the tip of Santa Isabel, where they off-loaded the boats and personnel. Colonel Oka ordered the barges dragged ashore, camouflaged, and hidden where possible, intending to make two jumps down the southern coast of Santa Isabel by traveling at night. The third jump—a sixty mile stretch of open water to the northwestern tip of Guadalcanal—would take place on the fourth day of the operation.

Mangrum's air attack on September 2 was just the beginning of the Jap-anese trial by fire. That evening, an hour before sunset, Oka ordered the convoy to continue down the coast of Santa Isabel. His men flowed out of their concealed positions in the jungle to muscle the landing craft into the surf. Ramps dropped, the soldiers reboarded, and the convoy began to stream southeastward, winding through the labyrinth of islets until it reached the coast of Santa Isabel. The watercraft plied along at six or seven knots, grinding through the waves as they hugged the shoreline. By 0300, they reached calm waters around Finuana Island, about midway down Santa Isabel. There, Colonel Oka ordered the convoy to go to ground. The soldiers dragged the barges ashore and concealed them with bushes and palm fronds before they settled down in the jungle to sleep through the day.

But there would be no sleeping. The dive-bomber crews would see to that.

The morning searches were launched from Henderson only about an hour after the barges made landfall. They flew up the Slot in pairs or triplets, the crews scouring the island coastlines for any sign of the little vessels. The scouts quickly found the barge nest at Finuana Island and hurried home to deliver the news. At 0800, Dick Mangrum pulled together eleven SBDs for the first strike of the day. Baldy, who by now knew the area as well as any American, flew on Dick's wing. The rest of the group came from VMSB-231. Maj. Leo Smith flew this mission to get acquainted with the battle space and what these barges looked like from the air.

Mangrum's force found thirty-four of Colonel Oka's sixty-one boats, which were arrayed on a beach almost gunnel to gunnel. The Americans saw no troops among the barges, though, and assumed they were hiding in the triple canopy vegetation just inland from the sand.

This time, Mangrum's Dauntlesses seeded the beach with their 500-pound bombs, blowing up landing craft with direct hits and raking others with shrapnel. When they finished their runs, Mangrum ordered everyone back up to a thousand feet. There, the SBDs flew a wagon-wheel pattern over the barges, banking to give their rear gunners the best and longest possible shots at the vessels below. They circled the target area, the rear-seaters hammering away with their twin .30s until they sent every round aboard downrange.

All day long, the SBDs refueled, rearmed, and returned to Santa Isabel to pummel Colonel Oka's boats, whose crews fought back with rifles and a few machine guns. Rivers Morrell and Rex Jeans from John L.'s squadron joined one of the 231 strikes, adding their six .50s to the steady diet of strafing the Americans inflicted on the Japanese.

Still, it didn't seem to be enough. These watercraft proved exceptionally hard to kill, even when stationary. They were small targets, and the firepower available to the dive-bomber crews was at best unsatisfactory.

Marines tend to foster creativity, and this unique challenge saw several of 232's gunners rise to the occasion. Frustrated by their rifle-caliber machine guns, Lewis Macias and Ed Eades visited a mud Marine 81 mm mortar platoon and convinced the men there to part with some of their ammunition. That afternoon, when Tommy Thomas and Don McCafferty joined the final strike of the afternoon, the two gunners had stacked a small arsenal of 81 mm mortar rounds in the rear cockpit. As Don and Tommy made runs over the barges, the two gunners stood up and flung mortar rounds down on the Japanese. It was a move straight out of the early days of combat aviation in World War I, but it made them feel better. At least it did until Ed dropped one of the rounds as he was trying to arm it. The munition fell into the rear cockpit and rattled around at his feet. After that, the gunners decided that World War I callback tactics were probably not the answer.

While the SBDs continued their attacks, Brig. Gen. Roy Geiger arrived on Guadalcanal from the New Hebrides to take overall command of all air units on the island. By now there was such a mélange of squadrons defending the island, the aviators needed a senior officer to run the show. General Geiger was the perfect man for the job—far better than Fike had been in the first days of the campaign.

Geiger was a Marine legend, an old-school aviator who earned a Navy Cross as a bomber pilot during World War I. A passionate advocate for naval aviation and close air support, he commanded the 1st Marine Air Wing at the start of the Pacific War. Now, he'd come to lead the cobbled-together Cactus Air Force, as the denizens of Henderson Field had started calling themselves after they learned that Guadalcanal's US Navy code name was Cactus.

He didn't waste a moment. From the Douglas R4D transport plan that had brought him to the island, he went straight to the Pagoda to get up to speed on the current situation. He ordered Colonel Wallace to keep battering the Japanese barges, and he let the MAG-23 staff know they were going to be aggressive wherever possible.

Throughout September 3 and 4, the Dauntless crews flew constant missions. Night searches swept the Guadalcanal shoreline for signs of the Tokyo Express. Morning patrols found and attacked landing craft wherever they could. The Marine and Navy crews had sustained this pace since at least August 28, the first American force to fly continuous twenty-four-hour combat operations in all weather conditions. Doing so without more men lost in operational accidents or combat was nothing short of a miracle.

The Americans' efforts paid off, forcing changes to Japanese plans, causing chaos with the enemy navy's and army's chains of command, and turning back multiple reinforcement efforts. Even when the Marines and Navy scored no hits or conducted no attacks, their presence disrupted the Japanese reinforcement runs. Mangrum's tiny force, joined now by another handful of SBDs, had a far greater impact on the defense of Guadalcanal than has usually been credited. The Japanese who did get through the aerial cordon arrived wet, exhausted, and often without their supplies, which were sometimes scattered in penny packets dropped by destroyer skippers eager to get out of harm's way.

The morning searches on September 4 found Colonel Oka's barges tucked into San Jorge Island on the southeast end of Santa Isabel. Stragglers were spotted all along the barge route as well, denoting damaged vessels that had been left behind for its crews to repair. At 1000, Dick led thirteen SBDs against their latest location. Eight VMF-224 Wildcats joined them, each armed with two 100-pound bombs. Bob Galer led the F4Fs while Tommy Thomas and Bruce Prosser joined Mangrum from 232. The rest of the SBD force was filled out by a mix of available crews from Flight 300 and VMSB-231.

The American planes reached the target area before lunch. The Japanese barges were scattered between San Jorge Island and the coast of Santa Isabel, just northwest of the channel between the two islands. The Americans counted about forty landing craft, about a third of which they estimated were the longer seventeen-meter Daihatsus; the rest were smaller. The aviators wasted no time in attacking with every gun and bomb they possessed. Three barges took direct hits and were blown apart. Others were sprayed with shrapnel and bullets until, by Japanese accounts, almost a third of their boats were crippled or badly damaged. Once again, though, the troops and barge crews remained out of sight. They suffered few casualties, if any.

In the afternoon, the Americans returned twice, forcing the Japanese to suspend repair work on their damaged vessels and take cover in the jungle. Several more landing craft were hit or blown up. The P-400s of the 67th Fighter Squadron took part on one of the afternoon missions, where they discovered that their 20 mm cannon and its high-explosive shells inflicted significantly more damage than did the .50s and .30s carried by the SBDs and F4Fs. From here on out, the P-400 would be the ultimate antibarge weapon available to the Cactus Air Force. Unfortunately, Dale Brannon's squadron could only field three functional Airacobras, one of which the ground crews miraculously cobbled together by pulling the wings and engine out of a wrecked bird and fitting them on another.

By day's end, the Marines had no doubt what the Japanese intended to do. San Jorge Island was clearly the last jump-off point before pushing on to Guadalcanal. These soldiers were destined to fight the mud Marines defending the perimeter. They were fifty-seven miles away from the northern tip of Guadalcanal—an eight- or nine-hour transit in calm seas.

The barges could reach Guadalcanal that night.

While Oka's men patched holes and fussed over engines, a massive Tokyo Express run raced down the Slot, intent on delivering another thousand men, including the Kuma Battalion and a detachment from the 2nd Sendai Division, which was new to the fray. Led by a light cruiser, eleven destroyers slipped into Savo Sound, their presence masked by the haze and unusual darkness of the night. The sliver of a moon provided little illumination and was often concealed by clouds. Like the moon, the weather shrouded the stars, and the haze just off the water offered perfect concealment for the Japanese warships. After reaching Taivu Point unharmed, the destroyers offloaded the troops and supplies successfully.

On the way back through Savo Sound, they shelled Henderson Field. The gunfire attracted two US Navy destroyer-transports, the *Little* and the *Gregory*, which in the worst possible moment were illuminated by PBY-dropped flares. Outnumbered six to one, with only a couple of WWI vintage four-inch guns for self-defense, the two old warships were demolished under a rain of Japanese shellfire, taking heavy casualties among the crews.

Meanwhile, the barge convoy began the last leg of its crucible several hours late, having been delayed by an unexpected low tide and battle damage inflicted by American aircraft. Instead of kicking off their night movement just before sunset, the lead boats didn't leave until 2130. Even at their best speed, the landing craft would be unable to reach Guadalcanal before daylight.

The Marines' morning search caught the convoy in mid-transit. Not only had the barges not reached Guadalcanal by dawn, but heavy seas and the damage inflicted from previous raids slowed the convoy down. Landing craft fell behind the main force as water flowed into them through dozens of bullet and shell holes. Others suffered engine malfunctions. They limped along, the seasick soldiers vomiting as their NCOs ordered them to bail the water out faster and faster.

Dick Mangrum and Dennis Byrd looked down on this scene from two thousand feet. It was a gorgeous morning; the sun was shining over crystal-blue seas, small fluffy clouds dotting the sky. Only minutes after beginning their patrol, they found two groups of six barges about a mile apart. The landing craft chugged along, rolling in the heavy swells and trying to maintain a formation of two columns of three each. Dennis could see the men inside, their helmets slick with ocean spray, looking like shiny coconuts packed into the cracker-box-shaped Daihatsus.

Dick dove to the attack, dropping his bomb and pulling up into the wagon-wheel banking turn that gave Dennis the best shot at them. He flayed the barges, swinging his gun back and forth across the formations until the barrels grew hot and his ammunition ran out.

Meanwhile, Dale Brannon and one of his second lieutenants took off from Henderson to attack the landing craft with their P-400s. They raced westward up the Guadalcanal coast toward Cape Esperance, where about fifteen of the boats were about to come ashore. Dale made pass after pass as the desperate Japanese headed full speed for the beach. All the boats made it, but the two US Army Air Forces pilots shot up most of them. About thirty minutes later, six F4Fs from 224 reached the area and went to work on the boats. Most of the Japanese men splashed out into the surf and charged for the safety of the jungle tree line. Still, their supplies and equipment remained in the vessels, which were hit again and again.

The Japanese fought back with their rifles and machine guns. They shot down one Wildcat. Its pilot, 2nd Lt. Robert Jefferies, went straight into the water off the beach and was killed instantly.

Undeterred, Brannon and his second lieutenant raced back to Henderson to rearm and refuel, then returned before 1000 to hit the Japanese again.

As the landing site was raked with cannon and machine gun fire, another SBD search team discovered some of the lagging barges on the south shore of San Jorge Island. Knocked out of commission by earlier attacks, these drew the ire of Danny Iverson and 2nd Lt. Yale W. Kaufman, one of 231's pilots.

While the barges endured repeated attacks, another of the near-daily Japanese bombing raids sped down the Slot to try to suppress Henderson Field and give the embattled Japanese soldiers some measure of relief. Warned by members of the Coastwatchers stationed up the Solomon chain, and with the help of the newly arrived SCR-270 radar set, eighteen F4Fs from the two squadrons rose to intercept.

The aerial brawl that followed saw the Wildcat pilots suffer a serious beating. Rivers Morrell, leading 223's eight ready-alert pilots, managed to get his men into the bomber formation. He and Zen Pond claimed a Betty each, but then the escorting Zeroes pounced on the Marines. Cannon and machine gun fire shredded Zen's F4F, severing the oil line just forward of the cockpit. His engine seized, and Pond rolled into a desperate dive to escape the Japanese predators. He dove all the way back to Henderson Field to belly-land his crippled aircraft in a spray of mud.

Amazingly, he emerged with only a grazing bullet wound to his left arm, but his aircraft was a total washout, fit only for spare parts.

As Pond dove out of the fight, Zeroes hammered Rivers Morrell's F4F. A cannon shell burst through the side of the cockpit and exploded between Morrell's legs, studding both limbs with serious shrapnel wounds. In tremendous pain, Rivers fought like a demon to shake the Zeroes. He was hit again. This time, like so many others, bullets and cannon strikes tore up his cowling and punctured the oil reservoir. The hot, viscous liquid sprayed through holes in the firewall to coat him. As he dove clear of the fight, the cockpit was full of blood and oil.

Despite the damage, his engine failing, Rivers was determined to save his aircraft. He cranked the wheels down, lined up on the runway, and somehow coaxed the battered F4F onto the ground. Rescuing Marines swarmed over his wings to get the canopy open and pull him out of the wrecked cockpit. Like John Lindley and Pond before him, he was covered in oil, his bare skin burned from the terrible stuff.

Bob Galer's 224 pilots fared little better. He and another pilot claimed a Zero each but lost one of their NAPs, Staff Sgt. Clifford Donally Garrabrant. Galer's plane was also badly shot up and would take days to repair.

John L. Smith went to check on Rivers Morrell later in the day. He found his old friend crammed into the hospital tent. His legs were bandaged, and he was heavily sedated with morphine. He was an urgent evacuation case and would be flown out on the first available transport in the morning. Rivers would live, probably, but 223 had lost its pugnacious warrior of an executive officer. John L. wished him the best, then set off to find Marion Carl. He would be the squadron's new executive officer.

While the fighter pilots gathered before dusk that evening to find quiet solace in one another's company, Mangrum's men continued to attack the barges. The search teams found them all over the place, scattered along the northwestern coast of Guadalcanal, San Jorge, Santa Isabel, and even Savo Island, where about 450 troops staggered ashore. Tommy Thomas, ever up for anything Mangrum threw his way, added his SBD to a three-plane strike led by Leo Smith. The group bombed and shot up the landing craft on the Guadalcanal beaches, hoping to destroy as much of their supplies as possible.

It had been a weird, desperate effort to stop Colonel Oka's force. The Americans had failed to prevent the Japanese from landing on Guadalcanal, but the SBDs, P-400s, and F4Fs ensured that those who did arrive were disorganized, sick, exhausted, and lacking much of their equipment. Instead of landing as a complete reinforced battalion, the Japanese came ashore in two pockets on the opposite end of the island from Taivu Point and Kawaguchi's main force. When Oka counted heads that evening, he found that only about three hundred men had made it to Guadalcanal. They may have reached their destination, but with minimal supplies and few heavy weapons, Oka's men were marooned. The other seven hundred were either dead, wounded, or scattered. For the next seven days, the Imperial Japanese Navy would help round up the scattered survivors of the convoy, bringing them to Guadalcanal under the cover of darkness. They were more like shipwreck victims than combat-capable, organized fighting formations.

Altogether, the American air strikes killed about 10 percent of Colonel Oka's men, with presumably at least another 10 percent wounded. It was a telling blow to a major element of Kawaguchi's brigade—a blow from which it would not recover. In the days that followed, the significance of what Mangrum's little force and the other SBD crews had accomplished would come into better focus. For the moment, the men knew they had inflicted significant destruction on a key Japanese reinforcement element.

General Geiger wanted to keep the pressure on. The search teams would continue to attack the landing craft wherever they were found in the days that followed, but he wanted to deal a surprise blow to one of the anchorages used by the Tokyo Express and, presumably, by the barge convoy. This was Gizo Harbor in the New Georgia group of islands in the Central Solomons, about 240 miles from Henderson Field. Long-range reconnaissance aircraft had spotted Japanese activity there. Destroyers came and went. So did transports and possibly seaplane tenders.

The mission was given to Leo Smith and VMSB-231, with ships being the priority and shore installations in the harbor the secondary targets if no vessels were to be found. Fletcher Brown and Charley McAllister would go with them, along with their gunners, Corp. Robert S. Russell and Corp. V. K. Humphreys, who had shot up his own tail by accident a few days earlier while strafing barges.

Before the mission, Dick Mangrum met with Brownie. The executive officer had lost a lot of weight from his five foot nine, 140-pound frame and was looking gaunt and haggard, but his brown eyes were still full of vigor. That said, Brownie was clearly as exhausted as Dick felt. Neither man had slept the night before. Some Japanese destroyers had shelled Henderson for an hour just after midnight, waking everyone up and sending them again into sloppy, mud-filled holes. There, they clung to the earth as the shells exploded around them, mosquitoes feasting on their exposed flesh.

The two men were as close as anyone on Guadalcanal. Squadron command was a lonely position, and Dick was much more an island than John L. was. He kept the "proper" boundaries between himself and his men while never coming across as uncaring or aloof. It was a tightrope he walked with great care.

Brownie was the exception here. Dick lowered the wall with his executive officer, and the two men had forged an exceptional bond.

On this morning, September 6, 1942, Dick surprised his friend with the news that Brownie had been promoted from captain to major. Then he produced a pair of gold oak leaves, the rank insignia that officers wore on their collars. Dick had worn this pair up until the first of the month. He'd tucked them away in hopes of being able to give them to his friend when Brownie received his own promotion.

As Brownie stood at attention, Dick pinned the insignia on the man's threadbare collar. Major Fletcher Brown. He'd proved himself with his energy, intelligence, and relentless optimism, and he richly deserved this promotion. Someday soon, he'd take a squadron of his own into combat, and Dick had no doubt he would lead it well.

"Remind me to write my wife about this," Brownie quipped as Dick shook his hand warmly.

Sometime before 1100, eleven SBDs warmed up beside the runway, each carrying a 500-pound bomb for the day's raid on Gizo. Bob Galer's squadron provided escort with six precious F4Fs. They would be going into an area not well known by any of the Americans, flying to the edge of the operational radius. It would be a challenging mission.

Dick went down to the flight line to see his pilots off. Charley McAllister, still on a high from the news that he would be a father early next year, was strapped in and ready to go, engine turning over. Dick wished him well, then walked down the line to find Brownie standing on the wing root of MB-21, his usual SBD. He saw Dick and shouted down at him over the sound of warming engines, "By the Great Horn Spoon, tell Gruenke I want some decent chow this evening!"

Dick burst into laughter and promised he would.

Brownie waved toward the squadron-ready tent, adding, "And try to keep those kids out of mischief while I'm gone."

The mission was a complete mess. The formation ran into a massive storm front, which hived off at least one of the 231 pilots, who returned to Guadalcanal without reaching the target. Those who made it to Gizo found no shipping to attack. They bombed the meager harbor facilities and a building thought to be the radio and communications facility. On the way home, the storm front scattered the SBDs. One by one, they trickled back to Henderson Field. By 1450, the last one to arrive had set down.

Fletcher Brown and Charley McAllister never returned home. The rest of the men waited at the runway, pacing and calculating fuel reserves in their heads. But as the afternoon wore on, it became clear their friends were out of fuel.

The waiting men tried to look at the bright side. Some of the downed pilots walked in after bailing out. The latest was a 224 pilot, Dick Amerine, who went down on the squadron's first mission. He'd been out in the jungle for days, eating bugs and killing Japanese with rocks and his pistol until finally finding his way to the perimeter.

So there was hope that Brownie and Charley, along with their gunners, Corp. William Proffitt and Corp. Robert S. Russell, had alighted on an island somewhere up the Slot and they'd see them again someday.

But in their hearts, the men could not shake a sense of dread. By early evening, morale had tanked. Mangrum, hurting worse than at any other time since getting to the island, retrieved a precious bottle of brandy.

He found his men sitting together in near silence, faces stricken. Through his own pain, he poured a shot of brandy for each man, then led a toast for them. After they downed the fiery liquor, Dick knew he had to say something.

"Boys," he began, "there isn't anything I can do or say that's going to make you feel the loss of Major Brown and the other boys any less. But I think you might be able to bear your burden a little easier if you'll just not think of them as dead."

The men looked puzzled. Dick explained, "Just regard them as having been transferred."

The Corps had many duty stations stretching from the South Pacific to the Caribbean. Life in the prewar service meant establishing fast friendships, then parting ways after a tour and orders to a new unit and station. The bonds remained, but the person was no longer present. Letters would keep them connected, and maybe another posting would throw them together again in the future. When they did see each other, the old bonds ensured they would simply pick up where they had left off.

This was the only psychological defense Dick could offer, because it was the only one he knew. Brownie wasn't gone. He was just transferred off the island. Charley was out there, too, throwing himself into a new assignment.

When they got off the island, they could face reality and find the courage to grieve. For now, their friends were still out there, somewhere, still alive.

The Red Devils embraced their skipper's defense. From that moment on, anyone lost would not be killed in action or missing. They were transferred. It would work for a while, but such defenses ultimately became toxic self-deception. In time, the pain and grief this mind game held at bay would almost certainly break through. For Dick, that moment would probably come when he sat down to write Brownie's brilliant wife, Elynor, and Charley's pregnant bride.

That was a problem for later. Right now, they just needed to get through another day.

THIRTY-THREE

TRIPLE THIRTEEN

Henderson Field, Guadalcanal
September 9, 1942, morning

W ITH THE ARRIVAL OF VMF-224, JOHN L. NO LONGER NEEDED TO
send every pilot and plane into the sky to intercept the Japanese.
The full-squadron scrambles made sense until help arrived, but they came
at the cost of burning the pilots out. After almost three weeks of continuous combat, minimal food, and the environmental hell of Guadalcanal,
that bill was being paid in full. Marion Carl could see it on the faces
of every man around him on the morning of September 9. John L. had
split the squadron into thirds and started rotating them through intercept duties. They were short of pilots, especially after Rivers Morrell was
wounded, so in practice there was a lot of overlap between the thirds.

On the morning of the ninth, Carl sat with an exhausted,
hollow-eyed, and sick bunch of pilots. He had two divisions of four
men each that morning, including Scotty McLennan, Red Kendrick,
Clayton Canfield, Robert Read, Willis Lees, Eugene Trowbridge,
and Conrad Winter. Only Canfield and Winter were remotely fresh.
The others had flown to the edges of their endurance, surviving bombardments from the ground while being shot to pieces in the air by
Zero pilot marksmen. Canfield had flown on Carl's wing at Midway

and barely survived after being shot up and then shot down. He had belly-landed back at Midway, his aircraft reduced to spare parts and bullet holes. Trowbridge had dead-sticked a battered F4F on August 29 after being shredded by Zeroes. Read had been shot down and wounded. Lees had nearly been shot down on August 30, saved twice by John L. and Marion Carl as he limped home in an F4F crippled by Zeroes. Kendrick had belly-landed his F4F on August 21, then got shot up again on the thirtieth when a 20 mm shell exploded in his cockpit and slightly wounded him with shrapnel. McLennan had also been shot up during the squadron's first fight.

Twenty days in at Guadalcanal, and everyone had his war stories. And scars. The pilots, strangers two months ago, were now closer than blood family. They sat together playing cards, reading, smoking, or shooting the breeze not far from their waiting F4Fs. They looked like the ragged, over-taxed veterans they were. Most of the squadron suffered from one ailment or another. Men flew with malaria, fevers over 101 degrees. Others battled dysentery or gastroenteritis, unable to hold anything down. Dehydrated, sleep-deprived, their skin now pockmarked with open sores the Marines dubbed jungle rot, all they could do was hang on, keep flying the missions demanded of them, and pray for relief soon. Already, some of them required hospitalization. John L. sent one of the squadron's NCOs back to the naval hospital in the New Hebrides earlier in the month. Now John Lindley, still suffering from his half-healed wounds, was so sick the divisional docs decided to evacuate him as soon as possible.

Marion made a point of taking care of himself. Because he didn't smoke, he had clear lungs and could go higher without oxygen than anyone else. Nor did he drink much, if at all. He took pride in his physical fitness, having grown up rugged on an Oregon dairy farm. Yet nobody was spared the effects of life on Guadalcanal. He had lost significant weight and didn't eat much. When he did, he usually stuck to canned Japanese fruit or meat. He was careful about the water he drank. The caution didn't matter; either dysentery or gastroenteritis caught up with him and knocked him out of action from August 31 to September 3. In the last ten days, he'd gone from lanky to almost emaciated.

Such was the case with almost everyone in the alert tent that morning. They were weak, worn-out, and subdued, thanks to the events of the previous night, when MAG-23 had ordered both fighter squadrons aloft to attack a Japanese raid.

Control thought it was going after two APDs and two YP boats that had carried Col. "Red Mike" Edson's Marine Raider battalion to Taivu Point, where they had debarked earlier in the day and destroyed much of the supplies landed for Kawaguchi brigade. Those ships needed to be protected, so Geiger felt it was worth the risk sending his fighters up just after sunset.

Heavy rains over the past several days had turned Henderson into a quagmire. Some of the more recent shell and bomb craters had not been properly filled by the overworked engineers. Rather, they laid down steel planks of Marston matting over the holes. The rain filled the holes with water, which splashed over the aircraft as they rolled over the matting. One of the 67th Fighter Squadron's P-400s had been lost on takeoff because of this expedient fix of the field. Most of the other Cactus pilots white-knuckled both the takeoffs and the landings.

Of the sixteen F4Fs that started the mission that night, one pilot crashed on takeoff. The remaining fighters wandered around in the dark, finding no Japanese planes, and then returned to the field about an hour later. As the squadrons landed in heavy ground fog, Rex Jeans collided with Willis Lees on the runway, destroying both Wildcats. Somehow, the men emerged from the wreckage without serious injuries. A few minutes later, Charley Hughes set his F4F down and landed right in front of a poorly repaired crater. The Wildcat struck it, flipped over, and landed on its back, a total washout. Hughes also managed to escape serious injury, but three of the squadron's fighters were total write-offs, including two of the four brand-new F4Fs delivered to John L.'s men the day before from Efate.

How Willis Lees could climb back into an F4F's cockpit after everything he'd been through in the past week and a half was anyone's guess. He was operating on sheer stubborn tenacity. Both John L. and Marion knew that this pace couldn't go on much longer for Lees. Every pilot had his breaking point. Every human can absorb only so much trauma, tension, and fear and so many repeated adrenaline bursts before the person simply becomes nonfunctional. In the worst situations, a man would break down completely. Carl could sense that the squadron was already beyond its peak—that balance between combat experience and exhaustion—and was now on the downward slide toward becoming combat ineffective. He calculated that his men had maybe twenty more days left before they hit that wall and had either no aircraft left or no remaining pilots who could still fly.

Bob Galer's VMF-224 bought them some time on that front. Their arrival at the end of August proved a huge shot in the arm for morale. The boost didn't last long though. On their first mission, 224 lost four pilots to oxygen system failures. Only one pilot had walked in. They had lost two more men in combat since then. Five of nineteen men in a matter of days. It was a tough introduction to combat.

Carl noted a few differences between the two squadrons. John L. cultivated an informal atmosphere, which Galer did not. As a result, 223 was a much-tighter-knit bunch of guys than 224. The closeness that eluded the new squadron was also probably due in part to its leaders. While Galer was universally admired as a leader and a pilot, his senior subordinates included Kirk Armistead of Midway infamy, and tough-as-nails John Dobbin, an incredible fighter pilot whose abrasive personality on the ground created unnecessary conflicts within 224 and with 223. Galer himself was upset with his Midway veterans, confiding in his diary that they really didn't want to be there—a pointed reference to Armistead.

The two outfits flew and fought together, but their cultural differences ensured no smooth intermingling of the squadrons, especially with the animosity between Marion and Kirk.

Though they were on alert that morning, Marion's two divisions weren't even sure they would be able to fly. Henderson was in such bad shape that even Mangrum's morning searches could not get aloft. With the weather clearing after sunrise, the hope was the field would dry out under the tropical sun before the Japanese arrived.

Meanwhile, a Navy construction battalion (the Seabees) had arrived at the beginning of the month and was busy creating a dedicated fighter strip next to Henderson. At the moment, the site was a morass of mud and soupy brown water. Figuring out how to drain it properly would be a complex challenge in the weeks ahead. Still, both 223 and 224 would move over to the new strip on September 10 and dub it the Cow Pasture. Officially, it would be known as Fighter One. While it would eventually help with congestion on Henderson, the Cow Pasture would suffer from the same problems as the main field.

Despite the strip's condition, the fighter pilots got the order to scramble at 1115. They grabbed their gear and ran to their planes. Marion jogged to Black Thirteen, the Wildcat he'd personally selected back at Ewa. As he reached the plane, it dawned on him that this would be his thirteenth mission since arriving on Guadalcanal.

The strip was as bad as the pilots had ever seen it. Mud splattered, props dinged and nicked from flying gravel, the F4Fs sloshed through the bog and rose into the air. One of Galer's pilots, 2nd Lt. M. H. Kennedy, crashed on takeoff. He escaped the cockpit with minor injuries.

On this day, the Japanese bombers soared over the perimeter at about twenty-three thousand feet without dropping their bombs. Instead, they followed the coast toward Taivu Point. Carl and Galer used the extra time to climb out north over Savo Sound, then swing east after the bombers. They gained the high ground, counting some twenty-six twin-engine G4M bombers escorted by about twenty Zeroes. Just like at Midway, the Zeroes positioned themselves above and behind the bomber vees. Once again, the gap between the two formations yawned wide enough to give the Americans an opening. If they pulled this off right, the Marines could make a slashing attack on the bombers and run for the water before the Zeroes could even get into the fight.

Well above the bombers now, Carl and Galer led their four divisions in a column and pushed out above and ahead of the Japanese. The G4Ms made for Lengo Channel; this entry point into Savo Sound was the closest to the Guadalcanal shoreline. On the water steamed two vital transports, the *Bellatrix* and the *Fuller*. Both carried desperately needed ammunition for the 1st Marine Division as well as some personnel, food, and medical supplies. This convoy had tried to get into Guadalcanal and unload the day before but had been turned around by COMSOPAC HQ because of fear that a Japanese surface force might intercept it. At 0300 on September 9, the transports received orders to double back and deliver their supplies to the Marines. The vessels had just reached the area, covered by the destroyers *Hull* and *Hughes* along with three converted destroyer minesweepers, the *Zane*, the *Southard*, and the *Hopkins*. The two APDs from Edson's raid on Taivu Point had also linked up to provide extra escort for the vital transports. Altogether, the nine-ship convoy made an inviting target.

Before the Japanese could release their bombs, Carl and Galer launched their attacks. Carl managed to get about a mile ahead of the Japanese bombers and perform an overhead head-on pass. He rolled into a split *S*, reversing course to come down nearly vertically on the Japanese bombers. The maneuver was textbook—exactly how John L. had trained his pilots. Tight on his wing flew Clayton Canfield, Carl's wingman from Midway. Canfield stayed right with him as they blew through the Japanese formation, all guns spewing lead.

Marion saw his targeted bomber drop out of formation, raked from cockpit to tail gun by his long, accurate bursts. The attack lasted only a few seconds and sent 223's fighters down below the bombers on an opposite course—heading directly toward the Zeroes now. Carl and Canfield zoom-climbed back up above both formations, even as the Zeroes waded into the fray, tangling with 224's pilots.

The safe bet would have been to keep going and run for home. But the ships below contained supplies that could mean the difference between success or failure in the coming fight with all the troops the Japanese had recently landed on the island. So Marion reversed course and came down on the bombers in another high-speed vertical pass, Clayton snapping out bursts just off his wing as the two F4Fs plunged on their targets. Marion's Japanese bomber began coughing smoke from its engines. It dropped out of the formation, losing altitude. He lost sight of it but was sure he'd gotten two. Black Thirteen on its thirteenth mission, scoring Marion's twelfth and thirteenth kills. It was a trifecta of looming bad luck.

On all his other missions, Marion had adhered to John L.'s tactical dictum: one pass, two max. Then get the hell out of Dodge. Like the other Marines, Marion would roll into a long dive for the deck and scuttle home to fight another day. This time, however, the stakes were different. There were sailors, probably Marines, too, and holds full of food and ammo down there. The fewer bombers to drop bombs, the greater the chance those ships would get through. He and Clayton pulled up and raced above the bombers, Clayton hanging right with him and calling that he, too, had scored a bomber on that last pass.

Perched atop the sprawling fighting again, Marion checked his tail. All clear. In fact, he didn't see the Zero escort anywhere. Maybe he could get away with another pass. He looked over at Clayton, who had loyally followed him through both runs. Marion's partner was good for another go. Both men had ammo left. Their guns all functioned.

They were almost to the convoy now. Marion dropped down into another pass, his Wildcat howling as it approached four hundred miles an hour. He focused on a G4M swelling in his sights. He was about to pull the trigger when his Wildcat suddenly shuddered wildly. The cowling exploded in flames. Cannon and machine gun fire laced Black Thirteen. Smoke filled the cockpit, blinding him and leaving him choking in his oxygen mask. Unable to see, he was left with no choice but to open his canopy to clear the air. As soon as he did, the added drag slowed the F4F almost as if he'd pulled a parking brake on a speeding car. He had made a serious mistake, and he knew he was easy meat. A second later, the unseen Zero on his tail unleashed a fusillade of bullets and shells that walloped his F4F. A sheet of flame licked into the cockpit, burning his face.

That was the deal-breaker. The one thing Carl feared above everything else was fire. Burning alive in the cockpit of a dying F4F as it spun earthward was his worst nightmare. With the canopy already open, he rolled inverted and released his seat straps. A second later, he free-fell straight through an aerial firefight. Zeroes and Wildcats and Betties filled the sky around him as he plummeted toward the water five miles below. At about seventeen thousand feet, he pulled his rip cord and opened his chute, but then everyone lost sight of him.

Canfield lasted only a few minutes longer than Carl did. Neither pilot saw the Zeroes that caught them in their third overhead passes, but Canfield's enemy proved unshakable. Even as Canfield dove for the deck, the A6M stayed with him, shooting his Wildcat to pieces. Twisting and turning as he dove to throw the Zero off, he headed for the convoy's bow, coming in from its northwestern side.

The sailors aboard ship watched as the A6M finished Canfield off. His F4F, engine dead and pouring smoke, skipped across the water before digging its nose into a swell. Clayton flung himself out of the cockpit, dragged his raft out, and inflated it. Thirty seconds later, the Wildcat sank. He spent ten minutes in the water, riding his raft, before the *Southard* scooped him up. He'd ruptured both eardrums in the ordeal and could hardly hear anything. Other than that, he was unhurt: the armor plating behind the seat had saved his life.

While Carl and Canfield went down in flames, the rest of 223 and 224 hammered away at the bombers. Eugene Trowbridge shot one down. Red Kendrick got another, then tangled with a Zero, which he claimed as well. Galer and one of his pilots, 2nd Lt. R. M. D'Arcy, each claimed a Betty while Midway vet 2nd Lt. Charlie Kunz was credited with two Zeroes.

Even as the Marines pressed their attacks, the Japanese began their bomb runs. Aboard the ships, the American sailors saw two Betties trailing smoke and flames, lagging behind the main formation yet doggedly determined to hit their targets. It wasn't long before the bombs began falling. Like American B-17 crews, the Japanese pilots scored no hits with this high-level approach, though one string of bombs sent a spray of shrapnel across the *Bellatrix* and wounded two men. The convoy would get through to empty its holds at Kukum Harbor, delivering the last supplies to reach Guadalcanal before the Japanese unleashed their ground offensive.

By Japanese accounts, they lost three Betties that day, with another six damaged, out of twenty-seven that carried out the attack. A third of the force shot up or shot down disrupted the bombers so thoroughly that they ensured the survival of the ships below. Saving this convoy from destruction proved to be one of the most important victories scored by MAG-23's fighter pilots so far in the campaign.

Like everything at Guadalcanal, the victory came at a price. Marion Carl was more than just John L.'s executive officer now. He'd become a symbol of resistance for all the aviators at Henderson and many of the mud Marines as well. Most in MAG-23 considered Marion the best pure fighter pilot on the island, if not the Corps. He bolstered his reputation by coming home from each mission with victories and a plane rarely full of holes. With eleven kills on the day he went down and with John L. hard on his heels with eight, Marion led the growing pack of aces. Now, no one knew where he was.

Losing their best pilot and top ace punctured morale in 223. If their cool Oregonian could get it, they all would, sooner or later. In four days, the squadron had lost two of its three senior officers. John L. would have to shoulder the bulk of the load now, as he was out of captains since Howard Marvin was still back at Efate. He would have to fly with the squadron every day again, the rotation system so recently implemented useless now without Morrell and Carl. Meanwhile, the second lieutenants would have to step up even more than they had already been asked to do.

Carl's loss was the biggest blow but not the only one that day. Returning to Henderson, the Wildcat pilots made harrowing landings on the swamp that had once been their runway. Conrad Winter came in with a battered F4F riddled with holes and no aileron control. He bellied into the runway and sloshed through the mud to collide with a parked SBD Dauntless. Somehow, he walked away mostly unhurt, his crash making it a clean sweep: everyone in Marion Carl's two divisions now had either been shot down or been forced to crash-land.

Galer lost two of his seven pilots on the mission. Second Lieutenant J. M. Jones went missing during the fight while another was wounded in both legs.

The survivors gathered solemnly at the Pagoda, where Lieutenant Colonel Fike waited with his ubiquitous little black notebook. They were five pilots short, a fact not lost on any of the eleven men left. They talked the mission over, discovering that nobody had seen Marion Carl go down.

Neither had anyone seen what happened to Canfield. Both Midway veterans had simply disappeared. It was a crushing blow.

The pilots stepped to Fike one at a time to relate their side of the fight. Dutifully, Fike scratched out notes, eyes in his book. Everyone felt the mood deteriorate as the scope of the losses began to sink in. Before too long, word came that Canfield was safe aboard the *Southard*. The ship would drop him off at Kukum in a few hours. There was still no news about Marion Carl, however. They waited well beyond the endurance of his F4F. When he didn't appear in the pattern over Henderson, John L. finally faced facts. Marion Carl was missing in action.

The shocked and dispirited Marines gathered back at their bivouac totally unaware that their missing ace was even then fighting for his life some thirty miles away.

THIRTY-FOUR

THE KINDNESS OF STRANGERS

Aola Bay, Guadalcanal
September 9, 1942, afternoon

T HE PARACHUTE CANOPY OPENED CLEANLY OVER MARION CARL'S head, jerking him hard out of his high-speed descent toward the convoy below. He looked around for any Zeroes as the pilots had a penchant for strafing Americans in their chutes. He saw none. From seventeen thousand feet, he had an extraordinary view of the entire battlespace he'd spent the last three weeks defending. Soon, though, the southeasterly trade winds carried him down the Guadalcanal coast to an area he'd not even flown over before. He splashed into the ocean about a half mile from the beach and about four hundred yards from a small island.

In the water, he quickly unhooked himself from his chute harness and inflated his Mae West life preserver by pulling down on a small tab by his right ribs. The tab broke a CO_2 cartridge that filled the Mae West and pushed him onto his back. Its straps were tight against him, holding his head just above the water between the inflated ring around his neck.

Marion looked around, trying to orient himself in the whitecap swells. The sea wasn't rough, but as he tried to figure out where he was, his wingless-duck vantage point proved useless. All he could see were the trees by the beach to the west and a bit of the little island and the surf there, crashing across a reef that apparently ringed it. Neither seemed too far away. The weather wasn't bad, and the water had to be at least eighty degrees and not rough at all. Swimming ashore didn't seem like it would be too difficult.

The Oregonian assessed his situation with a cold, practical eye. He'd endured countless crises and trials growing up on the dairy farm. These challenges had made him even-keeled, taught him that staying calm and thoughtful in a storm was the best way to find clear skies. So he didn't panic in the water that afternoon. Nor did he dwell on who might occupy that beach not too far from him. If the Japanese were there, he knew he'd be in dire jeopardy. Instead, he compartmentalized each task, distilling the overall situation to the immediate issues critical to his survival.

First, he had to make a decision about his standard-issue russet-colored chukka boots. They were like dumbbells on his feet. Without his Mae West, the boots would drag him to the bottom. He could also feel the weight of his Model 1911 Colt .45 tucked into its leather holster on his hip. If his Mae West started to leak, he'd be in real trouble. Yet he knew that once he got ashore, the chukkas would be the only way he could negotiate the jungle, and his .45 the only way he could defend himself. He decided to hold on to both despite their drag and weight, at least for as long as he could. He began to tread water, the chukkas making the task far less efficient than if he'd been barefoot.

His face hurt from the burns the fire had inflicted. The parachute risers had given him rope burns on the back of his neck as well. As the adrenaline drained out of his system, he felt sore and beaten up by the ordeal but otherwise okay. No broken bones. He'd be able to walk in to Henderson as soon as he got his chukkas on the beach.

He began to swim for Guadalcanal. Paddling in an inflated Mae West was never easy, as it kept the wearer at a thirty-degree angle, face up, away from the water. On his back, Marion looked like a water bug trying to scuttle across the white caps. Kicking didn't help much either, thanks to the boots. Doggedly, he kept at it, pacing himself as his breathing grew heavy. After a while, he paused to check and see how much farther it was to the beach.

To his surprise, he'd made no progress. Marion realized the current in the area must be both strong and dragging him out to sea. All he'd managed to do was hold his ground against it.

He kept going, feet kicking, arms stroking under the Mae West's floats. His strength began to ebb. Keeping his chin up out of the water grew difficult. Ultimately, he faced a choice: wear himself out completely or stop fighting and let the current take him out to sea.

With his shoes and gun and gear, he couldn't just float. He had to keep treading water to keep his face out of the waves. An hour passed. Then two. The current swept him away from both the shore and the reef-ringed island. He had no idea where it might take him, but at the rate things looked, he would find out the hard way soon enough.

Carl grew up self-disciplined, with a will like battleship steel. He believed there wasn't a problem or a crisis that could not be solved with sheer perseverance. Although he hated academics at Oregon State, he had bulled through his classes to graduate. Now, he began to wonder if he'd encountered the exception to his rule: a situation he could not control, could not outwork, and could not solve.

He knew that help from Henderson would not be coming. They could not afford to send planes out to look for him. Besides, he must have drifted ten miles or more in his chute. Even if they did send a PBY out, nobody would be looking for him where he had landed.

He could encounter a passing ship. Chances were slight, he knew. Besides, at this point, he had an equal chance of being pulled aboard a Japanese destroyer or an American one.

Rescue at sea seemed like a remote hope at best. What other options did he have? There weren't any. All he could do was keep his legs moving, keep his head above the chop, and hope something would turn the situation to his favor.

The minutes ground on as he scissored his legs back and forth until his thighs burned with the effort. Short breaks gave him respite but dropped his chin into the water. All too soon, he'd have to start treading again.

The salt water stung his wounds. His wrists began to ache, and when he examined them, he discovered he'd suffered burns on both from the engine fire. Hour three faded into hour four. Living became anguish. Everything hurt. His tormented legs sizzled with pain. His arms grew weak as he kept sculling with them to try to ease the load from his legs.

Even if he dumped the pistol and his chukkas, it was probably too late. He could just see the beach in the distance. Yet, he didn't have the energy reserves left to get there even unencumbered against the current. He clung to hope, ordered his legs to keep kicking. A little longer. A little more.

His arms grew leaden. His legs were sluggish now. His watch read almost 1600. He'd been in the drink fighting for his life since noon. He was on the dregs of his energy—and his force of will.

"America? America?" an accented voice called across the waves.

Marion twisted his head. Wearily, he saw a dugout canoe, perhaps a hundred feet away. A single Melanesian man paddled it, scribing a circle in the water.

"You Japan?" the local asked.

Hoarse and weak, Marion cried out, "American! American!"

Still suspicious, the man in the canoe circled Marion several times, getting closer with each revolution. He studied Carl, who was unsure which side of the war this Melanesian was on. Most of the locals hated the Japanese, thanks to the brutal way the imperial troops treated them, but there were always exceptions.

"America?" the man asked again.

"American!" Marion assured him.

The Marine could barely keep treading water now. The man in the canoe, seeing that Carl was at the end of his endurance, made a decision. He steered his canoe directly at the Oregonian and pulled to a stop beside him. It took several minutes to get him into the dugout. Finally, Marion sat in the bow, totally spent.

The local identified himself as Steven. He and the other members of his village had seen Marion's parachute drift by and land offshore. It triggered a debate as to whether they should go rescue the man. They feared the Japanese intensely. Should the pilot prove to be from Japan, then killing him could draw a reprisal, while bringing him to the village opened them up to contact with the troops on the island. Some of the villagers argued that it was better to just leave the man in the water. Eventually, however, Steven volunteered to give it a try on the chance that the pilot was an American. He paddled out alone in search of the downed aviator.

Marion introduced himself as Steven handed him a cup of coconut milk. The Melanesian man spoke almost no English, and the Marine was in no shape for conversation. He felt more dead than alive.

Steven turned the canoe south for Aola Bay. Battling the current as well, he made slow progress. It took until almost sunset to negotiate the two miles to Steven's village at the edge of the bay. There, Marion limped with him to Eroni Leauli's house. Eroni was a Fijian doctor who belonged to Maj. Martin Clemons's Commonwealth scouts. Clemons was a hard-nosed British officer who was the senior administrator for the Solomons. He organized the Coastwatchers throughout the islands, while his Melanesian Commonwealth scouts operated behind Japanese lines, rescuing aviators, conducting reconnaissance, and reporting on enemy movements via a network of radios stashed around Guadalcanal. Doctor Eroni, as he was called by the locals, had stayed at Aola Village with his wife and children after Clemons moved out of the nearby district office.

Though the Japanese were close and Marion was in grave danger, he was not in any shape to try an overland march back to Henderson. He was at least thirty miles from the perimeter as the crow flew. The jungle between was full of the Japanese troops that had gotten ashore despite the best efforts of Mangrum's dive-bomber crews. Marion knew that even at full strength, getting home to Henderson Field would be a serious challenge.

Marion spent the night of September 9 as a guest of Eroni's family. When he awoke in the morning, he was so sore from his four-hour ordeal in the water that his host made him rest. Throughout the day, Marion slept and regained strength. Later in the afternoon, his host showed him the sixteen-foot launch he and the villagers kept camouflaged in the jungle not far from the beach. The locals had pulled it through a little cove and up a slow-moving stream, then beached it and covered it with jungle bushes, knowing that if a Japanese patrol found it, the boat would be stolen and put to enemy use. Eroni told Marion that up until a few months ago, the engine worked fine. One day, it just died and nobody could get it started.

Marion had spent most of his life tinkering with small engines, both on the farm and, later, in the Corps, when he purchased a one-stroke Cushman scooter that he used to get around his assigned base. The Cushman followed him to Midway and back to Hawai'i and eventually found its way to Guadalcanal aboard the *Burrows*. The outboard wasn't much different from anything he'd fiddled with before, so he rolled up his sleeves and got to work on the little one-cylinder, five-horsepower gas engine. After a few hours of effort with minimal tools, he couldn't get it started either. He and Eroni decided the only option left was to try to walk through Japanese lines and get back to the perimeter on foot.

That first day, like Rapid Robert Read had discovered a few weeks before him, Marion discovered being castaway with the locals did have its perks. While the Marines in the perimeter continued to eat appalling, maggot-filled Japanese rice, Dr. Eroni stuffed Marion with fresh chicken from his henhouse. It was the best meal he'd had in a month, and it went a long way to revitalizing him.

On the morning of September 11, Marion put on his now-dry chukkas, strapped his M1911 to a web belt he'd taken to wearing, and presented himself to the Fijian doctor, ready for the long journey.

At least, he thought he was ready. When Eroni and a group of villagers led off the march into the jungle, it became abundantly clear Marion was nowhere near as in shape as he thought he was. The Melanesians moved through the rugged narrow trails like ghosts, leaving Marion in their wake as he panted in the heat. Covered in sweat, his clothes soaked, he limped along as best he could until the party reached Paripao. They found the village virtually deserted as most of the locals had fled from Japanese patrols after Martin Clemons had cleared out. Eroni led them to Clemons's old district office, where Marion discovered a two-way radio set. He played around with it but quickly discovered that it was nonfunctional. If they could get it working, he might radio the perimeter and get a PBY to come pick him up in Aola Bay. With some effort, they got the receiver functioning again, but the transmitter was damaged beyond their ability to fix it.

Disappointed, they settled down to make camp for the night, cooking duck eggs and a duck for dinner. By sunset, the jungle had turned pitch dark. Even with clear skies overhead, a tiny sliver of a waxing crescent moon provided virtually no light. That would be to their advantage as they pushed into Japanese-held territory.

The next morning, the group continued on along a narrow trail that ran roughly northwesterly. They hadn't gotten far when they ran straight into a group of panicked Melanesians fleeing back toward Paripao. The escaping people had run into thousands of Japanese troops several miles up the trail.

There would be no way through to the perimeter in this direction.

Frustrated, fearful, and sheened in sweat, Marion and Eroni's men turned around to follow the fleeing locals back to Paripao, then continued on to Eroni's home. It took most of the day to double back and reach Aola Bay. There they discovered that a Japanese foraging party had stolen most of the chickens in the village.

Japanese ahead of them. Japanese behind them. Marion was sandwiched in the middle, and only fortuitous timing saved him from capture or death.

For everyone's sake, Carl needed to get out of the area as soon as possible, lest the enemy return. Should they capture or kill him, Eroni and his team would be horrifically treated, of that the Oregonian had no doubt. He decided to take a second look at the outboard motor on Eroni's launch. While his hosts chased down the last few chickens that had escaped the clutches of the Japanese, Marion broke out the boat's tool kit and set to work disassembling the motor. He grew optimistic when he discovered that nothing seemed to be damaged or broken. Whatever was going on might not require a new part that they didn't have.

He worked through sunset, continuing after their chicken dinner and hoping they could get underway sometime after midnight. Fiddling with the engine in the dark was no easy feat, and the poor light slowed his progress. Working with minimal light, he labored away as Eroni and his men kept watch. Marion had been at it for hours and was still not done when, sometime around 2100, the sky to the west lit up. Through the jungle canopy, flashes of hellish red-orange light glowed soundlessly. The men paused their work and went for a better view.

On the beach, they could see the red-orange strobes of colors illuminating the horizon. Quick flashes and a brilliant white glare followed by total darkness for a second or two. Then more fiery hell flashes would reignite the distant sky. A moment later, they heard a faraway sound of thunder rolling across the water. Something big was happening at Henderson. Something awful. Whatever it was, Marion's friends were in the middle of it.

THIRTY-FIVE

THE PLACE BEYOND ENDURANCE

Henderson Field, Guadalcanal
September 12, 1942, 2115 hours

LOUIE THE LOUSE SHOWED UP FORTY-FIVE MINUTES BEFORE MID-night. The MAG-23 Marines heard its engine throbbing in the distance as the little Japanese floatplane put-putted over Savo Sound, its crew searching the darkness for Henderson Field. When such intrusions began, the Americans took to naming everything that annoyed them at night. Oscar was the generic moniker given for the Japanese subs that sometimes surfaced to lob a few shells at the airfield. Washing Machine Charlie was a twin-engine night intruder that would occasionally drop flares or bombs as it ranged overhead. Sewing Machine Charlie was another floatplane, but it was larger than Louie the Louse. All these noc-turnal raiders harassed the Marines, denied them sleep, and forced them to roll out of their cots and take cover in increasingly muddy and dank foxholes, slit trenches, and dugouts.

By September 12, VMSB-232's men were so sleep-deprived, malnour-ished, sick, and overworked that some lacked the energy or will to dive into those vile holes in the ground. Dick Mangrum's gunner, Dennis Byrd, came up with a novel idea to avoid those frantic runs to the dug-outs. He carved a shallow trench out of the hard ground beside his cot. It was barely deep enough to get half his body protected when he lay prone in it, but for ease of use, it couldn't be beat. When night raiders lumbered overhead, he'd simply slide off his bunk and into the trench, though sleep usually eluded him there.

The squadron's quartermaster, Lt. Ed Butler, spent one night running from the tent he shared with Dick Mangrum to their nearest dugout three times. By the second time, his clothes were so slicked with mud and filth, he cast them aside and tried to get some sleep in the nude, tucked under his mosquito netting. Of course, a third raider appeared to drop a few bombs, sending Butler into the night buck naked and bound for that sludge-filled dugout.

Mangrum had tried to keep the men's spirits and alertness up by making a game of seeing how fast some of them could get out of their bunks and into their dugouts. While drinking some captured sake one night, Dick and Don McCafferty sat beside their dugout and timed the squadron's flight surgeon, Lt. Jim Standard. Jim was always the last to get into cover during a raid, so they were eager to see him up his game. In light of the game, the doctor decided on a new route, and he bet his skipper ten dollars that he could get out of his quarters and into the dugout in ten seconds. Jim came flying out of the tent and promptly tripped over one of its guy lines, sending him sprawling right in front of Dick and Don.

On this night, the Red Devils silently listened to Louie the Louse's approach, trying to judge whether to expend the energy to get out of bed, wrestle through their mosquito netting, and go sit in mud at the bottom of their dugouts. As the bombers reached the coast and buzzed down from the west, nobody in 232's camp moved. The little floatplane passed right over the dive-bomber encampment, then puttered on over the airfield.

A moment later, a flare burst to life directly over 232's tents, bathing the men in greenish-blue light. The flare swung back and forth under its parachute, creating a kaleidoscope of shadows and unearthly colors amid the hundred-foot-tall coconut palms. The wildly moving display made some of the men on the ground dizzy. The flare didn't even seem to be descending. It was just hanging there above them like a lantern in the night, beckoning the monsters beyond its eerie halo to strike.

The monsters were out there, all right. Gliding through Savo Sound a few thousand yards offshore steamed a Japanese task force of four destroyers led by the light cruiser *Sendai*. The Marine aviators couldn't see or hear them. Like silent killers, they slid into firing position.

The flare was their aiming point.

The sky to the north suddenly lit up reddish orange as if the gates of an inferno had burst open. The sick and exhausted men struggled to their feet, but in seconds, the first 5.5-inch shell freight-trained overhead. With a whine and a whoosh, it struck less than a hundred feet from 232's row of tents. The explosion knocked the men to the quaking ground, filling them with instant, feral terror. Two more shells landed, rocking the palm grove, splintering the trees, and sending shrapnel whistling through the canvas tents.

Ed Eades panicked. He jumped to his feet and tried to flee through his tent flap and into the fires of the night. In the glow of the explosions, Lewis Macias saw the expression on Ed's face and knew that in the trauma of the moment, his friend was acting irrationally. He tackled Ed, pinning him to the ground. Lewis then hugged his friend fiercely as shell fragments knifed through their tent just over their heads.

Fifty feet from Ed and Lewis, Dennis Byrd lay in the too-shallow trench beside his cot, face down, desperately trying to mold himself into the earth. Now a cascade of shells walked through the bivouac, one exploding practically atop the other. Even with his eyes squeezed closed, Byrd could see the orange flashes of the blasts. The concussive waves hit him like a desert tornado, so hot it felt like his exposed skin was burning.

The ground undulated, spasming in seeming agony at every explosion. Bits of palm trunks spun crazily to the ground, smashing tents flat and trapping the men inside. Somehow, over the din of the explosions, a Southern accent rang out. It was a kid from Louisiana screaming out a prayer that ended with him promising God he would never gamble again if he'd just end this misery.

Another storm of shells raked the men. Dennis's entire world went green, then orange—a world of roiling flame and overwhelming sound. Something snapped inside him right then. Eyes closed yet his vision filled with something Dante could never have captured on paper, he gave up.

"God," he said weakly, his voice washed away in the din, "make those ships go away."

A white-hot sliver of shrapnel fell through his shattered tent and landed on his back, burning through his shirt and sticking to his skin. He cried out but didn't move. The coup de grâce was imminent and would surely take him soon.

Up the row of tents, Dick Mangrum, Jim Standard, and Don McCafferty lay flat in their GP medium, listening to someone nearby moaning in agony. The voice was distorted, mindless, pain racked. It sent spears of pure panic through each of them. Dick wanted to help, but the shells were coming too fast, too close. Standing in this maelstrom would be a death sentence. They couldn't even get to their dugout, so they clung to the ground beside their cots and waited for a lull.

When it finally came, the three men crawled out from under their tent to see the flare still burning, hanging from a tree a few hundred feet away. Its light revealed that their bivouac had been turned into a landscape of smoking shell craters stippled with splintered palm trunks and tree limbs. Some of the palms had been decapitated, leaving only a couple dozen feet of bare trunk, like skeletal fingers pointing into the night sky.

They followed the sound of moaning, working their way to the next tent over. It had taken a near miss from one of the cruiser's 5.5-inch guns. Inside, they found the torn remains of two men. Art O'Keefe lay among them, shocked and hollow eyed. Art's rescuers reached him and found their traumatized friend physically unhurt but covered in blood and brain matter from the two men who had been killed.

Next to Art, Danny Iverson lay wounded and groaning. Dick and Jim pulled the two survivors from the wreckage. Danny was bleeding and broken emotionally by the horror of what had happened.

Dick called for help. Corpsmen made their way to the tent and eased Danny onto a litter. First Midway, now Guadalcanal. Twice in ninety days, Danny had been wounded by the Japanese.

There were still two men inside the destroyed tent. Both men never stood a chance. Dick, Don McCafferty, and Jim went back into the wreckage to confirm what they already knew. In the harsh blue-green flare light, they found the remains of Baldy and Don Rose.

They're transferred. They're just transferred.

But the fiction couldn't hold this time, especially not for Art O'Keefe, who sat nearby wiping his friends' blood and brains off his face.

Dick fought to control himself. The rest of the squadron needed him now more than ever. The backbone of 232 had been eviscerated with one shell.

Baldy stood before Dick Mangrum. They had served together for months. Dick had made a point of hanging on to him through every division of 232 in the run-up to the summer's influx of second lieutenants. There at Ewa, he had pinned Baldy's butter bars on his collar.

Just as he did with Fletcher Brown a few days before.

Not dead. No. Transferred.

They're transferred.

Dick, Don, and Jim clambered out of the wrecked tent, shocked and numb with grief. They had to keep moving; the night was just beginning, and Dick knew Geiger would order them aloft as soon as the bombardment ended. He left Jim and Don with the dead and worked his way through the bivouac, checking on his men, focusing on the present moment so that his mind wouldn't go back to the scene in Baldy's tent.

A new salvo of shells landed in the 231 encampment beside their own, so close it sent Dick and the others diving for cover. The explosions ground through the palm grove like a threshing machine, tearing trees, tents, and gear to bits. Through the smoke and flames and the thunder of the blasts, the Red Devils heard their comrades screaming in anguish, calling for corpsmen. They were losing brothers too.

The shellfire lifted past 231's camp and began to fall south of the airfield complex. The reprieve was not wasted; the Red Devils rose to their feet, grabbed shovels, and started deepening their dugouts. Some sixth sense told them this wasn't over. The bombardment left their nerves frayed. Mangrum needed them to hold together. They would be pushed even closer to that boundary between sanity and the abyss in the hours to come, for even as the shelling ceased twenty minutes after it began, the sounds of a furious battle echoed down from the ridges a mile south of Henderson Field. Machine guns chattered out long, desperate-sounding bursts. Dull thuds of grenades and 75 mm shells punctuated the fight. Hair-raising bugle calls rose and fell, followed by torrents of gunfire.

Kawaguchi's attack had begun, and it had struck the weakest sector of the Marine perimeter less than two thousand yards from Henderson Field.

Adding to the misery of the moment, it began to rain intermittently. The Red Devils kept digging deeper with anything they could find. Dennis Byrd, his tent offering protection from the rain, frantically worked to deepen his trench beside his cot. Lacking a shovel, he grabbed a screwdriver and a mess plate. Others did the same. About thirty minutes after the initial bombardment ended, the Japanese sent another torrent of shells at the perimeter. The aviators pressed themselves into their muddy holes, swearing, praying, trembling under the strain of the night. This time, the shells came from a battery of Japanese 75 mm guns, not the ships in Savo Sound. The Japanese targeted the hills south of the airfield, then walked their fire down through Henderson Field, hoping to destroy as many aircraft there as possible. The men of the other squadrons huddled in their holes as the shellfire walked through their areas. Some of the men were lying two or three atop one another in slit trenches and foxholes. Such was the case with Bob Galer, who was crushed between John Dobbin and one of his second lieutenants all night. When one man began shaking, the terror was physically transmitted to the other men, and soon all three would be trembling. They took turns praying, two Catholics and one Christian Scientist, even as their physiological reaction to fear continued.

Galer wrote in his diary the next morning, "Everyone now has religion."

This round of shelling lasted thirty minutes, followed by another lull until just after midnight, when the *Sendai*'s task force returned and dumped an avalanche of high-explosive shells onto Henderson Field. Roiling mushroom clouds of flame boiled up over struck fuel caches; aircraft were blown apart. The runway was cratered over and over. The men kept digging, even as Japanese infiltrators crept around the bivouacs to snipe at the Marines.

It was total hellish chaos unlike anything these young Americans had ever endured. The bombardment lasted until 0200. Through their fear, some of the crew members still managed to wisecrack. After a five-inch shell arced overhead and landed beyond the bivouac, one Red Devil's voice rose in the night: "Goddamn. I swear I recognized that Model T engine block I sold to a scrap dealer a few years back."

The fighting in the hills moved closer to the airfield. Galer and the fighter pilots on the other side of Henderson's runway soon found themselves taking tracer fire from the south. Bullets stitched their bivouac so thoroughly that both 223's and 224's pilots huddled in their slit trenches, sidearms in hand, ready to fight for their lives if the Japanese broke through the lines.

Word reached Mangrum to get his bombers in the air as soon as possible to chase down that Japanese task force. Yet nobody knew if the runway remained in American hands. The same question was asked by the fighter pilots, who waited tensely for word one way or the other. The uncertainty was gut grinding to the men who had already endured so much that night. Finally, MAG-23 HQ ordered Galer to send a truck out to the runway to find out who controlled it.

The lucky men who landed that duty drove through rain and darkness to discover that the ground crews from both 223 and 224 had established a rough defensive line in the dispersal area beside Henderson. Armed with whatever was at hand—pistols, tommy guns, and bolt-action rifles—they had taken fire on and off throughout the night and thought they were the front line now. So far, the Japanese had not broken through. Henderson remained in Marine hands.

The truck returned to the 224 bivouac, and the news spread through the squadrons. John L. and Galer gathered their pilots and headed for their aircraft sometime around 0430, knowing they would be needed not just for intercept duty but also to support the mud Marines in the south hills.

At 232's shattered camp, Dick rounded up a few of his men along with a handful of Flight 300 guys. They made their way along a narrow trail through occasional sniper fire to their aircraft. The first two planes they reached were nothing but burned-out hulks, smashed by naval shellfire. Oddly, their propellers had survived. The Red Devils came across one standing before the aluminum ash that had once been an SBD's fuselage. The propeller had a .50-caliber bullet hole through one of the blades. It was Baldy's whistling wonder, MB-22. The Dauntless had outlasted its pilot by only a matter of minutes. Dick knew it, but the other pilots did not. Word had yet to spread that their beloved "Can't Miss" Czech had been killed.

Closer to the airstrip, the crews found a Marine guarding each one of their SBDs. When Hal Buell got to his bird, he noticed one Marine in the cockpit, cleaning a tommy gun. Hal walked around the tail to the right side of the aircraft and almost tripped over a dead Japanese soldier. He stepped over him and saw dried blood splattered from the side of the fuselage across the wing to the trailing edge.

The Marine in his cockpit explained that they had been posted up all night to protect the planes in case any Japanese broke through. He decided to sit in the cockpit and wait for any would-be saboteurs. Sure enough, sometime before dawn, a Japanese infiltrator climbed onto the wing and stepped up to the cockpit, probably intent on detonating a grenade inside. Instead, the Marine stuck the barrel of his tommy gun into the surprised man's chest and put a burst into him. He spun and fell against the fuselage, then dropped onto the wing. "Then I pulled him off the wing so you guys can fly this thing." With that, the Marine climbed out of the pilot's seat and shuffled off after Buell thanked him.

While the men from Flight 300 and VMSB-232 warmed up their SBDs and the sound of gunfire and artillery drummed through the night, the engineers repaired the shell craters in the runway. There were a lot fewer engineers at work than normal. The bombardment had scattered them all over the area and the nearby jungle, where they sought the protection of any hole or trench. Now, perhaps less than half the crew had returned so far to patch the strip.

All the SBDs made it aloft, but in the predawn blackness, they could not find the enemy ships. They returned after sunup and dumped their bombs on what they hoped were Japanese positions in the south hills while F4Fs took off from Fighter One's Cow Pasture to strafe and patrol. The Dauntless crews had no idea if their bombs had hit anything, but by then they were so numb with fatigue, they were beyond caring. They circled back to Henderson and landed.

On the ground, the crews gathered. They looked like zombies. Their uniforms were covered in dirt and drying mud; their faces, hands, and arms striped with cuts and lacerations; their shoes barely recognizable as brown. Their hands were black from digging all night. They shucked off their helmets, the pilots heading to the Pagoda to report in and get debriefed and the gunners trekking back to camp.

When Dick returned to the squadron area and passed the radio repair tent, he heard a man sobbing. Stepping inside, he found Sgt. Frank Willsey, the radio department's senior NCO, sitting on an upturned wooden crate next to Dennis Byrd. Both men were crying unashamedly and talking about Baldy. To the enlisted men, Baldy was a hero, one of their own who secured a coveted slot in flight school through sheer hard work and determination. Even after he became an aviator himself, he mentored the lower enlisted in the squadron. He never barked orders, but what he said was like God's word. If he asked, it got done.

Knowing that his gunner was especially close to Baldy, Dick knew that he himself should probably have told Dennis what had happened. Dennis found out on his way back to camp, when he ran into Frank, who broke the news.

"I owe my life to Baldy," Dennis said, tears streaking down his grimy face. Dennis had originally been assigned to be Fletcher Brown's gunner. Before they reached Guadalcanal, Baldy switched him into Mangrum's back seat. Had he not done that, he would have vanished with Fletcher after the Gizo raid.

There was no consoling these two. Frank and Baldy had been in the squadron together for two years. They'd been best friends. Dennis, as tough a Texan as Dick had yet encountered, clearly loved Baldy like an older brother.

Everyone would be hurting as the news spread. In this moment, though, Dick couldn't penetrate the strata of rank and face the emotion needed to connect. He couldn't do it—if only for his own sake. He had to keep his distance. His only job was to keep the squadron going, and he couldn't break in front of his men. He muttered a reminder to think of Baldy and Rose as transferred, then slipped back out of the tent to let the two friends cope with the grief together. As he walked away, wondering how he would find the strength to write Don Rose's mom and dad, and Baldy's wife, the stark loneliness of command had never felt so raw.

THIRTY-SIX

THE DARKEST HOURS

Henderson Field, Guadalcanal
Sunday, September 13, 1942, 1630 hours

THE AVIATORS OF VMSB-232 GATHERED IN THE REMAINS OF
their bivouac, drinking the beef broth soup that Sgt. Al Gruenke
had somehow managed to make, further cementing his reputation as
the best cook on Starvation Island. The squadron was at a crisis point,
and every creature comfort, no matter how little, helped keep the men
together.

They looked like walking skeletons now. Their belts were on their last
notches and still barely kept their pants on their hips. Some of the men
had lost twenty pounds or more. This was their first decent meal since the
chaos of last night and their first chance to be together since Baldy and
Don Rose were killed. Looking around at one another, they could see that
almost everyone was suffering from some sort of illness. Malaria cases
began to spike earlier in the month with the onset of the rainy season.
Several men, including Robert Fleener and Art O'Keefe, were shivering
from it. Others battled amoebic dysentery, gastroenteritis, an unidentified virus the docs thought was similar to dengue fever, catarrhal fever,
and general enervation from the nonstop pace of missions (ops tempo)
and the lack of food. The days and nights spent in muddy, dank dugouts,

combined with the long gaps between chances to bathe led to skin and fungal infections in their armpits, crotches, and "intergluteal folds."

As if the physical misery weren't bad enough, the loss of Marion Carl and Baldy hard on the heels of Fletcher Brown's disappearance tore their hearts out. Baldy had been buried with scores of other Marines that afternoon. Some of the ground crew recovered the whistling propeller blade from his shattered SBD and placed it as his grave marker. Such gestures helped ease their pain a little, but the reality they faced included a long and difficult grieving journey for their lost mentor and friend. Don Rose's friend and mentor from college, Chaplain Angsar South, would preside over a memorial service for both men, but that event would have to wait until the enemy stopped coming at them.

The day had been nonstop mayhem. Air raids. Crashes at the airfield. Sporadic firefights all around the perimeter. Artillery bombardments. And, for the pilots and gunners, mission after mission after mission. Most of the aircrews had flown three times that day, searching for Japanese ships or bombing the enemy in the jungle. Their ops tempo kept the ground crews in constant motion, as they quaffed salt tablets to prevent heat exhaustion or heat stroke as the temperature trended toward ninety when the sun came out. Still, they worked like automatons to rearm and refuel the squadron's few remaining SBDs.

Intelligence reports steadily flowing in from Ghormley's HQ said that a Japanese carrier was out there, somewhere to the north. The reports lent a sense of urgency to the search missions. If the reports were true, the enemy surely intended to launch another major resupply effort to Guadalcanal in the midst of its current land offensive. This meant more Cactus Express convoys that would need to be stopped. Somehow. The Red Devils had only four planes left, and Leo Smith's VMSB-231 was in little better shape. The Marines teetered on the edge of combat ineffective.

The Wildcat squadrons—223, 224, and the Navy's VF-5 ("Fighting Five")—were fighting for sheer survival against a growing tide of Japanese attacks. Instead of the usual lunchtime bombing raid, the Japanese started coming over several times a day, forcing the men to scramble again and again. On this day, the fighter pilots had taken a beating. The new Navy squadron lost several pilots during the day. John L. and his crew had lost several more. And morale for Galer's men was hitting rock bottom.

Before everyone had gathered that afternoon, two gunshots suddenly rang out, closer than the background tapestry of firefights and other skirmishes. Don McCafferty, who had been standing beside his shrapnel-scarred tent, jerked reflexively. Both bullets missed him by mere inches. It was a symbolic moment: the men had taken fire all day, no matter where they were located around the airfield. More than once, spent bullets fell out of the sky to tumble to the ground near the men. One actually landed on Danny Iverson's lap after he'd been wounded and carried away the night before. Where they came from or who fired them was anyone's guess. By this point, the men heard fights raging in several directions.

Dick Mangrum joined the men after Geiger had summoned him to the Pagoda. He arrived with a grim expression on his lean face. He was as sick as the rest of the men, but he maintained a facade of being fine. A squadron commander, especially during a crisis moment like this, had to project confidence. He had to be invulnerable to all the havoc that the enemy, the scarce food, and the difficult environment wreaked on the unit. He needed to be stronger, harder, and more even-keeled than everyone else. Unbreakable. That front would honor the faith his men invested in him.

He didn't sugarcoat the news. Rumors had swirled all day long over what had happened the night before and what might be in store. One minute, the gossip leaned toward the Red Devils' being relieved and sent home. The next, the scuttlebutt turned dark: The Navy had abandoned them again. The Marines were about to be overrun and they had been left to stand, fight, and die. The tenor of the rumor mill changed a dozen times that day. Now the men waited anxiously for their skipper to fill them in with the straight dope.

Dick began by describing what had happened the night before. The Japanese had struck Red Mike Edson's 1st Raider Battalion with a series of disconnected, badly coordinated attacks. The battle Dick's men heard last night focused on control of a ridge—dubbed Edson's Ridge by the

Marines—and a series of hills that were the last terrain obstacles between the Japanese and Henderson Field.

Edson's men fought tenaciously with machine guns, rifles, grenades, and artillery. As waves of Japanese overwhelmed them, the battle became a knife fight in the darkness. They battled hand to hand in countless life-and-death moments, slashing and clubbing one another like feral animals. The skirmish was supremely vicious and terrifying. The Japanese refused to quit until dawn. Marines captured by the Japanese were dragged off and tortured. Their brothers could hear them screaming in anguish over the din of battle. It was kill or be killed. No mercy. No quarter. No options but hold or die.

When the sun rose, the Raiders clung to the ridge on the last legs of their mental and physical endurance. Now down to only a few hundred men, Vandegrift expected them to be hit again. The division's reserves had been ordered to move to the ridge, but to reach it, the mud Marines had to cross the airfield complex. The Japanese air raids, the constant flight operations, and some snafus had delayed that movement.

The Navy was sending help in the form of squadrons of orphaned aircraft after the Japanese crippled or sank Navy flattops. That was it. There would be no surface forces to stop the bombardments. No remaining carriers would attempt to intercept the Japanese carrier presumably lurking to the north. Adm. Richmond Kelly Turner had promised to bring the 7th Marines in as reinforcements, but they wouldn't arrive for at least four or five days.

Earlier in the day, Vandegrift told Geiger that if the Japanese broke through tonight and took the airfield, the division would use amphibious tracks to move inland up the Lunga River, where they would hold out as long as possible while conducting a guerrilla campaign against the enemy. He told Geiger to be prepared to fly every available aircraft off the island if it looked like the Raiders wouldn't be able to hold that night.

Such an order meant a night takeoff while the airfield itself became a battlefield, followed by a long and dangerous flight to the New Hebrides at the very edge of the planes' range. The odds of surviving a takeoff and flight like this—especially for the F4F pilots—were slim.

Geiger made it clear he intended to stay and fight with Vandegrift. The ground crews would be left behind as well to fight and survive as best they could with the mud Marines.

For now, the Cactus Air Force would dig in and prepare to fight. After spending a backbreaking day keeping the aircraft fueled, armed, and repaired, the ground crews from all the squadrons were ordered to establish defensive positions around their bivouacs alongside the aircrews, to repel Japanese troops. Division intelligence suspected the enemy might launch an airborne attack on the airfield, using their paratrooper units that had helped seize critical oil facilities in the Dutch East Indies. If the enemy now used a similar tactic, there would be no front line, just Japanese in the front and rear, with possible attacks on the flanks or along the coast to boot.

Everyone would be a rifleman that night.

Thirty minutes before sunset, the afternoon search planes returned to Henderson. Some of the Flight 300 pilots had slipped away for a quick bath in the river before another night spent in muddy holes. Getting clean, if only for a few hours, had a rejuvenating effect on morale, and for some men, it was worth the risk of snipers at the bathing area.

As Hal Buell and Christian Fink walked back to camp, a VMSB-231 Dauntless swung into the pattern to prepare for landing. It was piloted by Owen D. Johnson, a young second lieutenant whom most of the junior officers knew. As they watched him with professional interest, Johnson dropped his gear and flaps and began to loop around onto his final approach.

At that moment, two float Zeroes bolted across the beach, barely above the treetops. The Japanese fighters appeared out of nowhere, catching everyone, including the antiaircraft gunners, by surprise. Johnson and his gunner never saw the threat. The flak crews raced to get their weapons trained on the marauders, who arced over the field and cut inside Johnson's turn. Thousands of Marines stopped whatever they were doing and turned their eyes skyward. The float Zeroes ran down the SBD like predators on a savanna. Johnson's Dauntless—low, slow, gear and flaps down, rear guns secured for landing—was a sitting duck. As they passed directly over Buell and Fink, the float Zeroes opened fire. The SBD exploded in flames and dropped into the jungle, where it exploded, killing both men.

The two Japanese fighters, totally unscathed, sped out to sea and vanished, leaving the Marines who witnessed the attack sickened with fury. Not long after, as the sun began to set, a formation of twelve Navy SBDs from an orphaned carrier air group appeared overhead. The antiaircraft gunners, now at full alert and filled with rage over what had just happened, assumed they were hostile and opened fire on them. Fortunately, their aim was bad; none of the reinforcing Dauntlesses were shot down.

With darkness came the swelling sounds of battle in the hills to the south of Henderson Field. The aviators kept their sidearms close and dug like gophers, knowing they would probably again be under the guns of a Japanese task force, as well as an overhead assault from Washing Machine Charlie. Across Henderson, some of the fighter pilots dug themselves into shell craters gouged out of the mud and soil by the previous night's bombardment, thinking the odds of another shell striking the exact same place were probably low.

At 2045, the Japanese launched their main assault against Edson's battalion. Three thousand imperial soldiers poured out of the jungle screaming, officers brandishing swords, bugles calling through the night. The Marines met them with a wall of firepower that savaged the enemy ranks. The Japanese stepping over their dead and dying were felled by volleys of grenades thrown by desperate Marines, yet the enemy's momentum didn't waver. The Marines were pushed back, and one flank nearly collapsed. Edson called in artillery fire almost atop his own positions, and the 11th Marines hammered the Japanese waves with saturated 105 mm bombardments. Before daybreak, those gun batteries sent nearly two thousand high-explosive shells downrange.

Still, the Japanese collided with the Marines fighting from their shallow dugouts. Brutal hand-to-hand fighting ensued once again. In the melees, an understrength company of Japanese troops broke through the American lines and rushed for the airfield, followed by part of a machine gun company.

Three Japanese, including a sword-wielding officer, stormed General Vandegrift's headquarters, which was located not far behind Edson's Ridge. A Marine flung his rifle at one of the charging Japanese, hitting him across the forehead and knocking him to the ground. Three more Marines jumped on the officer, who, when they crushed him, cut his own right hand off above the knuckles with his sword. A Marine warrant officer ran over, Model 1911 Colt in hand, pulled the officer's helmet off, and stuffed the muzzle of the pistol against his head. The trigger pull blew the front of his face off, spraying the headquarters area with gore. The Marine swiftly killed another Japanese soldier the same way. The third fled into the jungle.

As the melee continued, Louie the Louse droned overhead. A dreaded parachute flare ignited the sky over Kukum Harbor, sending everyone not already in a hole diving for cover. It didn't take long for a fierce storm of five-inch shells, fired by a Japanese task force somewhere offshore in Savo Sound, to smother the harbor area.

The Red Devils burrowed into the ground as the exploding heavy shells caused the ground to quake. They waited in dread for the bombardment to shift their way, but mercifully for a change, it never did. Kukum Harbor took the brunt of the shelling.

While the shelling continued, the engineer battalion shuffled its positions both to provide anti-paratroop defense at the airfields and to protect General Vandegrift's headquarters area. They moved through the night, thinning their defenses everywhere.

Near the Ilu River to the east of the MAG-23 encampments, battle sounds suddenly rolled through the night. The Japanese had hit the 3rd Battalion, 1st Marines, with a second assault. The fighting raged in the jungle and in the darkness along the slopes of Edson's Ridge. Again, the Japanese failed to detect the 2,000-yard hole in the Marine perimeter just to the left of their attack on 3/1. Had they discovered it, the assault force would have gone straight into Fighter One without any opposition.

Before dawn, Fighter One did become a battlefield. The southwest edge, defended by Marine engineers, was suddenly assailed by screaming, desperate Japanese led by a wounded officer. They flung themselves at the engineers, overran several of their machine gun nests, then got pinned down as teams of Marines fired on them from their left flank. Both sides poured lead at each other, making movement impossible. The engineers hung on, taking about twenty casualties as the deadlock continued.

At 0400, a new firefight broke out on the perimeter's west side. The Marines now faced attacks from three sides. The men defending that side of the line watched about three reinforced companies of Colonel Oka's barge travelers snake along jungle trails, making for the American lines. The Marines waited until the soldiers were less than a hundred feet away, then opened fire with machine guns and canister shells from 37 mm antitank guns. The mass fusillade ripped bodies apart and stopped the assault cold, with heavy losses. But the Japanese refused to accept defeat. They launched repeated infantry assaults to dislodge the Marines.

Back on Edson's Ridge, the Japanese kept charging forward, their ranks savaged by exploding 105s, machine guns sweeping back and forth cutting down even more men. Still the enemy did not recoil. Instead, the Japanese closed with the Americans until both sides were bludgeoning, stabbing, shooting, and punching each other in the darkness. Bayonets, grenades, Ka-Bar knives, and pistols played pivotal roles that night. The dead from both sides interleaved one another where they fell, sprawled beside shallow foxholes and machine gun nests. Raiders who survived reported that they simply lacked the firepower to stop these human-wave charges. For every Japanese soldier they dropped, seemingly six more took his place. The enemy rushed up the ridge with almost supernatural courage. Even the wounded crawled over the dead and dying to fight the Americans with their last breath.

Through the long hours of that terrible morning, amid the knots of men locked in hand-to-hand fights, the screams of rage and pain, and the flashes of artillery rounds blowing humans into fragments, the Marines did not break. Edson stood just behind the crest of the final hill, ignoring the bullets and shrapnel filling the air around him. He set an example of courage that few would ever match as he moved in the open, encouraging his men as they fought from shallow foxholes. He personally called in curtains of machine gun fire, walking the shells up the slopes closer and closer until they landed practically atop his own position. That night, Merritt "Red Mike" Edson and his leadership saved the perimeter, the 1st Marine Division, and America's first offensive of WWII.

By 0430, both fields remained in American hands, with one group of Japanese holding tenaciously to the southwest edge of Fighter One and locked in battle with the engineers and some of the MAG-23 ground crews. Into this maelstrom came the fighter pilots. The 67th Fighter Squadron possessed three flying P-400s. Though sick with dysentery, Dale Brannon met with the division staff to plan out a dawn strike against the Japanese near the ridge. He wouldn't be able to fly it—he was too sick—but he picked three of his best pilots to execute the mission.

As John L. Smith's men made their way to Fighter One, they took fire and dove for cover. They crawled at least part of the remaining distance to their waiting F4Fs. The SBD crews assigned to the morning search had an easier time. Henderson wasn't as dangerous as Fighter One, and the men reached their aircraft on Henderson without too much trouble.

The P-400s took off first, just as the sun began to show on the eastern horizon. The trio wheeled around the perimeter and made for the jungle at the base of Edson's Ridge, as briefed. There, in the growing golden-hour light, they spotted hundreds of Japanese troops in the artillery-flayed tree line. The troops looked to be massing for yet another attack. Edson's men, down to roughly three hundred effectives, clung to the last defensible positions on the ridge. Bodies littered the slope, hundreds upon hundreds of them. The 11th Marine's 105 mm bombardments had torn many bodies apart, leaving a bacchanal of horrors for the new dawn.

The massing Japanese would have to tread on their own fallen brothers to get to the Marines now.

Down the P-400s went, all guns spewing shells and lead into the Japanese troops. The troops fell by the dozen. Exhausted, dispirited, starving soldiers of the rising sun had displayed courage matched only by Edson's men. The arrival of the 67th's clunker Airacobras, so terrible in air combat yet so perfectly suited for ground support, broke the tide.

The Japanese fired back with everything they possessed: rifles, pistols, machine guns. Two of the P-400s took serious hits. One had its radiator shot out. Both limped back to Fighter One and crash-landed. The third stayed, making pass after pass until not a bullet or shell remained in the chambers.

That attack proved to be the final straw for Kawaguchi. While the Japanese on the flanks continued to attack throughout the day, their main effort at Edson's Ridge was totally spent. Kawaguchi's battalions had taken massive losses. The ranks were filled with wounded men he could not treat out in the jungle. There was only one option: slide around the perimeter to the west, and link up with Colonel Oka, using the supplies brought in by barge to replenish his men and get them medical care.

The Japanese had flung more than five thousand men at the Marines, three thousand alone against Colonel Edson's embattled Raiders. Despite the breakthroughs the night before, the Marines held their perimeter. Like a boxer in the tenth round on his feet from sheer tenacious will alone, the Americans were punch-drunk, traumatized, sick, half-starved, and grief racked over their brothers whom they had seen killed.

But the Marines were still in the fight.

THIRTY-SEVEN

WALKING IN

East of Henderson Field
September 14, 1942, 0300 hours

MARION CARL AND DOCTOR ERONI EASED THE LITTLE SIXTEEN-foot boat through the cove and down into the open sea. They had spent all of September 13 laboring over the outboard motor before Marion finally figured out what was wrong and got it running. They calculated that it would take six or so hours to skirt the coast and get back to the Marine perimeter. If they left too early, they might run into a Japanese resupply task force. If they left too late, they would end up on the water after dawn, still well behind enemy lines.

Marion calculated that their best window would be an 0300 departure. If the motor kept running and they didn't encounter heavy seas, they could arrive just after sunrise. Unless their fellow Americans proved trigger-happy, it would be an easy cruise to Lunga Point from there.

Needing to stay far enough offshore to be out of small-arms-fire range meant heavier seas and the potential of running into the Tokyo Express offloading troops at Taivu. They also knew there was a good chance a bombardment force would be out there in Savo Sound again. Running into any Japanese ships would be a death sentence for both of them.

It was a dark night with another sliver moon that provided little illumination. As they pitched through the surf line into open sea, though, the western horizon glowed crimson—the sign that another battle raged. Puttering along at about five knots, Marion and Eroni made their way north, silently praying the little motor would not quit. If it did, both knew it meant serious trouble. Drifting offshore was a ticket to capture, torture, and death.

They approached Taivu Point sometime after 0400. On September 13, the main Japanese noontime raid had eschewed bombing Henderson Field in favor of pounding Taivu Point instead. Marion knew Edson's Raiders had landed on the eighth and the Japanese must have thought they were still at Taivu. Of course they weren't, and the bombs fell on the surviving Japanese whom Kawaguchi had left behind to guard the few supplies that escaped destruction during Edson's attack.

As Eroni sat in the bow and Marion steered the boat from the stern, they saw no lights or movement at Taivu. Could it be abandoned? They weren't sure, but both breathed a sigh of relief as they rounded the point and steadied on a westerly course.

As the little boat closed on the perimeter, gunfire continued to strobe the western horizon. The fighting had gone on all night. Now, they were getting close enough to hear the artillery explosions and machine gun bursts. It looked to be coming from points inland, not along the coast like the first Japanese offensive they had endured the night of their arrival on the island. That was good news—they wouldn't have to chug through a firefight to get home.

The rest of the trip proved anticlimactic. The boat went unseen by both friend and foe. Marion and Eroni made it to the boat basin at Lunga Point sometime around 0930, just as three float Zeroes made a surprise appearance over Henderson. Though the Americans couldn't know it, the A6M-Ns had been sent down to determine who held the airfield, since Rabaul had lost communications with Kawaguchi several days before. The seaplane carrier *Kamikawa Maru* had established a base of operations in Rekata Bay on the northern coast of Santa Isabel Island and was the source for many of the recent nocturnal Louis the Louse flare droppers.

Marion's first act on returning to Marine lines was to turn his head skyward and watch those three float Zeroes charge after a US Navy R4D transport—the militarized variant of the venerable Douglas DC-3 airliner. The unarmed transport looked like easy meat for the Japanese, but suddenly a patrol of F4Fs dropped down on the A6M-Ns and surprised their pilots. With a professional eye and smiling with approval, Marion watched all three Japanese planes go down in flames. The Wildcats—flown by VF-5—made short work of them. That's the stuff Marion wanted to see. Better yet, he wanted to be the one back in the cockpit doing the shooting.

NOT LONG AFTER THE AERIAL SCRUM, MARION CARL DROVE OVER TO the VMF-223 bivouac in a jeep. He was stunned at what he found: fallen trees and some of the tents shredded or lying crushed under coconut trunks. He picked his way through branches and palm fronds until he found his own tent, which had survived the fusillade. Ducking inside, he discovered a Navy F4F pilot in his bunk. John L., thinking Marion was dead, had let one of the "Fighting Five" pilots use Marion's cot.

Marion's stuff was gone too. Everything, including his Cushman scooter, his locker box, his towel, spare items of clothing, and his shaving kit. Even his shower shoes, which he habitually stored under his cot, were gone. He'd only been gone five days. This seemed a little premature to the Oregonian.

Though John L. and most of the 223 pilots were standing alert duty that morning, word quickly spread from the bivouac that Marion Carl had returned from the dead. The news electrified the exhausted aviators after five days of brutal losses. Marion didn't seem to notice the sensation his reappearance caused—he was too busy trying to find his stuff.

When General Geiger heard that Marion had walked in, he sent for him. Marion dropped everything and hustled over to air operations, which the pilots had dubbed the Opium Den. After Geiger welcomed him back, Marion asked, "General, what's Major Smith's score now?"

"Sixteen" came the reply.

In five days, Marion had gone from top ace to second place and four behind.

"Guess I better get to work then," he replied.

One of the enlisted Marines working in the Opium Den that morning quipped, "General, can you ground Major Smith for five days and give Captain Carl a chance to catch up?"[1]

The comment elicited a much-needed laugh. It had already been a rough day, and it looked to get even worse as the Japanese kept the pressure on MAG-23.

Marion spent the rest of the day rounding up his personal items, many of which had been divided among the other pilots. The rest had been put in his locker box and stored in the squadron's admin tent. It wasn't until John L. came back from the flight line after another taxing day that Marion learned the full scope of what had happened to 223 while he was gone.

John L. looked shockingly bad. Wan, sick, belt cinched beyond his last notch. His raccoon eyes denoted stress and the lack of sleep. To those who cared to look closely, a hard look now replaced the perpetually sad expression. He was a leader to the core and would not emote around his men. This impassive front was exceptionally difficult for him, as he was a naturally emotional man, at once genuinely rugged and easily injured because he threw his heart into everything he did—and everyone around him.

The double-edged sword—getting too close to, and too informal with, his squadron's young pilots—had cut him to the quick these past five days. Marion's was the first blow.

On September 9, everyone thought he'd gone in at sea and died. Clayton Canfield came back to Henderson only long enough to catch a ride to the naval hospital at Noumea, New Caledonia. In four days, John L. had lost two executive officers: Morrell on the fifth and Carl on the ninth.

There was nobody left in the squadron with the seniority needed for the job, but Hyde Phillips was pressed into the role for a few days—at least until some senior pilots from VMF-212 back in the New Hebrides could come to help out.

In the meantime, the intercepts continued. While Marion picked his way through the jungle, the Japanese shot down Zen Pond on the tenth. Nobody saw him go down; he was another Marine who just vanished. Zen and Bailey, best friends from back home in rural Michigan, were gone. As the pilots packed up Zen's things, they found a letter he'd written to his parents, proudly telling them he'd become an ace.[2]

On the thirteenth, the squadron lost its young genius, Scotty McLennan. During an intercept in the early afternoon, his Wildcat was shot up badly and he was probably wounded. He was last seen diving away from the fight, waving goodbye to his brothers before slumping forward, head down. His aircraft went straight into the jungle. Also lost on that mission was 2nd Lt. Richard Haring, a VMF-212 pilot who had come up with Maj. Frederick R. "Fritz" Payne to backfill John L. Smith's squadron.

Some talk around the airfield suggested that Scotty and Haring were lost to faulty oxygen systems. Eighteen F4Fs arrived on the morning of September 13 as replacement aircraft. Four of those planes were lost that day. The remaining fourteen were split evenly between John L.'s men and Bob Galer's. These Wildcats were utter yard sale items—poorly maintained and riddled with bugs and other malfunctions. Some of them arrived with machine guns so corroded they couldn't be fired. The aircraft were pressed into service anyway. That rush to get these birds into the fight came at a cost. Guns failed in combat. Oxygen systems failed as the men climbed to altitude. And engines failed to perform at their peak. It was a nightmare.

The nightmare continued on the fourteenth, after Marion Carl returned to camp. During a squadron scramble, Eugene Trowbridge clipped a fuel drum that was sitting on the runway, sending his own F4F careening into another Wildcat, which was being driven by a pilot from 224. The two planes were totally destroyed in the collision. Although the 224 pilot walked away, Trowbridge was knocked unconscious and seriously injured. He was pulled from the wreckage and taken to the division field hospital. He'd be evacuated on the first available R4D transport plane, his war now over.[3]

That afternoon, Orvin Ramlo returned from the flight line after flying the day's lunchtime intercept mission. John L. had seen much promise in this dive-bomber pilot turned F4F driver (like himself) back in Hawai'i. He'd transferred Ramlo to 224 to give him more training time. After rejoining the squadron at Guadalcanal, Ramlo earned the coveted status of ace in only a few days, justifying John L.'s confidence in the young second lieutenant. On the afternoon of September 14, exhausted and filthy, all he wanted to do was take a bath. He and a couple of other pilots grabbed towels and headed down to the river to get clean. Sporadic fighting continued on all three sides of the perimeter while Marine patrols hunted snipers and infiltrators all around Vandegrift's HQ and the airfield.

A burst of machine gun fire tore through the bathing area, kicking up water spouts as bullets impacted the surface. The naked, vulnerable men dove for cover and waited for the mud Marines to find the shooter. Ramlo pulled himself to shore, bleeding severely. His brothers crawled to his aid and found he'd been shot through both buttocks. They stemmed the bleeding as best they could until some corpsmen arrived to take over.

Ramlo was carried off to the division hospital. He'd survive, but his time on Guadalcanal was over. He'd be evacuated as soon as possible with Trowbridge.

In the five days while Marion was trapped behind enemy lines, John L. and his squadron lost six pilots killed, missing, or wounded. While Carl's return gave hope that others would walk in, the sad fact was that 223 stood on the same threshold of collapse that Dick Mangrum's squadron was facing.

Events that afternoon shoved the dive-bomber boys even closer to the edge when the Japanese attacked the airfield for a third time. Just before sunset, a large formation of aircraft from the seaplane tender at Rekata Bay swept over Lunga, hoping to catch MAG-23's fighters on the ground. The attackers flew ancient float biplanes armed with light machine guns and antipersonnel bombs. Slow and vulnerable, they were the same type as the flare-dropping Louie the Louse.

They overflew two of Mangrum's crews as the Marines dragged their SBDs home from a long afternoon search. Arthur O'Keefe, despite having an active case of malaria and a raging fever, flew lead on this mission. His wingman was a young second lieutenant replacement pilot named Yale Kaufman, a Jewish Miami University graduate who had come over from 231 to help make up the losses Mangrum's unit had suffered. O'Keefe had been delighted at this development since Kaufman was a close friend from the training pipeline.

As they approached Lunga Point at about two hundred feet above Savo Sound, the Japanese raiders overflew them. Art looked over at his friend's aircraft. To his horror, he saw Kaufman glance up, then his head disappeared in a spray of blood. Kaufman's SBD nosed down and went right into the water, vanishing in seconds. Kaufman and Barry Arnold, his gunner, both died.

What had happened? Art's gunner thought an ambushing Zero had hit Kaufman's aircraft. Friendly antiaircraft fire? Nobody was sure, beyond the fact that two more SBD crewmen had died—and died right in front of Arthur O'Keefe.

The shock of seeing his friend die left O'Keefe grief-stricken. He brought his SBD into Henderson and dove into the nearest trench as soon as the plane rolled to a halt. After the Japanese departed, he was found sitting on a stump in a complete daze. Shivering uncontrollably from malarial fever, he was brought back to the 232 encampment by some Marines, who laid him down on a cot. As his fever spiked, he began to hallucinate.

As several members of the squadron looked after him, he suddenly drew his Model 1911 Colt .45, flung himself to the ground, and fired straight up through the tent while calling out, "Zeroes! Zeroes!"

The men tackled him, pulled the gun out of his hands, and called for medical help. O'Keefe, 232's rugged and determined pilot with courage to spare, had given his all and beyond for Mangrum and the squadron. He was carried off, emotionally crushed and physically overwhelmed by disease. As they carried him to a field hospital, he vomited and went into convulsions. Art O'Keefe, who never should have left sick bay and flown off the *Long Island*, given the severity of his hip injury, had given all he had to give. Now, as night fell, he lay fever racked, hands shaking, periodically sobbing at the thought he'd let his squadron mates down. His friends and his beloved skipper, what would they think of him now? The idea of failing his brothers was Art's worst nightmare come to pass.

O'Keefe would be evacuated on the first available R4D to face a long and difficult recovery, first in the New Hebrides, then in California. His departure left Mangrum, Fleener, Prosser, McCafferty, and Thomas as the only remaining pilots from VMSB-232. Three-fourths of the squadron was gone—killed, wounded, or missing. The squadron had only a couple of functional SBDs left. Fike's prophecy had come true. The Red Devils had been expended.

THIRTY-EIGHT

THE LAST MILK RUN

Henderson Field, Guadalcanal
September 18, 1942, morning

Dick Mangrum walked along his flight line, watching his men working to prepare their remaining planes for the day. It was a short walk that morning, as 232 had only three SBDs left: Prosser's MB-30, McCafferty's MB-26, and the irrepressible Thomas's MB-32. To fly those three planes, he could count on himself, McCafferty, Thomas, and Fleener. Bruce Prosser, his stand-in executive officer ever since Brownie disappeared, flew his last mission the day before. He was done: too sick, too exhausted, had seen too much. Mangrum wanted to get him off the island as soon as possible, but the number of wounded from Edson's Ridge choked the pipeline back to the New Hebrides. Prosser would go out on the first available seat. Hopefully, that would be tomorrow. In a single summer of combat, Bruce had been among the few survivors of two squadrons. Midway had been a three-day race for survival against insane odds. Here at Guadalcanal, it was a slower, dribbling exsanguination that ground the men to pieces.

Dick also knew his own flying days were numbered. He was sick, weakened from a host of jungle maladies, bad food, and calorie-deficient meals. The weight of command had taken its toll too. No longer did he have Baldy or Fletcher Brown to help him run the squadron. He'd lost men he'd served with for years. Such wounds take a steady toll, no matter how much distance a leader tries to put between himself and his men.

Seeing that VMSB-232 no longer had enough pilots or planes to be a fully functional unit, MAG-23's staff was talking about taking the squadron away from Dick, breaking it up and parceling the men out to the remaining SBD outfits. Lord knows, they could all use an infusion—especially of trained ground crews. Because the Navy squadrons had arrived without any maintainers, VMSB-232's dedicated enlisted men and NCOs had already stretched themselves to help take care of the Navy SBDs, a task made ironically easier as their own squadron's planes were lost.

Break up the Red Devils? Dick had been with the squadron so long, he recoiled from the idea. The Red Devils were one of the oldest aviation outfits in the Corps, dating back to World War I. The squadron's many internal rituals paid homage to that heritage and tradition. The destruction of the unit, its remnants passed out to other units, seemed like a violation.

Then there were the men. . . . his men. His responsibility. He couldn't just send them to other squadrons. Dick resolved to fight hard to keep the surviving nucleus of 232 intact for as long as he could.

He paused to look over at Don McCafferty's MB-26 and the plane captain, Corp. David Mehargue, who was busily filing down gravel nicks from the SBD's battered propeller blades. He was a determined guy, one of the brightest and most ambitious young men in the squadron. The Pennsylvania native had joined as a private with a year in service back in July during the great influx. His dad had lost his general store in the Depression. To keep a roof over the family's head, Mehargue's father went to work as a grocery clerk, scratching out a subsistence-level living. The hardships of his childhood tempered Mehargue, made him tough. That ruggedness was balanced by a keen intellect that never had the opportunity to grow in a university setting, though he'd been an honor student in high school. In a matter of weeks, he'd proved himself not only competent but also a swift learner. He went from raw new guy to plane captain in less than two months. A plane captain at nineteen.

At MB-32, Second Lieutenant Thomas; his gunner, Ed Eades; and their plane captain, Staff Sgt. Harold Dow, worked with some of the CUB-1 guys to patch the SBD's most recent shrapnel holes. All they had for that was hundred-mile-an-hour tape. The aircraft was a checkerboard of tape squares and scuffed metal. Its aluminum skin was cracked and wrinkled in places—the result of being repeatedly overstressed in combat. The perforated dive flaps were cracked and broken—almost to the point of being useless.

Thomas was as sick as everyone else, but illness hadn't dented his irrepressible nature. As he worked beside Eades, he kept up a steady patter of anecdotes and one-liners. Thomas could look at the gates of hell and find the bright side.

As Dick approached, Dow ducked under one wing and greeted the skipper and handed him the plane's yellow sheet. It listed all the things functional or known nonfunctional on the aircraft. As usual, there were a host of issues with the bird that could not be fixed on Guadalcanal, yet weren't severe enough to keep it from operational status. The forward-firing .50s were out of commission. They'd been going into combat like that for weeks now, so Mangrum wasn't alarmed.

He handed the sheet back to Dow and exchanged a few words. He was an older NCO, thirty or so, Dick figured. A prewar regular Marine who had been a Red Devil since the fall of 1940, serving alongside Baldy, Gruenke, Brownie's plane captain Jack Scales, and many of the other NCOs for two long years. Pilots and gunners came and went, but these guys were the heart and soul of 232, closer than brothers. Like everyone else, though, Dow felt a deep exhaustion and sadness, which showed in his blue eyes. Baldy had been a close friend. He'd also served with Brownie and Rivers Morrell.

Somebody had once asked Dow what he would do once all this was over. He didn't even have to think about it. Desperate for cash, he had joined the Corps in December 1939. Three squares and $360 a year looked good to a poor farmer from Iowa whose family teetered constantly on the brink of insolvency. All he wanted to do was get a fair crack at running a farm again. He loved the life, and he'd never make the Corps his permanent home.

Behind Dow and Mangrum, Don McCafferty and Lewis Macias joined Thomas and Eades standing beside MB-32. In seconds, the four men were laughing and telling stories. Don possessed exceptional comedic timing. Thomas's laughter was infectious. Dick watched them, eavesdropping, perhaps wishing he could join that circle and enjoy that level of closeness again.

It was Thomas's turn to spin a yarn. A few missions back, Thomas, Don, and their gunners had been on a search mission—just the four of them in their SBDs. When they were attacked by Japanese planes, Macias's twin .30s broke free from their mount after Don rolled into a dive. Defenseless, Don swung under Thomas's wing for protection. As he did, both Thomas and Eades watched as Macias drew his Model 1911 and opened fire with it on an attacking Japanese plane. It was an absurd Great War–esque moment that Thomas thought absolutely hilarious.

Where does the Corps find such men as these?

Jack Scales, who had been Fletcher Brown's plane captain, came over to pass along some news from VMSB-231. Maj. Leo Smith was done. He was sick as a dog and was due to be evacuated. The squadron was down to only four or five pilots, and two of them were sick. The Flight 300 crews were almost done in too. A few, like the irrepressible Chris Fink, were still flying missions, but most were also scheduled to be evacuated off the island in the next few days.

It made sense to consolidate the survivors from both 231 and 232, then parcel out the ground crews as needed. Mangrum didn't care. He'd fight to keep the Red Devils together for as long as he could, if only to make sure everyone got off the island as soon as they could be relieved. If his ground echelon ended up attached to units that had just arrived, it could be months before the ground crews got out. They were in the same condition as his pilots and gunners. The idea of leaving them behind on the island long after the flight crews had left was something Mangrum found unacceptable. They came in as a squadron; they would leave as one too.

Somebody came down from the Pagoda and told Thomas the air staff wanted to see him. He bid Don and the others goodbye and headed over.

Admiral Turner had come through for Vandegrift. As promised, he'd assembled a major convoy to carry in the 4,262 men of the 7th Marine Regiment plus an attached battalion of artillery. Turner had moved mountains to make this happen, and he pushed stubbornly forward after a Japanese submarine sank the carrier USS *Wasp* on September 15. A lesser admiral would have turned his ships around, preserving them and the Marines for another day rather than risking Japanese air attack without half his carrier support (only the carrier *Hornet* remained in the area).

Turner's transports, consolidated with some of the APDs coming in to deliver desperately needed avgas, arrived off Lunga Point at daybreak. Guadalcanal's Wildcats had been flying combat air patrols over them all morning as the ships offloaded men, equipment, and supplies to barges, lighters, and Higgins boats. It was crucial to maintain radio silence and not give the Japanese any indication that the ships lay at anchor offshore. The division wanted Thomas to drop a written message to the convoy's flagship, the heavy cruiser *Minneapolis*. Thomas grinned, took two copies of the message in case they missed with the first drop, and headed back to the flight line.

When he returned, Dow had just checked the ammo trays in MB-32's rear cockpit. As always, Eades had carefully loaded them himself. Don and Lewis Macias were over at their own bird, ensuring that it was ready to go. Both crews expected to join a strike against a Japanese cruiser–led task force that had been seen in the Central Solomons at Gizo Harbor.

A strike did go out after those ships, but only Prosser went with it from the Red Devils. The Dauntlesses ran into bad weather, got lost, and aborted the mission. They returned to Henderson Field without seeing the Japanese.

Those ships steamed down the coast and shelled Henderson after dark on the night of September 17. Now, MAG-23's staff hoped to find and catch them as they scuttled back up the Slot. It had been the same on the sixteenth, when thirteen SBDs, most from VS-3, went out after one of these task forces. Don and Lewis had been on that strike, tagalongs representing the last of the Red Devils.

When Thomas arrived with the news that he and Eades had been given a milk run and wouldn't have to face a long flight in dicey weather only to fly into the teeth of heavy antiaircraft fire, Eades breathed a sigh of relief. Thomas was always raring to go, but Eades wanted a break. An easy mission close to home would fit the bill nicely.

They left Don and Lewis on the flight line, taxiing out to the runway, with Dow sitting on the left wing to spot shell holes and other obstructions for them. The plane captains had been doing this for several weeks now. Before Brownie went missing, he'd actually forgotten that Jack Scales was on his wing one time and began his takeoff roll. Jack had to jump clear; the incident was something he hadn't quite forgiven Brownie for before the pilot had vanished on the first Gizo strike.

MB-32 reached the runway and got into position. Dow stood up and walked to the fuselage to wish Thomas and Eades luck before he slipped off the back of the wing root. Thomas opened the throttle as the SBD labored to get up to speed. Its engine was well beyond its overhaul time and was worn-out from over a hundred hours of combat flying. And the airfield, muddy and pitted, didn't help either. Finally, the bird bounced roughly into the air, and Thomas banked over the shattered stands of coconut palms, both men looking at the shell holes and wreckage still tangled amid the ruins of the grove. It was a sobering sight—how anyone survived that shelling was a miracle.

The convoy was not far away, spread out around Kukum Harbor to the west and Beach Green on the airfield side of Lunga Point to the east. It was an impressive sight. An anti-submarine screen of destroyers and minesweepers patrolled in an arc around the transports. Inside the cordon steamed the *Minneapolis*, the light cruiser *Boise*, and the Royal New Zealand Navy's cruiser *Leander*. At the heart of all this combat power lay the "Unholy Four": attack transports *McCawley*, *President Jackson*, *President Hayes*, and *Crescent City*, all anchored about fifteen hundred yards off Beach Green. To the west, the destroyer-transports along with the attack cargo ship *Alchiba* unloaded at Kukum. It was a huge force, the largest seen at Guadalcanal since the initial landing on August 7.

Thomas decided to approach the convoy from downwind, which meant circling around to come in southeast to northwest. This orientation would give them an approach on the convoy's port beam, coming almost straight from the end of Henderson Field. To maximize the drop's chances of success, he kept his landing gear down and lowered his flaps. Low and slow was the plan. As they passed over the *Minneapolis* at masthead height, Eades would toss the first message out. If he missed, they'd get one more chance.

Thomas's watch read noon when he finished the circling around Henderson and headed over to the convoy.

Noon. The bombing hour.

Thomas and Eades passed a pair of destroyers, then flew by the *Leander*. The *Hayes* and *Jackson* lay dead ahead. Nervous lookouts on all the ships called out a strange or an unidentified aircraft heading straight at them. To the sailors, it looked like the plane was making a torpedo run on them. It was a nightmare scenario: the transports were sitting ducks, anchored and unable to maneuver. A torpedo strike could kill hundreds of sailors and Marines. Halos of Higgins boats, all armed with machine guns of their own, surrounded the transports, moving between the beach and the line to get back to their assigned vessel to pick up another load.

The *Hayes* and *Jackson* opened fire. The minute they did, nearly every ship in range followed suit. The sky around Thomas's Dauntless suddenly swarmed with tracers and 40 mm flak bursts. It took both him and Eades a minute to process that their own fleet was shooting at them. Then the Dauntless took a direct hit. Then another.

Thomas banked hard to starboard, sending the SBD directly at the *Minneapolis*. His hands moved like a flurry in the cockpit, retracting the flaps and the landing gear and firewalling the throttle almost simultaneously.

They found themselves in a deadly cone of fire, tracers converging on them from every ship in sight. The little Higgins boats unleashed their machine guns, too, dozens of them filling the sky with streaking bursts of .50-caliber rounds.

Low, slow, and trapped in the middle of the convoy, the SBD was being shot to pieces. In sheer desperation, Thomas yanked back the stick, hanging the Dauntless on its prop in a last-ditch bid to climb out of the fusillade.

Aboard the *Crescent City*, somebody cried out he'd seen American stars on the plane's fuselage. The skipper ordered a cease-fire. Same with the crew of the *Hayes*—they quickly realized their mistake after sending only a dozen 20 mm shells and eight .50-caliber rounds at the SBD.

The other ships, including the *Minneapolis*, hammered the SBD and did not let up. In the back seat, Eades watched the heavy cruiser swing into his field of view as Thomas tried to climb away. They were so close that he watched an antiaircraft gun crew track his aircraft and open fire. A huge hole blew out of one wing. The dive flaps disintegrated as explosive shells impacted against the wing's trailing edge. Suddenly, part of one propeller blade and a chunk of the spinner tore away and gyrated wildly past the cockpit, almost as if in slow motion.

Eades held his sights on the gun crew, willing himself to pull the trigger and defend his dying aircraft. He could sweep the deck, make those sailors dive for cover, maybe give Thomas a bit of time to get away.

He couldn't pull the trigger. Not on fellow Americans. Even if it meant his own and his pilot's death.

The engine erupted in flames, long tongues of fire licking back over the fuselage and cockpit. The SBD stalled and twisted into a spin. Something hit Eades, but he felt no pain. The spin tightened as the plane accelerated in its death plunge. Eades felt the centrifugal force fling him out of his gunner's seat. He found himself pinned, half in and half out of the cockpit, tethered to the SBD only by the eighteen-inch lanyards connected to his gunner's belt. The wind screamed around him and slapped him, like a toy doll, over and over against the fuselage. The engine quit. Smoke and flames embroiled the two men.

The aircraft struck the water with such force that the twin .30-caliber machine guns snapped off their mount and smashed into Eades's face with such force that he was driven back through the gunner's seat, demolishing it.

Eades couldn't feel his legs. He couldn't stand. Blood poured into his eyes from his battered face. Concussed and confused, he thought of only one thing: Thomas. He pitched over the side of the cockpit into the water. The SBD was sinking fast, nose first. He dragged himself forward along the water and the wing root to the pilot's cockpit and found his brother in arms, face down against the instrument panel.

"Tommy! Tommy!" Eades cried, reaching for him through the partially open canopy.

His friend didn't answer. He clawed at Tommy's harness, trying to get him free and pull him out. The cockpit was a tangle of wreckage, the fuselage bent from the impact. The pilot had been crushed into the cockpit by the impact.

"Tommy!" he pleaded.

Thomas didn't respond. The SBD's windscreen dipped beneath the waves. Eades couldn't let go, couldn't give up. Water filled the cockpit, spilling over Thomas's knees. Eades kept trying to pull him clear, but Thomas's body, even free of the seat straps, refused to budge. Eades tugged and yanked, but he had little leverage, as his own legs crumpled every time he tried to stand.

The water reached Tommy's chest now. The Oregon-born son of an auto mechanic remained unconscious, face against the instrument panel. Eades grabbed him with both arms, clinging to his body as the water rose around them. He wouldn't let go. Couldn't. Blood in his eyes dimmed his vision. He was dizzy and badly concussed. He still kept trying to save his pilot. Eades begged God for a miracle, something—anything—that could get Thomas free of the doomed SBD.

The universe was out of miracles that day.

A few seconds later, Savo Sound claimed the SBD. Submerged now, Eades held on to his pilot a few agonizing seconds longer. Then finally—at last—he let go.

THIRTY-NINE

TO THE BITTER END

Henderson Field, Guadalcanal
September 18, 1942, afternoon

T HE ASS-COVERING BEGAN ALMOST AS SOON AS THE LAST ROUND WAS
fired at Thomas's SBD. On Lunga Point, the Marines on the beach
unloading supplies or coming ashore from the Higgins boats cheered the
sight of the Dauntless's comet-like end, thinking it was a Japanese raider.

The skippers of several ships quickly documented how many rounds
their guns fired. One noted that a single .50-caliber machine gun loosed
a single nine-round burst before the order to hold fire was given. The vessels most likely responsible either blamed the destroyers on barrier patrol
around the transports or recorded in their war diaries a general note that
the enemy aircraft shot down was later determined to be friendly.

There would be no repercussions from the tragedy, beyond the devastation the Western Union telegram would inflict on Thomas's family back
in Idaho. Friendly-fire incidents were unfortunately all too common in
1942, and Thomas's arrival over the transports coincided with the most
common daylight hour that the Japanese bombing raids appeared over
Guadalcanal.

It took several hours, but a boat found Ed Eades, barely conscious and
badly wounded, adrift a few thousand yards off Lunga Point. He was

pulled aboard and taken ashore, where the Marine docs went to work on his extensive injuries, which included internal abdominal bleeding.[1]

Thomas's death left Mangrum with two pilots: Robert Fleener and the indestructible Don McCafferty. Bruce Prosser was totally spent, just like Art O'Keefe and Danny Iverson. Sick, traumatized, and staggering on his feet from countless nights of little to no sleep, Jim Standard made sure Bruce was evacuated on September 19.

The losses meant that while Dick continued to fend off efforts to break up his squadron, Fleener and McCafferty would fly scout missions for another week. Both men functioned on sheer determination alone. Weakened by repeated illness, the lack of food, and sleep deprivation, they dragged themselves to their cockpits each morning, knowing that they were playing a supporting role to the fresher SBD detachments from the Navy. The supporting role may have grated against them earlier in the campaign. Now, these proud Marines were too few, their aircraft too worn-out, their bodies too racked by disease to feel anything other than relief. The onus was off them at last.

Flight 300 was in similar straits. On September 19, their deadeye pilot, Christian Fink, went down after a mission to Gizo Harbor. When Lieutenant Colonel Fike heard the news, he surprised everyone and drove to Kukum Harbor, where he climbed into a Grumman J2F "Duck" biplane floatplane. The only aircraft on Guadalcanal more vulnerable to marauding Zeroes or floatplane fighters were the R4D unarmed transports carrying in supplies and taking wounded men out. Fike's effort was a daring, courageous move, but after a late afternoon search, he was unable to retrieve Fink and his gunner. Fike went out the next morning, found them near Savo Island, landed on the water, and pulled them safely aboard.

Like 232, Flight 300 was down to just a couple of surviving SBDs. They were a rump of a detachment, a fragment of a carrier air group thrown into the fight six weeks earlier without any of their logistic support. Mangrum's ground crews flexed to arm, fuel, and maintain Flight 300 planes as well as their own, which stretched them to their limits. Caldwell's men were supposed to be on the island for only a few weeks, functioning as a stopgap until reinforcements could be scraped together and sent to Cactus. Now, they were all but wiped out, just like 232 and Leo Smith's VMSB-231.

A PILOT'S EFFECTIVENESS IN COMBAT LOOKED LIKE A BELL CURVE OVER time. During the first five missions or so, the green aviators were at their most vulnerable. They knew nothing of battle and the minute tactical and flying details that could keep them alive and help them be effective. Those first five fights were the initial crucible. Survive them, and your lethality to the enemy increased dramatically. Over the next few weeks, pilots would function at their peak capabilities, but eventually, the stress inflicted on mind and body by air combat would begin to degrade their effectiveness. At some point, they would be useless in combat and much more vulnerable as they reached the end of their endurance.

In most theaters, this curve took months to play out, allowing for long tours that sometimes (in the US Army Air Forces) stretched for a year or more. At Guadalcanal, everything was compressed because of the intensity and repeated trauma on the ground and in the air. There were no breaks from combat, just short breaks from flying. In Europe, the men in the 8th Air Force could unwind by taking leaves into local British towns and cities. The defenders of Port Moresby rotated frequently back to Australia for a rest. But there was no respite like that at Guadalcanal, where the mere act of bathing could get a pilot shot.

There was no respite for either side on what the Japanese began calling Starvation Island. It was an apt name for both sides.

In the circumstances, it isn't surprising that morale plummeted.

Effectiveness diminished. The men sleepwalked like zombies from their tents to their aircraft, a sense of increasing desperation pervading the ranks. Lt. (j.g.) Francis "Cash" Register, a VF-5 ace, penned one of the starkest descriptions of what this pervasive sense looked and felt like after only a week or so on the island:

Pilots are becoming exhausted and sick; it's a pitiful sight. Everyone is trying so hard and is driving themselves on. Am so tired I can't eat. I passed out today so had to stay at the field hospital for a day and a half. Lack of food and exhaustion from high altitude were the causes.[2]

The MAG-23 staff struggled over how to deal with this issue. Some on the staff wanted to pull the original contingent out and send them home. By the third week of September, they were a spent force, especially the surviving dive-bomber crews. Galer, John L., Caldwell, and Mangrum all saw what this was doing to their men. The pilots and their crew climbed into the cockpits every day knowing the only way out of this nightmare was death or a debilitating wound that would get them sent to the Navy hospital on New Caledonia. They were being physically and emotionally broken, one grinding mission, one nightly naval bombardment, at a time. Yet, they stepped up every day and flew the missions required of them. For most, hope was a distant memory, and thoughts of getting home had long since been abandoned.

The squadron flight surgeons wanted to ground almost the entire air group as unfit to fly. They clashed over this decision with MAG-23's chief of staff, Col. Louis Woods, who listened to the surgeons as they stated their case. He finally shut them down, barking, "They've got to keep flying. It's better than a Japanese bayonet stuck in their ass."

That ultimately was the choice. Fly and fight, or face being overrun by unchecked Japanese reinforcements flowing down the Slot. Woods realized, of course, that the surgeons were right. Nobody should have been flying in the physical and emotional condition these men were in. But it would be days, maybe weeks, before more aircraft and pilots could join the Cactus Air Force. John L. even let an Army Air Forces pilot and friend of Marion Carl's from Oregon State fly missions with them in one of 223's F4Fs. The severity of the crisis blurred the lines between the services. If you were on Guadalcanal that September, you were less a Marine, a Navy officer, or an Army pilot than you were a member of a polyglot: the cobbled-together Cactus Air Force.

Bloody Ridge gave the Americans little respite. Though the weather frequently thwarted Japanese air raids, the Tokyo Express ran the gauntlet down the Slot to deliver food, medicine, and ammunition to Kawaguchi's starving, battered survivors. They established a base at the northwest tip of Guadalcanal not far from Cape Esperance. Kamimbo was a village that wrapped around a small anchorage that the Japanese used to maximum effect. By running supplies and men to this location, they saved their ships hours of transit time that the Taivu Point base required.

These Tokyo Express missions usually included four destroyers sometimes towing barge-loads of supplies. Lt. Cmdr. Louis J. Kirn's VS-3 tried to stop them through night attacks, supported by what crews and planes were available from Flight 300, VMSB-231, and VMSB-232. The Americans had little success, however, despite using flares at times and trying other techniques. Weather, little illumination from the moon, crew exhaustion, and lack of night training combined to make these night attacks little more than nuisances.

The nightly runs convinced the Americans that the Japanese were getting ready for another offensive. As the third week of September began, the two sides found themselves locked together like exhausted boxers, refusing to quit the fight while mustering all their remaining reserves for a knockout punch.

On September 24, Don McCafferty and Lewis Macias climbed into VMSB-232's last remaining SBD. Its forward guns were nonfunctional, its aluminum skin torn and gouged in scores of places. With its worn-out engine, the aircraft could not reach anything approaching the maximum speed of a brand-new Dauntless. Its flaps were so battered and torn they were useless—the weary SBD mirrored the condition of its crew.

By then, Don had flown more missions than any other pilot in the squadron. He was as sick as anyone else, but he refused to stand down. Macias was equally devoted; wherever Second Lieutenant McCafferty went, he went too. That day, they teamed up with a Flight 300 crew from VS-5 for the afternoon search in what MAG-23 staffers now called Sector B. The innocuous-sounding Sector B denoted the Slot on a base

course of 300 degrees out of Henderson. It was where all the action went
down.

At 1500, they spotted the day's Tokyo Express, counting four destroyers led by a light cruiser. They radioed the contact report to Henderson,
which ordered a full attack on the Japanese task force. As Cactus assembled a strike force, Don and his Flight 300 wingman, Ens. Walter W.
Coolbaugh, rolled into a diving attack on the Japanese ships.

The destroyers studded the sky with tracers from their 25 mm antiaircraft mounts. Yet both veteran Americans shook off their own feverish
conditions to deliver two near misses. One bomb appeared to have landed
about twenty feet off the light cruiser leading the task force. Both pilots
pulled out of their dives and skimmed the wave tops, dragging their birds
south for home as the Japanese fired until the aircraft passed out of range.

Two strikes went after the task force that McCafferty and Coolbaugh
had found. The first, led by Capt. Elmer Glidden of 231, scored another
near miss while the ships were 150 miles from Guadalcanal. After sunset, Lieutenant Commander Kirn and eight other SBDs, plus a lone
TBF, found the Tokyo Express as the Japanese reached Cape Esperance.
Because the enemy ships were illuminated by a full moon and mostly
clear skies for a change, the American crews spotted the Japanese and
attacked with some success. Two destroyers were damaged, and the Japanese abandoned the resupply effort, turning north with a third of their
cargo still aboard.

That the Americans were getting better at night attacks sent alarm
bells ringing through the Japanese high command and prompted the suspension of further Tokyo Express runs for the rest of the month. McCafferty's sighting of the task force directly led to the squadron's subsequent
attacks and significant change in Japanese strategy. It was the last contribution VMSB-232 made to the campaign. Not long afterward, Robert Fleener and Don McCafferty were both grounded by Jim Standard,
the squadron flight surgeon. Mangrum became the last pilot on flight
status, but that position didn't last much longer. Standard saw to it that
his relentless skipper was also grounded, for he'd become as febrile as
Prosser, McCafferty, and Fleener.

The ground crew soldiered on, splitting the load with 231's maintainers as they covered VS-3, the remains of Flight 300, and the first elements of new squadrons that came in from VMSB-141 and VS-71 (part of the doomed *Wasp*'s air group). As long as his men continued to repair, fuel, and arm aircraft, Mangrum intended to be with them.

FORTY

THE OREGON AERIAL SNIPER

Henderson Field, Guadalcanal
September 27, 1942, morning

THE MEN OF VMF-223 SAT AROUND A POKER TABLE OR LOUNGED ON chairs inside their new ready tent beside Fighter One, waiting for the phone hanging on a pole to ring and order them aloft. Artillery boomed in the distance, punctuated by frequent strings of machine gun bursts. General Vandegrift was using the 7th Marines to attack the Japanese west of the perimeter. For three days and nights, the sounds of that battle echoed across the airfield complex.

John L.'s squadron was so short on pilots the 223 ranks now included three men from VMF-212 and three more from VMF-121 on temporary duty. He had seventeen total. The six fresh faces, which almost everyone already knew, were a welcome addition. Their units would be sent to Guadalcanal soon enough.

The past week at Guadalcanal had been relatively quiet for the fighter pilots. The Japanese raids ceased a few days after Bloody Ridge, probably because of weather. The rainy season hammered the Solomons with sudden squalls and shocking deluges that put several inches of water on the ground in surprisingly short intervals and made it impossible for the Japanese to push raids down to Guadalcanal. Instead, Betties and Zeroes went after targets in New Guinea and waited for the weather to improve over the Slot. There would be no rest for these aircrews, who were as tired and worn-out as the Americans defending the Marine perimeter.

The fighter pilots at Guadalcanal didn't get much of a respite either. They flew daily patrols and covered convoys that churned through Savo Sound to deliver more supplies to the island. They strafed and bombed Japanese positions to the west of the perimeter and flew escort missions to Rekata Bay, where the dive-bombers did their best to put an end to the seaplane operation the Japanese had established there.

For the last few days, rumors abounded that MAG-23 HQ was devising a plan to get the F4Fs to Gizo Harbor along with the Dauntlesses. Because the Japanese continued to use Gizo as a stopping point for the Tokyo Express, the harbor would be an important target. Each time the Cactus bomber force went after Gizo, though, the crews took heavy losses from weather and Japanese float fighters. Now, there was talk that the F4Fs would be sent up to cover the bombers on their way to the target and back. Gizo was 240 miles away from Henderson. The F4F-4 could fly about 175 miles before hitting its point of no return, so external belly tanks would be needed if the fighters were to pull this mission off. So far, no such tanks had materialized.

Red Kendrick, who had taken to writing songs about their predicament, saw how the rumors put his squadron mates on edge. He took up his pen and, working for two days, came up with a new song for the occasion, basing it on Kipling's poem "On the Road to Mandalay." Riffing on the nickname for MAG-23's operations tent (the Opium Den), he wrote:

> *In Guadalcanal Operations, where the*
> *needle passes free,*
> *They've cooked up a hot assignment for*
> *Marine Air Group 23*
> *As the wind howls through the palm trees,*
> *you hear Operations say,*
> *"Load the belly tanks with juice, boys, take*
> *the scouts to Gizo Bay."*

Hit the road to Gizo Bay
Where the Jap fleet spends the day,
You can hear the duds a-chunking from
          Rabaul to Lunga Quay
Pack a load to Gizo Bay
Where the float plane Zeroes play
And the bombs come down like thunder on
          the natives 'cross the way.
Take me East of Ewa
Where the best ain't like the worst
Where there ain't no Doug MacArthur
And a man can drown a thirst.
For the Army takes the medals, and the
          Navy takes the Queens
But the boys, what takes the beatings . . . is
          the United States Marines.

Red's song was an instant hit within the squadron, and it soon spread throughout MAG-23. Bob Galer liked it so much, he wrote the lyrics down in his diary so he wouldn't forget them. During moments of downtime, the guys would pester Red to sing it again and again, the others joining in.

Nobody wanted to go to Gizo Harbor. At least with the fighting over Guadalcanal, the crews who went down had a chance to get home. Get shot down over New Georgia, and the men had a slight chance of making contact with a local Coastwatcher. Other than that, they were likely to die after being captured and tortured for information. So they groused and sang Red's song and hoped that whoever came up with the idea would forget about it.

The morning of September 27 passed quietly. The men played poker, listened to records on a phonograph somebody had found, chatted, and smoked. By eleven, the tension level ratcheted up a notch. If the Japanese were coming, this was the time the Americans would get the call.

But the phone didn't ring. Their watches ticked past noon. Still no call. The weather report didn't seem to be that bad. Maybe the Japanese were ready to leave this hellish island to the Americans, after all.

The phone rang at 1312. Marion Carl stood up to answer it. "Bandits incoming, three hundred and ten degrees," said the voice on the other end of the line.

"How far out?" Marion asked.

"Hundred and fifty."

He turned and told the squadron. The field went to yellow alert, and the men wrestled into their gear and ran to their aircraft. Nearby, Galer's men did the same. The Marine F4F squadrons shared Fighter One, and the Navy's VF-5 used Henderson. In minutes, both fields buzzed with activity as pilots strapped into their planes and fired up their engines. What followed was a pell-mell rush to get into the air and reach fighting altitude. There wasn't time to carefully form up as squadrons. Instead, 223 and 224 interlaced, the pilots formed up on whoever was closest.

Marion Carl got off the ground first for 223. Eight others from the outfit trailed behind, taking off between runs by the 224 pilots. As a result, Marion tacked onto a flight of four from Galer's squadron.

It was led by none other than Kirk Armistead, the captain who took over VMF-221 at Midway after that Japanese raid wiped out most of the squadron. Although Marion detested Armistead, such feelings stayed on the ground. In the air, any friendly fighter a pilot could team up with usually meant the difference between life and death.

They climbed out to twenty-six thousand feet, Armistead leading five F4Fs. Four other 224 Wildcats still struggled to get to fighting altitude, along with the other eight 223 fighters. Another fourteen F4Fs from VF-5 got into the air but were several thousand feet below the Marines and still clawing for altitude.

Strung out, flying in patched-together divisions, the Marines ran nose-to-nose into the Japanese raid. Armistead's division looked to be a couple thousand feet above the bombers, in a perfect setup for overhead runs. Spotting a fighter escort of only a few Zeroes astern, above, and to the left of the bombers, the Marines calculated they couldn't intercept the F4Fs before they made passes at the G4Ms.

The Betties flew in two formations, line astern in vees. Carl counted eighteen total, nine in each formation. By a stroke of good luck, the Marines had reached the enemy before it started its bomb run on Henderson. A good pass, and they could totally disrupt the bombers' pattern, saving the men below from yet another pounding.

Armistead chose to go after the last bombers in the trailing formation. Carl and the others in the division followed after him, watching the lead Betties go under them. Two of the Marines couldn't resist those targets. They broke off and rolled into a reverse overhead pass, flipping on their backs and pulling through what amounted to a half loop until the bombers came back into sight.

Kirk and Marion started their runs and inadvertently picked out the same bomber. They hammered it until it burst into flames and dropped out of formation. Seconds later, Kirk went zooming past the rest of the Betties and kept going. So did the other members of the ad hoc division, one of whom suffered catastrophic mechanical failure in his dive and had to dead-stick back to Fighter One.

Marion, on the other hand, saw the escorting Zeroes diving after Fritz Payne and the rest of 223. The Wildcats had arrived at the same altitude as the Betties only seconds after Armistead rolled into his attack, and Payne led them into a side run against the formation. He aborted as soon as he saw the Zeroes coming after them. Better to fight another day. He called a warning on the radio and dove out of the fight. His three other F4Fs followed him down.

The Zeroes gave chase. A wild vertical game of cat and mouse ensued as the Japanese fighter pilots aggressively stayed on the Wildcats. The chase with Fritz's group left no Zeroes in sight as far as Marion could see. Instead of diving away, he decided to go up top again and make another pass at the bombers.

Flak bursts peppered the sky now, as Marine 90 mm antiaircraft guns opened up on the Betties. The G4M bombardiers took careful aim and opened their bay doors. Flying straight and level through the fusillade of bursting shells, they loosed a mix of 500-pound high-explosive bombs and 100-pound fragmentation "Daisy Cutters."

The bombs fell in a tight pattern that left a string of destruction from the edge of Kukum across to the parking area at Henderson Field. The rippling blasts destroyed or severely damaged sixteen aircraft and knocked out the 1st Marine Division's communications center right at a critical moment in the ongoing Battle of the Matanikau River. It was a devastating attack.

The Marine antiaircraft gunners scored near misses on several of the G4Ms. As the bomber formations turned slowly over Lunga Point and headed in a slow 180 over Savo Sound, Carl continued to stalk them. He cut inside their turn, gained a bit more altitude, and tailed them until 1417, when he made another overhead run on the trailing formation of Betties.

His guns chopped up one of the G4Ms, and as he dove through them, his target was already falling away, smoke billowing over its wings. Two kills, one of them shared with Armistead, was enough for the day. Pushing his luck earlier in the month had nearly got Marion killed. No more of that. He stayed in his dive and headed back for Fighter One.

Back at the strip, the pilots gathered to discuss the fight. It had been a sprawling affair that ranged from almost thirty thousand feet down to the deck. The Navy pilots of Fighting Five claimed four Zeroes that came their way as Payne dove away from them. The Marines thought they had shot down five of the bombers, plus a Zero.

Marion earned a half credit for the G4M he and Kirk shot down, plus credit for the second one he attacked as the Japanese tried to exit the area. Cactus lost no pilots during the interception that day, though two VF-5 pilots suffered wounds.

The Japanese fighter escort made plenty of mistakes that day, both seen and unseen by the Americans. There were actually thirty-eight A6Ms protecting the G4Ms, not the half dozen or so that Kirk Armistead saw. In an effort to keep the Wildcats off the bombers, the Japanese had split the escort force. A fighter sweep of twelve had flown ahead of the main force. Seventeen more Zeroes provided close escort for the bombers with two formations, one on either side of the G4Ms, behind and above. Above them, a high cover element of nine more Zeroes staggered aloft to thirty-one thousand feet.

On paper, this plan looked sound. In practice, the fighter sweep missed the action, and the seventeen providing close cover were initially so far out of position that Armistead's division attacked before they could react. Once engaged, though, the aggressiveness of the Japanese pilots may have chased the F4Fs down and away from the bombers, but it also left their charges virtually undefended. This gave Marion and several 224 pilots another crack at the Betties. They gave chase, climbing after the Betties and pursuing them for almost sixty miles before attacking.

Had it known the real figures, MAG-23 would have been alarmed by the number of Zeroes actually involved that day. The Wildcat pilots estimated they had seen a total of thirteen A6Ms. The disparity masked a change in Japanese tactics that would have implications later on. For now, the Marines noticed no change, and this oversight would cost them.[1]

FORTY-ONE

THE FIELD DAY

Henderson Field, Guadalcanal
September 28, 1942, morning

T HOUGH 223'S EXHAUSTED MEN DIDN'T KNOW IT, THE JAPANESE change of strategy after Edson's Ridge ensured that the dreaded escort to Gizo mission would never happen. After spending the last thirty days sending in reinforcements piecemeal and throwing more men onto an island already critically short of supplies, the Japanese high command decided that victory on Guadalcanal could only be achieved by a massive, concentrated offensive using all means at their disposal. The strategic value of Guadalcanal to both sides was significant. It could be used by the Japanese as a springboard into the New Hebrides and to Fiji, cutting off American sea lanes to Australia. At the same time, it could be the first rung on the Solomons ladder for the Americans, and the Japanese saw Guadalcanal as a dagger pointed at the heart of their defensive network in the Southwest Pacific: Rabaul.

Beyond the strategic value of the island, there was also Japanese pride. The surprise offensive had struck a deadly blow to the military's pride. Both the Japanese army and navy had lost face. They were willing to pay any price to atone for that blow and drive the Americans off the island.

After suspending the Tokyo Express following the attacks on September 24, the Japanese reinforced their air units in the area with fresh bombers and fighters. Some of the weary veterans who had carried out the attacks in both New Guinea and the Solomons were stood down, soon to be sent home to Japan.

The Coastwatchers on Guadalcanal kept Vandegrift informed of the state of the Japanese troops they encountered on the island. The survivors of Bloody Ridge and the Ilu River were starving and disease racked. On the withdrawal and march to the western side of the island, many had thrown their weapons away as their strength failed them. They were in desperately bad condition, in need of food, medical supplies, arms, and ammunition. The Tokyo Express runs earlier in the month provided only a trickle of what was needed to sustain the men already on the island. Much of those supplies sent down the Slot never reached the Japanese on Guadalcanal, or they were destroyed shortly after arrival. The Cactus Air Force's premier ground attack aircraft, Dale Brannon's P-400s, made a living taking out supply concentrations and exposing enemy troops in thankless low-altitude missions flown nonstop for weeks.

Losing most of the supplies at Taivu Point after Col. Red Mike Edson's troops made their surprise raid there made this situation even worse for the Japanese. By the end of September, they faced a choice: go all in at Guadalcanal, or abandon the island and shift to a defensive posture somewhere up the Solomons ladder. They chose to go all in, pulling reinforcements from all over the empire to drive the Marines out once and for all.

To get those reinforcements to Guadalcanal, the Imperial Japanese Navy planned a coordinated effort to resupply the island using not just the Tokyo Express but also small convoys of barges that would better utilize the islands in the Central Solomons than Kawaguchi's first attempt had. Along with the destroyer and small-boat runs, the seaplane carrier *Nisshin* would bring in heavy weapons, including 150 mm field artillery batteries. Each destroyer run to Guadalcanal would feature the tin cans towing barges filled with supplies. As these runs built reserves, a massive reinforcement effort, using fast transports well supported by the Imperial

Japanese Navy, would be assembled to push an entire infantry division with tanks and artillery onto the island.

For now, the Tokyo Express and barge runs would resume on October 1. This time frame gave the new aerial units about a week to crush the Cactus Air Force. Their inaugural effort began on September 27. The next day, the Japanese planned their heaviest blow yet. The stage was set for the biggest air battles of the campaign so far.

The field telephones at Fighter One and Henderson proper rang at two minutes before 1300 hours that day. Coastwatchers on New Georgia, plus the new radar sets established on Guadalcanal, almost simultaneously detected a large Japanese force heading for Cactus.

With these reports, MAG-23 scrambled every available F4F. Thirty-five climbed off the dusty runways, twenty Marine Wildcats and fifteen from VF-5. John L. Smith led the way up to the battlesphere, sixteen F4Fs tucked in tight with him. Another three led by Bob Galer trailed John L.'s group but had a little more altitude.

Then something strange happened. The Japanese usually came straight down the Slot on a southeasterly course. The Marines countered that by flying at them on an opposite, northwesterly approach, most often around 310 degrees. This time, the raid changed course, passed over northern Guadalcanal going almost due south, then turned east to make its approach on Lunga Point. The fighter direction officer on Guadalcanal, Maj. Joseph "Joe" Renner, watched this development and ordered John L. to head southwest. John L. did so, continuing to climb with the twenty Marine fighters. Fighting Five also changed course.

Renner set the Marines up perfectly. The F4F pilots spotted the incoming raid from twenty-eight thousand feet. They were four thousand feet above their targets, ample space for overhead runs and fast getaways. Even better, they didn't even see any fighter escort at first. Scanning the sky, John L. finally picked them out far behind and *below* the Betties.

The Japanese had made a catastrophic mistake. The Americans would have ample time to make their attacks without any interference from the Zero escort.

The Americans peeled off and rolled into their attacks. It was a slaughter. Bombers burst into flames, exploded, or dropped out of formation with crippled, smoking engines. Debris cascaded down like aluminum rain. One oversized division of six 224 pilots claimed three G4Ms in that first pass.

Galer and his trio waded into the fray, approaching the bombers head-on, then flipping inverted to pull through screaming overhead passes. Galer crippled two bombers in one pass, an exceptionally difficult thing to do, given the mere seconds on target the tactic produced. Both Betties fell out of formation, their pilots dumping their bombs to lighten their battle-damaged birds. Joe Bauer, flying with Galer that day and seeing his first combat, cut another bomber out of the herd with a masterful pass. He pulled up and got back above the fight, even as more F4Fs piled on the Japanese.

Marion Carl, now back almost two weeks from his escape and evasion ordeal, led his wingman, Rex Jeans, diving into the fray. Willis Lees and Fritz Payne went after one of Galer's cripples. Lees hit his target, which burst into flames. Payne finished off the other one, then nearly collided with a third. Carl attacked Bauer's cripple, sawing his spray of .50-caliber bullets across the engine nacelles and cockpit.

John L., now leading Bill Brooks, Robert Read, Dean Hartley, and Charley Hughes, hit the formation with a high side pass. There were so many diving and climbing F4Fs over the Japanese that John L. decided to come in from the flank to avoid colliding with them. High side passes required excellent deflection shooting. As John L. dove, banking his F4F into a pursuit curve, the sudden negative g-forces sent dirt and grime from the cockpit floor into the air around him. Wearing his goggles on his forehead proved to be a bad move. Dirt flew into his eyes, obstructing his vision for just a second or two. But in air combat, where split seconds meant the difference between success or failure, the distraction was enough to blow his attack. He plunged out below the bombers, crossing their formation again at over three hundred knots. Angry and frustrated, he checked the sky for Zeroes, saw none nearby, and decided to try again.

He swooped back up a few thousand feet and to one side of the bombers, flying parallel and well out of range of their defensive armament. He studied the scene. The bombers had their bay doors open, even though they were miles from Lunga Point. To his surprise, they jettisoned their loads to help effect an escape. The entire formation bombed the hell out of uninhabited jungle nowhere near the Marine perimeter.

John L. banked and dove back toward the G4Ms, speeding down on them from abeam, banking into a curving approach again. This time, he had his goggles down, and dirt did not foul his eyesight. He selected a bomber at the trailing edge of its formation. Behind him, Brooks stayed tacked onto John L.'s wing. The two opened fire with long bursts as their speed rapidly ate up the distance to their targets. At the last second, they eased off their triggers and dove under the formation. The Betties looked like goners to them as the bombers ran for home.

As John L. finished his second run, the Navy pilots from Fighting Five showed up and joined in the slaughter. The Zeroes had still been unable to get into the fight. But after one pass by VF-5, they finally waded in after the F4Fs.

The bombers banked for home, their battered formations awkwardly pulling an aerial U-turn. A scrum developed between the Zeroes and the Wildcats and soon devolved into a vertical race, F4Fs diving away from the lighter A6Ms. A few Wildcat pilots stayed above the dogfight and hunted crippled bombers. There were several G4Ms limping along, falling farther and farther behind the main pack of Betties.

When it was over, and the Wildcats set down on the two strips, not a single American fighter had been lost. Five F4Fs had taken damage, but nobody was even wounded. Claims for the day totaled twenty-three Betties and one Zero. Willis Lees, John L. Smith, Marion Carl, Rex Jeans, and a temporarily attached pilot, 2nd Lt. Frank Drury, all were credited with one bomber each. Howard Marvin, who had come up from Efate after a long illness to rejoin the squadron, shot down a Zero on his first mission with 223.

Bob Galer was the high scorer of the day, getting credit for three G4Ms—two in that first pass and another later in the fight. A pair of VF-5 pilots were credited with two bombers each as well.

It was the biggest single victory to date for the fighter pilots of the beleaguered Cactus Air Force. They thought they'd nearly wiped out an entire group of Japanese bombers without losing a single F4F. In fact, they did inflict a devastating defeat on the Japanese that day. Five Betties, including the strike leader's aircraft, went down over Guadalcanal during the fighting. One more ditched en route home, another crash-landed in the Northern Solomons, and the one that did return to base crash-landed and became a total loss. Altogether, eight G4Ms were lost, forty-one crewmen killed in action, and of the remaining seventeen Betties that reached Guadalcanal, none returned home unscathed. The F4F pilots managed to put holes in every one of them.

Day two of the renewed Japanese air offensive to destroy the Cactus Air Force resulted in such a devastating defeat that the imperial leaders conducted a thorough analysis of what had happened. On September 28, the fighter sweep of twenty-seven Zeroes took off late and didn't lead the way. Instead, the fighters ended up chasing the bombers down the Slot and never got in front of the main raid. That was the first mistake. The second misstep came about halfway to Guadalcanal, when the close escort leader's Zero suffered mechanical failure and began losing altitude. Without radios in their aircraft, the leader couldn't report his problem. As a result, the close escort followed him down, which put them below and behind the bombers. The strike leader detoured south and arced over eastward to give the escorts time to catch up, but they didn't get back in position before the Americans attacked. Mistakes on mistakes set the table for the disaster.

In two days, the Japanese G4M units lost 20 percent of their available strength. Because such a loss was unsustainable, the Japanese switched tactics again. Knowing there were Coastwatchers somewhere in the Central Solomons reporting on their aerial movements, they crafted a plan to send a small bomber force down toward Guadalcanal, escorted by a large number of Zeroes. But before they got to the island, the Betties would turn around and go home—after presumably being seen by the watchers.

The Zeroes would continue on to Lunga Point, overfly Henderson, and shoot down any opposing Wildcats climbing to intercept the reported bombers. Meanwhile, small groups of Betties would venture down the Slot at sunset to strike the perimeter with night bombing attacks. The shift to attacking under darkness resembled the change in strategy the Luftwaffe employed during the Battle of Britain in 1940.

The Japanese tried this new attack plan the next day, on September 29. Two hours into the raid, the nine bombers accompanying the Zeroes turned back—a move that the Coastwatchers noted. The Zeroes continued on to Guadalcanal. All three Wildcat squadrons launched to meet them, though John L. and Bob Galer's pilots never saw the Japanese among the cloud layers over Guadalcanal. Instead, Fighting Five made contact, claiming three Zeroes for the loss of one pilot. The Japanese thought they'd shot down fifteen Wildcats, at the cost of two Zeroes lost over the target, two more as battle-damage write-offs. From the Japanese point of view, the outcome seemed like a victory—though a costly one.

Such an apparent success required a follow-up, but the weather closed in on September 30 and the next day, preventing further raids for the moment.

Adm. Chester Nimitz, commander of the Pacific Fleet, chose this moment to fly into Guadalcanal and see for himself the conditions on the island. He had already met with Admiral Ghormley in the New Hebrides and had been shocked at his old friend's attitude and mental condition. Ghormley was demoralized and out of touch. He had not even visited Cactus, and he had repeatedly shown that he wasn't even fully aware of his command's capabilities. The seed had been planted in Nimitz's mind to replace him with Adm. William "Bull" Halsey. In the meantime, Admiral Nimitz set an example by going to Guadalcanal himself, his actions only highlighting just how derelict Admiral Ghormley had been on that front.

Nimitz arrived on September 30 and spent a miserable night on the island, which was bombed by several G4Ms. He was scheduled to fly out on October 1, but before he left, he wanted to surprise the weary pilots of MAG-23.

Just before 0630, a select group of pilots gathered, as ordered the night before, at Vandegrift's headquarters. There, they encountered a waiting group of mud Marine officers and NCOs, including Colonel Edson and several of his Raiders.

The aviators lined up in a formation beside their Marine brothers. It had rained all night, and the ground was a boggy mess, but for now, the sky had cleared. They stood at attention as Admiral Nimitz stepped out in front of them. One by one, he called the men forward to give them awards.

John L. approached Admiral Nimitz and stood before his theater commander, who presented him the Navy Cross, saluted, then shook his hand. Nimitz pinned the medal on the aviator's chest, just above his left breast pocket. Bob Galer was next. The VMF-224 commander stepped up to the admiral and received a Navy Cross as well. Then Marion Carl's name was called. Nimitz pinned a Navy Cross on the lanky Oregonian's shirt.

What of Mangrum? When his name was called, the dive-bomber skipper was given a Distinguished Flying Cross. Galer and Smith exchanged glances. This seemed like a slight to a man who had led his men on so many critical missions. In his diary, Galer confided bitterly, "The distribution of medals was just like everything else: all done at the last minute to suit the number of medals the admiral brought with him instead of the medals recommended for the pilots that went in."

It wasn't intended to be a slight. Nimitz had simply run out of Navy Crosses to give to Richard Mangrum.

One by one, the other pilots received Distinguished Flying Crosses. Of John L.'s pilots, Willis Lees and Red Kendrick were so recognized. Don McCafferty stood beside his skipper, also wearing the Distinguished Flying Cross by the end of the event. Four men from VF-5 and two from 224 also rated Distinguished Flying Crosses. For some of the men, this surprise honor was a humbling life moment they never forgot. Fighting Five's Lieutenant Register thought of how his family would react, and he took pride in being recognized. Marion Carl admired Nimitz greatly. He'd encountered the admiral once before, after the Battle of

Midway. Now, seeing him sharing the same bad food and the same rain of bombs that the fighting Marines faced daily ratcheted up Marion's admiration for him. The ace took the Navy Cross on the same even keel he always had, though the honor was a significant one that gave him a deep sense of pride.

There was a dark side to this moment though. Nimitz clearly meant well, but medals have always been a touchy subject in the service. That Mangrum was somehow seen as less worthy than the fighter pilots to receive America's second-highest valor award was nothing short of outrageous. He'd flown and fought just as effectively as Marion, John L., and Bob had, and his squadron had more directly affected the flow of the campaign than any other so far. That imbalance alone did much to destroy the goodwill the ceremony was supposed to bring.

For leaders like John L., Dick Mangrum, and Bob Galer, those awarded medals only highlighted their men who deserved them but who got nothing. Instead of boosting morale, the brief ceremony left them spitting acid over who got left out. The skippers had a point: if awards were to be given at this point in their deployment, they should have been for everyone who had been written up or deserving. They should not have been based on how many the admiral's staff had packed for the trip.

Walking back to squadron bivouac that morning, Dick Mangrum resolved to make sure that all his men received the awards they deserved. The living, the wounded, and the dead. If he lived through this, he would make it a personal mission to see they were properly recognized. They deserved at least that from their skipper.

The ceremony underscored the Marines' general feeling that nothing the high command could do was thought-out or well planned when it came to Guadalcanal. They were right. They were at the tip of a deeply dysfunctional spear, clinging to a patch of real estate most in Washington, D.C., had already written off as a lost cause. No amount of Navy Crosses could counter that morale bomb.

They would fight on, not for the command, not for medals, but out of survival. And for one another.

FORTY-TWO

VERTICAL RUN

Henderson Field, Guadalcanal
October 2, 1942, morning

THE AIR RAID SIREN CAUGHT EVERYONE BY SURPRISE. MARION CARL was off duty that morning, so he'd gone down to the river to bathe. When the siren wailed to life, he was walking back to the 223 bivouac. He looked up, puzzled. The clear sky that graced the decoration ceremony the day before vanished only a couple of hours later. For twenty-four hours, the weather teetered between tropical polarities: deluges and blue sky with a broiling sun. Now, as the lunch hour approached, Marion could see in the cloud cover some holes revealing overcast layers, stacked one atop the other like a wedding cake.

Who bombs through that?

He heard the alert pilots firing up their Wildcats. John L. had the duty that morning, just in case. He and his men had been playing poker in the squadron's ready tent when the call came through to scramble.

John L. only had one division: five guys. Marion realized at once that his skipper would need help. He rounded up Ken Frazier, Red Kendrick, and Charley Hughes and raced over to the Fighter One flight line, where four F4Fs sat unused. As they strapped in, the last of fourteen Fighting Five Wildcats lifted off from Henderson to disappear into the overcast.

Marion and his three other pilots soon followed Fighting Five into the scud. They were several minutes behind John L.'s division and Bob Galer's and John Dobbin's two divisions from VMF-224. Better late than never. Joe Renner, the fighter direction officer, called out over the radio that the radar showed lots of small returns. Single-engine bombers, maybe? Or Zeroes. Either way, every second counted in the race to get to altitude in their beer-bellied Wildcats.

John L. Smith, Howard Marvin, Willis Lees, "Rapid" Robert Read, and Fred Gutt, who was fresh back from a hospital stay at Efate, formed the tip of the vertical spear. They arrowed upward, their F4Fs straining as they passed through alternating layers of blue sky and cloud cover. Finally, at twenty-five thousand feet, John L.'s F4F burst into crystal-blue skies. Below him stretched a veritable ocean of gray-white clouds.

He looked up and froze. Zeroes. Lots of them. Seventeen-plus. His division had popped out of the clouds directly below the deadly Japanese fighters. Already, six had peeled off and were plunging down on him and his men.

John L. called out a frantic warning. This was the worst-imaginable tactical situation. The Wildcats were slow and sluggish, still climbing as hard as their engines allowed. The Zeroes had the high ground and energy from their dives to dictate the fight.

Before the Americans could roll into dives of their own and get away, the six Zeroes slashed through their formation. John L.'s Wildcat shuddered and bucked as 20 mm cannon shells struck home. Rows of gouges ripped across both wings. The cowling took hits. John L. willed the aircraft's nose down for the safety of the clouds, but the aircraft mushed and waddled in its low-energy state. Another torrent of shells and bullets hammered the F4F. The engine was hit. He glanced down to his left at the cylinder-head temperature gauge; it was rapidly spiking. That meant his oil system had been damaged. His gauge redlined, and he knew his engine would seize at any moment. The cloud layer below was his only hope.

Right then, a Wildcat exploded in flames. It was the F4F piloted by Willis Lees, the Northeastern blue blood. The aircraft twisted away in a spin, trailing smoke and debris. Somehow, Lees got out of the cockpit. A split second before John L. reached the cloud layer, he caught a glimpse of Willis's chute opening.

They were at twenty-five thousand feet. Zero pilots made a point of killing Americans in their parachutes, and the Marines and Navy pilots sometimes repaid the deed.[1] This was not a war of gentlemen. It was not the ridiculously overblown *Hollywood Knight of the Air* imagery so often presented for the World War I generation. This was a cold, bitter, merciless battle to the last man.

Lees had a long, long way to go before he'd be safe.

John L.'s division scattered, every man for himself. Read and Marvin plunged into the overcast and did their best to shake the pursuing Zeroes. John L. kept going in his steep dive until he burst out the bottom of the highest scud layer. In a wild turn of events, he suddenly appeared almost directly over three A6Ms. But his engine was running rough now. Not much time left. Anyone else in that situation would probably have just kept going, bent on their own survival. John L. rolled after the trio, intent on doing as much damage as he could. If anything, distracting these three might help the other men in his division escape.

He shot up the number three plane in the Japanese formation. But now his engine was coughing and missing as it overheated. These were the last sounds of a dying engine before it succumbed to the incredible heat and lack of lubrication. He dove past the Zeroes, believing he'd gotten at least one of them. Two of the Zero pilots used their planes' remarkable agility, winged over, and managed snap shots as John L. dove for his life. They rocked his F4F with more hits seconds before he hit the next layer of clouds.

Then he was free, at least for the moment.

Behind and above him, the rest of his division dropped out of the top cloud layer right onto John Dobbin and his three 224 pilots. Dobbin had no idea there were Zeroes in the area, and his men were caught absolutely flat-footed as Read and Marvin arrowed past his Wildcats, with Zeroes in hot pursuit. The four surprised Marines rolled inverted and headed downstairs, running for their lives just like John L.'s men.

Bob Galer was next. Seconds after John L. was attacked, Bob and his four F4Fs climbed out of the weather and ran straight into the same nightmare trap: Zeroes above. This time, twelve A6Ms fell on the Americans. Two of the four Wildcats dove away, but Galer and his wingman began to scissor back and forth, scraping Zeroes off each other's tails. What followed was a three-minute running fight to the death, the Japanese attacking from above, the side, and behind while the two F4Fs wove back and forth to protect each other, taking whatever shots presented themselves. Galer took a few hits in his wing tips, but the Wildcat wasn't seriously damaged.

At nineteen thousand feet, just under the top cloud layer, Galer and Hartley found themselves alone. Over the radio, Galer heard news that bombers were incoming. Rather than dive away to fight another day, he and Hartley began climbing to look for the Betties. Before they could get to the overhead clouds, seven Zeroes jumped them. The two Americans went back to weaving, and with one snap shot, Galer thought he'd nailed one of the Zeroes. Then he fixated on a trio, boring after them with his guns pouring fire. He lost Hartley and found himself alone. The other Zeroes had piled on Hartley, ripping his F4F to shreds. Hartley dove out of the fight and made for Fighter One, his Wildcat crippled.

Alone, Galer battled at least six remaining Zeroes. He fought with cold fury and pure desperation. He stayed on one Zero as it tried to dive away from him, and as he unloaded on his target, the other Japanese chased after him. One tacked onto his tail, closed quickly and riddled his Wildcat. Bullets and shells stitched across both wings and tore into the fuselage, the engine cowling, and the cockpit. His instrument panel shattered, and a bullet shot away one rudder pedal right out from under his foot. A cannon shell exploded in the cockpit, its shrapnel ripped through his pant legs. Instinctively, he rolled inverted and did a split S maneuver. As he did, his engine quit. His Wildcat fell into the sea of clouds below and vanished.

At eighteen thousand feet somewhere south of Tulagi, Ken Frazier, Red Kendrick, and Charley Hughes climbed into one of the clear spaces between the cloud layers. Behind them, Marion Carl struggled to keep up. His engine had started running rough, and Frazier took the lead. Still, Marion doggedly pressed on after his division.

Right then, Frazier spotted seven Zeroes below and in front of them. Frazier, Kendrick, and Hughes winged over and dove after them, guns spewing tracers. The Zeroes dove into the cloud layer below them, all three Marines hard on their heels.

Behind them, Marion watched them dive, his engine still acting up. Before he could go after them, he glanced up to see even more enemy fighters drop out of the top cloud layer. They headed straight for Marion's lone F4F, thinking they had easy meat.

Marion had no choice. He dropped his nose, rolled inverted, pulled through a split S, and vanished into the lower overcast. Had he stayed, the Zeroes would have made short work of him.

Meanwhile, Frazier and Kendrick lost their Zeroes in the scud. They climbed back out of the layer together, looking for Charley Hughes as they got into position for a second overhead pass should the enemy fighters materialize again. They pitched into another cloud, and when Frazier came out of it, Kendrick was nowhere in sight.

Down low over Savo Sound, Bob Galer's F4F glided along off Florida Island. He chose to ride the doomed bird into the waves rather than bail out. He ditched about a mile off a small island not far from Florida's coastline. The distance didn't seem that far at first, but Bob had been battered, burned, and slightly wounded. He swam for an hour before finally making it to the beach, where he crawled ashore completely exhausted and filled with fear. Four local Melanesian men approached with machetes drawn. Unsure if they were friendly or hostile, Galer initially "captured" them with his pistol. One of the Melanesians touched his chest and said, "Michael. Me Christian. Me friendly."

One of the younger locals climbed a tree and chopped some coconuts out of it. The five men shared an impromptu meal of coconut milk, the war for the moment a million miles away.

Meanwhile, John L. was in dire straits. His engine seized on his way back to the perimeter. He was now trading altitude for airspeed and time. As he glided for Fighter One, Marion Carl appeared. He'd gathered two other Wildcats with him as he headed for home. Marion realized his skipper was a sitting duck should any marauding Zeroes pounce on him. He and the other two F4Fs took station to protect him.

John L. knew the Wildcat couldn't make it to Fighter One. It was a simple equation: altitude, speed, distance. He didn't have the altitude, and he wouldn't have the speed when he ran out of it.

He judged he was about four to six miles from Marine lines when he picked out a grassy ridge poking out of the jungle. It was the best-looking place he could see to belly-land a Grumman, so he eased his F4F into a gentle turn around the ridge and lined up an approach. He set the F4F down as gently as he could. The bird slid through the grass and rough terrain, throwing him around in the cockpit until it finally came to a halt.

He was down southeast of Marine lines with about five hours of sunlight left. Marion dove down and passed over him to make sure he was okay. He saw John L. climb out of the cockpit and run down the ridge for the tree line. Marion and the other two F4Fs stayed overhead to make sure he made it to cover, then they bolted for home to report his exact location.

Back at the Pagoda, the men were shocked and silent. Colonel Fike, notebook in hand, quietly asked questions of each pilot. None of them wanted to talk much. Six men were missing: Smith, Kendrick, and Lees from 223; Bob Galer and another man from 224; and one VF-5 pilot. They had been ambushed in the worst possible position—nose high, airspeed low—and the ambush had cost the Cactus Air Force both Marine fighter squadron skippers and four of the five men honored by Nimitz at the award ceremony the day before.

The Marines knew John L. was in the jungle, but all the others were missing. Though most of the Japanese had migrated to the west side of the perimeter, John L.'s route back to Henderson would be a dangerous one. The word went out to the 1st Marine Regiment that the skipper of 223 might be entering their lines later this afternoon. The news prompted something that rarely happens in the Corps: a host of mud Marines volunteered to patrol out into enemy territory to see if they could find their great aerial leader. Day after day, they had seen John L. lead 223 into the bombers that tormented them. They had watched the contrails of his dogfights. They had seen his targets fall in flames. He was more than just a major in charge of a fighter unit, more than just an ace. To the Marines on Guadalcanal, he was a symbol of the irrepressible fighting spirit they all needed if they were to survive this ordeal.

They weren't going to leave him out there.

Col. Clifton Cates studied the map and the point where MAG-23 HQ told him John L. had crashed. He looked over the contours of the terrain and settled on what would have been his route back to the perimeter. Then he took out a patrol of his own to find him.

JOHN L. MOVED STEALTHILY THROUGH THE JUNGLE, MAKING GOOD TIME despite his many bruises from the crash. Being out in enemy-held jungle at night was not something he wanted to do, so he moved as quickly as the terrain, the heat, and his own physical state allowed.

After fording a stream and crossing a creek, he soon came to a debris field in a clearing. As he approached, he could see the battered remains of a Wildcat's propeller. Little else was left of the aircraft, but something in the site convinced John L. he'd found Scotty McLennan's aircraft. He looked around for any signs of life. Scotty had gone down three weeks ago and had just vanished, like so many others. If John L. could confirm it was his craft, the family would at least have closure.

He noted the location as well as he could, then pushed on back into the jungle. Late in the afternoon, he ran into Colonel Cates and the patrol he was leading. A happy American reunion ensued, and the mud Marines brought their lost aviator back to the airfield, where his return was met with cheers. It was a bit of good news in a day of awful events. The men celebrated as much as they could, but Red Kendrick and Bill Lees were not far from their minds.

Of the original eighteen 223 pilots who launched from the *Long Island* in August, only eight remained. Marion Carl did some grim math in his head. Wearily, he figured none of them would live to see November.

FORTY-THREE

THE COCKPIT PRAYER

October 3, 1942, morning

THE MARINES OF MAG-23 GATHERED FOR SATURDAY MASS ON the morning of October 3, a sober and quiet bunch. Mangrum was the sole representative from VMSB-232, as his last two pilots, Don McCafferty and Robert Fleener, had been evacuated the previous afternoon. Both were exhausted skeletons, sick with jungle maladies, and covered in sores.

His squadron was finished now, but Dick refused to be evacuated too. His ground crew labored on, working on the SBDs around the field, no matter whose they were. The crew members were vital to continued antiship operations and would have to stay until VMSB-141's ground echelon arrived. Dick would leave only when his ground echelon received their orders for home.

Don Rose's friend from school and home, Chaplain Angsar South, presided over the Mass that morning. He intended to honor the missing and the lost, starting with Bob Galer, but just as he was about to begin the service, Galer walked into the gathering. His Melanesian friends had brought him to Tulagi by dugout canoe, where he'd been picked up by the J2F Duck floatplane that Fike had used to rescue Ensign Fink and his gunner. Dinged up and badly bruised, his face baked crimson by the sun, Galer

looked like how everyone felt. He moved into the gathering gingerly—
there was not a spot on his body that wasn't sore—and shook hands with,
and hugged, his brother aviators. Galer's surprise appearance brought a
moment of levity and happiness to the solemnity of the service.

THE MASS ENDED, AND THE MEN DISPERSED TO THEIR DUTY ASSIGN-
ments. Marion Carl, Ken Frazier, Ike Winter, and Floyd Lynch (on loan
from VMF-121) headed for the squadron's ready tent. After the disaster
of September 28, they were all that VMF-223 could field that day. Just as
they were about to pile into a jeep, Lt. Col. Joe Bauer approached Marion
and asked if he could take a 223 fighter up and join them. He'd checked
with John L., who had told "the Coach" it was Marion's decision that day.

Before Pearl Harbor, flying Marines considered Joe Bauer the best
fighter pilot in the Corps. In countless mock dogfights, he had defeated
every challenger—except Marion Carl. The two men were evenly
matched in flight skill, aggressiveness, and the willingness to take calculated risks. Bauer had held the edge with his experience, but Marion
always tested him to the limits in those prewar scrums.

Now, things had changed. Marion's experience was matched only by
the handful of Marines left from 223. Joe was fresh and eager to fight,
having been stuck defending the New Hebrides with his squadron for
months. Marion was exhausted, wrung out, and more disciplined in the
air since he had been shot down.

The Coach and his A-plus student, in the air together again—this
time against an actual enemy? No matter how time and combat changed
the dynamic between them, this was a no-brainer for Marion. "Hell yes,
come on!" he told Joe. Bauer climbed into the jeep, and the five men
drove to the ready tent.

As they waited for the field telephone to ring, the five pilots discussed
the ambush from the day before and how to avoid it again. They decided
to go for even more altitude.

How high could an F4F go? The oxygen shortage had been worked
out, but the Wildcats were in such poor condition nobody was really
sure what their ceiling would be now. Officially, the F4F could get to

thirty-eight thousand feet, but that was certainly way beyond the ability of these weary birds.

The phone rang at 1154. Marion picked it up and listened. A Japanese raid was inbound, 145 out. Without prompting, the men grabbed their gear and rushed to their waiting F4Fs. The plane captains waited for them on the wings to help strap them into their seats. Marion looked left. Looked right. On either side of him down the flight line, his pilots fired up their engines. Everyone looked good to go.

He watched them, his friends. Ken Frazier had more than earned his respect. The scrapper from New Jersey was almost a double ace now. He'd survived every fight and seemed as unflappable as Marion. On the other side of him was Joe Bauer, his mentor of over two years. Joe was the epitome of a Marine fighter pilot, the one man in the prewar service whom every young tiger emulated.

They were flying into the unknown together. Just like yesterday, the weather was garbage. Nine-tenths cover with cumulous clouds towering thousands of feet and creating canyons of clear sky between them. Lots of places for Zeroes to hide. Lots of places for ambushes. Today could be a repeat of yesterday if they weren't careful.

Marion pulled his goggles down over his dark-ringed eyes. He felt so weary, every movement seemed freighted with extra weight. As 224's seven available F4Fs gathered on the runway to make a speedy launch, he waited and brooded, lost in a sense of dread. Never a praying man and always one to rely on himself and his skills, in that moment Marion reached a point beyond endurance. Perhaps the Mass had moved him. Perhaps he found the courage and strength to ask for help, something a proud and self-reliant man like him could rarely do. Or perhaps it stemmed from pure desperation as he clung to the last shreds of his morale. Whatever motivated him, Marion broke character and began to pray.

God, I'll give you anything you want from me. I'll sell my soul if that's what it takes. Just give me one more week of life.

The last of 224's Wildcats rolled down the runway. All too soon, it was Marion's turn again. He checked one more time on his division, then led his men into the air.

FORTY-FOUR

A WARRIOR'S GRAVE

Over Guadalcanal
October 3, 1942, early afternoon

THE FIVE WILDCAT PILOTS SCRATCHED AND DRAGGED THEIR WAY to thirty-four thousand feet, the highest any of them had ever been in an F4F at Guadalcanal. The aircraft were barely airworthy at that altitude, limping along at max power just above stall speed. Nobody had ever seen a Zero this high, so getting bounced from above seemed unlikely.

From the ground, Joe Renner reported that the Japanese raid split into two groups. It looked like one was orbiting a hundred miles from Cactus while the other—smaller signatures—pressed on. The radar signatures suggested the Japanese were sending in another fighter sweep ahead of their bombers.

The sky was a mass of cumulous clouds and canyons of dead space between them. Terrible weather, like fighting in a forest for the infantry—you'd never know the enemy was there until they were at point-blank range. Carl's division sat atop the worst of the weather, all five sets of eyes scrutinizing the sky around them for any sign of the Japanese.

Forty minutes after takeoff, Marion spotted the enemy. Nine Zeroes down low—so low they were but tiny dots scything through one of the canyons of open sky east of Lunga Point. They were so low and far away,

Marion deemed them no threat to him or his men. He could have stayed high and patrolled on, looking for the bombers that were their primary target. Renner's report of the radar signature of this raid suggested they were facing only Zeroes, so the chance of encountering bombers were slim. Marion knew that some of the American pilots had gotten to the point where they just wouldn't engage if they could avoid a scrap. Bob Galer also suspected this of some of his own men, as well as some in VF-5.

Avoiding combat was not in Marion Carl's nature. He was duty bound and naturally aggressive. No matter how spiritually exhausted and physically worn-out he was, he would never let an opportunity like this pass him by. Below him was the enemy, probably some of the same pilots who had shot up the Americans so badly the day before. So the battle was personal, and this attack would be payback.

He signaled his division and began to let down, gaining speed in his stubby little F4F. He kept upsun, spiraling downward in gentle banking turns to maintain that position relative to the Japanese. As he did, Lynch missed one of the turns and lost the division. It would be four versus nine now. With luck, numbers wouldn't matter. Marion's group had the high ground—and, hopefully, the advantage of surprise.

Down they went past twenty thousand feet. Nine thousand feet below them, the Japanese seemed completely unaware of their presence. The Zeroes flew along serenely in an extended, wide vee, turning from an easterly course back toward the northwest and probably for home. In doing so, they put the Marines almost directly behind them. It was a perfect setup.

A few thousand feet above now, Marion abandoned his spiraling approach and dove straight at the trail Zero on the far right of the formation. It was killing time. Each Marine picked a target, with Joe Bauer angling over to hit the far left wing of the vee with Ike Winter. Ken Frazier stayed tacked onto Marion, ready to protect him should more Zeroes burst out of the clouds and fall on them.

The Japanese didn't see the Marines until they were less than three hundred yards away. By then, it was too late. The trail A6M swelled in Marion's sight. He waited a split second longer, then unleashed all six guns on his target. From dead astern, with zero deflection, and at a hundred yards or less, the fusillade simply blew the Zero apart. Marion pulled up sharply and headed for a perch above the fight to determine his next move. Meanwhile, Frazier hammered the next Zero in line, sawing its wing off with a point-blank and deadly accurate burst. He was so close, spinning debris ricocheted off his F4F as the doomed fighter gyrated wildly out of control, flames spewing from its ruptured fuel tanks.

As Marion raced for altitude, one of the Zeroes arrowed almost vertically in pursuit. Frazier passed his first victim and saw the threat to Marion's tail. He pulled up sharply, bleeding off precious speed at an alarming rate. The Zero kept climbing—this bird and all the other A6Ms extraordinarily agile craft. Frazier half looped and got a quick sight picture. He opened fire from almost dead astern and cleared the threat off Marion's tail.

In mere seconds, the Marines had killed three of the nine Zero pilots. Almost simultaneously, Joe Bauer struck the other side of the formation. He flayed the trail Zero on the left with a long, accurate burst. The A6M spewed fire and smoke, rolled over, and fell off into the clouds below. Without missing a beat, Bauer pulled up and went after the next man in line. The Zeroes were trying to scatter now. His new target plus two others started to bank and climb to the left. Bauer still had speed and held the initiative. He cut inside their turn and pulled up to go after the next man in line. A long burst. Tracers vanished into the targeted Zero. Then one of his guns jammed. Two others followed suit. But Joe kept shooting, and his rounds struck home. A tongue of flame licked back from the Zero's engine, engulfing the fuselage and cockpit. As he eased off the trigger, Bauer realized he only had one gun functional now.

Ike Winter entered the fight in time to see a trio of Zeroes falling in flames. It was a massacre. The surprised Japanese did everything wrong. He made a pass on another A6M climbing after Marion, then used his speed to race for more altitude.

Like Bauer's guns, Marion's had also jammed. Immediately at the end of his pass, all six of them had quit. As he climbed, he tried unsuccessfully to clear them. He'd just scored his sixteenth kill, a number that put him only two behind the skipper. He wanted to do more damage, deal out more payback, and catch John L. But his luck ran dry this day. The guns refused to fire.

Right then, another formation of Zeroes broke out of the clouds and dropped on Marion and Winter. Both Americans were low on airspeed from the climb and terribly vulnerable. As they rolled into dives, Lynch appeared out of nowhere dead astern from one of the Zeroes. It blew up. He dove past, the other Zeroes scattering to save themselves.

Somewhere below, Frazier was alone and slow from his climbing half loop. He ducked into the side of a cumulous cloud, gaining speed in the safety of its milky depths. He popped out a minute later, ready to fight. A Zero saw him first. From below, it pulled up after him and unleashed a deadly barrage of 20 mm cannon shells that ripped open the Wildcat's vulnerable belly. The engine chuffed and gagged, and flames poured out of the cowling. Banking back toward the cloud, he plunged into it. The fire grew. His fuel gauge needle sagged toward empty. He realized the enemy shells had punctured his fuel line. He'd either explode or run out of fuel at any second. He had no choice. He jettisoned his canopy, released his seat harness, and rolled inverted. He fell right out of the cockpit, his body careening through space in the near-zero visibility of the cloud.

Suddenly, he tumbled into clear sky. Still thousands of feet above Savo Sound, he pulled the D-ring that deployed his chute. It streamed out from its backpack and jerked open. Now he hung there just below the fight, his chute's canopy a gigantic bull's-eye to predatory Japanese pilots. He instantly regretted not waiting longer to open his chute.

It didn't take long for a Zero to come after him. Its pilot banked along the cloud and bored in for the kill. Ken dangled from his chute, helpless. There was no way to run. No way to hide. No way to fight back.

The Zero chewed up the distance between it and Frazier in seconds. As it pulled into range, the Japanese pilot pulled his trigger. Tracers speared toward Ken.

Right then, Joe Bauer bounced the Zero from behind, firing furiously with his only working gun. His bullets tore into the A6M's fuselage, struck the engine, and totally distracted the Japanese pilot, who fired one last wild burst that missed Ken completely. Then, the Zero rolled and dove desperately for the nearest cloud. Joe made a wide turn around Ken, watching him descend into the water. On the dregs of his fuel, he dove for Fighter One.

In the parking area, Marion Carl climbed out of his F4F and waited for Joe Bauer to return. Bauer was the last man to land. When he climbed out of the cockpit, Carl called over to him. "How many?" he asked.

The Coach grinned ear to ear and held up four fingers. He didn't stay around long though. Bauer jumped into another F4F and went out to find Ken Frazier. Beyond Fike and the Duck floatplane, there was no organized search and rescue force at Guadalcanal, so it was often up to the pilots to locate their downed comrades.

Joe located Ken Frazier in the water floating in his Mae West and stayed with him until the destroyer *Nicholas* fished him out. Frazier was shaken, bruised, and slightly wounded in the leg. But he was alive.

While Carl and the others scrummed in the clouds, Rex Jeans and Charley Hughes set off into the jungle with a mud Marine captain and a platoon of riflemen. The day before, Rex had seen an F4F in a clearing about five miles south and two miles east of the perimeter. He made a pass over it and thought he saw movement. When John L. returned that evening, Jeans asked for permission to go out and find the crash site.

They spent the afternoon working their way through the jungle until they finally came upon an intact Wildcat resting upside down. Because its wheels had been pulled up, the pilot had clearly attempted a belly landing in this small and rugged patch of open ground. But the F4F's nose had struck something and flipped. Rex and Charley saw the number on the fuselage and recognized it as a VMF-224 aircraft. This could not be Scotty's plane.

They reached the cockpit and peered inside, where they found Red Kendrick dead and hanging from his seat harness, right hand still gloved and still holding the control stick. He died instantly from the impact when the aircraft flipped on its back.

Carefully, Rex and Charley slid under the F4F and undid Red's lap belt. They pulled their friend from the cockpit as the mud Marines rushed to help carry him clear of the crash site. The platoon had brought shovels, and as the sun started to sag in the west, they dug a shallow grave for this beloved member of VMF-223. Charley and Rex took turns digging along with the somber and respectful riflemen. They all knew what this felt like. Everyone on Guadalcanal had lost somebody close to them. It was the universal commonality that bound the defenders of Lunga Point, aerial and ground, together for the rest of their lives.

They laid Red in his warrior's grave, covering him quickly while others set fire to the F4F to deny the Japanese any intel from it. A few words were shared over the grave. What words could there be for such a moment? Nothing could ever ease the grief of this day, and they had no time left to search for some phrase or higher meaning that might stanch the pain. The platoon stood by and watched Red's two friends say a final goodbye, then they headed back to Henderson, the F4F's wreck burning like a funeral pyre in their wake.

FORTY-FIVE

THE GOD-GIVEN WEEK

Guadalcanal
October 5, 1942, late afternoon

T HE NINE REMAINING PILOTS OF VMF-223 SAT TOGETHER AT THE
end of another long day of patrols. The Japanese had not returned in
the air for two days, giving the alert pilots a bit of a break after the intensity of the previous week. The bit of downtime gave John L. a chance to
write home to his wife. He was as tired and war-weary as Marion Carl,
and the letter reflected that:

> *Dear Louise,*
>
> *. . . Have lost the best I started out with. Lost one the same day I was
> lost (Oct 2), would have rather it had been me instead of him. Hope I can
> see his family when I get back and tell them what a swell Marine he was.
> I know they will be proud of him. He just received the Distinguished Fly-
> ing Cross the day before. Really no justice in war, or he certainly would
> have gotten through.*
>
> *I have gotten 18 of them so far and am getting sick of seeing them burn
> and blow up in my face. Several times I have had to duck to get out of the
> debris. It isn't so funny when I am on the receiving end of it. An Admiral*

pinned the Navy Cross on me the other morning. I am proud to get it,
except that they think that it is good payment for seeing young pilots who
are sharing my tent go down in flames day after day. I don't mind saying
that I am sick of the whole mess.

All my love to you,
John

If the Japanese raids had ceased, the Tokyo Express runs had ramped
up again. It seemed like a mirror of the first week of September when the
enemy was trying to build strength for another offensive. That left the
torpedo bombers and SBD crews overworked, flying day and night again
to try to interdict these reinforcement runs. At some point soon, the Japanese would unleash another massive assault on the perimeter, and the
airfield would probably once more become a battleground. John L. and
the men of 223 would have to go through it again. At least this time, they
knew what to expect.

Bombers came at night to disrupt sleep. The flare-dropping Louis the
Louse harkened the arrival of yet another bombardment force offshore,
whose guns would rain high-explosive shells down on the Marines. Life
was reduced to a broken record, stuck on a single measure: *patrol, alert*
duty, get shelled, try to sleep in a hole.

John L. and his men now represented the best and most experienced
Marine fighter pilots in the entire Corps, closely followed by Bob Galer's 224. Through almost eight weeks of fighting, their numbers halved
from combat and illness, these nine survivors formed a hard-core veteran elite. Despite their battle fatigue, 223's aggressiveness never
flagged. It sometimes led to friction between them and the other two
F4F squadrons on the island. Nobody could argue with VMF-223's
success. The squadron claimed to have shot down almost ninety planes
since that first day on the island back in August. John L. had eighteen
of those, Marion sixteen and a half. Ken Frazier and Fred Gutt counted
themselves aces as well.

This was how the week Marion Carl prayed for played out: patrols and bombardments. On October 9, seven men of the squadron scrambled to intercept a reported inbound raid. One of the Fighting Five F4Fs that joined them suffered oxygen failure, and its pilot was lost. The squadron found no enemy planes.

When they returned to Fighter One, John L. learned that the entire squadron would be evacuated at the earliest possible moment. There were new F4F units coming in, Marines who had been furiously preparing to take 223's spot on the island.

Orders were issued. The men were told. There was relief. There was joy. There was a numb sense that this nightmare could actually be coming to an end.

Except, not. That night, MAG-23 ordered John L.'s men to fly one more mission. The indignation was palpable. Let somebody else do it. They had done their duty. They had their orders in hand. But the door to that blessed R4D that would carry them away from this hellhole would have to wait. Another Japanese task force had been sighted, and a maximum effort would go after them first thing in the morning. John L. would lead the escort force—fifteen F4Fs, including five from 223 plus three 212 pilots on temporary duty with them. It was his division's duty day, so Marion Carl and his pilots stayed behind. With John L. were Howard Marvin, Rapid Robert Read, Fred Gutt, Rex Jeans, and the three 212 men. John Dobbin and 224 filled out the remainder of the formation.

The strike force found the Tokyo Express. As the US bombers went in to attack the Japanese ships, a gaggle of floatplanes went after Smith's escort force. Seeing these aged biplanes charging them, John L. keyed his radio microphone and called out, "A suicide squad, boys. Follow me, and we'll give them what they want."

The Marines turned into their Japanese attackers. It was a massacre. In a matter of minutes, John L.'s men claimed nine of fifteen floatplanes shot down. Smith, Gutt, Jeans, Read, and Marvin all scored a kill each. The floatplanes were slow, vulnerable, and easy prey for the well-blooded Marines.[1]

All the F4Fs returned home. It was a banner way to end the worst and most defining period in their lives, and that night, they celebrated in the highest fashion. Long-hoarded bottles of Wild Turkey were pulled from hiding places and delivered to the squadron area. The men gathered in pajamas and pieces of uniforms to celebrate not only their last mission but Fred Gutt's twenty-third birthday as well. A group of mud Marines heard the news that John L. and his men were leaving in the morning. They somehow rounded up enough ingredients to bake a chocolate cake topped with white frosting that read "To VMF-223, From Rocky's Raiders."

The squadron had shot down ninety-five planes in fifty-two days of combat. John L. reigned as the high scorer. Marion could never make up the ground he had lost during his week in the jungle. That said, number two wasn't a bad position, especially since everyone—including John L.—knew that Marion had no peer in air-to-air battle. He was the best of them, second-place score be damned. Nobody flew like the lanky Oregon farm boy. Now, new units and new pilots—like Joe Bauer and Joseph "Joe" Foss—would take their place and shoulder the mantle that 223 had so furiously carried. The mud Marines would not be left without air cover. Instead, the blanket of F4Fs would only grow larger in the weeks and months to come.

John L.'s men had held the line until America could catch up with its own offensive and get the needed planes and pilots to where the fighting raged.

The next morning, the men stacked their locker boxes for shipment home, grabbed their duffel bags, and settled down to wait. Some of the men went out aboard the USS *Zeilin*. About half the ground echelon was forced to wait for another ride while Marion and John L. received priority travel orders. They would fly out of Henderson and island-hop home to San Francisco.

Dick Mangrum left Guadalcanal a day after John L. and Marion departed. He, too, had the golden ticket—the priority travel order—that would get him posthaste to Honolulu and then to San Francisco. He refused to leave until he knew his ground echelon would be pulled out and sent home too. But MAG-23 still needed these ground crew members to fuel and maintain the dwindling number of SBDs at Henderson. Finally, it was agreed that the VMSB-232 men would fold under VMSB-231 until the last half of the month, and then they would be put aboard the first possible ship.

That deal done, Dick flew to the New Hebrides, where he made sure the squadron's sick and wounded in the hospitals would not be sent back up to Guadalcanal once they returned to duty. Ed Eades was the exception. He *wanted* to get back. He returned from the hospital and got to Guadalcanal in November for at least several days before being ordered home.

The fact was, the Navy wanted Marion Carl, John L. Smith, and Dick Mangrum stateside as soon as possible for propaganda purposes. The men duly obeyed orders, but when they left, the ground echelons from both squadrons ended up more or less orphaned. Capt. Howard Marvin became 223's skipper, but he was already well on his way home to San Francisco with the other pilots. Ultimately, it meant small groups of enlisted men, led by corporals and sergeants, ended up going out at different times.

Their misery didn't end when the flying stopped. On the night of October 13/14, two Japanese battleships steamed into Savo Sound and hurled a thousand 14-inch shells at the Marine perimeter. The bombardment was unlike anything the Marines had ever experienced. Even the World War I vets among them had no frame of reference for the ferocity and power of these massive naval guns. Men broke down. Others simply vanished in the nightmare of flames and shrapnel. The shelling set fire to the bulk of the aviation fuel supply, which burned for hours and cast the airfields in a hellish glow through the early-morning hours of the fourteenth. When dawn broke, forty-eight of the ninety airplanes around the airfields lay smashed and broken. Most of the rest were riddled with shrapnel. It was a catastrophic event that scarred those who lived through it for the rest of their lives.

Two days later, the last men of VMF-223 were ordered to board the destroyer-transport *McFarland*, which had raced to Guadalcanal to deliver desperately needed aviation fuel. As the gas was offloaded, 223's skeletal, disease-racked maintainers climbed aboard ship.

Thirty minutes later, a Japanese air raid reached the area, spotted the *McFarland*, and attacked. A bomb struck the fantail, destroying a barge tied up alongside the transport and detonating some of the avgas. At least four enlisted men from 223 died in the conflagration.

The vessel limped to Tulagi, where about fifty surviving 223 ground crew members debarked. They spent four days marooned there before hitching a ride aboard the USS *Southard*, which dropped them off at Efate.

The saga of the ground echelon turns particularly grim at this point. As if being bombed, shelled, stricken with illness, and burned alive by flaming avgas on their ride out of the nightmare weren't enough, at Efate they ran into REMF officers—Rear-Echelon Motherfuckers— who pitied nobody and cut these men zero slack. These were noncombat support types whose jobs were vital but who experienced far safer conditions than what the combat veterans went through. The natural tension between the two groups was made worse by the spit-and-polish demands of the REMFs. When a man doesn't even own a complete uniform after months in combat, and a lieutenant without a sweat stain chews him out for his lack of military bearing, the cruelest side of the service was laid bare for those men who had endured so much.

The senior man in this contingent of fifty exhausted ground crew members was a corporal. Without an officer, these men had zero pull and no authority. This was the collateral damage the Marine Corps inflicted on VMF-223 when the Corps pulled John L. from command to send him on the hero tour. By then, Smitty was being shuffled before reporters and cameras, out of communication with his squadron. He had no idea of the trouble the ground echelon endured until years later.

After a few days marooned on a small island in Vila Harbor, on Efate, they boarded the cargo ship *Castor*. That's where the trouble began. The martinet skipper of this vessel was so appalled by the condition of his Marine passengers that he banned them from the dining areas aboard ship until they could find "proper" uniforms.

These men had escaped from Guadalcanal with literally the clothes on their backs and nothing more. Their clothing was filthy, bloodstained, tattered rags by the time they reached the *Castor*. Denied food after eight weeks of starvation rations, they were thrown into an empty forward hold without even blankets or bedding and told by the tin-pot tyrant commanding the ship that they would be put to work for the duration of their journey.

Some of the sailors took pity on the Marines and donated clothing until enough men had at least something resembling proper attire to get some food. Other Marines broke into the hold next to theirs and discovered supplies originally slated to go to the cruiser *Indianapolis*. They quickly appropriated everything they could to make their own space a little more comfortable.

The captain then ordered them to scrape and paint the ship as it sailed to New Zealand. Day after day, these Marines spent the journey on their knees laboring away. Two of the 223 men collapsed while working deep belowdecks in an enclosed space, overcome by paint fumes. The Marines retaliated by raiding the paint locker one night and tossing all its contents overboard. So much for that duty.

A brief stop in Auckland revealed that not only did the 223 castaways lack proper uniforms for shore liberty but they also hadn't been paid in months. Nobody had any money. A major managed to secure ten dollars for each man, and the men went into the town for a twelve-hour respite from their nautical tormentor. When they returned to the ship, they saw that a load of fuel drums had been taken aboard in their absence. One Marine, thinking that this meant they were going to head back to Guadalcanal, turned and walked away from *Castor*, never to be seen by the 223 vets again.

The rest of the men reboarded and enjoyed a truly miserable, mind-numbing monthlong voyage back to San Francisco. They steamed under the Golden Gate in mid-December, about a week behind the men who had gone out on the *Zeilin* on October 11. Captain Marvin met them as they came ashore and gave them money and a twenty-four-hour liberty before they headed to San Diego, their ultimate destination.

Marvin meant well, but he unleashed a furious band of Marines on the San Francisco bars. They drank, fought, and fornicated their way through the Tenderloin neighborhood in righteous fury, like springs suddenly uncoiled. The next morning, Marvin discovered that half his new arrivals were sleeping off benders with black eyes and bruises in local jail cells. He spent the day bailing everyone out.

That afternoon, the squadron, mostly united for the first time since leaving Guadalcanal, headed for the train station for the trans-California ride to San Diego. By then, the men knew that John L. Smith and Marion Carl were national heroes. They saw their skipper on the cover of *Life* magazine, heard John L. and Marion interviewed on the radio, and saw their names in the paper. The two men were still carrying out what was derisively called the "rubber chicken tour" for the Navy Department. The squadron headed south without them. But when they boarded their train, the officer in charge of their meal vouchers had somehow lost the coupons. Without money, clothes, or food, they rolled through the night and reached San Diego the next morning, pissed off, bitter, and yearning for another brawl that would let them bleed off the rage they felt.

It had been a hell of a hard way to come home from war.

MANGRUM'S MEN HAD IT A LITTLE EASIER. WHILE A FEW WENT OUT with 223 aboard the *McFarland* or on other lifts, the last bunch departed the island on October 21, care of the USS *Hovey*. Gradually, VMSB-232's men made their way in dribs and drabs back to California. The last man back was Leland Thomas's gunner, Ed Eades. He reached San Diego sometime in mid-December, when he was greeted with open arms by Lewis Macias. The two friends turned brothers by combat promptly went out to celebrate their reunion with a grand pub crawl.

Wearing fresh dress blues, they entered one club, sat down at a booth, and did their best to catch up. Macias related how Don McCafferty, on his first day back in San Diego, went out to get a new uniform ordered— and was very nearly killed by a falling desk. Of all the things that could have happened to their pilot, who had flown to the ragged edge and beyond, being crushed by incompetent movers trying to get a desk into a high-rise office building seemed something straight out of one of Tom Moore's cartoons.

As they talked, both men noticed a pair of attractive blondes sitting at the bar. The Marines made eye contact with them. The night seemed to be developing well. The flirting from across the bar continued until, properly encouraged, the Guadalcanal vets stood to go introduce themselves. They didn't get the chance. Two sailors, clueless to what had been going on, crashed the party and got to the women first.

Lewis and Ed eyed each other, nodded, and waded into the fray, fists flying.

The sailors, no veterans of Starvation Island, never had a chance.

EPILOGUE

Aftermath

Amazing how one cab ride and a good-night kiss can change a life.

Marion Carl fell in love with Edna Kirvin that first night in New York. Until that evening, he'd been exchanging letters with a woman in Pensacola, Florida. He ended the Florida relationship immediately and spent every spare moment he had with Edna. Courting her. Loving her. Sharing his story with her. She became the one person in his life to know everything. For her, that knowledge was a sacred trust.

He proposed in December. She accepted. He took her back to Hubbard, Oregon, with him to meet his mother and extended family. When they rolled into town, Marion was greeted as a returning hero. Behind their hands, though, the town gossiped about the unlikely match: Oregon farmer and New York model. People said it would never last.

The wags had a point. Marion and Edna's differences were many. His first Christmas gift to her was a hunting rifle. She'd never held a gun. But she learned to shoot it, and despite the distinct lack of romance in the gift, it became a treasured part of the family's belongings. Marion was stoic, rough and tumble, with many edges. Still he had presence and knew exactly how to be a gentleman. The Marine Corps gave him that polish.

They married after a whirlwind wartime romance. Within the bond of marriage, they began to get to know each other. Countless such marriages failed during or just after the war, or they led to miserable unions and dysfunctional families. Marion and Edna went through all the phases of marriage. They fought. They were headstrong. They loved each other with passionate intensity that they rarely let others see. For all their differences, the commonalities they sensed in each other that first night in New York entwined them in a way that carried them through every challenge, every storm.

Marion went on to lead VMF-223 in a second tour in the Solomons in 1943, scoring two more kills before he was pulled from combat again. He never caught John L.'s score and missed tying him by half a plane, the other half of which went to Kirk Armistead.

The score didn't matter. Marion went on to have one of the most illustrious careers of any Marine aviator. As a test pilot, he set countless records. He flew higher and faster than any other naval aviator. He was the first Marine to fly a helicopter. The first to fly a jet. The first Marine to land a jet on an aircraft carrier. He carried out high-altitude, top-secret recon missions in unarmed F2H Banshee straight-wing jets over Communist China in the 1950s, and he took one of the first Marine brigades into Vietnam in the mid-1960s. There, he was one of the few brigadier generals to fly frequent combat missions—in helicopters.

He retired as a two-star general in the early 1970s, one of the last Guadalcanal Marines to shed the uniform.

Marion outlasted Dick Mangrum, who retired in 1967. Dick had gone on to command the Corps of Cadets at NAS Corpus Christi after the war bond tour in 1942. He was an exceptional, conscientious officer who never forgot the men of 232. A year after the pilots of 232 returned home, most of them or their families received belated Navy Crosses and Distinguished Flying Crosses. Dick made sure his enlisted men were taken care of as well, and he helped several of them—including his gunner Dennis Byrd and Ed Eades—secure orders to flight training. Both men went out as F4U pilots and saw combat in the final year of WWII, carrying the spirit of 232 with them against the tattered remains of the Japanese empire.

After a short stint commanding a dive-bomber training group in the Southeast, Dick returned to overseas duty and combat in January 1945, first as a staff officer and later as the skipper of MAG-45 in the Central Pacific.

Over the next fifteen years, Dick's career crossed paths with both Marion's and John L.'s. The three men were part of the rugged heart of the postwar Corps, forged in the fires of Guadalcanal and tempered in subsequent deployments. But Dick added a layer of intellectual acuity that elevated his thinking beyond that of most of his peers—and superiors. While on the faculty of the Naval War College, he wrote dense, broad-minded policy papers as the new Cold War developed with the Soviet Union. During Korea, he led MAG-12 into combat in 1951 before becoming the Marine liaison officer to the 5th Air Force.

In 1956, Dick earned his first star and played a major role in the shaping of Marine Corps training, education, and strategic philosophy through the next decade. In 1965, he became the first Marine Gray Eagle—the naval aviator who had earned his wings before anyone else still active and in uniform.

He retired as a three star after having served as the assistant commandant of the Marine Corps from 1965 to 1967. He settled on the East Coast not far from Cherry Point, North Carolina, and lived quietly in retirement until his death in 1985. His two children grew up to have successful lives and careers, his daughter marrying a naval officer who later made admiral.

Dick's beloved wife, Virginia Mangrum, passed away a few years before he did, and life without her left Dick deeply depressed and missing her terribly. Their marriage had begun in the depths of the Great Depression and had lasted through wars, seismic world events, space flight, and the dawn of the digital age. It had been a half-century adventure together through the highest circles of the Marine Corps.

In 1991, Marion Carl invited a young graduate student from the University of Oregon to his retirement home on the Umpqua River, just outside Roseburg, to discuss his career and memories of Guadalcanal. This was a risk for Marion. The university was not known for producing graduate students with favorable opinions of the military, and he must have been worried when an out-of-shape twenty-two-year-old with a mullet rolled up in a 1956 Ford Victoria.

He gave the kid a chance, invited him into his living room, and spent the day recalling the early days of his Marine Corps career. When he told the story of bringing Edna home to Hubbard, Marion added, "Those townspeople said it would never last."

"Well, did it?" his guest asked.

Marion offered a sly grin. "Wanna meet her?"[1]

They loved each other fiercely, weathered all the ups and downs of a military marriage. In the end, they built an amazing life together. They had two children, a son, Bruce, and a daughter, Lyanne, both of whom grew up to have successful, happy lives.

Marion often told people that his first star was all Edna's. The old adage "Anyone can make colonel. It takes a great wife to make general" was absolutely true in the postwar Marine Corps. The social events surrounding a life in the Corps could sometimes be as important as the best fitness reports. She was dynamic on his arm—a charming, brilliant, and charismatic woman with verve and energy to match Marion's. She loved life in the Corps; it exercised her inner extrovert. Marion was the opposite, an introvert more at home in a cockpit than at a cocktail party. She drew him out and stayed on his wing. And in the roughest moments of his career, she was always there for him, the one rock-solid source of support he could trust implicitly.

On the night of June 28, 1998, the couple were home alone in their house built above the river. Marion was in declining health by then and had withdrawn from public events, living with the first stages of Alzheimer's disease. A local teenage methamphetamine addict kicked in the front door, wielding a double-barreled shotgun. Edna had been sitting at the kitchen table. He leveled the shotgun at her. Marion, asleep in the nearby primary bedroom, awoke to the commotion and rushed to his wife's aid. She saw him come through the doorway and called out to him. He flung himself in front of her just as the home invader pulled the trigger. Marion took the full blast from both barrels and died instantly. With his last act, he shielded his beloved wife and saved her life. She was hit by several pellets in the head, but the wounds were grazing and she recovered.

The killer was run down and captured in California. He became the youngest man in Oregon to be sentenced to death following his trial. He languished in solitary confinement and then death row.

A few years after Edna's death in 2007, Bruce Carl asked the state of Oregon to commute the sentence of his father's killer. He was taken off death row and given a new sentence: life without the possibility of parole. When asked why he did it, Bruce replied, "My dad was dead. Nothing was going to bring him back. What was the point of taking another life?"

FINAL NOTE

John L.

Lexington, Oklahoma
June 1953

B RIG. GEN. CHARLES FIKE WAS THREE YEARS IN HIS GRAVE AT
Arlington, but the words he had spoken that day on the *Long Island*
in August 1941 remained burned in the memories of every man who had
heard them. Fike had displayed courage and skill rescuing Ens. Christian
"Chris" Fink and his gunner back in September 1942, but the opinion of
most who served with Fike on Guadalcanal never really changed. Those
blunt words spoken on the little carrier's flight deck poisoned the well,
and whenever he didn't lead from the tip of the spear or at least fly some
combat with John L. or Dick, he was never able to recover the respect
he'd lost with that speech.

Fike left the service and went to work as an executive engineer for the
A. G. Budd Company in Pennsylvania. In the spring of 1950, he lost
control of his car during a rainy late Sunday night's drive home. Fike's
car slammed into a tractor trailer, and the impact catapulted him through
the windshield. Rescue crews found him pinned under one of the tractor
trailer's tires. Though they rushed him to a hospital, he'd suffered extensive injuries, including a compound fracture of the right leg and bleeding

in his brain. He lived for three days, developed gangrene in his injured leg, and died on May 3, 1950.

The irony of it all, John L. came to discover, was Fike had been right. John L. and his pilots had been disposable Marines. They bought the time the country needed. They became heroes in a moment of desperation when the country still wrestled out of its prewar cocoon.

In 1953, John L. Smith stood beside US Route 77 at his family's old house in Lexington, Oklahoma. As he thought about those words from 1942, they took on new meaning. He had returned home a couple of times since the end of the war. He'd stopped in to see old friends and family when he came home from his second Pacific tour in 1945. And he had returned in 1948 when his dad passed. Now, he'd come to Oklahoma one more time to see two aunts and some old friends before he headed out the door for his third combat deployment—this time in Korea.

The family house looked about the same. But the sign that his dad's friend, Ted Keller, had erected in 1942 proudly proclaiming it the "Birthplace of Marine Ace Major John L. Smith" lay on the ground, shattered and mud covered. A storm had blown through Lexington a year and a half ago, knocking it down. The sign had not been repaired or replaced.

Discarded.

One of the photos taken at NAS Anacostia graced the cover of *Life* magazine's December 7, 1942, edition. He'd been feted and celebrated wherever he went. Yet at home, after the honeymoon period that most returning vets experience with their wives, Louise began to turn bitter. From the outside, John L. was a man with his future secured and with the backing of a nation that worshipped his exploits at Guadalcanal. The humble Midwest grace he projected made him even more popular, especially when he said such things as "I was a Marine rifleman in charge of a fighter squadron." In the Corps, everyone was above all a rifleman. Not even fame shook that identity from John L.'s sense of self.

In February 1943, he and Louise traveled to the White House, where they met President Franklin D. Roosevelt. FDR presented him with the Medal of Honor in a brief but memorable ceremony that culminated with

John L. bending at the waist so the president in his wheelchair could place America's highest award for valor around the Oklahoman's neck.

He returned to combat as the executive officer of MAG-32, which supported MacArthur's troops during the Philippines campaign. Later, when John L. was acting commander of MAG-32, his men helped support the 41st Infantry Division as it landed on Jolo Island in April 1945. By war's end, his men had flown thousands of bombing sorties during close air support missions that saved countless lives of American and Filipino troops locked in fierce combat with Japanese defenders who routinely fought to the death.

It all looked so promising. In the years that followed, Smith polished his pedigree with a NATO tour and another as a staff aide to the chief of naval operations, Adm. Forrest Sherman. On New Year's Day 1951, he earned a promotion to colonel. His first star lay just on the horizon.

For now, Korea awaited. It would be his third combat tour and second war. The multiple tours weren't that unusual for the Guadalcanal Marines who remained in the Corps. They were professional warriors, some of whose service stretched the distance from those first hours at Ewa during the Pearl Harbor attack to the final missions before the Japanese called it quits in August 1945.

There was a dark side to all this. Louise and he had constant problems. Where the outside world venerated John L., she tore into him whenever she had the chance. The tension and bitterness that grew between the two fostered infidelity, which spun things even further out of control. At night in their unhappy marital bed, John L.'s subconscious revisited the ghosts of 223. Nightmares followed him through the rest of the war and beyond. He self-medicated with alcohol, which exacerbated everything. It also made him more crusty and more willing to speak his mind. Professionally, his utter devotion to aviation and his willingness to say or do anything to protect and foster that part of the Corps made him enemies. Some were jealous peers who took political shots at him from the wings. Others were officers above him in the chain of command who wielded considerable influence on his career prospects. He didn't care, but he was surprised to learn that when his nation made him a hero, it also put a target on his back.

The service, at its worst, could be warped by petty envy.

THAT DAY IN JUNE 1953, JOHN L., LOST IN THOUGHTS OF THE PAST, went into his hometown only to discover that most of the people he'd known in his youth had either died or moved away. He was thirty-eight now, approaching middle age. His hair was thinning and flecked with gray. His eyes were flanked by spreading crow's feet and dark bags beneath them—signs of stress and tormented sleep.

As he walked down Main Street, he recalled the canvas banner welcoming him home the first time he had returned. It stretched across one block, hung from the buildings on either side just before the makeshift platform the residents had built for his homecoming. In gratitude for his flying on Guadalcanal, they had given him the watch he now wore on his wrist.

He'd been America's Ace of Aces then.

Richard Bong of the US Army Air Forces eventually took that title, and the banner was long gone. Somebody had told him that the Bryant family purchased it and used it on their covered wagon, since canvas was unavailable during the war. For the last few years before peace broke out, John L.'s father watched the wagon, pulled by a pair of horses, pass by his house every morning and afternoon as the Bryants carried schoolkids between Denton and Stovall, where the roads were too muddy and rutted for bus and car traffic.

It was a surreal thing, seeing an icon of the nineteenth-century migration across the prairie sporting the remains of a canvas banner as its covering, *Home of John L. Smith* still visible to onlookers. Eventually, better roads and better vehicles kicked the Bryants' wagon into retirement, and the remains of the welcome-home banner disappeared altogether.

There were no signs in downtown now, no trappings of hometown pride for their native son who had joined the president at the White House and had fought his way across the Pacific. During that walk along Main Street, he did run into a few old family friends. Roy Sherman and

John Washburn rushed to greet him. They had been pall bearers at his father's funeral in 1948. They were embarrassed about the sign on the outskirts of town and quick to mention the town had already raised funds for a replacement. John L. just laughed it off. Underneath that reaction, though, lay the deeper question. *What happens to America's heroes when they're no longer needed?*

An impromptu fried chicken lunch at the Shermans' house followed. John L. learned the goings-on of old friends and schoolmates, then excused himself to go visit Cora Burkett, his old teacher who had given him the watch the day he came home in 1942. She was the last of the major influences of his life, retired now, hair gray. She was delighted to see him.

The visit lasted only a short while before he said his farewells. It was his last solo trip through Lexington.

JOHN L. SMITH COMMANDED MAG-33 IN THE FINAL WEEKS OF THE Korean War. He earned a Bronze Star with Valor for his service that summer. He spent his off-hours helping refugee and orphaned South Korean children and then returned to the States in 1954 to attend the National War College—the next step on the road to his first star. He had shone through every command and duty station. Those who served under him considered him the best natural leader they had ever known in the Corps. Marion Carl thought him the "strongest squadron commander and finest combat leader" he'd encountered during his career. John L. was always a task master, demanding the best out of everyone in his command. He balanced that attitude with quiet compassion and steadfast loyalty. He never shied away from going toe-to-toe with anyone—peer or superior—on behalf of his men.

The old Guadalcanal gang leveled up through the 1950s. Marion Carl got his star. So did Robert Galer and, of course, Dick Mangrum. John L. served time at Quantico and became the number two officer in the Division of Aviation. It seemed a lock that he'd get what he wanted more than anything else out of life: a chance to be a general in his beloved Corps.

But John L. never got his star. In 1959, the selection board, composed of six ground Marines and three aviators, recommended he not be made a general. Some thought the decision was payback for his abrasive and fanatical defense of Marine aviation. Others thought his drinking might be a factor. This explanation seems unlikely, however, given how many senior Marines drank copiously after World War II. Louise was no Edna Carl, which didn't help matters either.

There were also dark rumors that one of the aviators on the selection board had been one of the Guadalcanal vets John L. did not get along with during the 1942 deployment. Some people believed that this member used his spot on the board to drive a knife in John L.'s back to settle the old score.

Despite the speculation and rumors and no matter what the real reasons were, the Corps was an up-or-out organization. When John L. didn't get promoted, it was the death knell for his career.

His being passed over was a devastating blow. His entire life, entire identity, was consumed by the Corps. Now, well into middle age, he had to start from scratch without a plan B. He'd struggled with depression since Guadalcanal, carrying the wounds of grief for twenty years for the pilots he lost. The double-edged sword of relaxing the barriers between ranks had made VMF-223 the best, tightest-knit squadron in the Marine Corps in 1942, but his bonds with the men he had lost left him a tortured soul.

His marriage, long frayed and tension-racked, started to fall apart. He spiraled so deeply into depression that he voluntarily checked himself into Bethesda Naval Hospital just before New Year's Eve of 1959. He'd done perhaps the most courageous thing of his life: he'd asked for help.

The mid–Cold War Navy had no effective treatment system for combat veterans dealing with depression. By now, the shine of his Medal of Honor was dimmed by seventeen years. The pull and prestige it once carried in wartime were long gone. To the Bethesda staff, he was just another WWII veteran, another Marine colonel, and nothing more.

He was told the psychiatric staff was on vacation. It was the holidays, after all. They admitted him, then locked him in the psych ward, where he spent twelve days in confinement.

When Marion Carl heard the news, he rushed to see his old skipper. He found John L. in terrible condition. He did what he could to bring some comfort to his old friend, but Smith needed real professional help, along with a proper diagnosis. Of course, the understanding of combat-related post-traumatic stress disorder (PTSD) was decades away. The Navy and the Corps tended to see any sort of psychological issue as weakness, and most officers avoided what little treatment there was for it out of fear that it could impact their careers.

In mid-January, after confining him for almost two weeks, Bethesda arranged for John L. to receive seven 30-minute sessions with a flight surgeon. The surgeon had no background in psychiatric care. Nevertheless, he diagnosed John L. with depression. Bethesda took no further action beyond releasing him later in the month.

John L. was honorably discharged and retired from the Marine Corps eight months later. He held America's highest award for valor, the Medal of Honor, the Navy Cross that Nimitz bestowed on him, the Distinguished Flying Cross, a Silver Star, a Legion of Merit, and five Bronze Stars. There were few Marines in 1960 who wore as many awards for courage in combat as John L. Smith.

Cast aside by the service he loved, he turned to a civilian career with Grumman Aviation. The company that produced the aircraft he flew on Guadalcanal seemed like a good fit for him initially. Grumman made him their foreign sales rep. It was a chance at a new life and a fresh start.

He and Louise separated in February 1961, only a few months after he left the Corps. The courts finalized the divorce in May 1962, and on June 9, 1962, he remarried to a woman also named Louise.

Things looked up for John L. that year. He was invited to the White House and met John F. Kennedy in the Rose Garden. The president took the time to speak to him for several minutes during the event.

It was a rare highlight. Less than two years after getting the job at Grumman, John L. moved on to North American Rocketdyne Corporation. He and his second wife moved to California and bought a home in Encino. Working again as a foreign rep, he made many trips to Europe to help convince NATO allies to purchase the company's rocket systems, some of which were being used in US strategic missiles and NASA satellite launchers.

At face value, John L.'s career seemed to thrive. In reality, he'd become a one-man dog and pony show for an aerospace corporation. He was the war hero with the Medal of Honor the company trotted out to potential buyers. His job was to schmooze, play golf, and be the aging war hero endorsing the company's products.

It was a hard, steep fall for a man who once had been a lynchpin in the defense of Guadalcanal. Another such Marine, Red Mike Edson, faced a similar fall a decade before. He'd been the man atop Bloody Ridge, standing in a bullet-torn night, urging his men to fight and hold the waves of Japanese storming the slopes. That history-defining moment cast a long shadow over the rest of Edson's life. Nothing he achieved afterward ever measured up. Thirteen years later, his life came to a tragic end. He died by suicide in 1955, using the carbon monoxide from his car's exhaust.

John L. battled depression and almost certainly PTSD throughout the 1960s. While in France on a business trip, he attempted suicide by driving a car into a brick wall. He survived, but the underlying issues he couldn't cope with were never treated.

In 1970, as his career with Rocketdyne slowly failed, he plunged into another suicidal depression. He attempted to kill himself again, this time with a shotgun. When he pulled the trigger, the weapon misfired. The luck or fate or destiny that carried him through Guadalcanal's worst moments gave him another chance.

In 1972, he was fired from his job as director of foreign sales at Rocketdyne. He was fifty-seven years old. The search for a new job did not go well. He was told he was too old. The final words of his employer at Rocketdyne burned him to the core. As he was being fired, his superiors called him worthless, washed up. The subsequent rejections at every place he applied seemed to confirm the opinion. Thirty years after Fike's speech, the skipper of 223 had been expended by the Corps he loved and by the country he loved even more.

In May that year, some of the veterans of Guadalcanal held a reunion to honor the thirty-year anniversary of the battle. When John L. arrived, the hundreds of veterans in the conference center gave him a standing ovation. Three decades and a lifetime later, he was still the man who symbolized the spirit of resistance to all those who had held the perimeter against every Japanese attack.

The gesture lifted his spirits, and for the weekend, he was the John L. of old. Charismatic, happy, he caught up with the men of his squadron who attended the reunion. He projected himself as a man entering his senior years happy, fit, and healthy.

It was all an affectation.

On June 9, 1972, a month after the reunion, John L. and his second wife were preparing to go out to dinner to celebrate their tenth wedding anniversary. Louise had just showered and was blow-drying her hair in the upstairs bathroom.

John L. had retrieved one of his prized souvenirs from World War II—a 7.65 mm Japanese Hamada Type 1 pistol. Based on the Model 1910 Colt, it looked like a rougher version of the American-made weapon. The Japanese intended to replace the ubiquitous 8 mm Nambu with it as the Imperial Japanese Army's standard sidearm, but production ended in 1944 after only a few years. Only a few thousand had been produced, and most of those ended up in units based in Manchuria. A few found their way into the Pacific, however, when the Japanese army redeployed units from the mainland to defend the Philippines or other islands. John L. likely had acquired it in the Philippines on his post-Guadalcanal deployment.

He carried the weapon to the backyard, sat down, racked it, and put the barrel to the right side of his head, just behind his temple. He pulled the trigger.

The weapon misfired. The same luck, the same fate or destiny, had held yet again. He had cheated death at the hands of the Japanese, the Chinese, and the North Koreans in service of his country. And now, he had cheated it three times by his own hand.

He'd been given one more chance at life.

He could have stood up, walked back to the house with Louise none the wiser, and put the gun away. A night on the town awaited. He had his Marine Corps retirement pay. He had the stipend that comes with the Medal of Honor. He could have retired and lived a life of comfortable leisure.

The life he wanted, he never got. He wanted what Marion Carl and Dick Mangrum had—a career that led to the highest circles of Marine Corps leadership. Instead, he became a corporation's captive Medal of Honor winner. Discarded now, his self-esteem in tatters, and the ghosts of Guadalcanal his constant companions, he lived a life of quiet torment and desperate sadness.

He racked the slide again. The 7.65 mm round that misfired flew out of the chamber, its brass dented by the firing pin.

He chambered another round and put the gun to his head again. Enough. The universe kept sending him messages that it wanted him to live. He kept pushing back. This time, the universe—and the country that had so disastrously failed him—lost. John L. pulled the trigger and died instantly.[1]

NEWS OF JOHN L.'s SUICIDE SWEPT THROUGH THE VETERANS OF GUA-dalcanal and left 223's pilots stunned. Fred Gutt in particular was shocked by the news. His skipper had looked so good, so dynamic, at the reunion the month before. It seemed impossible he'd been hiding such demons. Bill Brooks later said he was devastated by the news. He had no idea his old skipper was struggling—if he had, he would have done anything for him. Clayton Canfield echoed those sentiments. Even ten days before his own death in 2003, even mentioning John L.'s suicide took an emotional toll on him.

A few brief news articles of his death hit the wire services. None of those mentioned his suicide. The papers back in Oklahoma largely ignored the story. He'd long since left his roots behind, and his old community had moved on. The *Van Nuys News*, a local Southern California paper, covered the story in perhaps the most detail, focusing on the fact that John L. Smith, a Medal of Honor recipient, could not find employment after his termination from Rocketdyne.

Gone was an American who brought a group of young second lieutenants into a cauldron of violence on the ground and in the air—a cauldron that, until that point, had no peer in American history. Under his leadership, the men went from half-trained, raw greenhorns to the Corps' most deadly fighter squadron, credited with officially shooting down 111½ Japanese aircraft in the fifty-three days they served on Guadalcanal.

John L.'s death underscored so many problems with the way America treated its war heroes and veterans. These same issues are challenging Americans today after twenty years of war in the Middle East and Afghanistan. Hopefully, when generations to come look back, they will conclude that today's generation learned the lessons that John L.'s did not and that today's military and citizens did a better job providing the treatment and care our veterans need. Only then will John Lucian Smith's death be less of a tragedy and more of a signpost on the way to understanding combat trauma.

In 1998, Lexington, Oklahoma, placed a beautiful granite marker at a city park off Route 77, honoring John L. Smith. It took almost half a century, but Ted Keller's storm-tossed sign was finally replaced.

THEIR LEGACY

FOR FIFTY-THREE DAYS, JOHN L. SMITH AND DICK MANGRUM LED their squadrons during the most crucial campaign of World War II. Had Guadalcanal fallen in August or September 1942, the effects of that disaster would have been incalculable. At a minimum, almost twenty thousand Americans would have almost certainly been killed or captured. Positionally, the Japanese would have been in better shape to push an offensive forward into the New Hebrides. The offensive on New Guinea to take Port Moresby would have been renewed, and how the Allies could have held in the Pacific with Guadalcanal lost and the Japanese singularly focused on that island again is hard to imagine.

The loss of Guadalcanal would not have altered the ultimate outcome of the war, however. The atomic bombs were coming. It was just a matter of when they would be unleashed on the Home Isles. That said, the entire subsequent history of the Pacific War would have looked radically different and would probably have been more costly to the Allies. Moreover, in the fall of 1942, Guadalcanal took on greater importance than just the strategic equation in the South Pacific. It became a titanic test of national will. Could the United States, struggling to create a globally deployable military, defeat the blooded veterans of Imperial Japan? Could a nation so isolationist rise to the occasion and overcome its own inexperience in offensive amphibious warfare to prevail after so many mistakes?

Holding Guadalcanal that fall settled all those questions. It came at a terrible cost. When John L., Dick, and Marion were introduced to their

American audience that November 1942, the country still did not recognize the true nature of this global war or what it was going to cost to win it. The peacetime trappings left the vets in shock and disgust after so many weeks of starvation rations on Guadalcanal. A college football game, dining in the capital, the fashions worn, and the parties thrown all seemed divorced from reality.

November was the turning point for that home-front fantasy. With the North Africa invasion, the fury of the fighting on Guadalcanal, and the start of the air campaign against Germany, the trickle of War Department telegrams that spread from the Pentagon to Main Streets everywhere began to grow. About twenty thousand had been sent out by the time the three Marines came home—a shocking number to Americans today but one that represented a fraction of the losses experienced in the Civil War or in World War I. The twenty thousand killed were diffused throughout the 150 million people then living in the United States.

After November 1942, that sentiment changed. The trickle of deaths became a stream. And at times, the stream became a torrent. As the losses piled up, every street in every town seemed to have a Gold Star family. Some lost every son in the service. Others lost their only child. Each death resonated out of those households and affected neighborhoods and communities in ways that could not be fully understood for years. If Marion, John L., and Dick found the United States not serious about the war in November 1942, the next year produced a grim and tenacious American resolve to see it through despite every heartbreak the Axis inflicted. The War Department sent out nearly 410,000 of the dreaded "We regret to inform you" telegrams by August 1945. Additionally, about 68,000 American workers—men and women—were killed in industrial accidents from 1942 to 1945. Some 300,000 more were permanently disabled by injuries in the war factories.

The Americans of 1942 were playing at war. The Americans of 1945 were hardened, tempered, and heartbroken by it. The nation was a veteran war maker; its military had gone from a force smaller than that of the Netherlands in 1940 to a force unsurpassed by any other nation, with only the Soviet Union as a peer. That metamorphosis began at

Guadalcanal. And the two squadrons that held the line during those desperate weeks in August and September proved to be the edge that carried the day against the Japanese. The repeated destruction or scattering of Japanese reinforcement convoys and the debacle of Colonel Oka's barge force ensured that Kawaguchi attacked Red Mike Edson without the heavy weapons, supplies, and additional manpower needed to overwhelm the Raiders and break the perimeter. John L. Smith and VMF-223 ensured that Japanese raids could not destroy Henderson Field or knock it out for long. Ultimately, the men of the squadron did exactly what Lieutenant Colonel Fike required of them: they bought time with their lives, time the Navy and Corps used to get just enough men and matériel into Guadalcanal to sustain the defense that summer and fall.

It was a near-run, exceptionally costly victory. The Marines proved up to the task. Few if any others would have been so capable.

Today, the experiences of the likes of Ken Frazier and Art O'Keefe have largely been forgotten. Marion Carl, John L. Smith, and Dick Mangrum are remembered by an increasingly small number of Americans. We've moved on to other things, and the people who defined our past are often left behind in it.

Such men, their wives, and their families—their experience is part of our American DNA. Their struggles to overcome everything from the Depression to those horrific nights on Guadalcanal represent our marrow, our strength. They deserve to be remembered, not just for overcoming the odds stacked against them but to remind us of an important part of our legacy.

We're tougher than we think we are.

The proof lies in the lives of average Americans. Zen Pond. Fred Gutt and Leland Thomas. They came from all over the country and from every socioeconomic class and had nothing in common with one another when the Corps threw them into a collision course with history. Lewis Macias, son of Mexican immigrants who grew up near penniless in a Wyoming company town. Don McCafferty, the working-class kid from New York. Scotty McLennan and Red Kendrick, scions of blue-blood families, complete with their Ivy League pedigrees. Oliver Mitchell, whose family of Greek immigrants fought their way into the middle class in prewar California.

These men had nothing in common but the uniform of their nation. They were as diverse and different a lot as had ever fought for our nation. Yet they came together and bonded in a way that, for the survivors, lasted a lifetime. That bond drove them to fight and die for one another. It was a fate worse than death to let anyone down. They loved one another in a way unique to anything they would experience at home in later years.

Sure, there was plenty of conflict in the ranks. Plenty of animosity existed there, especially toward those who didn't give everything they had or who made a miserable situation worse with their attitude or actions.

Nevertheless, both squadrons fused into a fighting force that went toe-to-toe with the better-equipped, better-trained, and more-experienced Japanese. The Americans fought them to a brutal, bloody standstill, these American kids from everyday corners of the country, and played a key role in seizing the initiative away from the Empire of the Rising Sun.

Average Americans, with minimal training and experience, achieved that monumental task and bent the tide of history to their will.

In these days, when we forget the good and dwell all too much on the richness of our nation's many failings, this is a legacy worth remembering. For at our core, our hearts are the same.

APPENDIX

Fates of the Fifty-Three-Day Veterans

VMSB-232
Don McCafferty

D ON RETURNED TO HEMPSTEAD, LONG ISLAND, TO A HERO'S WEL-
come. Local civic clubs competed for his time as a guest speaker.
Children asked for his autograph wherever he went in town. The local
celebrity status was further enshrined when *Liberty* magazine contacted
the Marine Corps looking for a story on Guadalcanal from an aviator's
perspective. The Corps' public relations department arranged a meeting with Don, and from that flowed two exceptional articles Don wrote
about his time with VMSB-232 on the island. He included some of his
photographs, which remain among the only surviving images of the Red
Devils' fifty-three days on the island.

While in New York, he met Broadway actress Choo Choo Johnson,
who was part of the cast of *Early to Bed*. He gave her his gold wings,
which she wore on her costume during every subsequent performance.

In January 1943, the Marine Corps assigned him to NAS Miami to
serve as an instructor pilot. Promoted to captain in June, he also received
the Distinguished Flying Cross for his service on Starvation Island.

When asked how he got it, the matter-of-fact and self-effacing McCafferty would say, "I earned it for showing up to every muster."

The following year, he was stationed at Cherry Point, North Carolina. On March 1, 1944, his mother arrived at Cherry Point and, for the first time, was able to see her son fly. Two days later, he kissed his mom goodbye and took off on a dive-bombing training flight. Thirty miles offshore, his aircraft went straight into the Atlantic, killing both Don and his rear gunner, Sergeant Clabby. The base chaplain broke the news to Don's mother a few hours later.

Danny Iverson

AFTER BEING WOUNDED DURING THE BLOODY RIDGE BOMBARDMENTS that killed Lawrence "Baldy" Baldinus, Iverson was evacuated off Guadalcanal and flown back to recover in a California hospital. Finally well enough to be discharged in late November 1942, he drove home to Florida and surprised his Presbyterian minister father a few days after Thanksgiving. Wounded twice—once at Midway and once at Guadalcanal—Danny was welcomed home in Miami as one of the most experienced Marine dive-bomber pilots, having battled both the Kidō Butai and the Tokyo Express. Awarded the Navy Cross and the Distinguished Flying Cross, he spent his medical leave giving talks, attending his father's church, and courting Margaret Hough Fisher, the daughter of a senior executive at Westinghouse. They married February 10, 1943, and the Corps assigned Danny to be an instructor at NAS Miami.

The next year was a happy one for Danny. He was posted locally, close to family. He and Margaret had a little girl in late 1943. Yet, as the trauma of his final night with VMSB-232 receded, he yearned to return to combat. In early 1944, he received orders to head to the West Coast to join an operational squadron preparing to ship out to the Pacific.

On January 23, 1944, on one of his last assigned instructor flights in Florida, a student flying on his wing lost situational awareness and collided with Danny over Vero Beach. He was killed instantly.

The SBD Dauntless that Danny flew at Midway was brought back to the States to serve as a trainer for new naval aviators. The 219 bullet and cannon holes it suffered were repaired, and the aircraft served until June 1943, when another pilot crashed it into Lake Michigan while attempting to land on the training carrier USS *Sable*. In 1993, the aircraft was discovered, recovered, and determined to be the only veteran aircraft of the Battle of Midway to have survived the war. It was restored and is now on prominent display at NAS Pensacola's National Museum of Naval Aviation.

Arthur O'Keefe

ART O'KEEFE, THE BRAVE SECOND LIEUTENANT WHO FLEW HIS SBD OFF the *Long Island* despite a painful injury, suffered terribly on Guadalcanal. During the Bloody Ridge bombardment, he survived the night covered in the blood of his dead tentmates. A few days later, on his twenty-ninth combat mission, he witnessed the death of 2nd Lt. Yale Kaufman, one of his close friends from flight school. Racked with malaria, half-starved, and battling dysentery, Art was finally defeated by the strain and sickness. Evacuated after seeing Kaufman die, Art was diagnosed with psychoneurosis at the hospital on Efate. The casualty pipeline took him eventually to Mare Island, California, where a Navy doctor diagnosed his condition as a preexisting one and recommended he be discharged from the Navy. This would have left Art without any future care or ability to serve his country. He and his father fought furiously against this diagnosis, even getting their local Congressman involved to assist.

Art was transferred to Balboa Naval Hospital in San Diego, where his examining doctors completely disagreed with the Mare Island doc's findings so thoroughly that the head of the hospital send the Mare Island doctor a letter telling him what he had done was both illegal and unethical.

Balboa cleared Art for active duty again in July 1943, and he joined Dick Mangrum and Henry Hise at Corpus Christi as an instructor. Hise became Art's daughter's godfather, and Dick was there to shake his hand when Art received a Distinguished Flying Cross for a solo attack he'd made on Gizo Harbor on September 8, 1942.

Art returned to combat in February 1945 as the 4th Marine Division's assistant air officer. This was a non-flying billet, and he went ashore on the first day of the invasion to help coordinate air support for the front-line Marines. He could not stay out of the air, though, and on February 28, he became one of the first Marines to fly from one of Iwo's freshly captured airfields. Piloting an OY-1 light observation plane—roughly akin to a civilian Piper Cub—he braved mines on the runway, plus machine gun and antiaircraft fire from the moment he began his takeoff roll.

On that first flight, he marked targets for fighter-bombers, using smoke pots that he dropped on cave entrances and other defenses. He returned to the air later, armed with phosphorous grenades he flung out his side window. He continued to fly in extreme adverse conditions, sometimes carrying a photographer with him to get low-altitude imagery to the 4th Marine Division's HQ staff.

For his actions on Iwo Jima, Art received a second Distinguished Flying Cross.

He stayed in the Corps after World War II, when he took command of John L. Smith's old unit, VMF-223 in 1947. He served at the tail end of the Korean War and rose to the rank of lieutenant colonel while flying some thirty-six different aircraft throughout a career that ultimately spanned three decades. Invariably, the squadrons he commanded ranked among the best-performing in the Corps. No wonder: he'd learned about leadership from the best of the best—Dick Mangrum and John L. Smith.

On retirement in the early 1960s, he sailed a yacht down the Eastern Seaboard with his family, stopping in North Carolina to spend several days with his old skipper, Dick Mangrum. They remained friends until Dick's death in the 1980s. Art passed away at age ninety-two in 2013, one of the last of the MAG-23 veterans.

Art's son Michael O'Keefe continued the family's long tradition of military service and became a naval aviator, flying (among others) P-3

Orion anti-submarine and maritime reconnaissance aircraft in the Pacific during Vietnam and the Cold War. During the Vietnam War, he accrued 130 combat hours while searching for enemy shipping.

Henry Hise

EVACUATED OFF GUADALCANAL IN SEPTEMBER 1942 AFTER HIS BACK and pelvis were broken, Henry Hise found himself first in New Zealand, recovering in a hospital there. Sent home to the West Coast for further medical treatment that fall, he finally made it back to his hometown of Shamrock, Texas, in December. He spent his medical leave there, recovering from his injuries and deflecting questions about his time on Guadalcanal.

In December 1943, he returned to combat with VMTB-143, this time flying TBF Avenger torpedo planes in the Northern Solomon Islands. A third combat deployment took him to Okinawa, where he commanded VMTB-132 and operated off an escort carrier.

Henry stayed in the Corps after V-J Day and made a career out of the service that spanned thirty years. He flew sixty-six combat missions in Korea, flying F9F Panther jet fighters, then saw combat in Vietnam a decade and a half later as the deputy commander of Marine Air Wing One.

He retired as a brigadier general in 1971 after having flown five combat tours in three wars. He died in 2010 as a result of complications from a fall in which he broke his hip.

Dennis Byrd

DENNIS RETURNED TO THE STATES WITH THE REST OF 232'S SURVIVING air echelon. After his post-deployment leave back in Texas, he applied for flight school with Dick Mangrum's recommendation and was accepted as an aviation cadet at NAS Corpus Christi, where Mangrum was then serving as the commandant of the cadet regiment. The two made headlines when reunited, and later, Byrd's beloved former skipper pinned his wings on him when he graduated and received his commission. In March 1944, he married Mary Ruth Green—and Dick Mangrum stood up as Dennis's best man.

As a freshly minted Marine fighter pilot, Dennis deployed to the Philippines and spent ten months flying F4U Corsairs against the Japanese on Mindanao and Palawan.

When the war ended, he left the service as a first lieutenant and settled in Utah. After Thomas Miller's book *The Cactus Air Force* was published in the late 1970s, Dennis made it a personal mission to publish his own account of Guadalcanal and VMSB-232's role in it. He reached out to Dick Mangrum and the other surviving Red Devils and gathered personal recollections and stories from them. The manuscript, he hoped, would set the record straight and highlight the Red Devils' many achievements. Dick and the others were all terribly disappointed at how VMSB-232 was remembered in the secondary sources published on Guadalcanal, and they wholeheartedly supported Dennis's efforts. In one early 1980s letter, Dick mentioned offhandedly that it was probably too late to capture the truth about the deployment and that the record would never be corrected.

In 1992, Dennis discovered a flight simulation video game called *Aces of the Pacific*. One of the historic missions featured included flying with 232 on one of its dive-bombing missions against the Tokyo Express. Dennis was dumbfounded that a new generation had found a unique way to tell the story of his comrades. He wrote to Dynamix, the company that produced the game. He explained that whenever his grandkids asked him what it was like to fly at Guadalcanal, he showed them the missions included in *Aces of the Pacific*.

The letter landed on my desk—I was the team's aviation historian at the time—and his words had a profound effect on me and my own life. Dennis and I corresponded for many months, and after I left Dynamix to pursue a writing career in 1996, I interviewed him extensively over the phone. Dennis shared many stories and documents with me during our correspondence, and several times I approached military historian Eric Hammel in hopes that his Pacifica Press would publish Dennis's book.

But he and Dennis had a falling out, and Eric declined to publish the manuscript.

Dennis's memoir never reached print. I undertook this book in part to realize Dennis and Dick's wish that 232's full story be told. I hope that someday, perhaps, Dennis's manuscript will surface and be published. It would be an excellent addition to the history of Guadalcanal's early weeks.

Dennis passed away at age eighty-five in 2007.

Lewis Macias

DEADEYE MACIAS MADE A HOME OF THE MARINE CORPS, AND throughout his thirty-two-year career, most of the world felt the touch of his boots from Spain to Cuba, California to China. He served two tours in combat during the Korean War, saw action in Lebanon a few years later, and, at forty-eight, completed a combat tour in Vietnam as the first sergeant for Force Logistics Command. Along the way, beyond his native fluency in Spanish and English, he learned Thai, Greek, and Italian. Before he retired, he sometimes served as an unofficial linguist and translator on his deployments.

Lewis retired as a master gunnery sergeant in 1975 and died in North Carolina at age sixty-three in November 1984.

Edward Eades

EIGHTEEN-YEAR-OLD PFC. EDWARD EADES SURVIVED HIS INJURIES from the crash that claimed the life of his pilot, Lt. Leland Thomas. After his recovery in the States, he earned a slot as an aviation cadet, following Dennis Byrd into F4U Corsairs. He served a second tour in the Pacific, flying close support missions off an escort carrier during the final campaigns of the war.

Yet Thomas's death cast a long shadow over Ed's life, and he later wrote, "I never again flew over a ship without remembering that day and the helpless, hopeless frustration as we were shot from the sky."

On February 28, 1944, Eades attended the commissioning ceremony for the USS *Leland E. Thomas*, a destroyer escort that would ultimately serve in the Pacific for the final year of World War II. Thomas's mother christened the vessel, which served until 1946 and was finally scrapped in 1973.

Eades made a career of the Corps, retiring as a sergeant major. He died in 2010.

VMF-223
Charles Kendrick

THOUGH A PATROL FOUND RED KENDRICK'S AIRCRAFT AND BURIED HIM alongside it, postwar efforts to relocate the grave failed. In 1947, his father traveled to Guadalcanal and, working with locals, finally found his son and brought him home. He was laid to rest in Holy Cross Catholic Cemetery in Colma, California, the same final resting place as Joe DiMaggio. Red's sister later joined the Marines and served in honor of her beloved brother. After the war, the Kendrick family established several scholarships at Stanford University and the University of San Francisco in his name.

Scotty McLennan

SCOTTY WAS DECLARED OFFICIALLY DEAD IN 1943, A YEAR AFTER HE went missing in action. As was the case with so many of his brother aviators, his remains were never found and he is still on the World War II MIA list.

His brother Don honored the request Scotty had made in the letter he mailed at Efate shortly before reaching Guadalcanal. Scotty asked Don to take care of his wife, Peggy, should he not return. In February 1945, Don married Peggy while he was serving as a lieutenant commander in the US Navy.

Four months after their wedding, the war dealt Peggy another cruel blow. Her brother George was killed in action on Okinawa during one of the last major engagements on the island.

According to one McLennan family member, Don and Peggy's union was troubled from the start. Peggy struggled with the loss of her beloved Scotty and her brother for years. Ultimately, her marriage to Don failed. She remarried Hulburd Johnston, a wartime staff officer in MacArthur's headquarters, and moved to Florida. Her second husband died in 1991. She passed in 1996 and was laid to rest in Lake Forest Cemetery in Lake County, Illinois, beside her second husband, not far from Scotty's memorial and the McLennan family plot.

Ken Frazier

KEN RECEIVED THE NAVY CROSS FOR HIS SERVICE ON GUADALCANAL. He returned to combat in 1943, serving under Marion Carl in the Solomons during VMF-223's second combat tour. He went out a third time and saw combat in the Central Pacific as the ops and executive officer of VMF-216 before finally returning home in late 1944 to become a fighter instructor.

He stayed in the Corps after the war, rising through the ranks as he served with distinction in Korea, where he earned a Bronze Star with Valor during his 1952–1953 tour.

On July 17, 1959, he took off from the old Brewster factory's airfield in Hatboro, Pennsylvania, at the controls of an FJ3 Fury. According to some accounts, a wrench left inside the fuselage by a careless mechanic jammed Ken's controls, causing the aircraft to stall and crash into a cornfield. He was killed instantly, leaving behind his wife and four daughters. Ken was among the best Marine Corps aviators of his era. His awards included the Navy Cross, three Distinguished Flying Crosses, the Bronze Star for Valor for his Korea deployment, and twelve air medals awarded for specific missions carried out from 1942 through 1944.

Eugene Trowbridge

AFTER BEING WOUNDED ON SEPTEMBER 14, 1942, EUGENE WAS EVACUated back to the United States, where he recovered in hospitals on the

West Coast and in Illinois. On returning to duty, he transitioned to the F4U Corsair and deployed again to the Philippines, serving on Mindanao with VMF-218. He left the service after the war and became a high school music teacher in Minnesota. He died in 1994.

Rivers Morrell

AFTER RECOVERING FROM HIS WOUNDS, RIVERS MORRELL EARNED HIS first command, VMF-216, which he took to the Northern Solomons in late 1943. He served with the 1st Marine Air Wing in Korea before retiring as a brigadier general in 1959. He passed away in 2002.

Fred Gutt

FRED COMPLETED THE FIFTY-THREE-DAY TOUR AND WENT BACK OUT with VMF-223 under Marion Carl the following year. Flying an F4U Corsair, he shot down three Japanese Zeroes in five minutes during a December 1943 fighter sweep over Rabaul. He finished the war with eight confirmed victories. He died in 2012.

MAG-23
Charles Laird Fike

FIKE COMPLETED HIS TIME ON GUADALCANAL AND RETURNED STATE-side to give a thorough debrief of the experience at Henderson to the Navy's Bureau of Aeronautics. He was given stateside posts through 1943. The following year, he was embroiled in controversy surrounding the US Navy's reluctance to adopt a quick-release parachute. In response to the press, he defended the Navy's decision to delay its operational use. He retired in 1946 as a brigadier general and went to work in Pennsylvania for the Pullman railroad car division of the Budd Company. In 1950, he was badly injured in a car wreck and died a few days later. His son, born in 1925, also served in the Marines.

Robert Galer

BOB GALER CONTINUED TO LEAD VMF-224 AFTER JOHN L. SMITH AND the rest of 223 were evacuated from Guadalcanal. He was shot down three times, scored eleven kills, and received the Medal of Honor for his leadership and courage during that deployment. After spending 1943 stateside, he was posted to staff duties as operations officer for the 3rd Marine Air Wing during the Battles of Peleliu and Iwo Jima.

In Korea, he served as the supply officer for the 1st Marine Air Wing through 1952. In May 1953, he received command of MAG-12 and led it from the tip of the spear as he'd done on Guadalcanal a decade before. He earned a Distinguished Flying Cross for courage in combat during a strike on the North Korean capital. Not long after, he was shot down behind North Korean lines and was miraculously saved from captivity by a daring helicopter rescue.

Bob retired as a brigadier general in 1957, a legend in the Corps for his tenacity and aggressiveness in combat. He ranks as one of the greatest aviation leaders in Marine Corps history. He died in 2005 in Dallas.

ACKNOWLEDGMENTS

FIFTY-THREE DAYS REALLY STARTED ON THE DAY I VISITED MARION and Edna Carl at their house outside Roseburg, Oregon, in January 1991, while I was a graduate school student at the University of Oregon. Writing Marion and Edna's story has been on my bucket list ever since. General Carl's hospitality and kindness to me resonated for thirty years and struck me again while I was listening to the interview tapes from that day.

This book would have remained an unrealized dream without the consistent support and understanding of Brant Rumble, my editor at Hachette. His patience through repeated delays, rewrites, and additions has been a godsend. Thank you, Brant, for all you've done for me, the men and the families of MAG-23, as well as my own family.

Mollie Weisenfeld, your relentless attention to detail and editorial acumen played the central role in taming the original manuscript while sculpting the narrative to be tighter and much more readable. The success of this book will be your success as much as mine. Thank you for the guidance.

Before my agent and dear friend Jim Hornfischer passed in June 2021, he kept abreast of all the developments in my writing career, despite surgeries and hospitalizations. He looked out for me to the very end of his life and beyond. Before he died, he arranged for me and my career to be entrusted to Folio Literary Management and an old friend from 2008, Will Murphy. Will and I worked together on Fred Burton's *Ghost* and have reconnected to work together again. Will immediately jumped in to help steward my career and the completion of *Fifty-Three Days*. His support and encouragement have been pivotal as I grieved for my lost friend who was my trusted guide through the publishing world. Jim Hornfischer's effect on my life was nothing short of transformational. He is the reason these books of mine have been written. I'll miss him for the rest of my life.

Many people provided critical assistance in the completion of this book. By opening his own interviews and research on VMF-221 and VMF-223, Larry Lassise jump-started the book and ensured that stories and recollections from the aviators themselves, all of whom are now passed on, were included. Larry, your friendship and support were a godsend, and working with you and visiting Bruce Carl with you will always be one of my life's highlights. Thank you for making this book a reality.

Renee Bruning, my daughter, spent her first months of Covid lockdown accumulating and organizing Marine muster rolls for VMSB-232. Renee had just graduated from Willamette University and brought all the enthusiasm, energy, and fun imaginable while helping to build the document archive that would serve as the backbone of the book. There's nothing more fun than getting to work with you, Renee. Finding the Grumman newsletters from 1942 was an absolute coup, one that allowed me to include, in the chapter about the Grumman War Production Corps, the details straight from eyewitnesses and the pictures that Grumman's photographers snapped that day. Thank you for all your many contributions to *Fifty-Three Days*.

Jack Cook, my brother from another mother, thank you for all the assistance, photographs, reads of the manuscript to catch errors, and encouragement through some really trying times. Sitting in your kitchen and talking history with you was like decompressing. Your loyalty and unwavering friendship, plus your willingness to clock me when I made a historical mistake—no matter how arcane—have made me a better historian and writer. Thanks, brother, for everything.

Gus, your fourth-quarter research Hail Mary yielded many gems for *Fifty-Three Days*. Taking time out of your frantic schedule to help move the manuscript across the goal line was above and beyond. But then again, everything you do is above and beyond. Your friendship, eyes on the manuscript, advice, and suggestions were instrumental. Thank you for all you've done.

Eddie and Jenn Bruning worked hard to support me through the writing of this book. There is no way I would have gotten through the pandemic, the Santiam Canyon wildfire, and everything else without you two in my corner. Thank you for all you've done for me, and for the book.

To the Pullmans, Annelizabeth and Jeff—you've given me a quiet place to write in the beautiful Oregon woods for the last fourteen years. Some of my life's best memories have been shared at Timberspirits, and the best writing I've done has been up there among God's grace in the Cascades. I will forever be grateful to you both. Thank you for everything, but especially your friendship.

As always, in every book I've written since 2009, I must mention Taylor Marks. Taylor was killed in Iraq in August 2009. The news broke while I was driving to meet Brian Stann to work on *Heart for the Fight* in New Mexico, where Brian was training for his next mixed martial arts fight. Taylor was like family to me, a young man full of energy, creativity, and ideas. He joined my volunteer OPFOR (opposing force—we were the bad guys in field exercises) group that provided training support to the 2nd Battalion, 162nd Infantry. The experience convinced him to enlist in the Guard out of high school, and he repeatedly volunteered after Advanced Individual Training to join the Oregon National Guard on its 2009 deployment to Iraq, even though he'd been assigned to the Defense Language Institute in Monterey, California, to learn Cantonese before joining his military intelligence unit.

Six weeks into that deployment, he and his truck commander, Earl Werner, were killed by an Iranian-made roadside bomb. When I gave Taylor's eulogy, I swore to live with his sense of adventure and to carry his spirit wherever I went. The year after Taylor died, I traveled to Afghanistan to embed with Task Force Brawler, 3rd Combat Aviation Brigade, 3rd Infantry Division, and spent the summer and fall in Regional Command East, flying from Forward Operating Base Shank in Chinooks and Blackhawks. The twin experiences of Taylor's crushing loss and my own days in combat completely changed how I write military history. The heart of *Fifty-Three Days* comes from those twin events in my own life.

Taylor, you were the best of us, and there has not been a day since 2009 that I haven't thought of you and all the potential this country lost when you were killed on that Baghdad overpass. When I wrote of Oliver Mitchell, Leland Thomas, Scotty McLennan, Red Kendrick, and Baldy Baldinus, I did so knowing firsthand what their deaths inflicted on those who loved them.

THE GREAT TAKEAWAY FROM *FIFTY-THREE DAYS*, AND ONE I HOPE OUR contemporary leaders both in and out of the military absorb, is this: an unprepared, underequipped military may help ease budget constraints, but America's warriors will be forced to pay the balance with their blood.

BIBLIOGRAPHIC ESSAY

THE HISTORIOGRAPHY FOR THE GUADALCANAL CAMPAIGN IS A MASSIVE one. My interest in the campaign began when I was a kid, and it developed when I wrote my senior thesis at the University of Oregon on the six-month long battle. My original master's thesis focused on naval aviation training before the war and how doctrine and tactics that were developed in the 1930s fared in combat during the first year of the Pacific War. That project led me to Marion Carl's door.

To that end, I've collected books, articles, documents, and interviews since 1987 from a variety of sources.

Interviews

William Brooks (via Larry Lassise)
Dennis Byrd
Clayton Canfield (via Larry Lassise)
John F. Carey (via Larry Lassise)
Bruce Carl
Marion Carl
Chambers Family
Fleener Family
Robert Galer (via Larry Lassise)
Fred Gutt (via Larry Lassise)
Dean Hartley (via Larry Lassise)
Howard Marvin (via Larry Lassise)
McLennan Family
O'Keefe Family
Frederick Payne (via Larry Lassise)
Jesse Rollow (via Larry Lassise)
Smith Family (John Bruning and Larry Lassise)

Richard "Dick" Truesdale
Sumner Whitten
Leon Williamson (via Larry Lassise)

Oral Histories

Dennis Byrd (Library of Congress Veterans History Program)
Marion Carl (USMC Oral History Program)
Charles Fike (Bureau of Aeronautics; hereafter cited as BuAir)
Henry Hise (Nimitz Museum)
Richard Mangrum (BuAir + USMC Oral History Program)
John L. Smith (Fighter Aces Association, Seattle Museum of Flight)

Letters and Correspondence

Harold Buell
Dennis Byrd
Marion Carl
Chambers Family
Ed Eades
Lewis Macias
Richard Mangrum
Mike O'Keefe
Bruce Prosser Family (via Larry Lassie and Jack Cook)
Jack Stanner

Primary Source Material
Archives Visited and Utilized

Air Force Historical Research Agency, Maxwell Field, Montgomery, AL
Fred Waring Collection, Penn State University Libraries and Archives, University Park, PA
Hoover Institution Library and Archives, Stanford Campus, Palo Alto, CA
Marine Corps Archives, Quantico, VA
National Archives, College Park, MD
National Archives, Laguna Niguel Branch, Laguna Niguel, CA
National Museum of Naval Aviation, Pensacola, FL
Naval History and Research Center, Washington Navy Yard, Washington, DC

Notes on Primary Sources, Non-Archival

Among the many gems collected for *Fifty-Three Days* over the years were the flight logs of many of the VMSB-232 and VMF-223 pilots and gunners. The information in these logbooks filled in many gaps and shed new light on how many missions 232 actually flew in September

1942—after the unit disappears from traditional narratives of the period. Most logbooks were collected by Dennis Byrd, who shared them with me. Larry Lassise contributed several from VMF-223's veterans.

Robert Galer's personal diary from September and October 1942 was another rare gem that came via Larry Lassise. Galer's frank assessment of the situation and the men around him revealed much of the thinking behind the decisions made during those hectic weeks. The diary is a historical gold mine, and I'm deeply appreciative to the Galer family for letting it be used in the construction of this book.

Mike O'Keefe shared with me his father's complete medical history after Art's evacuation from Guadalcanal. Mike also provided me with extensive documentation on his dad's subsequent service and career in the Marine Corps, including the award citations he received both after Guadalcanal and after his second combat tour on Iwo Jima.

Online Documentary Archives

To further delve into the lives and backgrounds of the MAG-23 Marines, I used a variety of primary sources found in Fold3.com and Ancestry.com. Among the best sources are these two:

- **Census data:** The 1920, 1930, and 1940 census reports played a key role in building the socioeconomic backgrounds of the Marines.
- **Marine muster rolls:** These documents noted where each Marine was stationed, from his induction into the Corps through his post-deployment years. We accumulated every surviving one for every pilot and gunner in the two squadrons.

The websites www.newspapers.com and https://newspaperarchive.com provided hundreds of stories on the MAG-23 veterans, including reportage on their combat experiences while the men were still on the island, their post-deployment speaking tours, their homecomings, and their other activities both before joining the military and after World War II.

An independent research effort called the Missing Marines Project (https://missingmarines.com) provides a wealth of information on the MAG-23 aviators still unaccounted for after more than eighty years.

To round out what could be gathered online, I tracked down and purchased the college yearbooks for Fletcher Brown, Dick Mangrum, and John L. Smith, acquired through eBay.com and its community of rare-book dealers.

Archival Source Notes

OVER THE LAST THIRTY YEARS, I COLLECTED DOCUMENTS RELATING TO Guadalcanal, naval aviation, the US Marine Corps squadrons that fought for Henderson Field in 1942, and the surface engagements around the island. The most useful documents for the book included the following:

Eric Hammel Collection: Material in this collection located at the Marine Corps Archives in Quantico, Virginia, included correspondence between Eric Hammel and veterans of the campaign, as well as further correspondence between Dennis Byrd and other members of the Guadalcanal veterans.

First Marine Division Records: Located in Quantico, the battalion and regimental war diaries, histories, and reports provided plenty of details and gems, especially related to the stories of the downed VMF-223 pilots Charles Kendrick and Scotty McLennan and the patrols sent to find their aircraft.

Additionally, MAG-23 and 1st Marine Division communications to higher commands provided a wealth of insight into the ebb and flow of the campaign, as did the CINCPAC war diary.

VMSB-241 and VMF-221 war diaries and after-action reports from the Battle of Midway also provided further information.

MAG-23 Records: The war diary for MAG-23 is a tale unto itself. There are actually at least two versions of the war diary: one written at the time and then one written later in October, after VMF-223 and VMSB-232 left Guadalcanal. As best as I can assemble, Lieutenant Colonel Fike rewrote the original after his return to the States and based the war diary on his copious postmission notes scrawled during the debriefings at the Pagoda. Though we searched to see if Fike's black notebook survived, we could not locate it or ascertain whether it still exists. The VMF-223 Reunion Association included the different versions of the war diary in the 1990s, when the group decided to put together all the known VMF-223 documents. The documents included not just the war diary but also personal accounts of the VMF-223 Marines who sought to correct the official account's many errors. Dick Truesdale, who flew later in the war with 223, gave me the entire collection in 1999 when he was urging me to write a history of his unit. I will forever be in Dick's debt, as so much of the material the squadron's historians pulled together for this collection exists nowhere else.

Additionally, I consulted the war diaries from every ship, task force, or task group mentioned in the book to reconstruct their movements and how the naval side of the campaign affected the men of MAG-23. On the Japanese side, I used the Tabular Record of Movement (TROM) to document the movement of the ships and convoys VMSB-232 attacked through August and September 1942.

Books

HUNDREDS OF BOOKS HAVE EITHER BEEN WRITTEN ON GUADALCANAL or touch on the battle. The following were the most useful and important ones to the completion of *Fifty-Three Days*.

Alexander, Joseph. *Edson's Raiders: The 1st Marine Raider Battalion in World War II*. Annapolis, MD: Naval Institute Press, 2001.

Alexander, Joseph, and Marlin Groft. *Bloody Ridge and Beyond: A World War II Marine's Memoir of Edson's Raiders in the Pacific*. New York: Caliber Books, 2014.

Baeza, Bernard. *Guadalcanal, Cactus Air Force Contre Marine Imperiale*, vol. 1. Le Vigen, France: LELA Presse, 2015.

Baker, A. D. *Japanese Naval Vessels of World War II, as Seen by U.S. Naval Intelligence*. Annapolis, MD: Naval Institute Press, 1987.

Ballard, Robert D. *Return to Midway*. Washington, DC: National Geographic/Madison Press, 1989.

Bartsch, William H. *Victory Fever on Guadalcanal: Japan's First Land Defeat in World War II*. College Station: Texas A&M University Press, 2014.

Bertke, Donald A. *World War II Sea War*. Vol. 7, *Day to Day Naval Actions September Through November 1942*. Dayton, OH: Bertke Publications, 2014.

Boomhower, Ray. *Richard Tregaskis: Reporting Under Fire from Guadalcanal to Vietnam.* Albuquerque, NM: High Road Books, 2021.

Brand, Max. *Fighter Squadron at Guadalcanal.* Annapolis, MD: Naval Institute Press, 1996.

Buell, Harold. *Dauntless Helldivers: A Dive-Bomber Pilot's Epic Story of the Carrier Battles.* New York: Orion Books, 1991.

Carl, Marion, and Barrett Tillman. *Pushing the Envelope: The Career of Fighter Ace and Test Pilot Marion Carl.* Annapolis, MD: Bluejacket Books/Naval Institute Press, 1994.

Chastain, Bill. *Jackrabbit: The Story of Clint Castleberry and the Improbable 1942 Georgia Tech Football Season.* Thomaston, ME: Cadent Publishing, 2011.

Christ, James F. *Battalion of the Damned: The 1st Marine Paratroopers at Gavutu and Bloody Ridge, 1942.* Annapolis, MD: Naval Institute Press, 2007.

Clarinbould, Michael John. *Pacific Adversaries,* vol. 2. Australia: Avonmore Books, 2020.

———. *Nemoto's Travels: The Illustrated Saga of a Japanese Float Plane Pilot in the First Year of the Pacific War.* Australia: Avonmore Books, 2021.

———. *Pacific Profiles.* Vol. 8, *IJN Floatplanes in the South Pacific 1942–1944.* Australia: Avonmore Books, 2022.

Clarinbould, Michael John, and Peter Ingman. *Solomons Air War.* Vol. 1, *Guadalcanal August–September 1942.* Australia: Avonmore Books, 2023.

Coggins, Jack. *The Campaign for Guadalcanal: A Battle That Made History.* Garden City, NY: Doubleday, 1972.

Dechant, John. *Devilbirds: The Story of United States Marine Corps Aviation in World War II.* Washington, DC: Zenger, 1979.

Dull, Paul S. *Battle History of the Imperial Japanese Navy.* Annapolis, MD: Naval Institute Press, 1978.

Ferguson, Robert L. *Guadalcanal, the Island of Fire: Reflections of the 347th Fighter Group.* Blue Ridge Summit, PA: Aero, 1987.

Frank, Richard B. *Guadalcanal.* New York: Random House, 1990.

Hammel, Eric. *Guadalcanal: Starvation Island.* New York: Simon & Schuster, 1987.

———. *Carrier Clash: The Invasion of Guadalcanal and the Battle of the Eastern Solomons, August 1942.* Pacifica, CA: Pacifica Press, 1997.

Hammel, Eric, and Thomas McKelvey Cleaver. *The Cactus Air Force: Air War over Guadalcanal.* Oxford, UK: Osprey, 2022.

Hoffman, Jon T. *Once a Legend: "Red Mike" Edson of the Marine Raiders.* Novato, CA: Presidio Press, 2000.

Hubler, Richard, and John A. Dechant. *Flying Leathernecks.* Garden City, NY: Doubleday, Doran & Co., 1944.

Izawa, Yasuho, and Ikuhiko Hata. *Japanese Naval Aces and Fighter Units in World War II.* Annapolis, MD: Naval Institute Press, 1989.

Keeney, L. Douglas, and William Butler. *This Is Guadalcanal.* New York: Quill, 1998.

Kendrick, Charles. *The Memoirs of Charles Kendrick.* San Francisco: privately printed, 1972.

Kiplinger, William M. *Washington Is Like That.* New York: Harper & Bro., 1942.

Lee, Clark. *They Call It Pacific.* New York: Viking, 1943.

Lengerer, Hans, and Lars Ahlberg. *Fubuki-Class Destroyers: In the Imperial Japanese Navy During World War II*. Atglen, PA: Schiffer, 2022.

Lundstrom, John. *The First Team*. Annapolis, MD: Naval Institute Press, 1984.

———. *The First Team at Guadalcanal*. Annapolis, MD: Naval Institute Press, 1994.

McEniry, John H. *A Marine Dive Bomber Pilot at Guadalcanal*. Tuscaloosa: University of Alabama Press, 1987.

Mersky, Peter. *Time of the Aces: Marine Pilots in the Solomons, 1942–1944*. Washington, DC: USMC Historical Office, 1993.

Miller, John Jr. *The War in the Pacific: Guadalcanal, the First Offensive*. Washington, DC: Historical Division, US Army, 1949.

Miller, Thomas G. *The Cactus Air Force*. New York: Harper & Row, 1969.

Moore, Thomas. *The Sky Is My Witness*. Auckland, New Zealand: Pickle Partners Publishing, 2015. First published 1943 by G. P. Putnam's Sons (New York).

Morison, Samuel Eliot. *The Struggle for Guadalcanal*. Annapolis, MD: Naval Institute Press, 1949 and 2010.

Nelson, V. A. *An American Hero: Eugene Trowbridge*. 3rd ed. Houston, TX: Squall Line Publishers, 2017.

O'Sheel, Patrick, and Gene Cook, eds. *Semper Fidelis: The U.S. Marines in the Pacific 1942–1945*. New York: William Sloan, 1947.

Parshall, Jonathan, and Anthony Tully. *Shattered Sword: The Untold Story of the Battle of Midway*. Annapolis, MD: Naval Institute Press, 2005.

Peattie, Mark R. *Sunburst: The Rise of Japanese Naval Air Power, 1909–1941*. Annapolis, MD: Naval Institute Press, 2001.

Richter, Don. *Where the Sun Stood Still: The Untold Story of Sir Jacob Vouza and the Guadalcanal Campaign*. California: Toucan Publishing, 1992.

Sherrod, Robert. *History of Marine Corps Aviation in World War II*. San Rafael, CA: Presidio Press, 1980.

Sims, Edward H. *Greatest Fighter Missions of the Top Navy and Marine Aces of WWII*. New York: Harper & Bros., 1962.

Tagaya, Osamu. *Mitsubishi Type 1 Rikko "Betty" Units of World War 2*. Oxford: Osprey, UK, 2001.

Thomas, Lowell. *These Men Shall Never Die*. Philadelphia: John C. Winston, 1943.

Tillman, Barrett. *Wildcat, the F4F in WWII*. 2nd ed. Annapolis, MD: Naval Institute Press, 1990.

Tregaskis, Richard. *Guadalcanal Diary*. New York: Random House, 1943.

Umemoto, Hiroshi. *Air War over Guadalcanal August–October 1942, Volume 1*. Japan: Dai Nihon Kaiga, 2021.

US Marine Corps, ed. *History of Marine Corps Operations in World War II*. Vol. 1, *Pearl Harbor to Guadalcanal*, by Frank Hough, V. E. Ludwig, and H. I. Shaw Jr. Washington, DC: US Marine Corps, 1958.

Wildenberg, Thomas. *Destined for Glory: Dive Bombing, Midway, and the Evolution of Carrier Airpower*. Annapolis, MD: Naval Institute Press, 1998.

Willcock, Roger. *Unaccustomed to Fear: A Biography of the Late General Roy S. Geiger*. Princeton, NJ: privately published, 1968.

Articles

Mangrum, Richard. "Guadalcanal Diary." *American Magazine*, February 1943.

McCafferty, Don, as told to Alan Hynd. "On Guadalcanal with the Marines." Pts. 1 and 2. *Liberty*, January 30, 1943; February 6, 1943.

Mrazek, Robert J. "No Ordinary John Smith." *Naval History*, August 2012.

Wilcox, Richard. "Captain Smith and His Fighting 223." *Life*, December 7, 1942.

NOTES

Chapter 4

1. Officially, SBD stood for Scout Bomber, Douglas, in Navy/Marine-speak. The aviators nicknamed it "SBD—Slow But Deadly."

2. The Buccaneer never went into combat with US Navy or US Marine Corps units. Instead, the planes remained stateside as training aircraft for Marine night fighter squadrons. The Bucks County factory managed to produce about 735 F3A Corsairs before Brewster lost all its contracts in late 1944. Half the F3As went to the British navy, the rest to the US Navy, which deemed them unfit for combat. They were used as fighter trainers stateside until the end of the war. Meanwhile, Chance Vought built over 12,000 F4U Corsairs. The disaster at Brewster was thoroughly investigated by Congress, and the report from the 1944 hearings is an eye-opening account of waste, mismanagement, chaos, and graft. It was a sad chapter in the American mobilization for total war and reflective of the darkest side of that endeavor.

Chapter 7

1. Merrill, twenty-eight at the time of the Battle of Midway, had graduated from the University of New Hampshire in 1937. He joined the Corps in 1939 and, by the time of the attack on Pearl Harbor, was married. While he was in the Pacific, his wife gave birth to twin girls. Merrill recovered from his wounds and returned to a combat unit, serving with VMF-211 in the South Pacific. On March 24, 1943, he crashed while flying an F4F through a heavy thunderstorm. His body and aircraft were never found. He never met his twin girls.

Chapter 8

1. In November 1942, Smith recalled in his Bureau of Aeronautics debrief that they were not told whom they were going to support, what the mission was, or where they were going. They only knew they had six weeks max to be ready to fight the Japanese.

Dick Mangrum remembered things a little differently. He recalled Larkin telling them they would be going to Guadalcanal and that the location of their future operations was to be shared with nobody. Yet when Dick returned to his squadron, his sergeant major's first question to him was "Sir, where is Guadalcanal?" The NCO network always stayed one step ahead of Joint Staff Operations Security (OPSEC). Whatever the case, the rank and file pilots had no idea of their destination until August.

Chapter 9

1. *Graying out* was the term used for the absolute edge of unconsciousness as *g*-forces drained blood from the pilot's brain. If pushed too far, the pilot would black out and become unconscious.

Chapter 11

1. The pilots John L. traded were 2nd Lts. John Jones, Clarence Moore, Dean Hartley, and Robert D'Arcy. In return, VMF-223 gained 2nd Lt. Fred Gutt, Midway veteran 2nd Lt. Charles Hughes, 2nd Lt. Robert Read, Orvin Ramlo, and Willis Lees.

Chapter 12

1. Officially, SBD stood for Scout Bomber, Douglas, in Navy/Marine-speak. The aviators nicknamed it "SBD—Slow But Deadly."

Chapter 14

1. The two VMF-212 pilots who went with 223 on the *Long Island* were Everton himself and Henry B. "Tex" Hamilton.

2. Film of at least one of those crashes can be seen on YouTube.

Chapter 15

1. The *Long Island*'s angled catapult has largely been forgotten by historians. The original conversion from the merchant ship hull took only three months. There must have been belowdecks problems that prevented building the catapult to standard specs— straight off the bow—so the hasty solution was to set it at an angle. It is possible that in either 1943 or 1944, when the ship underwent several refits and upgrades, the original catapult was replaced with a conventional one running along the port side of the forward flight deck to the bow. This iteration of the *Long Island* included additional 20 mm antiaircraft guns and has been used as the basis for many three-view drawings of it over the years. The Marines who launched that day were probably the only ones ever to use that catapult system operationally, and they remembered it with a mix of shock and incredulity.

Chapter 16

1. The Marine maps were incorrectly labeled. The Tenaru River was actually farther east, and the 1st Marine Regiment had anchored its defenses on the Ilu River, sometimes called Alligator Creek. The Japanese attack was led by Col. Kiyono Ichiki of the 28th Infantry Regiment, 7th Infantry Division, Imperial Japanese Army. The Ichiki detachment consisted of about 2,000 men, of which 917 were landed first from six Japanese destroyers on August 18, 1942. Ichiki had been ordered to wait to attack the Marines until the rest of his unit could be brought in aboard slower-moving transports, but the impetuous colonel elected to attack immediately. He force-marched his

men from Taivu Point to the Marine defense line along the Ilu River, covering about twenty miles over the next forty-eight hours. At 0200 on August 20, about 200 of his men opened the battle with a human wave assault across the sandbar at the mouth of the river. They ran headlong into well-entrenched Marines supported by 37 mm anti-tank guns, heavy machine guns, mortars, and artillery. The Japanese were annihilated. Ichiki continued to throw his men into further banzai charges that did succeed in getting across the river. The Marines stopped these attacks in brutal hand-to-hand fighting in the predawn darkness. After daylight, the Marines counterattacked, trapped the Japanese in a palm grove, and wiped out Ichiki's detachment. Ichiki either killed himself or was killed in the fighting, along with about 800 of his men. The Marines suffered 34 dead, 74 wounded. The fighting would later be called the Battle of the Tenaru River.

2. The Type 95 collapsible boat could carry sixteen fully armed troops or about a half ton of supplies. The three boats under Sergeant Ogasawara's command that morning were primarily loaded with supplies. Their crews were supplemented with a few men dispatched to cremate the remains of thirty-eight Japanese killed during a leader's recon that a Marine patrol had ambushed on August 19. Along the beach and in the jungle where the F4Fs strafed were an unknown number of Colonel Ichiki's men, fleeing the destruction of their unit and trying to return to their base at Taivu Point. Exactly how many there were is unknown, and Japanese sources don't detail casualties from the air attack beyond the twelve or thirteen corpses seen by one survivor. In the final analysis, there was no way 223 strafed five hundred troops, let alone a thousand. The number was probably somewhere between forty and sixty, with an unknown number killed and wounded. The reality matters to the postwar historian. The perception in the moment mattered to the aviators and the Marines on the ground defending the perimeter. To them, on the morning of August 21, the pilots of VMF-223 had more than proved their worth, boosting morale after a night of incredibly violent and merciless fighting.

Chapter 17

1. The MAG-23 War Diary states that John L. Smith's flight was at 14,000 feet, and most secondary sources repeat that altitude. A December 7, 1942, *Life* magazine article on Smith and VMF-223 says that they were at 8,000 feet. In a 1960s interview with the Fighter Aces Association, John L. concurred with the *Life* magazine article and mentioned they were at 8,000 feet. Either way, the aviators were probably not on oxygen, and the Japanese they encountered had the initial altitude advantage of between 500 and 2,000 feet.

2. In his 1942 interview with the Bureau of Aeronautics, John L. Smith only mentions that he took a shot at a Zero and that, later, Marines on the ground reported seeing it crash. The story is related differently in the December 1942 *Life* magazine article, and Smith's 1960s interview with the Fighter Aces Association conforms with the *Life* version. The fact is, Japanese records obtained and translated postwar show they lost no fighters that day. But perception in the moment was far more important than the postwar reconciliation of who shot down whom. The Marines had their first scalp, and John L.'s first kill helped demolish the myth of the Zero's invincibility.

3. Kawai's name came up repeatedly during a 1950 war crimes trial on Manus. He was one of the few combat fighter pilots who faced trial as war criminals of World War II.

Chapter 18

1. Every effort to tow the *Blue* failed. Ultimately, the decision was made to scuttle the ship, which sank around 2230 hours on August 23.

2. The Japanese transports (there were actually three) carried fifteen hundred battle-hardened troops, some from the elite 5th Special Naval Landing Force, the rest coming from Colonel Ichiki's rear echelon. The transports carried heavy weapons, including artillery, and ample ammunition. A couple of runs like this one would have put the Japanese in a very strong position to attack the Marine perimeter.

Chapter 19

1. In thirty-three years of writing aviation and military history, I've never encountered a more confused, poorly reported, and chaotic air battle than what happened on August 24. Reconstructing it has bedeviled historians for decades. My version and the squadron's internal dynamics that day come from my interviews with Marion Carl in 1991, when I was in graduate school at the University of Oregon, and oral histories with Fred Gutt, Marion Carl, John L. Smith, and Doc Everton. Secondary sources include Lundstrom's *First Team at Guadalcanal*; Hammel's *Guadalcanal: Starvation Island* and *Carrier Clash: The Invasion of Guadalcanal and the Battle of the Eastern Solomons, August 1942*; Tillman's *Wildcat, the F4F in WWII*; Baeza's *Guadalcanal: Cactus Air Force Contre Marine Imperiale*; Miller's *Cactus Air Force*; Sherrod's *History of Marine Corps Aviation in World War II*; Carl's book with Tillman, *Pushing the Envelope: The Career of Fighter Ace and Test Pilot Marion Carl*; and Frank's seminal work, *Guadalcanal*. Primary source documents include the MAG-23 and VMF-223 war diaries. Additionally, the participants that day were interviewed and observed by two civilian reporters and one Marine reporter. These articles, which recorded some of the comments of the pilots themselves, provide especially significant perspective.

2. Some of the pilots thought there were two waves of bombers, one composed of carrier-based Kates and the other a formation of G4M Betties launched from Rabaul. The Americans thought the second wave—the Betties—turned back after the Marines had savaged their ranks. This aspect of the mission colors many of the contemporary reports and caused much confusion in the secondary sources. The account was only resolved when Japanese records became available to American writers and historians.

3. There were no twin-engine bombers involved, though that had been the Japanese plan. The Betties were supposed to link up with the B5N Kates (from the light carrier *Ryūjō*) and hit Henderson Field together. The B5Ns were tasked with bombing the anti-aircraft emplacements defending the strip while the Betties, with their larger payloads, were to render the runway inoperable.

Because weather forced the Betties to return to Rabaul, they never made the rendezvous. The incoming strike that afternoon consisted of a first wave of six Kates in an arrowhead formation, closely escorted by six Zeroes off their starboard wing. Marion Carl initiated the battle by taking out Petty Officer 2nd Class Nojima Jinsaku's A6M Zero. Marion had mistaken his target as a Kate, probably because of how tight the formation had been—a defensive move that bombers used to maximize their firepower. Fighters usually flew looser formations.

Behind the first wave, the *Ryūjō* launched an additional nine Zeroes. They were the designated strafers, a second wave intended to capitalize on the bombing with a follow-up low-altitude attack on the airfield. As the two waves approached Guadalcanal, the nine strafer-assigned Zeroes dropped through the cloud cover and spread out in three formations of three planes each to attack Henderson from different directions. Those Zeroes were the ones that dogged Robert Read and fought with MacLeod and Bailey. Altogether, the *Ryūjō*'s strike lost four of its six Kates (three over the target, another crash-landed at Ndai Island off the northern tip of Malaita), plus three Zeroes.

4. Reportage for this mission was chaotic at best. Both the MAG-23 war diary and VMF-223's war diary list sixteen total kills for the day. The pilots on the mission included the four from Marion Carl's division plus Morrell, Jeans, Pond, Frazier, Bailey, Read, King, Taylor, Massey, and MacLeod. Yet somehow in Frank Olynyk's study of Marine Corps credits for aerial victories, Eugene Trowbridge is listed as shooting down two bombers that day. He is also credited with two Zero kills on August 21 plus a bomber on August 22. That would have given him five kills and shared status, with Marion Carl, as the first Marine Corps ace. However, there was no enemy contact on the twenty-second, Trowbridge wasn't with John L. Smith's flight on the twenty-first, and none of these five kills are listed in the squadron war diary or MAG-23's. The discrepancy arose from interviews conducted in 1943, a year after the fact, and the claims made in those interviews were added to the victory credits in Olynyk's work.

Chapter 20

1. Contemporary newspaper accounts of Macias refer to him as "Luis." In most of his official US Marine Corps paperwork, and his headstone, he went by the Americanized version of his name, "Lewis." Later in life, his friends called him "Rick." For consistency, I've used "Lewis," the name Macias himself used throughout his life.

2. The *Saratoga*'s air group found and attacked the *Ryūjō* that afternoon, crippling the light carrier and forcing its abandonment. Two further strikes by US Army Air Forces B-17s attacked the sinking vessel through the late afternoon and early evening but failed to do additional damage.

Chapter 21

1. At the time of the bombardment, clouds obscured the nearly full moon and made it impossible for the Japanese ships to see the airfield. The shelling was desultory at best, but it did deprive the Marines of desperately needed sleep. Like so much reporting on the Guadalcanal campaign, there are conflicting accounts of the number of ships involved in the bombardment force. Frank, *Guadalcanal*, and Lundstrom, *The First Team*, describe three destroyers. In a 1956 *Proceedings* article, Rear Adm. Raizō Tanaka said that there were five. Hammel's *Guadalcanal: Starvation Island* and Miller's *Cactus Air Force* use that number. According to the Tabular Record of Movements (TROM) of Japanese warships, three destroyers from Destroyer Squadron 30 made the run to Guadalcanal from the Shortland Islands to execute the bombardment: the *Mutsuki*, the *Yayoi*, and the *Isokaze*. Before they shelled the perimeter, the vessels

linked up with the *Kagerō* and the *Kawakaze*, two destroyers detached from Tanaka's own transport force. Tanaka had sent the *Kawakaze* forward to relieve the *Kagerō*. All five destroyers rejoined his task force later in the morning. Complicating matters was the arrival of the *Uzuki*, another destroyer sent from Rabaul to deliver food and ammunition to Kokumbona, Guadalcanal, that night. The *Uzuki* then moved to Ndai Island to rescue the *Ryūjō's* B5N Kate crew forced down on August 24 by VMF-223. This act is attributed to the *Mochizuki* in Lundstrom and Frank's account, though the ship's TROM states that the *Mochizuki* was undergoing a refit in Japan and did not rejoin the campaign in the Solomons until August 29. All this confusion has obscured which ships VMSB-232 and Flight 300 actually attacked on two of the four missions flown on August 25.

2. The two naval aviators spent twelve days with these local people, who filled them with plenty of great food, including roast duck. When they returned to Guadalcanal, they were the best-fed aviators at Henderson.

3. After Dick, Danny, and Baldy took off, a flight of Japanese floatplanes bombed the perimeter. The attack caused little damage, but it did deny the Marines their much-needed sleep.

Chapter 22

1. There were a small number of Nakajima A6M-2N "Rufes" in the area. These were derivatives of the Zero designed to operate from water. They were excellent for areas with no local airfields and would often be used in conjunction with a seaplane carrier. Instead of wheels, they were equipped with two small wing floats and a main pontoon under the fuselage.

Chapter 23

1. A fast-moving, narrow target free to maneuver in any direction turned out to be an exceptionally difficult target to hit with dive-bombing tactics, a lesson also learned at Midway when fifty-eight SBDs attacked a single Japanese destroyer at the end of the battle. All fifty-eight bombs missed. Not long afterward, a squadron of B-17s attacked the same ship, dropping another seventy-nine bombs on it. The skipper of that tin can deftly evaded all of them in what had to have been a record.

Chapter 24

1. MacLeod ended up in the same hospital with Gutt, who overheard him talking to a mud Marine about how he, MacLeod, was going to make sure he never had to go back to combat again. After the war, he went into the publishing business, making a name for himself at *Cosmopolitan* magazine. Later, he helped found *Seventeen* and *Teen Beat*. MacLeod was inducted into the NCAA Athlete's Hall of Fame in 1977, but he was not remembered fondly by those who flew with him on Guadalcanal in 1942.

Chapter 26

1. Marines examining the wreckage of Carl's victory found the plane's oxygen bottle and presented it to the Oregonian as a gift. The fate of the bottle is unknown, but Marion did take it home with him in 1942.

Chapter 28

1. The field's main radio system had been badly damaged by the Japanese raid on August 26.

2. The MAG-23 records give Barker credit for a hit, along with Fink and Caldwell. In a 1998 article in *Echoes*, the Guadalcanal veterans' newsletter, Caldwell wrote that his bomb was a near miss. Miller credited Moore with a hit, McCafferty with one during the search force's pile-on, and Fletcher Brown with another one. Trying to unsnarl who hit what at this juncture is probably impossible. The important thing is that the raid sank one destroyer, crippled another, badly damaged a third, and lightly damaged the fourth, forcing the abandonment of the reinforcement mission.

Chapter 29

1. McQuiston, a 1921 Naval Academy graduate, served aboard the battleship *Arizona* and the cruiser *Astoria* and commanded several submarines in the interwar period before ending up in charge of a recruiting center in Michigan as the European War broke out. He finished his tour with the *Burrows* and later in the war was given command of the USS *Sibley*, a Victory ship commissioned in October 1944. He saw the *Sibley* through the Iwo Jima landing in February 1945 and the Okinawa landing in April 1945. He stayed in the service, was promoted to commander in November 1945, and eventually retired with a bump in grade to captain in 1951 after thirty years of service. In fairness to McQuiston, the charts for the Tulagi channel and anchorage were primitive at best, making navigating those difficult, shallow waters treacherous. Nevertheless, the decision to toss cargo overboard had a painful effect on the units depending on it.

Chapter 30

1. Shingō lived a charmed life. He flew at the Battle of Santa Cruz with the *Zuikaku*'s air group in October 1942. Later, he commanded a Kawanishi Shiden Kai group in the defense of Japan. He survived the war and served in the Japanese Self-Defense Forces from 1954 to 1962.

Chapter 31

1. A reporter changed the name *Cactus Express* to *Tokyo Express* to conceal Guadalcanal's code name. The moniker stuck, and for the succeeding eighty years, *Tokyo Express* has been the term used for these fast Japanese resupply runs, usually composed of patrol boats, destroyers, and the occasional fast minelayer.

2. This patrol boat happened to be carrying elements of the Japanese 8th Independent Anti-Tank Company, which had been aboard the *Boston Maru* on August 25. Its soldiers witnessed the sinking of the *Kinryu Maru* that day before being taken to the Shortlands and transferred to four "patrol boats"—the Imperial Japanese Navy equivalent of the US Navy's overage destroyer-transports (APDs).

Chapter 32

1. This section is an example of the chaotic nature of the source material. Most secondary sources note that the strikes on Kawaguchi's barge convoy didn't start until

September 3. One version of the MAG-23 War Diary (there are at least three versions) says these attacks began on September 2. Dennis Byrd, in his unpublished manuscript, agrees with the September 2 date. The MAG-23 history also confirms the attacks started on the second. Don McCafferty's account of his search mission in *Liberty* magazine gives no date for it. So the date was a judgment call on my part, given the sequence of events and McCafferty's descriptions of what followed. Either way, the mission that begins this chapter happened either on the morning of September 2 or the morning of the third.

2. Don and Baldy had probably come across the beginnings of Kawaguchi's barge operation, which began with the landing craft being carried by two Imperial Japanese Army transports down from the Shortlands to an island just off the northwestern coast of Santa Isabel. The transports had arrived around 0300 on September 2. Baldy might have hit the *Asakasan Maru*. After this mission, the ship did not take part in any operations until late February 1943, and then it wasn't in the South Pacific but was in the Indian Ocean. If he didn't hit the *Asakasan Maru*, he probably hit one of the larger landing craft used in the operation, such as one of the 17-meter Daihatsus that could carry both men and vehicles.

Chapter 37

1. The classic story about this encounter goes as follows: Marion entered the Opium Den and asked about John L.'s score. General Geiger needled him a bit after telling him Smith had pulled ahead to become the top ace. At that point, Marion quipped, "Goddammit, General, ground Smitty for five days so I can catch up!" There are multiple versions of this story, but it seems like they stemmed initially from Robert C. Miller's article on Marion's escape and return to the perimeter. When John L., Dick Mangrum, and Marion were on their war bond tour, they were asked about this moment. Marion laughed it off and said an enlisted man, not himself, had suggested grounding John L. Over the years, the story morphed and Marion playfully recounted it, as the version where Marion does the quipping makes for a great yarn in the midst of an exceptionally grim period at Guadalcanal.

2. Zen Pond's fate may have been exceptionally terrible. Japanese sources relate how a captured Marine flyer was tortured for information on September 12. The pilot broke and told the Japanese that the south side of the perimeter was largely undefended, confirming for Kawaguchi the wisdom of his attack plan. The captured Marine has never been positively identified, but he was either VMF-224's 2nd Lt. J. M. Jones or Zen Pond. The Japanese did not record the fate of their captive, but he surely was executed or left to die.

3. Eugene made it back to the States as the third-ranking ace in VMF-223. He was hospitalized in San Diego and later in Great Lakes, Illinois, until the end of January 1943.

Chapter 39

1. Eades was flown out to the New Hebrides, where he spent five weeks in the hospital. When he was cleared for duty, he voluntarily returned to Guadalcanal for several more weeks in November 1942. By then, the rest of VMSB-232 was back in the States.

2. Francis Register, quoted in Eric Hammel and Thomas McKelvey Cleaver, *The Cactus Air Force: Air War over Guadalcanal* (Oxford, UK: Osprey, 2022).

Chapter 40

1. Actual Japanese losses that day were two G4Ms lost over the target area; a third limped to Rekata Bay and ditched. Marion's second victim crash-landed at Buka Island in the Northern Solomons, a total loss. All the remaining fourteen bombers took some level of damage from either flak or fighters. The trailing formation that Armistead picked out belonged to a new air group that had just arrived as reinforcements for the Japanese. Based at Kavieng, New Ireland, Papua New Guinea, the Takeo Air Group sent nine bombers south for the unit's inaugural raid on Guadalcanal. The veterans of Rabaul, the Kisarazu Air Group, led the way. The group's previous experience probably explains why the bombing was so accurate and did extensive damage. One Zero was lost, but the A6M pilots claimed six Wildcats in return. Ultimately, the raid cost nearly a third of the G4Ms. With the other bombers shot up, it was a bad day for the G4M crews.

Chapter 42

1. A few weeks before, several US pilots shot up a Japanese pilot in his chute. Appalled by what he'd seen, another pilot reported the shooters to MAG-23 HQ. The incident was brushed off. Again, this wasn't a gentleman's war. There was no mercy on Guadalcanal.

Chapter 45

1. Postwar research revealed that there were four Japanese floatplanes involved in this action. All four were shot down.

Epilogue

1. That visitor was me—a twenty-**three**-year-old graduate student from the University of Oregon who arrived at the house in a 1956 Ford Victoria. I sported a mullet back then. Not a good look. Marion was exceptionally kind and gracious to me, and that day is the reason I wrote this book.

Final Note

1. The police report and medical examiner's report of John L.'s suicide state that the misfired round was 7.65 mm in caliber. The police assumed the Japanese pistol was a Nambu, which was a generic name for all Japanese military pistols back then. The Nambu chambered the 8 × 22 mm round, but the Hamada chambered the 7.65 mm. I've based my call on the assumption that the police would recognize the caliber more than they would a rare and unusual Japanese WWII sidearm. The only Japanese pistol to chamber the 7.65 mm round was the Hamada Type 1.

INDEX

Aces of the Pacific (video game), 464

Advanced Carrier Training Group
program
reputation of, 76, 84, 98
training at, 94–95, 138

African Americans, 30

aircraft. *See also specific aircraft*
air medals, 467
antiaircraft guns, 139, 168, 232, 261,
273, 401
against Axis powers, 38
from Brewster Aeronautical
Corporation, 30–31, 33, 44
with Double Wasp engines, 199
Douglas Aircraft Company, 266–267
duels, 252–256
economics of, 33, 39–40
in Europe, 391
fuel, 125, 158, 173
Grumman Aircraft Corporation, 36,
42–48, 71, 449
at Guadalcanal, 153–161
in Hawaii, 68–74
to Hicks, 31–32
history of, 469
from Japan, 1, 26, 46–47, 66, 233–234,
244–251
to John L., 34, 63–64
in Korean War, 463, 468
MIA pilots and, 203, 231, 332,
342–343, 377, 379, 417–419, 466
at Midway, 46, 74

at National Museum of Naval
Aviation, 461
Navy, 381
oxygen systems for, 376
at Pearl Harbor attack, 75
for Red Devils, 181–182, 363–364
reinforcements and, 125–126
for Royal Air Force, 284–285
in storms, 189–190
strike, 70
training, 85–86
Vandegrift and, 157
weight of, 151–152
in World War I, 32, 222–223
with Wright Cyclone engines, 40, 102,
149, 214, 232, 264

aircraft carriers, 98–107. *See also specific
carriers*

Alchiba (cargo ship), 386

alcohol, 5, 62, 431

alcoholism, 448

Alhena (transporter), 186–188

Alwyn, USS (ship), 128

Amagiri (destroyer), 280–282

Anderson (destroyer), 100

Ant Freight, 320–321

antiaircraft guns
accuracy of, 401
in combat, 232
at Guadalcanal, 261
range of, 273
in World War II, 139, 168

Arizona, USS (ship), 61, 107

Armistead, Kirk
  Carl, M., and, 5
  in combat, 399–401
  leadership of, 2–3, 62
  at Midway, 337
  reputation of, 438

Army, US
  Air Corps, 138
  Air Force posts, 70
  B-26 Marauders, 4–5
  bases, 73
  to media, 26–27
  US Navy and, 33, 39
  in World War I, 94

Arnold, Barry, 378

Asagiri (destroyer), 280–282

Asia, 90, 321. *See also specific countries*

Astoria (cruiser), 123

Atlanta, 23–29

Atlanta, USS (ship), 23–24

Australia, 123

autobiographies, 464–465

Axis powers, 38, 48

B-17 Flying Fortress bombers. *See* Flying
  Fortress bombers

B-26 Marauders, 4–5

Bailey, Elwood
  death of, 376
  in service, 76–78, 82, 197, 202–204,
    257
  Taylor and, 242

Baldinus, Lawrence
  in combat, 213–214, 224, 226
  death of, 356, 359, 360–361, 363, 381
  in flight, 151, 228
  Hise and, 223
  Iverson and, 215–216
  legacy of, 460
  McCafferty and, 317–320
  reputation of, 94–95, 114, 117–119, 382
  Sewell and, 210

Baldinus, Wencel, 117

Barker, J. T., 273

Barner, Duke, 105–106, 143–144,
  146, 148

Barnes, Lois, 54

Barnes, Lucille, 54

baseball, 37, 265

Battle of Midway. *See* Midway

Bauer, Joe
  Carl, M., and, 143
  in combat, 424–425
  Foss and, 431
  Frazier to, 426
  Galer and, 5
  John L., and, 261
  MacLeod and, 243
  reputation of, 69, 127, 420–421
  training with, 167
  Winter and, 423

Bell Aero Corporation, 300

Bellatrix, USS (transporter), 338–339

Betties. *See also specific topics*
  in combat, 123, 245–246, 407–409
  for Japan, 251, 341–342
  protection of, 261
  strategy against, 247–250
  Zeroes and, 396–397, 399–402

Betty Boop (cartoon), 132

Blue (destroyer), 186–187, 191

Boise, USS (cruiser), 385–386

bombers. *See specific topics*

Bong, Richard, 446

Boston Maru (transporter), 236–237

boxing, 36

Boyington, Gregory, 126

Brannon, Dale
  reinforcements and, 404
  reputation of, 261, 295, 300
  as scout, 310
  squadron of, 325–327
  strategy of, 370

Brewster Aeronautical Corporation
  aircraft from, 30–31, 33, 44
  business operations of, 36–37
  factories, 39–41
  reputation of, 34
  after World War II, 467

Brewster F2A Buffalos. *See* Buffalos
Bronze Star medal, 449, 467
Brooks, Bill, 69, 105, 406–407
Brown, Bernie, 228–229, 232
Brown, Elynor, 262, 333
Brown, Fletcher
    death of, 331–333, 363, 380–381
    Dick and, 265
    in flight, 272–273, 278
    leadership of, 228
    McAllister and, 330
    O'Keefe, A., and, 233
    promotions for, 330–331
    reputation of, 114, 117, 129, 152, 382
    as scout, 305–306, 311–312
    with soldiers, 262
Brownings, 232
Buccaneers
    Buffalos and, 38
    Dick in, 39–41
    factories for, 36
    reputation of, 34
Bucks County, Pennsylvania, 32, 36–41
Budd Company, 468
Buell, Harold
    in combat, 281–282, 359
    as dive-bomber, 305
    Fink and, 366–367
    injuries of, 320
    Moore, T., and, 210–211
    reputation of, 275–276
Buffalos
    on aircraft carriers, 101–102
    Buccaneers and, 38
    in Central Pacific, 3
    designs for, 33–34, 66
    at Midway, 34–35
    reputation of, 64
    Wildcats and, 1–2, 6, 89–90, 99–100, 130
    Zeroes and, 40, 67
Bureau of Aeronautics, Navy, 468
Burkett, Cora, 13–14
business
    in US, 37–38

    in US Navy, 80–81
    in World War II, 30–32
Butler, Ed, 353
Byrd, Dennis
    Baldinus, L., to, 360–361
    in combat, 214, 236–237
    death of, 465
    Dick and, 120–121, 148–150, 230–235, 326
    in flight, 276–277
    after Guadalcanal, 463–465
    ingenuity of, 352–353, 357
    Japan to, 218
    Mitchell, O., and, 278
    psychology of, 158, 280, 303, 354–355
    reputation of, 120–121, 147–150
    Rose and, 309–310
    with soldiers, 307–308

Caldwell, Turner
    Dick and, 290, 390–391
    John L., and, 392
    reputation of, 211, 274–276, 280
    strategy of, 215–216
California
    China and, 465
    Hawaii and, 76
    Hollywood, 71, 76, 131–132
    San Diego, 69, 72, 75–76, 84, 94–95, 98, 434–435, 461
    University of San Francisco in, 466
Canberra (cruiser), 123
Canfield, Clayton
    Carl, M., and, 342–343
    in combat, 339–341
    experience of, 66, 85, 261
    injuries of, 375
    reputation of, 334–335
Carey, John, 66
Carl, Bruce, 441
Carl, Marion
    Armistead and, 5
    authority of, 467
    Bauer and, 143
    Canfield and, 342–343

Carl, Marion (*continued*)
Chambers and, 85–86
in combat, 164–165, 200, 244, 259, 289–290, 298, 399–402, 422–423
death of, 440–441
in debriefings, 92
Dick and, 10–12, 15, 154, 439, 452
experience of, 420–421
family of, 47–48, 57–58
Frazier and, 423–426
friends of, 392
Galer and, 338–339, 410
at Guadalcanal, 23, 344–351
at Henderson Field, 162–163
Hughes and, 415–416
with jammed guns, 424–425
Jeans and, 406–407
John L., and, 44–46, 49, 70–72, 328, 336–337, 412–413, 431–432, 439, 447–449
against Kate bombers, 2
Kirvin and, 51–58, 437–438, 440
leadership of, 100–101
Lees and, 298–299
legacy of, 455–456
Lindley and, 99, 199–200
McLennan and, 300–301
to media, 44–45
at Midway, 33, 69
Morrell and, 73, 81–82, 93, 100, 102–104, 243, 257
nightlife to, 50–51, 63
opinions of, 145–146
on patrol, 295
in plane crashes, 31
PR to, 17–22
psychology of, 5–6, 47, 334–335, 340–341, 418, 430
on radio, 52–53
reputation of, 129–130, 203, 220, 267, 339–340, 342, 410–411, 428–429, 435
return of, 374–376
in service, 84, 96, 155
with soldiers, 85

strategy of, 372–374, 416–417
in surprise attacks, 4
test-flying by, 36
Trowbridge and, 128
in VMF-221, 88
for VMF-223, 283–284, 468
Wildcats and, 3, 195–196
wingmen of, 193–194
before World War II, 294
against Zeroes, 252–256
Castor, USS (ship), 434
casualties
to Dick, 279–280
to dive-bombers, 4–5
to Japan, 168–169
to John L., 87–91
memory and, 19
at Midway, 62–63, 88–89, 115, 206, 460
to Moore, T., 279–280
of Morrell, 375–376
psychology of, 26–27, 35–36, 220–229
recovery from, 467–468
trauma and, 132–133, 460
from U-Boats, 44
to VMF-221, 4, 61–62, 67
to VMF-223, 11, 86, 87–91
Western Union and, 41
from Zeroes, 2–3
Cates, Clifton
leadership of, 418
Thomas, G., and, 157–158
Vandegrift and, 166
Chambers, Clyde, 86
Chambers, Oliver Kenneth, 79–80, 82–86, 89–91
Chanel No. 5, 51–52
Cherry Point, North Carolina, 40
Chesterfield cigarettes, 52
Chin, Ben, 36
China
California and, 465
Japan and, 36, 180, 301
Philippines and, 111
US and, 126, 157, 438

Choi, Clarence, 67
Civil War, 34, 56, 456
civilians, 31, 348–350, 372–373
Clemons, Martin, 348–349
Coast Guard, 26–27
Coastwatchers
  from Great Britain, 241–242, 348
  at Guadalcanal, 260
  reports from, 261, 294
  safety of, 398
  Vandegrift and, 404
  warnings from, 327
  Wildcats and, 287
  Zeroes and, 408–409
Cold War
  geopolitics, 439, 456–457
  US in, 465
  US Navy in, 448
  Vietnam War and, 463
college education, 18
college football, 24–29, 456
COMSOPAC (South Pacific Command)
  Fike with, 174
  Guadalcanal and, 122, 161, 172
  headquarters, 186, 339
  Vandegrift with, 241
Congress, US, 37–38
construction battalions, 337–338
Conzett, Elmer, 305
Coolbaugh, Walter W., 394
Copacabana Club, 54–55
Corry, Roy
  death of, 247, 250, 256
  experience of, 244
  Hamilton and, 246–247
  Pond and, 99
  psychology of, 129
  reputation of, 69
Costello, Frank, 54
Crescent City, USS (attack transport), 385–387
CUB-1
  fuel from, 183
  Polk for, 181–182
  reputation of, 173–174

sailors for, 285, 287–288
supplies from, 210–211
Cuba, 465

Daisy Cutter bombs, 401
D'Arcy, R. M., 341
Dauntlesses. See also specific topics
  against bombers, 217
  from catapults, 150–152
  designs of, 34, 40–41, 149
  against destroyers, 216
  Dick and, 40–41, 156, 220–221
  before flight, 147–148
  gunners on, 166
  Japan and, 276–277
  at Midway, 264, 461
  for Red Devils, 125
  reputation of, 88, 94–95, 115,
    118–120, 397
  scouting with, 324, 386–388, 393–394
  success with, 280–282
  Tracers and, 231, 277–278
  Wildcats and, 139, 143, 154, 189,
    210–211, 233, 303–304
  Zeroes and, 115, 150, 217–218, 222,
    224–225, 230–231
Dawn Patrol (film), 76
death. See casualties
Delaney, Jack, 36
Dick. See Mangrum, Richard (Dick)
DiMaggio, Joe, 466
Distinguished Flying Cross medal, 127,
    410–411, 438, 449, 459–460, 462,
    467, 469
dive-bombers
  accuracy of, 359–360
  Buell as, 305
  casualties to, 4–5
  crews of, 66
  danger for, 460
  designs for, 34, 39–40
  to Dick, 106
  from Japan, 182–183
  John L., and, 125–126, 221
  against Kidō Butai, 87–88

dive-bombers (*continued*)
    at Midway, 88
    for Red Devils, 72, 75, 117–118
    at San Diego, 75
    squadrons, 64
    training, 438–439
Dobbin, John, 337, 357, 413, 430
Double Wasp engines, 199
Douglas Aircraft Company, 266–267
Dow, Harold, 382–385
Drake, Gaston, 82
Drury, Frank, 407
dust bowl, 97
Dutch air force, 39
Dynamix, 464

Eades, Edward
    in combat, 323
    death of, 466
    after Guadalcanal, 465–466
    Macias and, 323, 354, 384, 435–436
    McAllister and, 184–185
    psychology of, 432
    reputation of, 158–159
    rescue of, 389–390
    Thomas, L., and, 207–208, 225, 227,
        319, 382–383, 385–388
Edson, Merritt
    Kawaguchi and, 457
    leadership of, 364–365, 367, 370–371
    reputation of, 306, 336, 339, 410
    strategy of, 369–370, 404
    after World War II, 450
Efate, 128–137, 153, 173, 261, 433, 466
El Morocco, 53–54
Elks magazine, 82
Elrod, Henry, 127
enlistment standards, 138
Enterprise, USS (fleet carrier), 141, 211,
    235–236
Europe. *See also specific countries*
    aircraft in, 391
    North Atlantic Treaty Organization
        and, 449
    World War II in, 267

Everton, Loren
    in combat, 165, 168–169, 246–249
    Hamilton and, 244
    John L., and, 196
    leadership of, 202–203
    on patrol, 167–168
    reputation of, 143
    for VMF-223, 166–167
Ewa Field
    culture of, 63–64, 68–74, 82
    Midway and, 87–91
    training at, 96–105
    VMF-223 at, 92–96

F2H Banshees, 438
F4F Wildcats. *See* Wildcats
F4U Corsair, 34, 45, 464, 468
F6F Hellcats, 45
fashion industry, 49–50
Felt, Don, 217
Fike, Charles
    Barner and, 144
    with COMSOPAC, 174
    Dick and, 142–143, 148, 256, 271, 279
    Frazier and, 201–202
    after Guadalcanal, 468
    Hayes and, 165–166, 190
    John L., and, 122, 154–155, 159–160,
        201, 343, 457
    leadership of, 125–127, 153–155,
        203, 417
    legacy of, 443–444
    Polk and, 174–175
    reputation of, 145–146, 161, 234, 379,
        419–420, 426, 450
    with soldiers, 216
    Vandegrift and, 289
    in Wildcats, 152–153
Fink, Christian
    Buell and, 366–367
    in combat, 281–282
    injuries of, 383, 390
    legacy of, 443
    reputation of, 235, 275–276, 419–420
Fisher, Margaret Hough, 460

FJ3 Fury, 467
Fleener, Robert
  McCafferty and, 390, 419
  O'Keefe, A., and, 362–363
  Prosser and, 379, 394
  reputation of, 233
Fleischer, Dave, 131–132
Fletcher, Frank Jack, 123
Florida
  culture of, 82
  training in, 97–98
  University of Miami, 83
  US Navy in, 39–40, 86
Flying Fortress bombers, 66
Fomalhaut (transporter), 186–188, 191
Foss, Joseph, 431
France, 52
Frazier, Ken
  Carl, M., and, 423–426
  in combat, 199, 424
  death of, 467
  Fike and, 201–202
  after Guadalcanal, 467
  Gutt and, 429
  Hughes and, 412–413
  Kendrick and, 415–416
  MacLeod and, 197
  Morrell and, 99
  on patrol, 295
  reputation of, 79, 84, 101–102, 220, 421
  Trowbridge and, 244, 252–253
Fred Waring Show (radio Show), 52–53
Fubuki-class, 280–281
fuel
  aircraft, 125, 158, 173
  in combat, 233–234, 249
  from CUB-1, 183
  in World War II, 173–175
Fuhrman, Lee, 27–29
Fuller, USS (transporter), 338–339

Galer, Robert
  Bauer and, 5
  Carl, M., and, 338–339, 410
  in combat, 328, 341, 406, 415

death of, 469
in diary, 357
Dick and, 392, 447
Dobbin and, 413
John L., and, 96, 99, 358–359, 364, 376
in Korean War, 469
leadership of, 94, 98, 324, 331, 399
missing in action, 417
psychology of, 358, 398, 416, 423
reputation of, 117, 337, 408, 411, 429
in service, 75
South and, 419–420
for VMF-223, 105
for VMF-224, 92–93
Wallace and, 303–304
Garrabrant, Clifford Donally, 328
Geiger, Roy
  Dick and, 364
  leadership of, 374–375
  reputation of, 323
  strategy of, 329, 336
  Vandegrift and, 365–366
  Wallace and, 323–324
Georgia Tech, 23–29
Germany
  for Axis powers, 48
  in France, 52
  Soviet Union and, 267
  U-Boats from, 26
  US and, 456
  to US Navy, 44
Ghormley, Robert, 172, 186, 409
Gilbert, Paul, 44
Glidden, Elmer, 394
glide-bombing, 318–319
Grant Field, 23–29
Great Britain
  Coastwatchers from, 241–242, 348
  Royal Air Force of, 284–285
Great Depression
  culture of, 120–121, 269
  Oklahoma and, 96–97
  psychology of, 55, 62, 183
  World War I and, 82–83
Green, Mary Ruth, 464

Gregory, USS (transporter), 326

Gruenke, Al, 308–309, 331, 362

Grumman, Leroy, 44–47, 49, 53

Grumman Aircraft Corporation, 36, 42–48, 71, 449

Guadalcanal. *See also specific topics*
  aftermath of, 437–441
  aircraft at, 153–161
  antiaircraft guns at, 261
  blunders at, 283–292
  Carl, M., at, 23, 344–351
  Coastwatchers at, 260
  combat at, 193–203, 278–280, 353–361
  COMSOPAC and, 122, 161, 172
  defense at, 412–418
  Dick at, 156–158, 181–184, 188–191
  Efate and, 153
  Henderson Field at, 160, 162–170, 193–194
  in history, 455–458
  Imperial Navy at, 212
  Japan and, 9, 35, 122–123, 174, 191–192, 230–237, 280–282
  legacy of, 444–445, 455–458
  life after, 459–469
  Long Island and, 147–154
  MAG-23 at, 241, 288, 419–421
  media and, 13, 21, 23–29, 197, 266–267
  Midway and, 32, 58
  psychology at, 19, 203–204, 238–243, 362–371, 422–427
  Red Devils at, 11, 158, 161, 184–188, 303–308, 311–316, 374–379, 391–395
  reinforcements at, 389–391, 396–402
  reputation of, 38–39
  reunion, 450–451
  routines at, 262–269
  search missions at, 308–311
  Smith, L., on, 303–305, 312–313, 322
  soldiers at, 16–22, 205–212, 220–229, 244–251, 428–436
  Solomon Islands and, 138–146
  strategy at, 252–259, 270–278, 380–388, 403–411
  to US Navy, 122–131

VMF-223 at, 171–180, 293–302

VMF-224 at, 334–343

Wildcats at, 46

World War II and, 213–219

guns
  antiaircraft, 139, 168, 232, 261, 273, 401
  efficacy of, 285–286
  gunners, 166
  gunnery training, 84–85, 103
  jammed, 3–4, 249, 424–425
  machine, 190–191
  on Wildcats, 85, 168–169, 263–264

Gutt, Fred
  on birthday, 431
  death of, 468
  Frazier and, 429
  after Guadalcanal, 468
  Hamilton and, 193–194
  injuries of, 242
  Jeans and, 430
  Marvin and, 413
  Pond and, 457–458
  reputation of, 200

Hallyburton, Claude, 307–310, 316

Halsey, William, 409

Hamilton, Tex
  in combat, 248
  Corry and, 246–247
  Everton and, 244
  Gutt and, 193–194
  reputation of, 166, 169

Hammel, Eric, 464–465

hand-to-hand combat, 368–370

Haring, Richard, 376

Hartley, Dean, 406–407, 415

Hato, Kazushi, 180

Hawaii. *See also specific topics*
  aircraft in, 68–74
  California and, 76
  Long Island in, 64, 98–107
  Palmyra Atoll near, 98–103
  soldiers in, 61–67, 95–96, 103–106

Hayes, Charles, 158, 165–166, 190

Helena (cruiser), 139–140

Hell's Angels (film), 76
Hemingway, Ernest, 53
Henderson, Lofton "Joe," 87–89, 115–117,
        119, 160
Henderson Field
    attacks against, 289
    communications at, 273–274
    Japan at, 353–361
    soldiers at, 160, 162–170
    Wildcats at, 193–194
Henley (destroyer), 186–187
Hicks, T. E.
    aircraft to, 31–32
    Dick and, 31–32
    Grumman and, 49
    leadership of, 36, 45, 52
    in PR, 16–22, 24
    for US Navy, 11–12
    Van Dusen and, 33–34
Hilo, USS (ship), 64, 75–79
Hise, Henry
    Baldinus, L., and, 223
    in combat, 224, 312–314
    death of, 463
    Dick and, 271–272, 461–462
    in flight, 151–152, 154, 273
    after Guadalcanal, 463
    injuries to, 11, 315–316
    landing by, 158
    Mitchell, O., and, 277–278
    Prosser and, 267
    reputation of, 138–139
    as scout, 304
Hollywood, 71, 76, 131–132
Hope, Bob, 114
Hopkins, USS (converted destroyer), 339
Hornet, USS (ship), 73, 93, 99, 384
Hovey, USS (ship), 435
Hughes, Charley
    Carl, M., and, 415–416
    Frazier and, 412–413
    Hartley and, 406–407
    Jeans and, 426–427
    reputation of, 153, 261, 336
Hughes, USS (destroyer), 339

Hull, USS (destroyer), 339
Humberd, William C., 6
Humphreys, Josiah, 214, 308
Humphreys, V. K., 330
Hurricanes, 33

Iden, Rubin, 312–313
immigration, 48, 117, 268, 457–458
Imperial Army (Japan), 321
Imperial Navy (Japan)
    at Guadalcanal, 212
    reputation of, 258–259, 281
    strategy of, 404–405
    in World War II, 32, 143
Indianapolis, USS (cruiser), 434
injuries. *See* casualties
INS. *See* International News Service
intelligence reports, 363, 366,
        398–399, 405
International News Service (INS), 18,
        20–21
investigative reporting, 27–29
Iverson, Danny
    Baldinus, L., and, 215–216
    in combat, 213–214, 232–233
    death of, 460
    in flight, 151, 306
    after Guadalcanal, 460–461
    injuries of, 355
    McCafferty and, 273
    Moore, T., and, 191, 206–207
    O'Keefe, A., and, 390
    Prosser and, 217, 274
    psychology of, 327, 364
    reputation of, 114–115
    as scout, 304, 307
Ivy League Schools, 78–79, 175

J. Franklin Bell, USS (ship), 68, 74
James, Harry, 266
jammed guns, 3–4, 249, 424–425
Japan. *See also specific topics*
    aircraft from, 1, 26, 46–47, 66,
        233–234, 244–251
    Ant Freight for, 320–321

Japan. (*continued*)
in Asia, 90, 321
against USS *Atlanta*, 23–24
attacks from, 164–165
Betties for, 251, 341–342
bombers and, 20, 65, 72, 74
to Byrd, 218
casualties to, 168–169
China and, 36, 180, 301
Coastwatchers to, 241–242
in combat, 109–110
culture of, 445
Dauntlesses and, 276–277
on defense, 370–371
destroyers for, 192
to Dick, 160–161, 226
dive-bombers from, 182–183
Guadalcanal and, 9, 35, 122–123, 174,
    191–192, 230–237, 280–282
at Henderson Field, 353–361
Imperial Army of, 321
Imperial Navy of, 32, 143, 212,
    258–259, 281, 404–405
in intelligence reports, 398–399
Japanese Americans, 96
John L., on, 131
Kawaguchi for, 310–312, 373
Korean laborers for, 261
machine guns for, 190–191
to MAG-23, 336
to media, 38–39
at Midway, 139
in Pacific, 123–124
at Pearl Harbor attack, 19
Philippines and, 10, 464
prisoners of war and, 344–351
raids by, 11, 215, 283–292, 313–315,
    369–370, 377–378, 392–393,
    412–418, 421
Red Devils and, 209, 261, 293–302,
    325–333
reinforcements for, 235–236, 304,
    373–374, 392
reputation of, 1–2, 36, 43, 46, 61–62,
    75–76, 89–90, 260–262, 301–302
to soldiers, 362–371, 458
strategy of, 3–6, 20–21, 172, 194–202,
    317–319, 368–369, 396–397,
    401–402
success against, 236–237
Tainan Air Group for, 179–180,
    258–259, 301
task forces from, 139–140, 187–188,
    216, 271, 358–359, 366–368
at Tenaru, 166–168
Tulagi for, 186–187
US and, 21–22, 35, 185–186, 252–259,
    267–268, 281–282, 359–360,
    403–411, 455
to US Navy, 45, 162–163
veterans of, 280–281
Wildcats against, 246–247
after World War II, 438
Zeroes for, 220–221, 223, 338–341
Jeans, Cloyd
    Carl, M., and, 406–407
    Gutt and, 430
    Hughes and, 426–427
    reputation of, 96, 203, 336
Jefferies, Robert, 327
Jinstū (cruiser), 236–237
John L. *See* Smith, John Lucian
John Roberts Power Agency, 49, 55–56
Johnson, Choo Choo, 459
Johnson, Owen D., 366–367
Johnston, Hulburd, 467
Jones, J. M., 342

Kagerō (destroyer), 192, 236–237
Kalvelage, Walt, 152
Kamikawa Maru (carrier), 373–374
Kate bombers, 2, 194, 195
Kate Smith Hour (TV show), 12
Kaufman, Yale W., 327, 378, 461
Kawaguchi, Kiyotake
    Edson and, 457
    for Japan, 310–312, 373
    reputation of, 281–282, 307, 310–311
    strategy of, 320–321, 357–358, 371
Kawai, Shiro, 180

Kawanishi H8K seaplanes, 261
Keller, Ted, 444, 453
Kendrick, Charles
  in combat, 341
  creativity of, 397–398
  death of, 426–427, 466
  Frazier and, 415–416
  after Guadalcanal, 466
  John L., and, 299–300
  Lees and, 295, 417
  legacy of, 457–458
  Lindley and, 179
  McLennan and, 289–290
  reputation of, 220, 296, 410–412
  in service, 96
  as wingman, 175–176, 178–179
Kennedy, Donald, 261
Kennedy, John F., 449
Kennedy, M. H., 338
Kidō Butai
  attacks against, 132
  dive-bombers against, 87–88
  Humberd against, 6
  at Pearl Harbor attack, 1
  Red Devils and, 116
  reputation of, 194, 216–217
  Zeroes and, 20
Kimberlin, Milo, 235
King, John, 201, 252
Kings Wharf, 122
Kinryu Maru (transporter), 236–237
Kipling, Rudyard, 397–3989
Kirn, Louis J., 393–394
Kirvin, Edna, 51–58, 437–438,
    440–441, 448
Knudson Trophy, 77
Korean Americans, 67
Korean laborers, 261
Korean prisoners of war, 286
Korean War
  aircraft in, 463, 468
  Galer in, 469
  soldiers in, 467
  US in, 439, 444, 447
  Vietnam War and, 465

Kunisuke, Yuki, 258
Kunz, Charlie, 66, 341

Langley, USS (ship), 117
Larkin, Claude, 71–73, 75, 110
Leander (cruiser), 385–386
Leauli, Eroni, 348–350, 372–373
leave, 9–15, 61, 82
Lebanon, 465
Lees, Willis
  Carl, M., and, 298–299
  in combat, 296–297, 407
  Jeans and, 336
  John L., and, 413–414
  Kendrick and, 295, 417
  Payne and, 406
  psychology of, 336–337
  Read and, 413
  reputation of, 410–411
  in service, 79, 244, 247
Legion of Merit, 449
Leland E. Thomas, USS (destroyer
    escort), 466
Lend-Lease Act, 33
Leslie, Maxwell, 264
Lewis, Joe E., 54
Liberty magazine, 459
Life magazine, 12, 54, 444
Lindbergh kidnapping trial, 27
Lindley, John
  Carl, M., and, 99, 199–200
  in combat, 176–177, 328
  injuries of, 177–178, 183, 335
  Kendrick and, 179
  leadership of, 175
  reputation of, 65, 96–97, 102
  as wingman, 193–194
Little, USS (transporter), 326
Lohr, Billy, 183
Long Island, USS (ship)
  to Efate, 128–137, 143
  group dynamics on, 111–113
  Guadalcanal and, 147–154
  in Hawaii, 64, 98–107
  Midway and, 115–119

Long Island, USS (ship) (*continued*)
    at Pearl Harbor attack, 96–97, 103–107
    soldiers on, 108–111, 113–115,
        119–121, 138–146
    strategy on, 122–131
Long Island City, New York, 30–36, 44, 71
Lufbery, Raoul, 294, 296
Lynch, Floyd, 420, 423, 425

MacArthur, Douglas, 445, 467
machine guns, 190–191
Macias, Luis
    in combat, 225–228
    death of, 465
    Dick and, 272
    Eades and, 323, 354, 384, 435–436
    after Guadalcanal, 465
    legacy of, 457–458
    McCafferty and, 383, 385, 393–394
    reputation of, 208
    as scout, 318
MacLeod, Robert S., 197, 202–203,
    242–243
MacPhail School of Music, 68–69
Mae West life preservers, 344–346, 426
MAG-23. *See* Marine Aviation Group 23
malaria, 125
Mangrum, Bryan, 28, 447, 455
Mangrum, Harriet, 28
Mangrum, Richard (Dick)
    authority of, 431–432, 463–464
    Brown, F., and, 265
    in Buccaneers, 39–41
    Butler and, 353
    Byrd and, 120–121, 148–150,
        230–235, 326
    Caldwell and, 290, 390–391
    Carl, M., and, 10–12, 15, 154, 439, 452
    casualties to, 279–280
    in combat, 165–166, 230–237
    Dauntlesses and, 40–41, 156, 220–221
    death of, 462
    dive-bombers to, 106
    on duty, 263
    estimations of, 147–148

    family of, 266
    Fike and, 142–143, 148, 256, 271, 279
    in flight, 150–151, 303–307
    Galer and, 392, 447
    Geiger and, 364
    at Guadalcanal, 156–158, 181–184,
        188–191
    health of, 380–381
    Hicks and, 31–32
    Hise and, 271–272, 461–462
    Japan to, 160–161, 226
    John L., and, 23–29, 50–51, 64,
        108–109, 127–128, 184, 292, 377
    Larkin and, 72–73
    leadership of, 92, 95, 105, 108–109,
        118–119, 145–146, 213–219, 268
    legacy of, 443, 455–456, 462
    Macias and, 272
    McCafferty and, 353, 355, 379
    Mehargue to, 381–382
    Mitchell, O., to, 114–116
    nightlife to, 53–57
    to Nimitz, 410–411
    PR to, 17–22
    at press conferences, 45
    promotions for, 410
    Prosser and, 191
    psychology of, 109–110, 126, 356–359,
        383–384, 419–420
    with Red Devils, 223–226, 228–229,
        244–245, 263–264
    reputation of, 282, 330–333, 435–436
    retirement of, 438–439
    in service, 33, 75, 115
    with soldiers, 117–118, 145, 206–211,
        274–275, 308–310, 355–356
    speeches by, 34–35, 38–39
    Stanner to, 111–114
    strategy of, 122–125, 222–223,
        235–236, 276–278, 321–322, 395
    tact of, 360–361, 364–365
    Thomas, L., and, 328–329
    trauma to, 115–116
    Vandegrift and, 158
    in youth, 270–271

Mangrum, Virginia, 50–51, 110, 439
Marine Aviation Group 23 (MAG-23)
  with fuel, 158
  at Guadalcanal, 241, 288, 419–421
  headquarters, 104, 111, 397, 418
  intelligence reports for, 405
  Japan to, 336
  in Korean War, 447
  leadership of, 409–410
  orders from, 105–106, 430
  Red Devils and, 319
  reinforcements and, 292
  reputation of, 370
  staff of, 381, 393–394
  strategy with, 300, 384–385, 392
  VMF-223 and, 103
  for Wildcats, 183
  in World War II, 64, 96, 98
Marine Raiders, 159
Marines. *See specific topics*
Marsh, Adabar, 97–98
Marsh & McLennan insurance, 78
Marvin, Howard
  Gutt and, 413
  leadership of, 434–435
  promotions for, 432
  Read and, 414, 430
  reputation of, 82, 106–107, 407
Mason, Paul, 294
McAllister, Charles
  Brown, F., and, 330
  death of, 331–333
  Eades and, 184–185
  psychology of, 135–136, 310
  reputation of, 134–135
  as scout, 306–307
McCafferty, Don
  Baldinus, L., and, 317–320
  in combat, 224–228, 236
  death of, 460
  Dick and, 353, 355, 379
  Fleener and, 390, 419
  in flight, 272–275
  after Guadalcanal, 459–460
  Iverson and, 273

legacy of, 457–458
Macias and, 383, 385, 393–394
Mitchell and, 268–269
Prosser and, 380
psychology of, 314, 364
reports from, 234, 278–279
reputation of, 152, 205–206, 208, 212,
  410–411
in service, 264–265
Standard and, 355–356
Thomas, L., and, 217, 223, 323
after World War II, 435–436
McCain, John S., 187
McCawley, USS (attack transport),
  385–386
McConnell, Henry, 239
McFarland, USS (ship), 173, 183–184,
  196, 432–433, 435
McLennan, Bill, 136–137
McLennan, Don, 466–467
McLennan, George
  Carl, M., and, 300–301
  in combat, 335
  death of, 376, 418, 466
  family of, 136–137
  after Guadalcanal, 466–467
  Kendrick and, 289–290
  legacy of, 457–458
  on patrol, 295
  Phillips and, 83–84
  Pond and, 247
  reputation of, 78–79, 130–131
  as wingman, 175–176, 244
McLennan, Peggy, 136–137, 466–467
McQuiston, Edward I., 287, 291–292
medals
  Bronze Star medal, 449, 467
  Distinguished Flying Cross medal, 127,
    410–411, 438, 449, 459–460, 462,
    467, 469
  Medal of Honor, 127, 444–445,
    449–450, 452, 469
  Silver Star medal, 449
  in US Navy, 410–411, 438, 449,
    460, 467

media
  Carl, M., to, 44–45
  Guadalcanal and, 13, 21, 23–29, 197,
    266–267
  Japan to, 38–39
  Pearl Harbor attack and, 12
  propaganda with, 455–456
  soldiers in, 11–12, 14
  US Army to, 26–27
  at US Navy Department, 16–22
Mehargue, David, 381–382
Merchant Marine Academy, 131
Merrill, Herbert T., 67
MIA. *See* missing in action
Midway. *See also specific subjects*
  aircraft at, 46, 74
  Armistead at, 337
  Buffalos at, 34–35
  Carl, M., at, 33, 69
  casualties at, 62–63, 88–89, 115,
    206, 460
  Dauntlesses at, 264, 461
  defense of, 1–6, 67
  dive-bombers at, 88
  Ewa Field and, 87–91
  Guadalcanal and, 32, 58
  Japan at, 139
  to John L., 104
  Kate bombers at, 194
  leadership at, 64, 70
  leave from, 61
  lessons from, 130
  Long Island and, 115–119
  Pearl Harbor attack and, 73
  promotions after, 62
  to Red Devils, 132
  strategies at, 246
  trauma at, 206–207
  veterans of, 76, 105, 217
  VMF-221 at, 66
  Wildcats in, 19–20, 221
  Zeroes at, 195, 294
Miller, Bob, 256, 274, 277, 279
Mills, James, 239
Minneapolis, USS (cruiser), 384–387

missing in action (MIA)
  pilots, 203, 231, 332, 342–343, 377,
    379, 417–419, 466
  VMF-221 and, 4–5, 67
Mitchell, Don, 268
Mitchell, James, 268
Mitchell, Margaret, 268
Mitchell, Oliver
  Byrd and, 278
  death of, 280, 309–310
  Hise and, 277–278
  legacy of, 457–458
  McCafferty and, 268–269
  Moore, T., and, 261–262
  reputation of, 114–116, 118,
    207
Mitsubishi A6M2. *See* Zeroes
Mitsubishi G4M Betties. *See* Betties
models, 49–58
Moore, Clarence, 105
Moore, Tom
  Buell and, 210–211
  casualties to, 279–280
  in flight, 151, 155, 277
  injuries of, 307–310, 316
  Iverson and, 191, 206–207
  legacy of, 436
  Mitchell, O., and, 261–262
  O'Keefe, A., and, 304
  Prosser and, 148
  psychology of, 131–133, 135–136
  religion to, 133–135
  reputation of, 95, 114–115, 118
  as scout, 305–307
Morrell, Rivers
  Carl, M., and, 73, 81–82, 93, 100,
    102–104, 243, 257
  casualties of, 375–376
  in combat, 196, 199–200
  Frazier and, 99
  after Guadalcanal, 468
  John L., and, 92
  leadership of, 130
  on patrol, 295
  Pond and, 244, 327–328

reputation of, 117, 220, 322, 382
in service, 64–65, 73–74
Mustin (destroyer), 100
Mutsuki (destroyer), 237

Nakajima B5N bombers. *See* Kate bombers
NAP program. *See* Naval Aviation Pilot
  program
National Geographic (magazine), 9, 129
National Guard, 68–69
National Museum of Naval Aviation, 461
Naval Aviation Cadet (NAVCAD)
  program, 69, 77, 79, 83
Naval Aviation Pilot (NAP) program,
  96–98
NAVCAD program. *See* Naval Aviation
  Cadet program
Navy, US
  aircraft, 381
  bases, 73
  Brewster Aeronautical Corporation
    and, 33, 38
  Bureau of Aeronautics, 468
  business in, 80–81
  Coast Guard and, 26–27
  in Cold War, 448
  construction battalions, 337–338
  Department, 16–22
  economics, 43
  enlistment standards of, 138
  factories for, 32
  in Florida, 39–40, 86
  funerals, 86
  Germany to, 44
  Guadalcanal to, 122–131
  Hicks for, 11–12
  intelligence, 185
  Japan to, 45, 162–163
  John L., to, 41
  lookouts for, 140–142
  medals in, 410–411, 438, 449, 460, 467
  Naval Air Station Anacostia, 11–12
  at Palmyra Atoll, 98–103
  paratroops, 123
  politics, 389

PR, 459
preparations, 163–164, 172
radio, 205–206
reinforcements, 365
reputation of, 77
ROTC program for, 239
in San Diego, 461
Smith, L., to, 41
soldiers to, 283–292, 443–444, 449
statistics to, 267–268
strike and search system for, 271–278
TBF Avenger torpedo bombers, 4–5
training for, 80
urgency in, 38
US Army and, 33, 39
warships, 261
Wildcats to, 71
after World War I, 157–158
in World War II, 391–395, 457
NBC television, 52
Netherlands, 456–457
New Hebrides, 125, 128, 143. *See also* Efate
New York
  literary scene, 82
  Long Island City, 30–36, 71
  Merchant Marine Academy in, 131
  New York City, 37, 48–58
  Waldorf Astoria in, 49–58
New York Times, 17
New Zealand, 385–386, 434
Nicholas, USS (destroyer), 426
Nimitz, Chester, 141, 409–411, 449
Nisshin (seaplane carrier), 404–405
North Africa, 456
North American Rocketdyne
  Corporation, 449–450
North Atlantic Treaty Organization,
  445, 449
North Carolina, 39–40
North Korea, 469

Oahu, Hawaii. *See* Hawaii
Ogasawara (sergeant), 167, 485n2
Oka, Akinosuke, 321–322, 325, 329,
  369, 371

O'Keefe, Arthur
  death of, 462
  Fleener and, 362–363
  after Guadalcanal, 461–463
  injuries of, 140–141, 145
  Iverson and, 390
  Moore, T., and, 304
  psychology of, 152, 160, 355–356
  reputation of, 94–95, 233, 378
  trauma to, 378–379
O'Keefe, Michael, 462–463
Oklahoma
  Great Depression and, 96–97
  soldiers in, 12–14
  University of, 65
Oklahoma, USS (ship), 61
"On the Road to Mandalay" (Kipling),
    397–3989
Owen, Robert, 240–241
oxygen systems, 125, 173–174, 376

P-400 Airacobras, 186, 284–285,
    294–296, 299–300, 370–371
Palmyra Atoll, 98–103
Papa New Guinea, 267, 290
Paramount Pictures, 42–43
paratroops, 123
Parks, Floyd, 2–3, 117
Payne, Frederick R., 376, 400, 406
PBY Catalina flying boat, 61, 187–188
Pearl Harbor attack
  aircraft at, 75
  culture and, 53, 109–110
  Japan at, 19
  Kidō Butai at, 1
  Larkin at, 71–72
  Long Island at, 96–97, 103–107
  Marines at, 5–6
  media and, 12
  Midway and, 73
  Palmyra Atoll and, 98–103
  psychology of, 26, 44, 61, 112, 122
  significance of, 25, 445
  US before, 51, 127
Pennsylvania, 32, 36–41, 52, 443, 467–468

perfume, 51–52, 54–55
Philippines, 10, 111, 464
Phillips, Hyde, 69, 82–84, 290, 376
photographs, 19–20
pilot fatigue, 391–392
Piper J-2 Cubs, 76–77
Polk, George S., 173–175, 181–182
Pond, Zenneth
  Bailey and, 202
  in combat, 197, 199, 290
  Corry and, 99
  death of, 376
  Gutt and, 457–458
  to John L., 243
  McLennan and, 247
  Morrell and, 244, 327–328
  on patrol, 295
  psychology of, 204, 257
  resourcefulness of, 127–128
  in service, 76–78
Popeye (cartoon), 132
Portland, USS (ship), 126
post-traumatic stress disorder (PTSD),
    449–453
poverty, 382–383
Powers, John Robert, 49–50, 55–56
President Hayes, USS (attack transport),
    385–386
President Jackson, USS (attack transport),
    385–386
press conferences, 45
prisoners of war, 262, 286, 344–351
Proffitt, William, 184–185, 332
Prohibition, 53
propaganda, 42–43, 414, 432, 455–456
Proser, Monte, 54
Prosser, Bruce
  catapult launches to, 144
  Dick and, 191
  experience of, 142, 304
  Fleener and, 379, 394
  in flight, 272
  Hise and, 267
  Iverson and, 217, 274
  leadership of, 184–185

McCafferty and, 380
Moore, T., and, 148
psychology of, 206–207, 390
reputation of, 114–115
as scout, 311
Thomas, L., and, 324
PTSD. *See* post-traumatic stress disorder
public relations (PR), 16–22, 24, 459
Purves, Margaretta, 78–79
Putnam, Paul, 127

Quincy (cruiser), 123

radar scrambling, 1–2
Ramlo, Orvin, 377
Ranger, USS (ship), 126
Read, Robert
 Bailey and, 203
 Brooks and, 406–407
 as castaway, 349
 in combat, 197–199, 204
 John L., and, 242
 Lees and, 413
 Marvin and, 414, 430
 reputation of, 243, 257
Red Devils
 aircraft for, 181–182, 363–364
 assignment to, 138
 against bombers, 188–189
 counterinvasions by, 124
 culture of, 113
 Dauntlesses for, 125
 decimation of, 376–379
 defense with, 222, 232–233, 412–418
 Dick with, 223–226, 228–229,
  244–245, 263–264
 Distinguished Flying Cross medal for,
  127, 410–411
 dive-bombers for, 72, 75, 117–118
 at Guadalcanal, 11, 158, 161, 184–188,
  303–308, 311–316, 374–379, 391–395
 Japan and, 209, 261, 293–302, 325–333
 Kidō Butai and, 116
 leadership of, 186
 legacy of, 459–469

MAG-23 and, 319
 Midway to, 132
 morale of, 380–388
 practice for, 92, 94, 106
 promotions in, 117–118
 psychology of, 363–364
 scouting by, 317–325
 under siege, 353–360
 strategy of, 422–427
 training for, 364
 in transport, 108–109
 VMF-223 and, 124–125, 286, 288
 Wildcats for, 140
Register, Francis, 391–392
reinforcements
 aircraft and, 125–126
 blunders with, 286–292
 Brannon and, 404
 of food, 309
 at Guadalcanal, 389–391, 396–402
 for Japan, 235–236, 304, 373–374, 392
 John L., with, 334–335
 MAG-23 and, 292
 psychology of, 261, 395
 supplies and, 187–188
 US Navy, 365
 for VMF-223, 183–184
 Wildcats and, 185–186
 in World War II, 125–126, 183–184
religion, 133–135, 357, 419–421, 466
Renner, Joseph, 405, 422
reporters, 17–22, 27–29
rescue missions, 393–394
Richthofen, Manfred von, 258
Roberts, Eunice, 78
Rollow, Jesse D., 115–116
Roosevelt, Franklin D., 16, 72, 96,
 444–445
Roosevelt, James, 72
Roosevelt Field, 36
Rose, Don
 Byrd and, 309–310
 death of, 356, 361, 363
 reputation of, 233, 274–275, 277,
  278–279

ROTC program, 239
Rowell, Ross, 72
Royal Air Force, 284–285
Royal Hawaiian, 63–64, 66, 70
Russell, Robert S., 330, 332
Ryūjō (aircraft carrier), 192, 235

Sable, USS (ship), 461
sabotage, 48
San Diego. *See* California
Sara (fleet carrier), 141
Saratoga, USS (ship), 5, 33, 117, 141, 154, 190, 206
Sasai, Junichi, 180, 258–259
SB2A Buccaneers. *See* Buccaneers
SBD Dauntlesses. *See* Dauntlesses
Scales, Jack, 382–383
Schackman, Frank O., 279–280, 309–310
Sendai (cruiser), 354, 358
service record books, 111–113
Sewell, David, 210, 214, 218
Sherman, Forrest, 445
Sherman, Roy, 446–447
Shikinami (destroyer), 312
Shingō, Hideki, 301–302
Shirakuma (destroyer), 280–282
shock, 71
Shōkaku (destroyer), 192, 235–236, 301
shuttle bombing, 306
Silver Star medal, 449
Sinatra, Frank, 53
"Sleepy Lagoon" (song), 266
Smith, John Lucian (John L.)
  in air raids, 287
  aircraft to, 34, 63–64
  authority of, 426, 430, 433
  Bauer and, 261
  Caldwell and, 392
  Carl, M., and, 44–46, 49, 70–72, 328, 336–337, 412–413, 431–432, 439, 447–449
  casualties to, 87–91
  in combat, 175–176, 289–290, 416–418
  death of, 452–453

  Dick and, 23–29, 50–51, 64, 108–109, 127–128, 184, 292, 377
  dive-bombers and, 125–126, 221
  Everton and, 196
  experience of, 425
  with family, 240–241, 428–429
  Fike and, 122, 154–155, 159–160, 201, 343, 457
  in flight, 153
  Galer and, 96, 99, 358–359, 364, 376
  gunnery training to, 103
  on Japan, 131
  Kendrick and, 299–300
  leadership of, 66–67, 68, 80, 145–146, 165, 217, 406–407
  on leave, 9–15
  Lees and, 413–414
  legacy of, 443–451, 455–456, 462
  MAG-23 to, 98
  Midway to, 104
  missing in action, 417–418
  Morrell and, 92
  nightlife to, 53–57
  orders from, 164, 166–167
  on patrol, 294–298
  Pond to, 243
  PR to, 17–22
  at press conferences, 45
  problem-solving by, 171–173
  psychology of, 30–31, 73–75, 81, 238–240, 257–258, 374–375
  Read and, 242
  records by, 438
  with reinforcements, 334–335
  Renner and, 405
  reputation of, 47, 64–65, 118, 130, 167, 175, 410–411, 435
  in service, 33, 75, 84, 96, 115, 145, 155
  soldiers and, 104–105, 197–198, 204–205, 342, 375–376
  speeches by, 35–36, 128–130
  strategy of, 194, 196–197, 244–251
  training to, 93–94, 96, 339–340
  Trowbridge and, 170
  to US Navy, 41

Vandegrift and, 396
in VMF-221, 5–6
for VMF-223, 79, 124–125
Wildcats and, 106, 142–143,
    220–221, 232
Smith, Kate, 12
Smith, Leo, 303–305, 312–313, 322,
    328–330, 383
Smith, Louise, 88, 444–445, 448–449,
    451–452
Smith, Robert Hall, 188
Smith, Roy Lamont, 65
soldiers. *See also specific topics*
    ages of, 119–121
    alcohol to, 5
    autobiographies from, 464–465
    bombers and, 32–33
    Brown, F., with, 262
    Byrd with, 307–308
    Carl, M., with, 85
    in Civil War, 56
    civilians and, 31
    in combat, 412–418
    from CUB-1, 173–174
    Dick with, 117–118, 145, 206–211,
        274–275, 308–310, 355–356
    family of, 262–263
    Fike with, 216
    at Guadalcanal, 16–22, 205–212,
        220–229, 244–251, 428–436
    in hand-to-hand combat, 368–370
    in Hawaii, 61–67, 95–96, 103–106
    health of, 270
    at Henderson Field, 160, 162–170
    Japan to, 362–371, 458
    John L., and, 104–105, 197–198,
        204–205, 342, 375–376
    in Korean War, 444, 467
    leave for, 9–15
    in *Life* magazine, 12
    on *Long Island*, 108–111, 113–115,
        119–121, 138–146
    MacLeod with, 242–243
    Mae West life preservers for,
        344–346, 426

in media, 11–12, 14
morale of, 372–379
NAVCAD program for, 69
in Oklahoma, 12–14
psychology of, 218–219, 238–243,
    268–269, 353–361
with PTSD, 449–453
religion to, 133–135, 419–421
reunions with, 450–451
routines of, 262–269
in San Diego, 434–435
Sewell with, 218
suicide to, 221, 450–453
trauma of, 389–391, 445–446
in US, 455–458
to US Navy, 283–292, 443–444, 449
for VMF-223, 96–105, 196
from World War I, 71–72, 117
after World War II, 437–441, 459–469
Solomon Islands, 45, 129, 138–146. *See
    also specific islands*
Sousa, John Philip, 43–44
South, Angsar, 275, 363, 419–420
South Pacific Command. *See*
    COMSOPAC
Southard, USS (converted destroyer),
    339, 433
Soviet Union, 267, 456–457
Spain, 465
sports, 24–29, 36–37, 265, 456
Standard, Jim, 353, 355–356, 395
Stanford University, 466
Stanner, Jack, 111–114, 161
Stark, Albert "Dolly," 37
Stephenson, P. M., 37
Stork Club, 55–58
storms, 189–190
strike aircraft, 70
strike and search system, 271–278
suicide, 221, 450–453
Swirbul, Leon A., 44

Tainan Air Group, 179–180, 258–259,
    301
Takutsuka, Toraichi, 180

Tanaka, Raizo, 236–237, 291
Taylor, Lawrence C., 203–204, 242
TBF Avenger torpedo bombers, 4–5,
    191, 463
Teamsters Union, 57
Tenaru, 166–168
Thomas, Gerald, 157–158
Thomas, Leland, 158–159
    death of, 388–389, 465
    Dick and, 328–329
    Eades and, 207–208, 225, 227, 319,
        382–383, 385–388
    legacy of, 435, 457–458, 466
    McCafferty and, 217, 223, 323
    Prosser and, 324
    reputation of, 379
Time magazine, 26
Tokyo Express. *See* Japan
Tracers
    in combat, 115–116, 164, 167, 176,
        249–250, 253–255, 416, 424–425
    Dauntlesses and, 231, 277–278
    efficacy of, 284, 296, 312, 386, 394
    reputation of, 190, 215–216, 276–278
training
    at Advanced Carrier Training Group
        program, 94–95, 138
    aircraft, 85–86
    with Bauer, 167
    carriers, 461
    death in, 86, 89–91, 460
    to Dick, 111
    dive-bombers, 438–439
    at Ewa Field, 96–105
    in Florida, 97–98
    gunnery, 84–85, 103
    to John L., 93–94, 96, 339–340
    psychology of, 103–104
    for Red Devils, 364
trauma
    alcohol and, 62
    casualties and, 132–133, 460
    to Dick, 115–116
    memory of, 465–466
    at Midway, 206–207

to O'Keefe, A., 378–379
    PTSD, 449–453
    of soldiers, 389–391, 445–446
    World War II and, 459–469
Tregaskis, Richard, 197, 201, 234, 256,
    260, 287
Trowbridge, Eugene
    Carl and, 128
    in combat, 288–289, 341
    death of, 468
    Frazier and, 244, 252–253
    after Guadalcanal, 467–468
    Hamilton and, 166
    injuries of, 376–377
    John L., and, 170
    psychology of, 163–164
    reputation of, 68–69
Tulagi, 123, 186–187
Turner, Richmond Kelly, 365, 384
Twenty-One Club, 53

U-Boats, 26, 44
unions, 37–38, 57
United States (US). *See also specific topics*
    African Americans in, 30
    business in, 37–38
    China and, 126, 157, 438
    in Cold War, 465
    Congress, 37–38
    culture of, 437–441, 446–447
    dust bowl in, 97
    fashion industry in, 49–50
    Germany and, 456
    Great Depression in, 55, 62, 82–83,
        96–97, 120–121, 183, 269
    immigration to, 48, 117, 268, 457–458
    Japan and, 21–22, 35, 185–186,
        252–259, 267–268, 281–282,
        359–360, 403–411, 455
    Japanese Americans, 96
    in Korean War, 439, 444, 447
    Lend-Lease Act in, 33
    Lindbergh kidnapping trial in, 27
    Medal of Honor in, 127, 444–445,
        449–450, 452, 469

New Hebrides to, 125, 128, 143
before Pearl Harbor attack, 51, 127
poverty in, 382–383
Prohibition in, 53
propaganda for, 432
ROTC program in, 239
soldiers in, 455–458
Soviet Union and, 456–457
strategy, 391–395
Vietnam Veterans Memorial in, 16
in Vietnam War, 438
after World War I, 381
World War II and, 9–15, 28–29, 51
University of Alabama, 24–26
University of Miami, 83
University of New Hampshire, 67
University of Oklahoma, 65
University of San Francisco, 466
US. *See* United States

Van Dusen, C. A., 33–34, 36–38
Vandegrift, Alexander A.
    aircraft and, 157
    Cates and, 166
    Coastwatchers and, 404
    with COMSOPAC, 241
    Dick and, 158
    Fike and, 289
    Geiger and, 365–366
    John L., and, 396
    leadership of, 182–183, 189–190, 306
    Miller and, 274, 277, 279
    reputation of, 126, 278
    safety of, 368
    strategy of, 188, 216–217, 365
    Turner and, 384
    Wildcats and, 182
video games, 464
Vietnam Veterans Memorial, 16
Vietnam War, 438, 463, 465
Vincennes (cruiser), 123
VMF-221. *See also specific topics*
    Carl, M., in, 88
    casualties to, 4, 61–62, 67
    John L., in, 5–6

MIA and, 4–5, 67
at Midway, 66
reputation of, 74
veterans from, 71
Zeroes and, 2
VMF-223. *See also specific topics*
    to Barner, 148
    Carl, M., for, 283–284, 468
    casualties to, 11, 86, 87–91
    challenges to, 80
    Everton for, 166–167
    at Ewa Field, 92–96
    Galer for, 105
    at Guadalcanal, 171–180, 293–302
    John L., for, 79, 124–125
    leadership of, 63–64, 73–76
    MAG-23 and, 103
    morale in, 71
    rapport in, 96
    Red Devils and, 124–125, 286, 288
    reinforcements for, 183–184
    scarcity in, 242
    in service, 162–163
    soldiers for, 96–105, 196
    tours of, 438
    veterans of, 116
    after World War II, 462
VMF-224, 75, 92–93, 106–107, 334–343.
    See also specific topics
VMSB-232. *See* Red Devils

Waldorf Astoria, 49–58
Wallace, William J., 303–304, 310, 319,
    323–324
Walter, Howard, 100–101
Waring, Fred, 52–53
Washburn, John, 447
Washington Evening Star, 18
Wasp, USS (fleet carrier), 141, 384
Watkins, James, 265
Western Union, 41, 43–44
Wildcats. *See also specific topics*
    agility of, 93–94
    on aircraft carriers, 98–100
    against Betties, 245–246

Wildcats. (*continued*)
Buffalos and, 1–2, 6, 89–90, 99–100, 130
Carl, M., and, 3, 195–196
Coastwatchers and, 287
in combat, 167–170, 250, 252–256, 258, 406–409, 413–414
Dauntlesses and, 139, 143, 154, 189, 210–211, 233, 303–304
designs for, 33, 103–104, 173
Fike in, 152–153
at Guadalcanal, 46
guns on, 85, 168–169, 263–264
at Henderson Field, 193–194
against Japan, 246–247
John L., and, 106, 142–143, 220–221, 232
landing, 177–178
MAG-23 for, 183
in Midway, 19–20, 221
oxygen systems for, 125, 173–174
on patrol, 167–168
for Red Devils, 140
reinforcements and, 185–186
reputation of, 45, 74, 219, 243
TBF Avenger torpedo bombers and, 191
Tracers and, 176
in training, 86
to US Navy, 71
Vandegrift and, 182
Zeroes and, 3–4, 43, 115, 177, 180, 198–201, 289, 373–374, 414–417
William Ward Burrows, USS (transport), 106, 286, 290–292, 295, 300, 309
Willsey, Frank, 360–361
Winter, Conrad, 261, 334–335, 342, 423–424
women, as models, 49–58
Wood, Preston, 239
Woods, Louis, 392
World War I
aces in, 258
aircraft in, 32, 222–223
Civil War and, 456
destroyers from, 125, 172, 233–234
Great Depression and, 82–83
magazines in, 76
propaganda in, 414
Roosevelt in, 16
sabotage in, 48
soldiers from, 71–72, 117
strategy in, 323, 326
US after, 381
US Army in, 94
US Navy after, 157–158
veterans of, 432
World War II. *See also specific subjects*
alcoholism after, 448
antiaircraft guns in, 139, 168
Australia in, 123
Brewster Aeronautical Corporation after, 467
businesses in, 30–32
Carl, M., before, 294
Central Pacific in, 1–6
civilians in, 348–350, 372–373
college education and, 18
Edson after, 450
in Europe, 267
fuel in, 125, 173–175
Guadalcanal and, 213–219
Japan after, 438
Japan Imperial Navy in, 32, 143
leave in, 9–15, 61, 82
legacy of, 455–458
MAG-23 in, 64, 96, 98
McCafferty after, 435–436
morale in, 362–371
North Africa in, 456
propaganda for, 42–43, 432
reinforcements in, 125–126, 183–184
soldiers after, 437–441, 459–469
trauma and, 459–469
US and, 9–15, 28–29, 51
US Navy in, 391–395, 457
veterans of, 448–449
in video games, 464
VMF-223 after, 462
Wright Cyclone engines, 40, 102, 149, 214, 232, 264

Yale University, 78
Yamada, Yuji, 281–282
Yorktown, USS (ship), 126, 264
Yugiri (destroyer), 280–282

Zane, USS (converted destroyer),
    339
Zeilin, USS (ship), 96, 431, 434
Zerbe, Jerome, 53
Zeroes. *See also specific topics*
    Betties and, 396–397, 399–402
    Buffalos and, 40, 67
    Carl, M., against, 252–256
    casualties from, 2–3
    Coastwatchers and, 408–409
    Corsairs and, 468
    Dauntlesses and, 115, 150, 217–218,
        222, 224–225, 230–231
    Hurricanes and, 33
    for Japan, 220–221, 223, 338–341
    Johnson against, 366–367
    Kawai with, 180
    Kidō Butai and, 20
    at Midway, 195, 294
    in Pearl Harbor attack, 110
    reputation of, 66, 90, 121, 176, 189,
        412–414
    strategies against, 119, 130–131,
        216–217, 258–259, 422–427
    success against, 289–290, 295–301
    VMF-221 and, 2
    Wildcats and, 3–4, 43, 115, 177, 180,
        198–201, 289, 373–374, 414–417
Ziegfeld Follies, 54
Zimmerman, Peter, 34
Zuikaku (destroyer), 192, 235–236, 301